6/24/2019

MEDIA CONSTRAINED BY CONTEXT

MEDIA CONSTRAINED BY CONTEXT

International Assistance and the Transition to Democratic Media in the Western Balkans

Edited by

KRISTINA IRION and TARIK JUSIĆ

Central European University Press
Budapest–New York

Published in 2018 by
Central European University Press

Nádor utca 11, H-1051 Budapest, Hungary
Tel: +36-1-327-3138 or 327-3000
E-mail: ceupress@press.ceu.edu
Website: www.ceupress.com

224 West 57th Street, New York NY 10019, USA

ISBN 978-963-386-259-9

Library of Congress Cataloging-in-Publication Data

Names: Irion, Kristina, editor of compilation. | Jusic, Tarik, editor of compilation.
Title: Media constrained by context : international assistance and the transition to
democratic media in the western Balkans / edited by Kristina Irion and Tarik
Jusic.
Description: Budapest ; New York : Central European University Press, 2018. |
Includes bibliographical references and index.
Identifiers: LCCN 2018000793 (print) | LCCN 2018033293 (ebook) | ISBN
9789633862605 | ISBN 9789633862599
Subjects: LCSH: Mass media—Balkan Peninsula—History. | Mass media—Social
aspects—Balkan Peninsula. | Mass media policy—Balkan Peninsula. | Mass
media—Political aspects—Balkan Peninsula—History. | Democratization—Bal-
kan Peninsula. | Technical assistance, American—Bosnia and Herzegovina. |
Technical assistance, European—Bosnia and Herzegovina.
Classification: LCC P92.B28 (ebook) | LCC P92.B28 M425 2000 (print) | DDC
302.23/09496—dc23
LC record available at https://lccn.loc.gov/2018000793 Kristina Irion

Printed in Hungary

Table of Contents

List of Tables

List of Figures

List of Abbreviations

AJM – Association of Journalists of Macedonia
AMA – Authority on Audiovisual Media
AMPEK – Association of Independent Electronic Media of Kosovo
ANEM – Association of Independent Electronic Media
APJK – Association of Professional Journalists of Kosovo
BC – Broadcasting Council
BHRT – Bosnia-Herzegovina Radio and Television
BiH – Bosnia and Herzegovina
BIRN – Balkan Investigative Reporting Network
CAP – Crisis Assistance Program
CIMA – Center for International Media Assistance
CIN – Center for Investigative Reporting
CINS – Center for Investigative Journalism Serbia
CoE – Council of Europe
COHU – Organization for Democracy, Anticorruption, and Dignity
CRA – Communication Regulatory Agency
DANIDA – Danish International Development Agency
DPA – Dayton Peace Agreement
EAR – European Agency for Reconstruction
EBU – European Broadcasting Union
EC – European Commission
ERNO – Eurovision Regional News Exchange
EU – European Union
FCC – US Federal Communications Commission
FERN – Free Elections Radio Network
FOI – Freedom of Access to Information

FOIA – Freedom of Information Acts
FOSM – Foundation Open Society Macedonia
IFJ – International Federation of Journalists
IFOR – International Military Implementation Force
IMA – International Media Assistance
IMC – Independent Media Commission
IMF – International Media Fund
IREX – International Research & Exchanges Board
IRI – International Republican Institute
JDG – Journalism Development Group
KAS – Konrad Adenauer Stiftung
KEK – Kosovo Electric Corporation
KIJAC – Kosovo Institute of Journalism and Communication
KKRT – National Council of Radio and Television
KMI – Kosovo Media Institute
KOSMA – Kosovo Media Association
KRIK – Crime and Corruption Reporting Network
KTTN – Kosovo Terrestrial Telecommunication Network
KTV – Kohavision
LBA – Law on Broadcasting Activity
LDK – Democratic League of Kosovo
MAB – Media Appeals Board
MAJ – Macedonian Association of Journalists
MIM – Macedonian Institute for Media
MRTV – Macedonian Radio-Television
MSI – IREX Media Sustainability Index
MTF – Media Task Force
NATO – North Atlantic Treaty Organization
NED – National Endowment for Democracy
NUNS – Independent Association of Journalists of Serbia
OBN – Open Broadcast Network
OCCRP – Organized Crime and Corruption Reporting Project
OFA – Ohrid Framework Agreement
OHR – Office of the High Representative
OSCE – Organization for Security and Co-operation in Europe
OSF – Open Society Foundations
PSB – Public Service Broadcasting
PCK – Press Council of Kosovo
PDK – Democratic Party of Kosovo
PIC – Peace Implementation Council

RAEM – Regulatory Agency for Electronic Media
RBA – Regulatory Broadcasting Agency
RTK – Radio Television of Kosovo
RTP – Radio Television Pristina
RTRS – Radio-Television of Republika Srpska
RTSH – Albanian Radio and Television
RTS – Radio-Television of Serbia
RTV21 – Radio Television 21
RTVFBiH – Radio-Television of the Federation of Bosnia and Herzegovina
SAA – Stabilization and Association Agreement
SDSM – Social Democratic Union of Macedonia
SHC – Swedish Helsinki Committee
SIDA – Swedish International Development Cooperation Agency
SIMM – Strengthening Independent Minority Media
TMC – Temporary Media Commissioner
TRA – Telecommunications Regulatory Agency
UGSH – Union of Albanian Journalists
UNDP – United Nations Development Program
UNESCO – United Nations Educational, Scientific and Cultural Organization
UNMIK – United Nations Mission in Kosovo
USIA – United States Information Agency
VMRO-DPMNE – Internal Macedonian Revolutionary Organization–Democratic Party for Macedonian National Unity
WB – World Bank
YIHR – Youth Initiative for Human Rights

Preface

This edited volume is the outcome of a regional research project that explores the nexus between the democratic transformation of the media and international media assistance programs in five countries of the Western Balkans—Albania, Bosnia and Herzegovina, Kosovo, Macedonia, and Serbia. It aims to enhance the understanding of conditions and factors that influence media institution building in the region and evaluates the role of international assistance programs and their conditionality mechanisms. Of particular interest is the question of what happens to imported institutional models when they are transposed into the newly evolving media systems of transitional societies in the Western Balkans.

The book consists of ten chapters, organized into three distinct sections. The first chapter sets out the theoretical and methodological framework that underpinned the research project. It is followed by five chapters, one for each country covered in this volume, providing contextual information and detailed case studies. The third part consists of four comparative chapters that outline key lessons learned from the twenty years of media assistance efforts in the five countries of the Western Balkans.

In the course of our research one of the challenges we faced was the limited availability of data and documents on the media assistance programs and projects undertaken in the region during last twenty years. The task was further complicated due to restricted access to people who once played key roles in media development projects in the region, but have since moved on to other countries, institutions, and professions. An additional challenge was to keep up with the dynamic changes in the media environment in these countries and make sure that individual chapters are up to date.

We believe that this edited volume offers valuable insights into the nature and effects of media assistance and the strategies deployed by international aid agencies, local political forces, media professionals, civil society organizations and other actors, all of whom have shaped the development of media institutions in the region for over two decades. As such, it can be useful resource for researchers in the field of media development and development studies in general, students of media studies, experts and practitioners in the field of media development, as well as media professionals and decision-makers.

Acknowledgements

This book was produced as part of the research project "Development of Functional Media Institutions in the Western Balkans—A Comparative Study" implemented in 2012 and 2013 by the Center for Social Research Analitika (Bosnia and Herzegovina), in cooperation with the Center for Research and Policy Making (Macedonia), the Albanian Media Institute (Albania), and Democracy for Development (Kosovo). The project was funded within the framework of the Regional Research Promotion Programme in the Western Balkans (RRPP), run by the University of Fribourg under a mandate from the Agency for Development and Cooperation (SDC), Federal Department of Foreign Affairs, of Switzerland.

Special thanks go to Ms. Dženana Hrlović, who coordinated the research project on behalf of the Center for Social Research Analitika and provided the authors and editors with all necessary administrative and technical support throughout the implementation of the project and the subsequent preparation of the book. In addition, the book would not be possible without the generous support of the whole RRPP team, and especially Ms. Anđela Pepić, who at that time acted as the Local Coordinator of the RRPP program for Bosnia and Herzegovina, as well as Ms. Jasmina Opardija Šušnjar, who was RRPP's Program Manager at the University of Fribourg.

CHAPTER 1

International Assistance and Media Democratization in the Western Balkans: A Theoretical Framework

KRISTINA IRION and TARIK JUSIĆ

Introduction

Countries of the Western Balkans[1] are undergoing a process of democratic transition in the course of which media institutions are also being created and transformed. The transformation paths of media systems in the region emulate what is considered the European media model. This is not the least the result of media reforms to conform with accession requirements of the European Union (EU) and the standards of the Council of Europe, among others. With varying intensity international media assistance (IMA) programs accompanied the democratic media transition in Albania, Bosnia and Herzegovina, Kosovo, Macedonia and Serbia.

This edited volume is the outcome of a regional research project which explores the creation of sustainable and functional media institutions in the democratizing countries of the Western Balkans, and the discrete contribution of international assistance programs and conditionality mechanisms in the context of constraints posed by local political, cultural and economic conditions. Of particular interest is the question of what happens to imported models when they are transposed onto the newly evolving media systems of transitional societies in the Western Balkans.

While recognizing the progress made in various areas, sustainable and functioning media institutions are rare in these Western Balkan coun-

---

[1] In the EU's definition, the Western Balkans comprise Albania, Bosnia and Herzegovina, the former Yugoslav Republic of Macedonia (i.e., the Republic of Macedonia), Montenegro, Serbia, and Kosovo. Montenegro is not included in the research project behind this book.

tries. The reasons why the emergence of key media institutions has not been achieved are similar throughout the region, that is, the nature of local media markets, lackluster implementation of media reforms, political interference in the media sector, and weak professionalization but strong instrumentalization of journalism.[2] And while democratic media transformation has never been a linear process, retrogressive developments have already offset some of the progress made.

The transformation of local media systems is not considered in isolation but as part of a larger transformation process of the social and political system.[3] The research framework, which is deployed throughout this edited volume, combines three strands of literature: first, theories on democratization and democratic consolidation; second, transition in postauthoritarian countries and Europeanization, and; third, concepts of international assistance and development. The data collection in the five countries follows a unified methodology that revisits these theories in the local context. Building on the chapters with country studies cross-national analysis is used to query how the varying intensity of international assistance impacts the democratic transformation of media.

This chapter sets the scene and introduces the theoretical background underpinning the research into the processes of democratic media transformation in the five Western Balkan countries. The chapter is structured as follows: It starts with an explanation of the theoretical framework and the methodology that has been deployed by all authors contributing to this volume and its limitations. It continues with a brief introduction to the five Western Balkan countries and their sociocultural and historical traits and where they stand in political and economic terms before zooming in on the particular issues with the democratic transition of local media systems.

Theoretical Framework

In the following we will set out the research framework that underpins the methodology, which contributors have deployed throughout this edited volume. The theoretical framework combines several bodies of literature that we grouped as, first, theories on democratization and democratic

---

[2] Irion and Jusić, "International Assistance and Media Democratization" (2014).
[3] Jakubowicz, "Lovebirds?," 75.

consolidation; second, transition in postauthoritarian countries and Europeanization, and; third, concepts of international assistance and development. Conceptual contributions on democratic media transition, media reform and media institution building have been reviewed and incorporated in the theoretical framework.

There is a voluminous body of theories explaining democratization. As an umbrella, democratization covers the transition and the consolidation phase, whereby a country's development can meander back and forth without necessarily progressing to the stage of a consolidated democracy. Following Huntington, the countries in the Western Balkans form part of the third wave of democratization, which swept away communist regimes in Central and Eastern Europe, among others.[4] There is now agreement across the democratization and development literature that the transformation of local institutions is contingent upon the political context and the overall state of democratic consolidation in the country. The literature emphasizes that democratic development is a nonlinear and open-ended process.

Consolidation of democracy starts once critical institutions and procedures for democratic governance are in place. There may be situations where certain policy subsystems and institutions develop ahead of the average pace of democratic transition but the interdependencies with other state institutions and practices can severely obstruct their ability to consolidate.

The literature on media systems generally concurs that local media systems cannot be considered in isolation but they exhibit synergies with the attendant political system and culture.[5] While this research draws from Hallin and Mancini's seminal book *Comparing Media Systems*,[6] the theoretical framework for Western Balkan countries is more appropriately based on theoretical extensions for non-Western democracies.[7] In countries undergoing democratic transition, media reforms and media institution building form part of a larger transformation process of the social

---

[4] Huntington, "Democracy's Third Wave," 16.
[5] Jakubowicz, "Lovebirds?," 76; Hallin and Mancini, *Comparing Media Systems*; Humphreys, *Mass Media and Media Policy*; Voltmer, "Building Media Systems"; Zielonka and Mancini, "Executive Summary."
[6] Hallin and Mancini, *Comparing Media Systems*.
[7] Jakubowicz and Sükösd, "Twelve Concepts," 9f.; Sparks, "Media Theory"; Voltmer, "How Far Can Media Systems Travel?," 224f.; Zielonka and Mancini, "Executive Summary," 2.

and political system.[8] In postauthoritarian countries, media's transition is aggravated by "legacies of undemocratic structures, politicians, and traditions."[9] As Jakubowicz aptly observed, the media first has to disentangle itself from the structures of the state and political entities[10] and new media organization with previously unknown roles have to be constructed from the scratch.

It is not only the past that affects the development of democratic media institutions. Throughout the transition process an "enabling environment" is deemed necessary for media institutions to develop and to operate in the public interest.[11] Research on media systems in postcommunist Central and Eastern European countries pinpoints at shortcoming in the political system that seriously hamper democratic consolidation. Zielonka and Mancini identify in these countries that media, politics and business form an iron triangle, that is, a self-enforcing power structure serving local, albeit sometimes competing, elites.[12] Characteristics are the politicization of the state, weak rational-legal authority and floating laws and procedures in addition to business parallelism and fuzzy ownership.[13]

The politicized state means a situation in which political parties and other vested interests try to conquer public and state institutions in order to extract resources from them.[14] In short, public policy and administration are informed by the ad hoc needs of the politicians in power and the informality of rules to the detriment of formal institutions and the rule of law. As conceived by Weber, rational-legal authority connotes whether essential tenets of the rule of law are asserted in a country, namely public authorities' impartiality and adherence to formal rules of procedure.[15] This is contrasted by forms of clientelism where individual interests and private relationships can take precedent over impartiality and formality.[16] Floating

---

[8] Jakubowicz, "Lovebirds?," 76; Zielonka and Mancini, "Executive Summary," 2.

[9] Price, Davis Noll, and De Luce, "Mapping Media Assistance," 57.

[10] Jakubowicz, "Lovebirds?," 76.

[11] Kumar, "One Size Does Not Fit All"; Price and Krug, "The Enabling Environment" (2006), 95f.

[12] Zielonka and Mancini, "Executive Summary," 2f.; Irion and Jusić, "International Assistance and Media Democratization in the Western Balkans" (2014).

[13] Zielonka and Mancini, "Executive Summary," 2f.

[14] Grzymała-Busse, "Political Competition," 1123.

[15] Weber, "The Three Types," 1; Zielonka and Mancini, "Executive Summary," 55.

[16] Hallin and Mancini, *Comparing Media Systems*, 58.

laws and procedures are oftentimes the visible outcome of such informality but also a principle lack of governmental authority.[17]

Business parallelism connotes the overlap between media, its owners and politics, which is symptomatic in Central and Eastern Europe. Sparks observed the "close set of relations between politicians, businessmen and the media that leads to a routine interchange between different groups in post-communist countries."[18] Media ownership, in addition, is often fuzzy[19] and media outlets depend on subsidies, which are rarely transparent. All of this points to conflict of interests for the media toward its owners and their political affiliations.

Following the theoretical framework it is indispensable to explore the nexus between political and media systems and markets. The authors of the country chapters have been asked to consider and reflect on these theories in relation to the local political system and the media system. There are a variety of reasons for floating laws (for example, whether the political system is conducive to media reforms depends very much on the political system but also on the local capacity to implement).[20] The aim was to produce contextual information before describing international media assistance and the specific case studies. The common structure deployed also aids the type of cross-national comparison this edited volume is ultimately concerned with.

The next body of literature relevant to this research are Europeanization theories, which conceptualize how a country stirs toward greater influence by the EU. While most of these theories are set against the perspective of an already EU member state, Europeanization explains the dynamic of EU integration as an incremental process "by which domestic policy areas become increasingly subject to European policy-making."[21] Associate and candidate countries could be said to undergo rapid Europeanization by entering into accession negotiations with the EU. All five Western Balkan counties aim for EU integration.

EU conditionality refers to a strategy by which the EU sets rules ("conditions") that aspiring new members have to gradually fulfill in order to progress through the various stages until EU membership.[22] As a mech-

---

[17] Zielonka and Mancini, "Executive Summary," 6.

[18] Sparks, "Media Theory," 42.

[19] Zielonka and Mancini, "Executive Summary," 5.

[20] Tsebelis, *Veto Players*; Zielonka and Mancini, "Executive Summary," 2.

[21] Börzel, "Towards Convergence in Europe?," 574.

[22] Schimmelfennig and Sedelmeier, "Governance by Conditionality," 669.

anism to promote and reward political and economic reforms, conditionality is closely linked and intertwined with the wider transition process toward democracy and market economy. For the Western Balkan countries the catalogue of political, social, economic and administrative reforms has been extensive also in view of the recent armed conflicts and ethnic tensions in some countries and the overall challenging political situation.[23]

Research on international assistance ties in with democratization theories in that development at the local level is contingent on political, social and economic circumstances.[24] Moreover, it is not possible to orchestrate results but only processes that may be conducive to buttressing democratic values and practices. International media assistance can be delivered in various forms, including outright external intervention and soft power conditionality mechanisms, or through locally driven reforms with limited external assistance. Kumar's report emphasizes that all efforts to create and support democratic media institutions have to be highly specific to a country's societal needs.[25]

It is important to recall that international assistance to the media is not only motivated by building democratic media institutions but a means to promote democratic development, importantly appeasement, accountability and good governance.[26] International media assistance is thus motivated by the convoluting objectives to assist overall democratic transition and build independent media institutions. Rhodes's report "Ten Years of Media Support to the Balkans," which is central to this edited volume, summarizes that media assistance [in the Balkans] proved itself an effective way to promote democracy by removing barriers to the enjoyment of fundamental rights to information and expression as protected by international law, and without intervening in political choices themselves. When media support was perceived as being primarily driven by political objectives, it was in danger of being like the problem it sought to alleviate and obscuring the concept of independent media.[27]

---

[23] Anastasakis, "The EU's Political Conditionality," 365.
[24] For a literature overview, see Dietz, "International Media Assistance."
[25] Kumar, "One Size Does Not Fit All," 4.
[26] Norris, *Public Sentinel*; Myers, Dietz, and Frère, "International Media Assistance," 2.
[27] Rhodes, "Ten Years of Media Support," 36.

Research Questions and Methodology

The research project compares the extent to which the media institutions that have been significantly supported or established by international assistance programs and conditionality have actually been able to reach a level of sustainability and functionality.

Our comparison rests on a combination of a multilevel, case study approach within each studied country and a comparison across countries.[28] The research methodology allows us to combine country-level studies with embedded case studies on selected media institutions. The five Western Balkan countries are a suitable testbed for this combination of methodologies because across the countries fairly similar general conditions prevail but approaches to international media assistance have been distinct for a relevant period during which local media institutions underwent transformation.

Moreover, throughout the region the transformation paths of the media systems converge in what can be considered the European media model. This means that an independent media supervisory authority and a public service media organization have been set up in each country together with a number of other media institutions that play a role in this setup, which lend themselves to a cross-national comparison. It helps to appraise how the national context impacts on democratic media transformation, since the outcomes invariably differ from ideal institutions of the European media model.

The comparative "multilevel case study" approach entails two layers. First, within each country, the transformation of and international assistance to domestic media institutions are juxtaposed in order to investigate why certain policy subsystems flow better through transformational stages than others. Within each country three to four selected media institutions were studied in depth (table 1.1). For their central role in the national media system, the media supervisory authority and the public service media operator are covered for each country. Additionally, one or a couple of other country-specific media institutions are included—such as a commercial media outlet, a media self-regulatory body or a media advocacy organization—allowing for diversification across countries, provided the organization was the beneficiary of international media assistance.

---

[28] Sartori, "Comparing and Miscomparing," 243f.; Lijphart, "Comparative Politics"; Hopin, "Comparative Methods."

Table 1.1. Country Reports and In-depth Case Studies

Country	Media Regulatory Authority	Public Service Media Operator	Other Media Institution
Albania	National Council of Radio and Television (Këshilli Kombëtar i Radios dhe Televizionit, KKRT). In 2013 replaced by Authority on Audiovisual Media (Autoriteti i Mediave Audiovizive, AMA) .	Albanian Public Radio and Television (Radio Televizioni Shqiptar, RTS)	Union of Albanian Journalists (Unioni i Gazetarëve Shqiptarë, UGSH)
Bosnia and Herzegovina	Communications Regulatory Agency, CRA (Regulatorna agencija za komunikacije, RAK)	Public Service Broadcasting System, PSB (Javni RTV sistem)	Open Broadcast Network (OBN) Center for Investigative Reporting (Centar za istraživačko novinarstvo, CIN)
Kosovo	Independent Media Commission, IMC (Komisioni i Pavarur i Mediave, KPM)	Radio Television of Kosovo, RTK (Radiotelevizioni i Kosovës)	Press Council of Kosovo (Këshilli i Mediave të Shkruara të Kosovës)
Macedonia	Broadcasting Council (Sovetot za radiodifuzija)	Macedonian Radio Television (Македонска радиотелевизија, MRTV)	Macedonian Institute for Media (Македонски институт za медиуми, MIM)
Serbia	Republic Broadcasting Agency, RBA (Republička radiodifuzna agencija, RRA). In 2014 succeeded by Authority for Electronic Media (REM).	Public Service Broadcasting of Serbia (Radio-televizija Srbije, RTS)	B92 (Private TV station) Center for Investigative Reporting Serbia (Centar za istraživačko novinarstvo Srbije, CINS)

The chapters with country studies on Albania, Bosnia and Herzegovina, Kosovo, Macedonia, and Serbia briefly explain the political and media system. They are based on desk research, contact with donors and qualitative research.[29] The authors of the chapters containing country-level studies conducted between six and ten interviews with local media experts and representatives of international donor organizations about

---

[29] See the contributions of Londo, Jusić and Ahmetašević, Miftari, Dimitrijevska-Markoski and Daskalovski, and Marko in this volume.

the influence of IMA on media institution building. The chapters assess and compare the experiences between and across policy subsystems in a country.

Second, a cross-national comparison is used to query how the varying intensity of international assistance impacts the democratic transformation of media. Thompson's chapter in this book compares the evolution of public service broadcasting across these five Western Balkan countries. Ršumović contraposes two centers for investigative journalism, one in Bosnia and Herzegovina and the other in Serbia. A separate chapter is dedicated to a conceptual critique by Voltmer of explaining the democratic transformation of media institutions in the Western Balkans against media system theory and normative media ideals that were developed against the backdrop of Western democracies. Our concluding chapter synthesizes all country-level chapters to a cross-national comparison and derives high-level policy conclusions from it.

With regard to the comparative analysis, we assume that the contextual factors are similar enough across the five Western Balkan countries. The chapters covering five Western Balkan countries lay the basis for identifying variations in media assistance approaches and in outcomes in terms of sustainability and functionality of media institutions. Although there are inevitable differences among the five countries in terms of paths and dynamics of their media democratization and overall democratic transition, basic contextual characteristics surface throughout the chapters with case-level studies, namely the nature of the media markets, political interference in the media sector, weak professionalization but strong instrumentalization of journalism, and lackluster implementation of media reforms, to name only few.

This allows us to focus on the two aspects of interest to our study and compare them across the five countries: the extent to which media institutions are sustainable and functional in relation to the relevant international assistance programs and conditionality linked to those institutions in a given context. As media institutions in the Western Balkan region are often modeled after similar institutions in Western European democracies, the outcomes invariably differ from the prototype. The contributions shed light on the question of what happens to imported models when they are transposed onto the newly evolving media systems of transitional societies in the Western Balkans.

However, in spite of the efforts to gather new information, the research is limited by insufficient documentation of international media assistance. Available data is highly fragmented and does not permit reliable insights on funds invested across international media assistance projects in the Western Balkan countries. In fact, the estimations in Rhodes's 2007 report are still the most cited, including in the country studies in this project.

Table 1.2. Media Assistance in the Western Balkans, 1992–2006 (in million Euro)

	Training	Direct Support	Media Environment	Total Euro
Albania	6.9	1.8	1.9	10.6
Bosnia-Herzegovina	17.4	42	27.7	87.1
Croatia	2.4	19.7	14.5	36.6
Macedonia	3.4	9.2	11.2	23.8
Montenegro	1.3	2.9	3.4	7.6
Serbia	5.4	26.4	13.1	44.9
Kosovo	6.1	45.6	6.9	58.6
Balkans	42.9	147.6	78.7	269.2

Source: Rhodes, Ten Years of Media Support to the Balkans, 15.

Conditionality is even more difficult to approach empirically since local stakeholders carry out democratic reforms in order to comply with the requirements of third parties, notably in the run-up to EU membership. Thus, it is hard to determine which reforms were externally imposed and which correspond to local demands, or whether they (most likely) developed as a combination of both.

Moreover, economic indicators that would measure local media markets are not gathered systematically, thus obfuscating media revenues, such as from advertisements, subscriptions or subsidies. This lack of transparency makes it impossible to establish how local media are financing their operations as well as whether, and which, media can be considered sustainable businesses.

The Countries of the Western Balkan region: Common Traits and Differences

Although the countries of the Western Balkans share significant social, political, historical and economic traits, the region's recent trajectory has not been very coherent. Since the collapse of communism in the 1990s, all five countries are undergoing a difficult transition to democracy and a free market economy. They have in common a postauthoritarian legacy, relatively small territories and weak economies. However, these similarities should not obstruct the recognition of important differences in political traditions, local cultures and ethnic composition of the population throughout the region.

In the past, political traditions of statehood differed significantly, characterized by periods of bloom and decline as well as external influences, notably from the Ottomans and the Austrian empire. The region's conflict-ridden history has inspired the term "Balkanization," which is widely used to describe a process of geopolitical fragmentation. After the disintegration of Yugoslavia and war with the Serbian hegemon, Bosnia and Herzegovina and Kosovo were founded as modern states. Macedonia was also affected by a limited conflict between its two majority peoples— Macedonians and Albanians. NATO undertook extensive military interventions against Serb forces in Bosnia and Herzegovina in 1995, and in Kosovo and Serbia in 1999. Albania alone went through a peaceful transition albeit the country took in many war refugees, mainly from Kosovo.

All of the countries covered are multiethnic but their composition varies to a significant degree. In Albania and Kosovo, Albanians are by far the majority people but there is a significant Serb minority in the latter. Serbia's dominant majority are Serbs (83% of the population). In contrast, Bosnia and Herzegovina is the home of three constituent peoples (Bosniaks, Serbs, and Croats) and in Macedonia ethnic Macedonians and Albanians coexist, among others.

Today, out of these five Western Balkan countries two are in the antechamber of the European Union (EU). Macedonia (for some time) and Serbia (recently) have had candidate status, but the preaccession negotiations are open-ended. Bosnia and Herzegovina, Kosovo, and Albania are still potential candidate countries, and thus further away from their ultimate aim to accede to the EU. Striving for EU membership requires these Western Balkan countries to comply with its democratic and market

economy standards (the so-called "Copenhagen Criteria"). EU conditionality is a major driver of reforms in the region.

Media in Transition

When the communist era ceased at the end of the 1980s, the media
systems of all the countries in the focus had a similar point of departure.
Under communist rule, all broadcasting media was operated by the state
and print media was tightly controlled, while propaganda and (self)cen-
sorship were commonplace. The transition paths that local media systems
passed through, however, started to differentiate very early. It was evident
that any transition was delayed in those countries that were a party to the
latest series of conflicts in the Western Balkans.

During the 1990s media, in particular, was instrumentalized: During
the Milošević regime, Serbian mainstream media was serving government propaganda. In Bosnia and Herzegovina, the media was ethnically
divided and in most cases openly war-mongering. In Kosovo, broadcast
media in Albanian language had been banned entirely by the Serbian
regime.

Moreover, the legal vacuum that followed socialist rule and the
violent conflicts does not compare to orderly liberalization and deregulation; rather, entry into the media market has been more an ad hoc seizure
of opportunity. For Western Balkan countries most of the decade of the
1990s has been characterized as chaotic because the use of the broadcasting spectrum was disorganized and early commercialization of print
and broadcast media rushed in without a regulatory framework in place.
In all of the five countries studied, media outlets initially proliferated to
hundreds of press products and radio and TV stations. Subsequently the
issued regulation and its supervision had to assert itself before the market
eventually complied with it to a certain extent. For instance, Macedonia,
Serbia, and Bosnia and Herzegovina subsequently granted licenses to most
radio and TV stations in operation, and this was apparently only limited
by technical constraints. However, little consideration was given to the
strategic development of the broadcast media markets.

As of the early 2000s, the transformation paths of the media systems
in the five Western Balkan countries converged into what is considered
the European media model. The general characteristics of this model are
that, firstly, the law distinguishes between press and broadcast media with
a press that should be self-regulating while broadcast media is subject to

extensive regulation.[30] Secondly, the implementation and enforcement of local broadcast media legislation is delegated to independent media supervisory authorities, that is, public bodies that should be formally and in practice independent from both elected politicians and the broadcasting industry. Thirdly, originating in the broadcasting sector, the so-called dual media system provides for the coexistence of independent public service TV and radio and private broadcasters.[31]

With the exception of Kosovo, where the public service broadcaster was built from scratch,[32] the public service media organizations are the product of the reform of the former state broadcasters in the countries.

In the Western Balkans, democratic media transformation involves very intense and complex reform processes. In less than a decade, media systems in Western Balkan countries underwent four fundamental reforms. The first reform abolished monopolies and liberalized the national media sector together with the introduction of new media legislation and a media supervisory authority. Another reform transformed the state broadcaster (radio and television) to one or more public service media organizations. Local media systems saw the introduction of professional codes and other self-regulation alongside the development of professional supporting organizations, such as associations of journalists, specialized training centers, industry associations, etc. More recently, media reforms facilitate the analogue switch-off of terrestrial broadcasting, licensing of digital multiplexes together with the overall digitalization of media across all platforms. The cumulative media reform needs had to be tackled all at once, contributing to constant change in Western Balkan media systems, which hardly evokes perceptions of consolidation and stability.

The implementation of these key reforms needed supporting strategies, legislation and institutions. Characteristically, media transformation in countries that are undergoing a much larger democratic transition process is least likely to receive optimal support. Typically, local restraints on democratic media transition are threefold: Firstly, media reforms stall because important media legislation and strategies are not adopted while, secondly, pieces of existing media legislation or other norms that have an effect on the local media system are constantly put up for revision by successive governments. Lastly, media policy objectives and legislation on the

---

[30] Pursuant to EU developments broadcast media legislation is extended to audio-visual media services that are broadcast-like.
[31] Thompson, in this volume.
[32] Naser Miftari, in this volume.

one hand, and implementation and practice on the other hand, are out of step to varying degrees, since the rules and policies are often selectively interpreted and applied.

The chapters with country-level studies of Bosnia and Herzegovina, Kosovo, Macedonia, and Serbia provide ample evidence for all three deficits, sometimes cumulatively; however, issues may accrue over successive governments' terms. Albania is certainly not without setbacks in media transition but judging from Londo's chapter it appears that important media reforms have been tackled, albeit slowly, and central media institutions were left relatively undisturbed by legislative reforms.[33]

Although this research was not tasked with measuring the performance of the Western Balkan countries, a look at the trends from the International Research & Exchanges Board (IREX) Media Sustainability Index below (figure 1.1) reveals that compared to the point of departure in the early 2000s all countries show progress on specific key dimensions of free media.[34] However, Bosnia and Herzegovina, Macedonia and Serbia outperformed their peers in the recent past only to drop again to what is the regional average, or, in the case of Macedonia, even below.

Possible explanations for the initial progress in local media systems and the recent stabilization at moderate levels could be that early democratic transition was more motivated to correspond with democratic ideals and international best practices. With subsequent governments and political elites this motivation has gradually worn off compared to the will to reach and cement political power (see, for example, the chapters on Macedonia and Serbia). Also, democratic media transition was to a significant extent induced externally, notably as a result of powers given to international actors, such as, for example, in the case with the Office of the High Representative in Bosnia and Herzegovina; but this effect is not (yet) showing as forcefully for Kosovo. In many situations it is likely that an amalgamation of both strands, decreasing local motivation as well as retracting international media assistance and monitoring, in practice results in toleration of political influence extending (again) to key media institutions as well as economically fraught mass media being (re)enlisted by political and private interests.

---

[33] Londo, in this volume.

[34] The IREX Media Sustainability Index groups indicators in relation to five objectives: free speech, professional journalism, plurality of news sources, business management, and supporting institutions. Cf. IREX, "Media Sustainability Index (MSI) Methodology."

Figure 1.1. IREX Media Sustainability Index for Western Balkan Countries

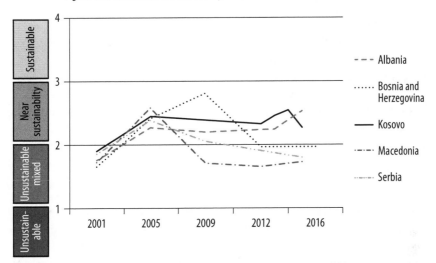

Source: IREX, sections of Albania, Bosnia and Herzegovina, Kosovo, Macedonia, and Serbia in the *Media Sustainability Index* between 2001 and 2015.

It is now widely accepted that imported media institutions and standards likely divert from the ideal-type models of similar institutions originating in Western democracies and media theory. The literature advances different theses that explain these variations as a result of the local context and conditions but also of the time required for democratic development and consolidation. Jakubowicz invokes "ontogenesis" as an analogy illustrating how local media institutions pass through similar stages of evolution as media institutions did elsewhere, although perhaps more compressed and with open outcomes.[35] Other authors stress the process of social construction during which imported values blend with local practices, as a result of which "atavistic" or "hybrid" media systems emerge.[36] Consequently, navigating the different trajectories on democratic media transition in the Western Balkan region requires a high degree of contextualization as well as an understanding of the evolutionary development and the social construction of the local media institutions.

---

[35] Jakubowicz, "Preface," xvi.

[36] Jakubowicz and Sükösd, "Twelve Concepts," 12; Voltmer, "How Far Can Media Systems Travel?"; Voltmer, in this volume.

Quality of Democracy

For the Western Balkan countries, the starting point has been anything but favorable because efforts toward democratic media transformation are confronted with "legacies of undemocratic structures, politicians, and traditions."[37] The chapters with the country-level case studies confirm a number of contemporary challenges to what would ideally amount to an "enabling environment" for the local media systems, notably that the rule of law and tenets of good governance are, even where they are in place, not effective.[38] As Marko aptly puts it for Serbia: "It has the form (laws, institutions, procedures, party pluralism, etc.) but lacks the substance of a meaningful democratic political culture."[39] The ethnic composition of the local population, which in some cases results in linguistic diversity, very much influences the political system. For Bosnia and Herzegovina as well as Macedonia, this has as a consequence that the mass media is also divided along linguistic and ethnical lines. Postconflict situations present in Bosnia and Herzegovina and Kosovo pose additional challenges because media can play a role in reconciliation but it can also work against it.

Western Balkan countries share many if not most of the characteristics Zielonka and Mancini identified in relation to other Central and Eastern European countries that undergo democratic transition, namely features that are indicative of the politicization of the state, weak rational-legal authority, in addition to a general implementation deficit.[40] In the country-level chapters accounts of the nexus between political and media systems exemplify a high degree of politicization, which are elaborated below.

Across the region, mass media editorial lines are often partisan; in the case of the public service media organization it was reported to favor the government at the time, whereas the political allegiances of the press and commercial television are distributed across the political spectrum.[41]

---

[37] Price, Davis Noll, and De Luce, "Mapping Media Assistance."

[38] That is, fairness, impartiality and objectivity of administrative processes. Cf. Kumar, "One Size Does Not Fit All," 14; Price and Krug, "The Enabling Environment" (2006), 97f.

[39] Marko, in this volume.

[40] Zielonka and Mancini, "Executive Summary," 2f.; Weber, "The Three Types," 1.

[41] In this context, Voltmer's contribution is very instructive because it critically engages with existing high notions of media pluralism and objectivity: See Voltmer, "Building Media Systems."

Albania, Macedonia and Serbia report a rise of clientelist media, while in Bosnia and Herzegovina there is a characteristic overlapping of ethnical with political patronage in the media. Partisan media tends to be even more pronounced during election times in Western Balkan countries. This was noted explicitly in the chapters covering Albania, Kosovo, and Macedonia.

In each of the countries covered in this volume political pressure on key media institutions is cited as commonplace, notably on the local media supervisory authority or the public service media organization. An additional characteristic is the significant postelectoral vulnerabilities when new governments in power repoliticize appointments to the boards of these bodies, for example, in Bosnia and Herzegovina, Kosovo and Serbia. New governments would change the legislation on the size of decision-making bodies and the rules for appointments or deploy other methods to disengage individual decision-makers.

Public money, which is a significant source of media revenues across the region, is often allocated in a nontransparent way and arguably follows clientelistic lines. This issue is especially flagged for Kosovo, Macedonia, Serbia and Bosnia and Herzegovina. The statutory independence of public service media is de facto undermined by the organizations' reliance on state funding.

Career paths of certain journalists signify a revolving door between media and political affiliations and jobs, as reported for Albania, Kosovo, Macedonia and Serbia. It has been established that many media owners in Kosovo and Macedonia were or are still elected politicians or cadres in the local partitocracy.

In relation to the media sector, the differences of the political systems in the Western Balkan region have not yet played out significantly. For example, for the local media systems it does not seem to matter whether the country's political system is majoritarian, as is the case for Albania, Serbia, and Kosovo, or polarized pluralist, as is the case for Bosnia and Herzegovina and Macedonia. Contrary to what is suggested in the theory developed in the context of Western democracies, neither political system has achieved better media policy stability or has protected independent media institutions better against partisanship and political influence.[42] In other words, neither constitutional veto points nor coalition governments are less likely to conflate political power with influence over the media and its key institutions. The pursuit of genuine public interest objectives,

---

[42] Hallin and Mancini, *Comparing Media Systems*, 298; Tsebelis, *Veto Players*, 6.

including media reforms, is often sidelined as a deliverable to satisfy EU conditionality, for example, in Serbia.

The two countries with strong ethnic differences grant veto powers to their respective ethnic constituencies, in the case of Bosnia and Herzegovina as a measure to secure peace and in the case of Macedonia in order to protect Albanian minority interests from Macedonian majority rule. The ethnic and corresponding territorial divisions are replicated in the political landscape; however, this polarization often cannot be bridged by consensus. In Bosnia and Herzegovina, where three public service broadcasters coexist, efforts to unify public service broadcasting under a common roof have not yet succeeded.[43] Interestingly, the politics of consensus appear to work best whenever elected politicians attempt to retain or increase their influence over the media but are less in favor of independent media institutions. The country report covering Macedonia describes a "pedantic distribution of spheres of influence" of Macedonian politicians over Macedonian media and Albanian politicians over Albania media.[44]

For all Western Balkan countries, civil society is not a decisive factor in public policy. Yet, for each country under consideration one or even more dedicated nongovernmental organizations specialize in media policy and advocacy, most of which have received funding from international donors for their work. They are crucial for claiming transparency and participating in legislative processes that concern the media and for being vigilant and vocal about interferences with media and journalistic freedoms. At the same time it becomes apparent from the country reports that many nongovernmental organizations that used to focus on media freedoms and freedom of expression discontinued or significantly limited their work often due to a lack of funding. Industry associations, however, became gradually more influential when representing commercial media interests in media policy making.

Media Economics

The democratic transformation of media systems in the Western Balkans faces comparatively difficult media economics. Local media markets are very small in terms of audiences, ranging from just below two million

---

[43] Jusić and Ahmetašević, in this volume.
[44] Dimitrijevska-Markoski and Daskalovski, in this volume.

inhabitants in Kosovo to seven million in Serbia. Advertisement-financed media competes for very limited sources of revenue, which is further exacerbated by the high number—in relation to the size of the media market and viewership—of print, radio and television outlets. All country reports note some degree of oversaturation in media markets the side effects of which are that private mass media ties in with politics and businesses for revenues. The overall unfavorable economic conditions after the 2008 global financial crisis have led to a further decline in advertisement spending, which disproportionately affects the print media.

In all Western Balkan countries, the public sector, including state-owned companies, is one of the most significant sources of funding for media that carry advertisements, campaigns and other public communications. This issue was specifically highlighted for Kosovo, Macedonia, and Serbia but appears to be present across the region. The resulting financial dependencies are a cause of concern whenever funds are not transparently allocated and possibly directed toward government-friendly media. Moreover, direct subsidies by the state to media outlets are quite common, for example, in Bosnia and Herzegovina and through local government in Serbia. This is regardless of the financing from public sources of the public service media in these countries, which in addition compete for advertising revenues with commercial media outlets.

Western Balkan media markets are highly susceptible to "business parallelism," which refers to the residual overlapping of "economics, politics and the media" in postsocialist countries.[45] Where there is no business in media, media becomes the business because it amplifies interests other than the public interest. Especially in highly polarized and politically fragmented contexts, media outlets that compete for rather limited resources can alternatively extract their revenue from political patronage and clientelism.[46] All country reports document fuzzy ownership issues where owners, financial stakes and political affiliations are not transparent. Compared to direct political influence, however, the issues of ownership and cross-subsidization are more subtle means to influence the editorial line of media outlets beyond the reach of constitutional and legal safeguards of media independence.

---

[45] Zielonka and Mancini, "Executive Summary," 4f.; Sparks, "Media Theory," 34f.

[46] Johnson, "Model Interventions," 80f.; Zielonka and Mancini, "Executive Summary," 3.

With a few exceptions, foreign media investors are not very prominent in Western Balkan countries. However, the international community did finance a fair number of media operations during the early 1990s in Serbia as well as in postconflict Bosnia and Herzegovina and Kosovo. The only notable development is the entry of Al Jazeera Balkans, which began broadcasting in local languages in late 2011.

Journalistic Profession and Professionalism

In these conditions, it is no wonder that the attractiveness of the journalistic profession suffers and that journalists' careers can take many directions. The country reports point out that the career paths of some journalists oscillate between media and political appointments. Moreover, it is important to note that the issue of media professionalism is not just about instilling adequate qualifications and journalistic values in fledgling and practicing journalists. As long as media patrons cannot afford and/or do not value certain qualities in journalistic professionalism even the most capable journalists may find it difficult to apply the highest standards in their daily work. Ršumović's comparison of dedicated centers for investigatory journalism in Bosnia and Herzegovina and Serbia illustrates well the dilemmas that led to the creation of such specialized journalistic hubs outside mainstream media.[47]

Other consequences of still developing journalistic professionalism are that across the region mechanisms of self-regulation and self-governance symptomatically lack acceptance and support from their own constituency, that is, press and media outlets, journalists and editors. Since under the European media model the press especially should be self-regulating this poses a Catch-22 situation between the local capacity and imported best practices.

Conclusions

The local media systems of Albania, Bosnia and Herzegovina, Kosovo, Macedonia and Serbia undergo transformations that are part of a larger democratic transformation process. Media reforms and institutions are

---

[47] Ršumović, in this volume.

formed in accordance with the contours of the European media model which is characterized by a separate regulatory treatment of the press and broadcasting media, a dual system of public service television and radio, on the one hand, and, on the other hand, commercial television and radio, as well as an independent media supervisory authority.

In spite of this familiar patterns, local media systems are distinct and created media institutions function differently than the ideal templates they were created after. As an outcome this is hardly surprising as this is recognized in the theory and literature on democratic transformation and institution building. The research framework underpinning this edited volume is thus conscious of the contextual and evolutionary development as well as the social construction of the local media institutions.

Owing to the literature this chapter maps out the characteristics of media systems of postauthoritarian countries, which have informed the methodology throughout this edited volume. Western Balkan countries share traits that are common to media systems in postauthoritarian countries and are additionally challenged by the economic conditions, given that media markets are often very small and oversaturated. The country-level case studies, assembled in this edited volume, follow a unified methodology that is suitable to trace the interdependency of media institutions from the wider political and economic context.

This chapter presents a comparative overview of the transition paths of the Western Balkan countries and summarizes relevant contextual factors. In particular, that in the early transition phase the market developed ahead of the legislative framework. Moreover, democratic media transformation involves very intense and complex reform processes; often not optimally supported and implemented. Western Balkan countries characteristically feature a significant degree of politicization of the state, weak rational-legal authority, in addition to a general implementation deficit. All these factors cumulate in the realization that—after initial progress—democratic media transformation in Western Balkan countries is stagnating.

The differences of the political systems in the Western Balkan region did not have a decisive effect on local media systems. Contrary to political theory developed in the context of Western democracies, neither political system has achieved better media policy stability or has protected independent media institutions better against partisanship and political influence.[48]

---

[48] Hallin and Mancini, *Comparing Media Systems*, 298; Tsebelis, *Veto Players*, 6.

The following chapters containing the case studies offer rich contextual explanations relevant to the democratic media transition. Against this background, the reminder of this edited volume queries how the varying intensity and means of international assistance impacts the democratic transformation of media in the Western Balkan countries. Our cross-national analysis concludes that international media assistance of varying intensity is not sufficient to construct media institutions when, in order to function properly, they have to outperform their local context.[49]

---

[49] Irion and Jusić, concluding chapter in this volume.

CHAPTER 2

Limited Assistance for Limited Impact—International Media Assistance in Albania

ILDA LONDO

Introduction

In the last twenty years Albanian media outlets and institutions have benefited from international assistance and aid, which, to some degree has contributed to shaping the media environment in the country. The assistance has spanned fields such as media law reform, support for independent and local media, media professionalism, and development of media institutions.

The development of Albanian media during the last two decades went through two phases. The first period, from early to late 1990s, marked by the so-called politically engaged media, was characterized by constant and severe struggle between the media and the government.[1] The pressure on the media became more sophisticated during the second period, from late 1990s onward, characterized by the expansion of clientelistic media. Open threats or assaults on journalists were replaced with problems of an economic nature, such as financial pressure, distribution issues, and transparency of funding, ownership, and labor relations.

Today, the country is characterized by a financially small and fragmented media market. The broadcasting system is a dual one, with public service broadcaster RTSH and a mushrooming commercial sector. The high number of media outlets cannot be economically sustainable in such a small market. As a consequence, transparency of ownership, especially transparency of media funding, remains a controversial issue. Concerns

---

[1] Baka, "Media vs. Politics," 3.

about the cross-subsidization of media outlets by their owners' other businesses, the owners' relations to politics, allegations of politically allocated state advertising, and the influence of big commercial advertisers have all led to doubts about media standards and editorial independence.

Media legislation efforts ranged from periods of strict and detailed regulation to periods of lacking or relaxed regulation. Currently the freedom of the press is guaranteed by the constitution and by law; there is no specific regulation for the print media, while regulation of broadcasting is a detailed one.

According to the IREX Media Sustainability Index, the Albanian media system has had significant progress over the years, but has experienced stagnation since 2005.

Table 2.1. IREX Media Sustainability Index for Albania, 2001–2015

Indicator	Year				
	2001	2005	2009	2013	2015
Free Speech	1.98	2.69	2.38	2.30	2.78
Professional Journalism	1.40	2.07	2.22	2.18	2.47
Plurality of News Sources	1.99	2.29	2.26	2.42	2.72
Business Management	1.41	1.88	1.87	1.69	2.10
Supporting Institutions	2.02	2.44	2.28	2.45	2.55
Overall Score	1.76	2.27	2.2	2.23	2.52

Source: IREX, "Albania," in Media Sustainability Index for the years 2001, 2005, 2009, 2013, 2015.

Despite international assistance and transformation processes, media in Albania face numerous challenges, such as slow legal reform, political influence on the regulatory body and the public service broadcaster, editorial influence of media owners and their political clients, informality of the labor market and journalists' poor organization, as well as disparity of development between national and local media.

Given all of the above, this chapter aims to provide an overview of the media system in Albania, focusing on its development in the context of foreign assistance and funding during the last two decades. The chapter will first describe the background of the political and media system in the country. It will also draw a picture of the main trends in international assistance to Albanian media, focusing on strategies, approaches, and aims of such assistance efforts. The nature and the effects of media assistance will be further analyzed in three case studies that have benefited from international media development and assistance programs: the National Council of Radio and Television (KKRT)/Authority on Audiovisual Media (AMA); the public service broadcaster, Albanian Radio and Television (RTSH); and the Union of Albanian Journalists (UGSH). The institutions in the case studies are key to the local media system and are often described as weak or politically influenced. Since international assistance was an important part of the history of these institutions, these cases would shed more light on the nature and effects of international media assistance in Albania.

Background: The Political System and the Media System

The Albanian media market is far from consolidated. Currently, twenty-six national daily newspapers are published, which is a significant number compared to its small population of around 2.9 million, but the total circulation is believed not to exceed 100,000 copies.[2] As of June 5, 2013, AMA listed in its website fifty-six local and two national radio stations. There were also two national television stations and seventy-one local televisions broadcasting in analogue, as well as two satellite stations and eighty-three cable TV stations.

The lack of reliable data on media funding does not allow for an accurate assessment of the economic size of the media market. The few public surveys and studies indicate that print media are constantly losing ground.[3] Competition from television and new media, combined with a stagnant quality of reporting, has led to a steady fall in the popularity of newspapers, especially among young people.[4]

Television advertising revenue seems to be increasing, or at least remain stable.[5] Television seems to receive the lion's share of the advertising spending, reaching almost 67% in 2011, as indicated in table 2.2.

---

[2] Ibid., 14.

[3] In 2010 the advertising revenue of daily newspapers dropped to €3–3.5 million, or 5–7% of the total media advertising market, compared to 10% in 2008. See Liperi, "Special," 52.

[4] In a survey of more than 2,000 people aged fifteen to thirty-nine, almost 72% said that they did not read newspapers at all. See Fondacioni Shoqëria e Hapur për Shqipërinë, "Përdorimi i Facebook."

[5] Instituti i Medias, "Roli i reklamave."

Table 2.2. Advertising Market Time-Series Spending Data in Albania, 2004–2011[6]

Media	2004	2005	2006	2007	2008	2009	2010	2011
Television	86.3%	81.1%	78.2%	63.6%	63.8%	68.7%	65.4%	66.8%
Radio	1.2	1.4	1.2	1.4	1.4	1.3	1.4	1.4
Press	6.4	8.1	5.8	20.1	17.8	8.5	10.7	8.5
Outdoor	6.1	9.4	14.3	15.6	17.4	21.8	20.8	22.4
Cinema	na	na	na	na	na	na	na	na
Internet	na	na	na	0.5	0.8	1.1	0.9	0.9
Ad Market (€ million)	14.5	19.8	24.38	27.18	42.23	49.3	57.4	54.34

Source: Abacus Research, November 2012, cited in Goga, "The Era of 'Cross-Platform' Media."

While advertising market trends vary, all sources point to conclusions that media outlets are not profitable businesses on their own, which leads to clientelism and negatively affects media professionalism and independence. According to the IREX Media Sustainability Index report for 2013, "most media are supported by other businesses of the media's main shareholders, which display a strong tendency to use these media as a tool to promote and protect their interests."[7]

Moreover, media content produced in the country closely mirrors the increasing political divide of the society. The trend of openly supporting one political party varies between different media outlets in degrees of subtlety, not in principle.[8] This becomes particularly visible during election campaigns, where media often serve as loudspeakers for political parties.[9] One important indicator of the level of political parallelism is the common tendency for the career paths of journalists to be shaped by their political affiliation.[10]

Against this background, it is hard to detect any signs of internal pluralism. Attempts of having different political voices and views within the same media have not been welcomed. According to the IREX report from

[6] Goga, "The Era of 'Cross-Platform' Media."
[7] IREX, "Albania" (2013).
[8] Ibid.
[9] OSCE and ODIHR, "Republic of Albania," 10.
[10] IREX, "Albania" (2009), 10.

2009, "not only are journalists unable to publish a story that the outlet owners or the political wing supporting the newspaper do not like, but they have started to adapt reports and comments in accordance with the preferences of owners or political parties."[11] As a result, the political stance is more or less uniform within one media outlet, which often leads to self-censorship.

In such a context, "the entanglements between business, politics and the media remain the greatest challenge in media independence."[12] The situation is further exacerbated by the general disregard of laws and procedure, and high level of informality—what Zielonka and Mancini describe as the context with "floating laws and procedures"[13] that is a common characteristic of postcommunist media systems. For example, the electronic media law has been amended seven times and it took five years to adopt the Law on Audiovisual Media in 2013. Similarly, the Strategy for Digital Switchover was approved only in May 2012, almost seven years after its first draft. Such a situation results in legal uncertainty and high level of informality.

It is therefore no surprise that journalism as a profession with its rules and norms remains underdeveloped. To this day, no media outlet has its own code of ethics, and the practice of self-regulatory mechanisms is largely unknown. Journalists have also found it difficult to organize themselves even for their own good. The current trade union organization was established in 2005 and is still weak. This situation naturally leads to low professionalization of journalists, with journalists lacking both autonomy and a distinct sense of their profession and purpose.[14]

Democratization and Media Assistance: An Overview

The bulk of the support in media assistance has come from aid agencies of Western states, but multilateral organizations such as UN agencies, the Organization for Security and Co-operation in Europe (OSCE), the World Bank, etc., have also been active. Until recently, some of the most active donors have included, among others, the Soros Foundation, DANIDA (Danish International Development Agency), the Swiss Development Agency, the German government, SIDA, USAID, Press Now, and

---

[11] IREX, "Albania" (2010), 9.
[12] FRIDE, "Democracy Monitoring Report."
[13] Zielonka and Mancini, "Executive Summary," 6.
[14] Ibid.

UNESCO. In recent years, the EU has also issued calls for projects that aim to assist media, either within the human rights or civil society program frameworks.

Media development assistance in Albania came in many forms: direct support for salaries, infrastructure, and capacity building of media outlets; journalism training; legislation reform; support for developing financial sustainability of media outlets; reform of public service broadcasting; helping self-organization of journalists; support for independent regulatory bodies, etc.

There is no accurate information on the amount of international assistance that was invested in developing the Albanian media system. According to the assessment by Rhodes, in the period 1996–2006, that support amounted to €10.6 million.[15] This sum constitutes just 3.9% of the donor support for the Western Balkans media, making Albania second only to considerably smaller Montenegro, in media assistance benefit.[16] Between 1996 and 2006, 64% of the €10.6 million in media assistance was spent on training, 17% on direct support and the remaining 19% on media environment, that is, projects related to media policies, media associations, self-regulation, etc.[17]

No formal structure for coordinating foreign media aid in Albania existed until 2005, when the Albanian government created the Department of Strategy and Donor Coordination. According to this department, in the period 2000–2008, the total donor commitment to Albania in the fields of civil society and the media amounts to approximately €20 million, with a disbursement rate of 58%.[18] The US was the largest donor in this sector, followed by the EU, Germany, Sweden, and the Netherlands.[19]

Albania continued to receive support for civil society and the media in the period 2009–2010, with the EU being the main donor, offering another €4.8 million, or 88% of donor support for this sector.[20] The 2011–2012 report shows donor commitment to media and civil society in the amount of €5.5 million, with Sweden as the main contributor.[21] The merging of the media sector within civil society programs reflects

---

[15] Rhodes, "Ten Years of Media Support," 15.
[16] Ibid.
[17] Ibid.
[18] DSDC, "External Assistance in Albania."
[19] Ibid., 18.
[20] Ibid.
[21] DSDC, "Analysis of Foreign Assistance Performance."

the overall withdrawal of important donors from media assistance in the Balkans, Albania included.[22]

Direct Funding for Independent Media

In the early period of media assistance direct funding for new and independent media outlets was the most common approach. The earliest biggest contributors in this respect were the US Information Agency (USIA), the International Media Fund (IMF), the Soros Foundation, and other donors.[23] The initial aid was elementary in view of the dire needs of Albanian media, including satellite dishes and VCR tapes for the state television to record international television programs, vans for newspaper distribution, setting up a computer lab for journalists, and providing newsprint for opposition newspapers.[24] Due to lower costs and easier bureaucratic rules, print media had a quicker start and enjoyed greater support. The most ambitious projects included the one by the IMF which in 1993 built the Demokracia printing house, at a cost of US$1 million, meant to be used by seven opposition newspapers that had emerged.[25]

Direct contributions to operational costs carried on for several years, targeting opposition newspapers first, but then expanding to include a wider diversity of voices. For example, in 1994 the Soros Foundation paid for the two first issues of fifteen newspapers and magazines for young people, paid transportation expenses for public broadcaster equipment that was purchased abroad, and bought equipment for the two existing associations of journalists.[26] Grants were given to independent and newly established press, ranging from US$3,000 to US$20,000.[27]

Development of local and minority media was viewed as another donor priority, at first through support for publishing expenses and later also through training for journalists.[28] In early 2000s Press Now provided

---

[22] Bagaviki Berisha, "Ndikimi i programeve," 154.

[23] Kornegay, "On the Road to Free Press in Albania," 5.

[24] Ibid., 6.

[25] Ibid., 7.

[26] Soros Foundation, "Albania Annual Report 1994," 32.

[27] Soros Foundation, "Albania Annual Report 1995," 28.

[28] Soros Foundation, "Albania Annual Report 1996," 25; Soros Foundation, "Albania Annual Report 1998," 27; Soros Foundation, "Albania Annual Report 1999," 28.

grants for printing houses and some operational support for three local newspapers based in Pogradec, Berat, and Gjirokastër.[29] Other donors, such as Swedish Helsinki Committee, supported a radio for the Macedonian minority and provided training and internship opportunities for Greek minority journalists and media in southern Albania.[30]

The majority of media that benefited from direct funding have disappeared through the years, unable to sustain themselves in a poor local media market. Out of the three local newspapers cited, only one is still running, while the Macedonian minority radio has stopped broadcasting. A survey of local and minority media cited financial hardship as the most acute problem, with none of these media being financially self-sustainable, relying on occasional donations or grants.[31]

Supporting Professionalization of Journalism

Improving professionalism of journalists has always been the most significant part of the assistance. This involved providing training and strengthening and sometimes even establishing associations of journalists and professional training centers, such as the Soros Media Training Center and the Albanian Media Institute. A number of professional associations have been created, some with more universal appeal, such as the Association of Professional Journalists, the League of Journalists, and the Union of Journalists, along with more specialized ones, based on thematic work or geography, such as the Association of Southern Journalists, the UN Press Club, the Association of Health Reporters, and the Association of Investigative Reporters.

Another dimension of supporting professionalism involved drafting norms for journalistic conduct and establishing self-regulatory bodies. A code of ethics was first drafted in 1996 and then in 2006, but its implementation has been slow.[32] After unsuccessful efforts to establish national self-regulatory mechanisms, attention turned to smaller-scale efforts, such as in-house training on ethics for newsrooms, but these did not result in adoption of codes by the media outlets or their involvement in self-regulation.

---

[29] Media Task Force, "Overview of Media Support to SEE," 19.
[30] AMI, "Annual Report 2005."
[31] AMI, "Minority Media in Albania in 2009," 19.
[32] Londo, "Albania," in *Freedom of Speech*, 34.

In addition to supporting self-regulation and establishment of ethical norms, the assistance was also offered for establishing a trade union, as a way of strengthening autonomy of journalists.

Overall, the assistance aimed at professionalization of journalism has had a mixed record. Even though there has been no success in establishing self-regulatory bodies, ethical dilemmas in media are increasingly part of the public debate. Moreover, professionalism of reporting, in spite of its limitations, has gradually improved, as the IREX Media Sustainability Index ratings show through the years. However, the organization of journalists still remains weak.

Legislative and Regulatory Reforms and International Assistance

Media legislation has been in the focus of the media assistance efforts in Albania from the early 1990s.[33] The OSCE, the Council of Europe (CoE), the EU, the Soros Foundation, USAID, German foundations, and other actors provided consultancy support for the drafting of laws, strategic documents, and other relevant policies. Assistance for legal media reform has been relatively successful, resulting in the introduction of regulation in all relevant media fields, though problems in implementation persist.

The legal reform of the media system started with the introduction of the Press Law in 1993, adopting, in a fairly closed process, the Press Law of the German state of Westphalia, without any effort to adjust it to the Albanian context.[34] The media community soon faced repressive legislation, and the law was annulled entirely in 1997.[35]

Pressured by the emergence of the first commercial TV stations, the Parliamentary Media Commission started drafting broadcasting regulation in 1995, with the expertise support provided through the CoE and the US embassy in Tirana in the subsequent years.[36] Through consultancy support, funding of study trips, and law reviews, this initiative involved an array of organizations and donors, such as International Federation

---

[33] Interview with Mustafa Eric, Media Development Officer, OSCE Presence in Albania, February 1, 2013.
[34] Londo, "Albania," in *Media Ownership*, 40.
[35] Ibid.
[36] Ibid.

of Journalists, the OSCE, the Soros Foundation, Article 19, the Federal Communication Commission in Los Angeles, IREX, etc.[37] The Law on Public and Private Radio and Television was approved in 1998.

In 2007, Albania signed an Action Plan for media legal reform with EU and CoE, who have since participated in the media legislation reform through legal analysis, consultancy and comments. This lengthy cooperation has focused especially on drafting Strategy to Digital Switchover and adopting a new law on audiovisual media, completed in 2012 and 2013, respectively.

Efforts to assist media legislation have also included regulation on libel and defamation. The Albanian Media Institute and the Open Society Justice Initiative worked on decriminalizing libel and defamation and amending civil provisions from 2004 to 2012, while the OSCE and Article 19 had also reviewed the regulation in 2004.[38] The efforts involved drafting legislation, lobbying with MPs and government, and raising awareness.[39] Since 2005, the Soros Foundation has also supported an initiative on amending the Access to Information Law.[40]

Moreover, an important part of the media assistance efforts directed at legislative reforms are activities focused on the transformation of the state broadcaster into a public service broadcasting model. International actors such as the OSCE, the Council of Europe, the EU, and the EBU have been essential in providing legal expertise in the reform that laid the basis for the creation of the public service broadcaster in Albania, as is described in more detail below.

More recently, media legislation has been linked to reforms that would speed up the EU integration process. Approval of the Law on Audiovisual Media, amendments to defamation provisions, and general implementation of the Action Plan of 2007 were made with the aim of bringing Albanian legislation in line with EU standards. While EU integration has certainly been a stimulus for amending legislation, it has not been a strong driver in this process, given the considerable delay in implementing this action plan.

---

[37] Ibid.
[38] For more information, see Pavli, "Running the Marathon," 2.
[39] AMI, "Albania Adopts Important Defamation Reform."
[40] Interview with Brunilda Bakshevani, Program Coordinator, Soros Foundation, February 20, 2013.

Media Assistance Effects

Overall, the scope of media assistance was rather ambitious, aiming to reform all key segments of the media sector, but the results have been mixed at best. The important elements of the regulatory framework have been put in place, but the reforms aimed at public broadcasters, the introduction of self-regulatory mechanisms, and the professionalization of journalism have proved to be particularly challenging. While external media assistance has been crucial for the development of the media system, endogenous factors such as the market, the culture of informality and weak institutions, and the nature of the interaction between politics, business, and media, have all negatively affected the outcome of donor efforts in the media field.

The following section provides a more systematic insight into the nature of media assistance in Albania by focusing on some of the most important institutions within the media system that have been affected by international aid efforts. Three case studies will be examined: the regulatory body for audiovisual media, the public service broadcaster, and the journalists' trade union.

National Council of Radio and Television (KKRT)/Authority on Audiovisual Media (AMA)

Këshilli Kombëtar i Radios dhe Televizionit (National Council of Radio and Television, KKRT), the regulatory authority for electronic media, started operating only in 2000, facing the task of regulating an already very dynamic landscape of electronic media. The regulator was set up as an independent body, whose main task was to oversee the broadcasters' abidance with regulation, guarantee fair competition among electronic media, and propose new legislation or strategies for further development of these media.[41] In March 2013, the parliament approved a new law on audiovisual media,[42] where the regulatory authority KKRT became Autoriteti i Mediave Audiovizive (Authority on Audiovisual Media, AMA.)[43]

---

[41] "Ligji nr. 8410 Per Radion dhe Televizionin Publik dhe Privat."

[42] AMI, "Parliament Approves the Law on Audiovisual Media."

[43] Irion, K., Ledger, M., Svensson, S. and Fejzulla, E. 2014. *The Independence and Functioning of the Audiovisual Media Authority in Albania*. Study commissioned by the Council of Europe, Amsterdam/Brussels/Budapest/Tirana, October, 2014.

International Assistance to the Regulator

International assistance to KKRT was primarily focused on providing support for the normal functioning of the regulator, for example, through capacity building and training. DANIDA, along with IREX through USAID funding, has contributed direct funding for equipment, expertise, training, exchange programs, and drafting the plan for frequencies.[44] A crucial step that enabled KKRT to start its activities was the assistance to complete the initial mapping of the frequency plan of the spectrum, by providing necessary equipment and training to KKRT staff.

Perhaps the most visible form of assistance to the regulator has been bringing expertise to legal reform, laying the legal ground for the creation of KKRT, and in general supporting the idea of an independent regulatory agency. This decision was made against a background that needed a proper balance between the dynamic regulation of an unregulated and booming electronic media market and the tendency of government to control other institutions and branches of power.[45] From 1998 to 2013 there have been seven amendments to the broadcasting law, affecting KKRT's structure and competencies, with the consultancy of international actors in almost all of them.

In addition, KKRT received assistance for issuing licenses after the approval of the law[46] while actors such as the OSCE and the Council of Europe have provided legal counseling on the regulation of digital broadcasting, audiovisual media, and the finalization of the Strategy to Digital Switchover.[47]

Initially, the support for KKRT/AMA was long-term and semi-continuous, but of a low intensity. However, with the exception of the legal reform and the early stage of the foundation of KKRT, assistance was rather sporadic. For example, the unlicensed emergence of the first commercial multiplex found KKRT unprepared to regulate digital broadcasting. The OSCE and the Council of Europe provided legal counseling on the drafts that emerged both for the strategy and the law on digital

---

[44] Interview with Andrea Stefani, IREX representative, February 28, 2013.
[45] Cela, "Mediat elektronike," 6.
[46] Ibid., 7.
[47] KKRT Materials on Digital Switchover project, located at: http: www://kkrt. gov.al. Accessed May 2, 2013.

Table 2.3. Amendments to Broadcasting and KKRT Regulations

Law	Content
Law no. 8410 (1998)	First broadcasting rules for public and commercial media KKRT established as regulator License terms specified for commercial media Content regulation introduced
Law no. 8655 (2000)	KKRT competencies expanded KKRT sources of funding increased Specifications to license conditions and limitations of ownership KKRT sanctioning ability increased
Law no. 8794 (2001)	KKRT internal structure further regulated Role and competencies of KKRT chair further detailed More rules on conflict of interest of KKRT Regulation of cable broadcasting License fees changed
Law no. 9016 (2003)	Majority to approve KKRT annual report specified
Law no. 9124 (2003)	Broadcasting rights regulated KKRT responsible for overseeing their implementation
Law no. 9531 (2006)	Membership reduced from seven to five, changing the quorum as well Mode of selection changed by shortlisting from professional organization proposals rather than political parties proposals Further limitations on conflict of interest potential Further details on ownership limitations
Law no. 9677 (2007)	KKRT membership go back to seven, changing the quorum again
Law no. 97 (2013)	KKRT transformed to AMA

broadcasting.[48] These actors have provided expertise through the eight years needed to finalize the Strategy to Digital Switchover, with the OSCE securing technical and legal expertise and being the main partner of KKRT in raising awareness among local operators in the country in the consultancy process that followed.[49]

---

[48] Londo, "Digital Television in Albania."
[49] KKRT Materials on Digital Switchover project.

Many of the efforts aimed at improving the operations and the standing of the KKRT were initiated within the European integration processes and the overall harmonization of the media regulation to EU and CoE standards.

Against this background, contextualization of the assistance has been generally successful, since the cooperation of the regulator with international actors has been constant. This has also been conditioned by the fact that, as a rule, legislation has followed rather than preceded developments on the ground.[50]

Although a formal coordination has been lacking, the assistance to KKRT has been generally coherent. The involvement of the same actors in legal support and consultancy (OSCE, CoE, and EC) operating on the same principles have helped avoid any particular conflicts in assistance provision.

Nevertheless, continuous monitoring and evaluation have been absent, perhaps due to the lack of continuous long-term projects. Aside from the more general but regular reports in the Media Sustainability Index by IREX and EU progress reports, there is no specific monitoring of KKRT's activities. KKRT's own annual reports, presented and discussed in the parliament, are an alternative source of regular reflection on the regulator's work.

Challenges to KKRT/AMA

In spite of the international assistance efforts and the progress made, KKRT/AMA's performance currently faces several challenges, stemming from political parallelism of the media, the politicization of the state, and the weakness of the rule of law and of other relevant institutions. These factors manifest themselves mainly through the election of members of the agency's governing bodies, and its decisions. An internal culture of independence has also proven difficult to develop, while the funding scheme and informality continue to challenge its normal operation.

---

[50] KKRT started working after the emergence of more than thirty TV and radio stations, and digital broadcasting regulation was approved many years after digital multiplexes had already operated. Similarly, KKRT approached OSCE for assistance in the digital switchover project after digital broadcasting had emerged.

For example, the formula for the election of KKRT members has changed several times.[51] Additionally, the lack of political consensus has challenged the smooth election of KKRT members: from 2000 until 2004, the opposition refused to propose candidates for KKRT,[52] while for most of 2009 the regulator lacked a quorum, since opposition withdrew its MPs from the parliament.[53] The influence of the political climate on KKRT was also visible in the interruption of the mandate of several members.

The second challenge has to do with the profile of KKRT members. Previous work experience of the chairs of KKRT or their future political career have cast doubts on the practical respect for criteria for appointing members of the Council.[54]

Third, one of the main objections to KKRT's performance has been related to concerns about politically biased decisions. These concerns have mainly been related to the application of a double standard in decisions related to licenses and broadcasting[55] and on decisions on cases of political advertising.[56]

---

[51] Until 2006, the president proposed one candidate based on professional merit and qualifications while the other six were proposed by the Parliamentary Media Commission and then elected through a simple majority vote. In 2006 the number of KKRT members was reduced to five and civil society associations and academia were involved in the nomination process. Later the majority and opposition agreed that two extra members would be appointed by opposition MPs from among the civil society candidates; Londo, "Albania," in *Television across Europe*, 79–82.

[52] Londo and Shuteriqi, "Albania," 12.

[53] Londo, "Mapping Digital Media," 76.

[54] Ibid.

[55] In 2004 TV Shijak, openly supporting the then opposition, was fined for violating broadcasting rights and its license was temporarily withdrawn. The station claimed that these sanctions were politically motivated, with the regulator applying a double standard. With the change of power and a new KKRT in 2007, an action to remove broadcasting antennas and free up spectrum was dubbed as politically motivated, as the antennas belonged to TV stations that criticized the government. See Londo and Shuteriqi, "Albania," 19; Londo, "Albania," in *Television across Europe*, 82–87.

[56] In 2008 KKRT fined News 24 TV for broadcasting an advertising spot ridiculing the government, claiming the law allowed political parties or associations to broadcast advertising spots only during electoral campaigns. By contrast, KKRT refused to act in 2010, when another movement broadcast an advertising spot against the then opposition leader. The comparison between these cases led to allegations on use of double standards that were politically influenced. See Londo, "Mapping Digital Media," 77.

The frequent changes in KKRT members and recent changes in its staff have made it difficult to strengthen a core that would create an internally independent culture.[57] KKRT is subject to audits by the Supreme State Audit, which are not systematic. KKRT has achieved a fair degree of transparency, publishing its decisions online and in the official gazette, but the decisions lack explanations. KKRT is also required to hold public consultations in regard to the development of national strategies for broadcasting.[58] In 2008 and 2009, KKRT, together with the OSCE, held discussion sessions with local and national operators regarding digital switchover and made the materials available online.

An additional challenge is related to the funding scheme of KKRT, which has several sources of income.[59] The regulator received state funding until 2006.[60] KKRT drafts its own budget, which is approved by the government. The KKRT budget has fluctuated through the years, and it also depends on the rate of payment of obligations and dues by operators.[61] This financing scheme makes it difficult for KKRT to function smoothly, especially in terms of needed investments. KKRT can still ask the government for funding for investment projects, but the funding success depends on the economic situation in the country.[62] Another source of funding is the percentage KKRT receives from fines imposed to electronic media, but the rate of payment of fines is low.[63] These continuous episodes point to the existing culture of informality, which weakens

---

[57] The opposition has recently pointed out that there have been politically motivated changes in internal technical staff. See Albanian Parliament, *Minutes*, 5.

[58] Ibid.

[59] These include the revenue from fees for administration of licenses, annual license fees, revenue from processing license applications, revenue from taxes applying to radio and television broadcasts, state budget funding, and donations.

[60] Londo and Shuteriqi, "Albania," 13.

[61] According to KKRT/AMA Annual Reports, in the period 2006–2013, the lowest budget was in 2007 with ALL66 million (€467,142) while the highest was ALL108.1 million (€707,214) in 2013.

[62] KKRT's 2013 draft budget asked for government funding for establishing a digital monitoring studio with the imminent digital switchover, but the Ministry of Finance suggested that funding should come from KKRT's own revenue. This was considered impossible, since the investment would cost half of the total annual revenue (ibid.)

[63] In 2012 KKRT had imposed seventy-four fines in the amount of ALL21,380 million (c. €150,271) but only ALL2.56 million (c. €18,285) were collected (ibid).

the regulator's authority.[64] A KKRT member also explained the selective implementation of decisions was due to political reasons: "When there is harmony between the decisions of the KKRT and government interests, the police or tax police also obey these decisions; when this harmony is not existent, KKRT decisions are not implemented."[65]

Overall, assistance to KKRT has been long-term, but of low intensity. It has been particularly focused, with specific aims, producing equally specific results. Initial efforts to provide technical expertise and build capacities for KKRT have been met, although not easily. Thanks to international assistance, KKRT was able to start the regulation process of a chaotic media landscape from scratch, fulfilling specific goals such as mapping the broadcasting spectrum, issuing licenses, and establishing rules of licensing with consultation from international actors. Independence of the regulator and a pluralistic, free, and independent media market have been only partially achieved. The explanation for this is complex, taking into account not only the way KKRT functions, but especially the social, cultural, political, and economic factors that affect the overall media landscape in the country, the regulator included.

Public Service Broadcasting: Albanian Radio and Television (RTSH)

RTSH, the public service broadcaster, is composed of Radio Tirana and Televizioni Shqiptar (Albanian Television [TVSH]). The approval of the Law on Public and Private Radio and Television in 1998 marked the formal transformation of RTSH from a state-owned institution into a public broadcaster.[66] The law establishes three governing organs of RTSH: the Steering Council, the director general and the Management Council.[67] The Steering Council is the highest governing body, while the director general is in charge of management of overall administrative, programming, and financial issues. The Management Council is an advisory body to the Director General on the financial and administrative issues, but not the content.[68]

---

[64] Ibid., 11.
[65] IREX, "Albania" (2009), 5.
[66] Londo and Shuteriqi, "Albania," 22.
[67] "Law no. 8410 on Public and Private Radio and Television," Art. 86.
[68] Ibid., Art. 104.

International assistance to RTSH

While there was no overall donors' assistance strategy, the assistance to the public broadcaster has generally been coherent. The aim has been to increase the professionalism of journalists and create a legal environment conducive to fulfilling the public mission of the broadcaster. In its early stage, the assistance to the public broadcaster included funding for its equipment, as well as content production and professional training for journalists. Several actors, such as DW, ZDF, IREX, and EBU, have organized or funded sporadic training courses for journalists or technical staff. ZDF has provided training of technical staff, while DW has provided editorial training.[69] Currently, RTSH is part of the EBU Special Partnership Program, which operates with EU support and consists of program exchanges, seminars on management, digital archiving and news production, consultancy on strategy and planning, etc.

Assistance has been rather successful in terms of content production, where RTSH has been a pioneer. For example, *Troc*, a program made by and for children with UNICEF support, has been a unique program of this kind for many years. Similarly, the radio soap opera *Rruga me pisha*, which addressed social issues and was made with UK support, was the only production of this kind in the country at the time. As a part of a regional program implemented by the Baltic Media Centre, RTSH participated in a daily TV news satellite exchange with other public broadcasters, organized through ERNO (Eurovision Regional News Exchange). This also included coaching and assistance to regionally coproduced prime-time TV series on topics such as youth issues, environment, youth and culture, etc.[70] However, content production and exchange has proven unsustainable. The production stopped once foreign support ended.

Legal expertise regarding RTSH has also been a significant part of international assistance, starting with the drafting process of the Law on Public and Private Radio and Television. The law imposed the model of the European public broadcaster, obliging RTSH to provide public service content and to respond to the diverse needs of society.

RTSH has benefited from legal consultancy provided by the OSCE, the Council of Europe, the EU, and the EBU as part of the general reform

---

[69] Media Task Force, "Overview of Media Support to SEE," 4–5.
[70] Ibid.

of media regulation, the general idea being to support the establishment of a functional and independent public service broadcaster. In 1997, Article 19 recommended that the government's priorities should include passing regulation that safeguards editorial and operational independence, while authorities should refrain from exerting pressure.[71] Similarly, the OSCE commissioned a review of the RTSH statute, recommending that the charter should clearly define the status of RTSH as a public institution which enjoys editorial freedom and institutional autonomy, along with a more specific definition of its program obligations and a change in the management system.[72] To this day no further changes have been made to the statute.

Long-term assistance to RTSH in developing strategies for reforming the broadcaster to a truly public one has been limited. An exception was the EBU assistance to draft RTSH's plan for digital switchover in 2007. As Londo and Shuteriqi argue: "While RTSH can certainly use any kind of foreign assistance, expertise in implementing satisfactory reform would be an important way to help TVSH successfully fulfill its public service mission."[73]

International assistance to RTSH has been less substantial compared to that offered to commercial media, a trend the Media Task Force report concluded for the whole region.[74] Some organizations saw RTSH as a part of the government propaganda machine, with no desire to reform itself.[75] Other donors tried to assist the reform, but were discouraged to do so. IREX intended to assist RTSH with improving its accountancy system, and especially control of its ad revenues. They soon gave up, seeing that there was not enough interest from RTSH.[76] This example indicates the institution's resistance to change, as well as a slow adaptation to the new reality in which advertising and funding are real concerns even for the public service broadcaster. Hence, initiatives that required a more substantial involvement did not succeed due to RTSH's resistance to change and donors' insufficient level of interest.

---

[71] Darbishire, *Analiza e ligjit shqiptar*, 70.

[72] Ibid.

[73] Londo and Shuteriqi, "Albania," 28.

[74] Ibid.

[75] Interviews with Andrea Stefani, February 28, 2013, and Mustafa Eric, February 1, 2013.

[76] Interview with Andrea Stefani, February 28, 2013.

Assistance to RTSH has not been regularly monitored and evaluated. RTSH drafts its annual reports, which are discussed in the parliament. IREX and the EU also tackle the public broadcaster in their annual reports. Both reports show concern that "the editorial independence of the public service broadcaster has not been strengthened,"[77] while the appointment of Steering Council remains political.[78]

Challenges to RTSH's Public Mission

Fulfillment of the public mission of RTSH has been an elusive goal ever since RTSH embarked on its transformation process; challenges to the broadcaster remain numerous.

For example, the Steering Council election formula has been a continuous source of controversy.[79] Similarly to KKRT, the election of KDRTSH members has largely reflected the political climate and tensions in the country, hindering its normal operation. In spite of the purport goal of transforming the Council into a more professional body, normal functioning of the Steering Council has remained sensitive to and dependent on political developments.

In terms of the broadcasting-politics relationship, Albania can be considered a country where the ruling majority always seeks to control the majority of seats in the regulatory authorities, the Steering Council included. The opposition's continual struggle against—and sometimes boycott of—these bodies highlights the fact that the regulatory practice in Albania is to institutionalize political dependence, making members of regulatory authorities dependent on (and reactive to) political moods rather than able to act in a professional manner to improving the institutions.

---

[77] European Commission, "Albania 2012 Progress Report."

[78] IREX, "Albania," 2013, 6.

[79] Until 2006 the Steering Council consisted of fifteen members, elected in equal numbers by ruling majority, the opposition, and civil society activists (Londo and Shuteriqi, "Albania," 11). In 2006, the Steering Council membership was halved from fifteen to seven, with the logic of replacing political balance with professional merits, and later it was agreed to increase to 11 ("Për disa shtesa dhe ndryshime në ligjin nr. 8410"). In 2013 the formula changed again with the change of the law. Currently the council should have 11 members, elected in a manner that respects political balance between propositions of ruling majority and opposition, respectively ("Për mediat audiovizive në Republikën e Shqipërisë").

There is also a visible politicization of content on RTSH, especially for its news and current affairs programs: for example, in July 2012 RTSH devoted approximately 34% and 31% of the broadcasting time to the prime minister and the government, respectively.[80] The ratio between the ruling party and the opposition in these news editions was 13% to approximately 5%.[81] Hence, *there has been a persistent criticism* of the public broadcaster's performance, especially regarding the political balance in news and current affairs.[82] Representatives of the public broadcaster have constantly opposed the claim that RTSH has been politicized, or at least have limited their validity to just the information department.[83] Even though the general public perception is far from positive, since we lack public data on audience share, it is impossible to measure the success or failure of RTSH.

The funding scheme presents another problem for normal functioning of RTSH. The funding is a mixed one, including sources such as license fee, advertising, services to third parties, and the state budget. Revenue from advertising and other sources have recently improved, while RTSH is still dependent on funding from the state budget for specific activities, such as funding of its orchestra and the annual song contest. The main source of funding for RTSH is expected to the be license fee. Although the license fee was recently increased, problems with its collection persist.[84] The continuous, yet unresolved, concern in the last twenty years over the proper way of collecting and transferring the license fee to the public broadcaster highlights the informality in Albanian society as a hindering factor in viability of public institutions, among others.

Furthermore, another concern has been that the law does not clearly determine the tasks and competencies of the three governing bodies, allowing for overlapping of competencies. In terms of staff integrity, there has been a high profile case of former RTSH director charged with corruption and mismanagement, but he was acquitted in court. Perhaps the biggest problem is related to the editorial independence of the newsroom, as described above. According to the IREX 2013 report, "the state media, which are not yet really public, are completely partisan, a permanent client

---

[80] KKRT, "Koha e Plote per Subjektet Politike dhe Institucionet Qendrore."
[81] Ibid.
[82] Londo, "Mapping Digital Media," 29.
[83] Albanian Radio and Television Steering Council, *Annual Report*, 11.
[84] License fee was ALL 600 (€5) per year, per household, until 2010, when the Government doubled it.

of each ruling majority, and do not serve the public interest."[85] It has also not been possible for RTSH to establish an internal culture of independence, given the continuous change of director generals, Steering Council members, and allegations that RTSH changes staff members to match the rotation of power in the government. The union of RTSH employees is hardly active.

RTSH reports to the parliament in annual public meetings, but the annual report or decisions of the Steering Council or other structures are not published. RTSH may be audited by the Supreme State Audit every three to four years. The last audit was in 2007, when some irregularities were found in labor contracts and other administrative matters.[86]

Overall, the assistance to RTSH has hardly been systemic, long-term, or of high intensity. Consequently, impact has been limited. Assistance has been limited to professional training, program exchange and networking, and legal analysis and recommendations. Resistance to change, especially in the early stage, coupled with the lack of a tradition of public service broadcasting have slowed down the reform of RTSH. Sustainability of successful programs that focus on various social groups has also proven difficult and dependent on donor funding. Hence, the doubts about the ability to transform RTSH into a public service broadcaster are still evident.

Union of Albanian Journalists (UGSH)

UGSH is a nonprofit organization, established in 2005 with the aim of protecting Albanian journalists.[87] The union has been active in protecting journalists' rights mainly through public statements, press conferences, media articles, and sometimes by following court cases against journalists. Moreover, the union has negotiated collective contracts with some of the main media outlets in the country.

---

[85] IREX, "Albania," 2013, 9.
[86] Londo, "Albania," in *Television across Europe*, 92.
[87] Unioni i Gazetarëve Shqiptarë, "Statuti." The highest organ is the General Assembly, followed by the steering board, which has a guiding and supervising role of the union. The Commission of Financial Control acts as the financial control of the union's activities.

International Assistance to the Trade Union of Journalists

The main advocate for establishing a trade union for journalists has been IREX. This organization supported the establishment of the first trade union of journalists in 1999, but the union was not able to rally sufficient support and interest from journalists, as "the reporters were too afraid to join because they feared losing their jobs."[88]

In 2005 the trade union was established again with IREX and USAID assistance.[89] As the initial support from IREX came to an end, other donors and organizations have supported the union, such as the UN, the Soros Foundation, the OSCE, and the Friedrich Ebert Foundation.[90] The interest of donors has not been exclusively on strengthening the capacities of the trade union as a way of improving journalists' rights, but also of organizing joint activities with the union as a way of reaching journalists, especially local ones. In general, the projects have reflected the local needs, though they were not as substantial or long-term as the union would have liked.[91]

Assistance has not been substantial and the tactics employed have been generally of low intensity and short-term.[92] The initial two-year IREX support consisted of operational support, capacity building, training, and consultancy. Subsequent assistance has been short-term and of a more product oriented nature, ensuing projects focused on attaining specific goals and producing concrete results, such as the website of the union, media monitoring, training for journalists, reports on the labor relations situation, and awards for journalists. There has been no formal coordination of donors; neither has there been monitoring nor evaluation of the assistance.[93]

Recently, support for the union has not been among the donors' priorities, focusing on joint events and interests at a particular time, slightly straying from the union's original mission.[94] Hence, the strategy of assistance to the union has been systemic and process oriented—at first focusing on incremental development of skills and infrastructure, and in

---

[88] IREX, "Albania" (2003), 10.

[89] IREX, "Albania" (2005), 13.

[90] Union of Albanian Journalists website: http://unioni-gazetareve.com/. Accessed on May 4, 2013.

[91] Interview with Aleksander Cipa, chairman of UGSH, April 12, 2013.

[92] Interviews with Andrea Stefani, February 28, 2013, and Aleksander Cipa, July 31, 2013.

[93] The exception is an internal evaluation report of UNDEF support (UNDEF, "Evaluation Report").

[94] Interview with Aleksander Cipa, July 31, 2013.

Table 2.4. Assistance to the Union of Albanian Journalists

Donor	Assistance Type	Duration
IREX[95]	• Direct operational support (equipment, office rent, salaries) • Training and capacity building (media freedom protection, negotiation tactics on labor relations) • Consultancy (drafting models of labor contracts and collective agreement)[96]	2005–2007
United Nations Democracy Fund[97]	• Capacity building (website establishment, distribution of membership cards, monitoring media freedom)	2010 (3 months)
Soros Foundation[98]	• Professionalization (monitoring media coverage of crime and corruption) • Establishment of investigative reporters' network	2011 (12 months)
FES and OSCE[99]	• Monitoring compliance with norms (conduct of survey on labor relations)	2012 (12 months)
UN Women[100]	• Training (gender issues coverage in Albanian media) • Funding (awards for journalists)	2012–2013 (6 months)
Japan International Tobacco[101]	• Funding (annual awards for journalists)	2007–2013 (annual event)

the later stage changing to a product-oriented one, focusing more on specific goals and objectives. For some donors, this decision has been influenced both by their own priorities and by UGSH's poor capacities in project implementation.[102]

---

[95] Interviews with Andrea Stefani, February 28, 2013, and Aleksander Cipa, July 31, 2013.

[96] Assistance in drafting a model of collective agreement and labor contract for journalists, mainly from Bulgarian experts, also considering similar experience in Hungary, Italy, Bulgaria, and Greece; Cipa, "Unioni i Gazetarëve Shqiptarë."

[97] UNDEF, Evaluation Report.

[98] Interview with Brunilda Bakshevani, Coordinator, Open Society Foundation Albania, February 20, 2013.

[99] Interviews with Aleksander Cipa, July 31, 2013, and Mustafa Eric, February 1, 2013.

[100] Interview with Aleksander Cipa, July 31, 2013.

[101] Ibid.

[102] Interviews with Mustafa Eric, February 1, 2013, and Brunilda Bakshevani, February 20, 2013.

Challenges Facing the Trade Union of Journalists

The union has established branches in the main cities in the country and at the moment it has about 500 members that regularly pay their membership fees.[103] UGSH estimates there are 5,000 media employees in the country, and 92% of journalists work without contracts.[104]

In a highly polarized country the union seems to have escaped the political bias. The impact of the union is limited by the social context and traditions of the media community, but the general opinion on the union is relatively good. The union has been active in protecting journalists, and bringing problems related to media freedom and the protection of journalists from pressure to the public agenda.[105] Journalists are still afraid of the unlimited arbitrary power of their outlet's owners, though.[106]

The formalization of labor relations continues to be an important problem in Albania, directly affecting the impact of UGSH. In 2005, 66% of journalists interviewed were pessimistic regarding the rapid empowerment of the trade union with the aim of formalizing labor relations, indicating the lack of confidence in journalism associations given their failure thus far.[107] The union has certainly been active in trying to pressure official authorities regarding labor relations in the media, but proper formalization of labor relations in society seems to be a lengthy process. Hence, the journalists are skeptical about organizing and putting their trust in the union, given the limited power the union has had in this context.

A key challenge is also the lack of any tradition of active organization among Albanian journalists. "The only gesture of solidarity among us is the reaction when a reporter is threatened by crime or politics, or when a media outlet confronts politics, the government, or the main parties."[108] The factors that affect the strength of the union's work are the relatively high mobility of journalists within the media market as well as some journalists tendency to dip into and out of the profession.

Finally, the funding model of the union combines external funding from donors with internal funding from membership fees, but so far has

---

[103] Interview with Aleksander Cipa, February 20, 2012.
[104] Interview with Aleksander Cipa, July 31, 2013.
[105] IREX, "Albania" (2012), 16.
[106] Interview with Aleksander Cipa, February 20, 2012.
[107] Cipa, "Unioni i Gazetareve," 7.
[108] Cipa, "Pushteti qe zhvishet nga dinjiteti," 9.

failed to ensure its financial stability. The statute of the union stipulates that the main income source is membership fees (of approximately €1.50 a month). While external funding is dwindling, missing membership payments are creating problems as well, linked to lack of trust of journalists in such associations. The lack of funding is also a limitation for the union to strengthen its capacities and achieve visible results, which would, at least in theory, increase income from membership and also expand the membership. Economic interests are against the odds of UGSH, since journalists have to see some benefits before starting to support the union.[109]

Concluding Remarks

The purpose of this chapter was to offer an overview of international assistance approaches and to analyze their eventual implications for the development of the media system in Albania during the last two decades. Considering the case studies and other examples mentioned, it is difficult to establish a direct let alone a causal link between the assistance received and the present situation of the media, partly because the assistance has been of low intensity and semi-continuous, but partly due to the complex interplay of a variety of contextual factors that have interfered with assistance efforts and their outcomes.

Nevertheless, one can safely say that media assistance efforts have succeeded in supporting a basic structure of a system (by helping the development of the regulatory agency and the trade union, for example) and have also contributed to the broader liberalization of the media sector and the creation of a legal framework. The media assistance started with support for independent media which could be labeled as the first phase "of direct support to besieged media against state-controlled outlets."[110] Then, attention turned to legal reform, establishment of regulatory authority, and reform of public broadcaster, mainly through drafting legislation and capacity building. Parallel to this, support for independent and local media outlets continued through direct funding and training. Establishment of education centers, later followed by self-regulatory initiatives, was another focus of media assistance.

---

[109] Interview with Andrea Stefani, February 28, 2013.
[110] Rhodes, "Ten Years of Media Support," 9.

However, there are many factors that limit the potential for the long-term sustainability of the results of media assistance efforts in Albania. Those factors can be classified into two groups: The first group of factors is related to the nature of deployed assistance strategies, that is, the way international actors and donors approached the reform process in terms of programmatic consistence, duration of engagement, focus, commitment, amounts of funds provided, coordination, and monitoring. The second group of factors has to do with the challenging nature of the local context—in particular, the weak media market, political and business influence on the media system, and the weak rule of law coupled with strong informal rules and mechanisms of doing business.

With respect to the first group of factors—the nature of deployed assistance—several key aspects should be underlined. First, the overall scale of assistance was rather limited in terms of funding, especially when compared to other countries in the region, which restricted the potential impact on the media system.[111] "The development of media as a means to an end rather than as an end in itself is a discernible trend over the years," a report on USAID media assistance notes.[112]

Second, most assistance can be considered short-term, intensifying usually in crisis periods, while long-term projects have been fewer. For example, during the Kosovo crisis there was a high intensification of media assistance aimed at informing and assisting Kosovo refugees through media services in Albania, producing special programs, taking journalists to refugee camps and other hot areas, producing publications, documentaries, etc. However, this was an ad hoc approach, one that was discontinued when the crisis was over. Long-term engagements were primarily focused on legal reforms and the creation of professional education centers, but such support was far from systematic and strategic. Moreover, predominantly short-term orientation and absence of strategy was combined with the limited coordination of donors' efforts, and weak monitoring of the results.

Third, some of the media assistance efforts suffered from what Berkowitz et al. term the "transplant effect"[113] or what Zielonka and Mancini call "opaque imitation of Western models."[114] The very early example of direct transplantation of a German press law led to resis-

---

[111] Ibid.
[112] Cary and D'Amour, "U.S. Government Funding for Media."
[113] Berkowitz, Pistor, and Richard, "The Transplant Effect," 167.
[114] Zielonka and Mancini, "Executive Summary."

tance and abrogation of the law. Conversely, local consent is not the only requirement for adaptability of norms and institutions. Even though there was nominal local support for self-regulation mechanisms, the council of ethics failed to materialize due to lack of sufficient interest from the media community and rather weak professionalization of journalism in general. Other contextual factors, such as different priorities of the media owners and a lack of independence and autonomy of journalists are also of crucial importance.

Fourth, funding strategies for media development varied according to the media institution targeted, and have proven to be one of the weakest aspects of the media assistance efforts. Public institutions established by law, such as the KKRT and RTSH, have depended on local funding, which offered them financial sustainability, but increased the risk of greater political dependence. Other institutions, as the union, depended mainly on international funding, having almost no local financial sources. This lack of funding poses a genuine problem especially for associations and media networks. For example, a regional network of media outlets established with OSCE assistance in 2010 has struggled after the first operational support ended and has almost disappeared.[115] Many local or minority media established with foreign funding ceased to exist after the funding ended, due to the limitations of the small markets where they operate.[116] An exception to the rule is the Forum for Protection of Audiovisual Authors, also started with IREX and USAID support. The members of this association see more tangible results in the royalties they receive and have greater trust in the organization.[117]

Fifth, it seems that there is a greater sensibility and pressure for media institutions to improve in the framework of the EU integration process. However, this influence should not be overestimated. Conditionality as a strategy of media assistance has had a mixed record so far and has mostly been effective in the legal reform of the media. It has failed to guarantee the absence of political and financial pressures on key media institutions.

With respect to the second group of factors which stem from the nature of the local context, the most important ones are the following. First, the assistance efforts have been hampered by the weak rule of law

---

[115] Interview with Mustafa Eric, February 1, 2013.
[116] IREX, "Albania" (2013), 12.
[117] Interview with Andrea Stefani, February 28, 2013.

and the strong culture of informality that pervades all aspects of life in Albania. Hence, the success of legal and institutional reform is dependent on and affected by other actors. The gap between good laws and good implementation remains. All three institutions under study have been affected by informality at some point, in implementing the media law, collecting license fees, or implementing the Labor Code.

Second, the general democratization process of the country, which is characterized by a high level of political interference in all spheres of life, including the media, is certainly a key factor that has affected all three institutions under review. The deadlock over the procedure to appoint members to the regulator is a direct effect of political influence. While politics, society, and media demand institutions that work in an independent manner, it seems that for politicians the greatest guarantee of this is the political balance of their members, rather than their professional merit. This phenomenon has often delayed and hindered the work of the regulator and the public broadcaster.

Third, the weak media market and slow economic development have significantly and rather negatively affected the development of the media institutions and the sustainability of media assistance efforts in Albania. The media market is small, overcrowded, and hardly transparent as regards its funding sources, so media outlets often turn to their owners or patrons for financial support. Furthermore, the weak media market has had a direct negative influence on the prospects for the financial sustainability of media outlets and institutions that depend on commercial income, such as commercial media, or on membership fees, such as trade unions. The provision of media assistance aimed to address this aspect, but there are limitations to what can be achieved, especially when local actors are not interested in changing the status quo and when economic conditions simply do not allow for the growth of the market.

Fourth, the low level of professionalization in the journalist profession and the lack of a tradition of self-organizing and self-regulation have hampered efforts aimed at establishing codes of ethics and self-regulatory mechanisms in the country.

Overall, international media assistance has been very important in shaping the current media landscape, though it has by no means been the decisive factor. The complete legal reform in the media and the establishment of its main institutions has seen the continuous involvement of international actors. International assistance has also been crucial in introducing new principles of journalism with the change of regime, and in improving level of professionalism among journalists. Although self-regulatory bodies have not materialized yet, the professional debate on ethics has become a significant part of the profession. Media assistance efforts have been less successful in terms of supporting member-based organizations, hindered by the lack of tradition in this field. Finally, although strengthening the notions of professional journalism has been the main focus of international support, Albanian journalism has ample room for improvement. However, the outcome of this dimension of assistance is certainly affected by the context, such as journalists' rights, media independence, and links between media, politics, and business. Similarly, strengthening of institutions and their sustainability might have been another focus that needed greater attention, though informality, the politicization of the state, and clientelism are all factors that greatly affect the outcome of any assistance.

CHAPTER 3

Media Reform through Intervention: International Media Assistance in Bosnia and Herzegovina

TARIK JUSIĆ and NIDŽARA AHMETAŠEVIĆ

Introduction

Bosnia and Herzegovina (BiH) is often considered one of the most promi-nent examples of international intervention into local affairs aimed at postwar state building, including institutions of the local media system. International actors played an important role in, inter alia, creating legis-lative frameworks and regulatory institutions for the media sector, intro-ducing the public service broadcasting (PSB) system, and supporting the development of independent media. These efforts have resulted in the elim-ination of outright ethnically charged hate speech and have opened up the media space to opposition voices and alternative sources of information.

However, although the efforts to reform the media system have achieved progress in many important areas, a general deterioration of the conditions in the media sphere has been witnessed in recent years. According to the IREX Media Sustainability Index (MSI), one of the international references of assessment of national media systems in democratizing and developing societies, after a significant increase in the MSI between 2001 and 2009, its overall score has continuously declined ever since (table 3.1).[1] Similarly, annual European Commission (EC) progress reports for BiH emphasize that "increased political and financial pressure on the media and intimidation and threats against journalists and editors are of serious concern."[2]

---

[1] IREX, "Bosnia and Herzegovina" (2014).
[2] European Commission, "Bosnia and Herzegovina 2014 Progress Report," 2.

Table 3.1. IREX Media Sustainability Index for Bosnia and Herzegovina, 2001–2016

Indicator	Year					
	2001	2004	2005	2009	2012	2016
Free Speech	1.95	2.83	2.80	2.94	2.45	2.46
Professional Journalism	1.37	2.23	2.11	2.30	1.68	1.67
Plurality of News Sources	1.84	2.71	2.65	3.02	2.16	2.20
Business Management	1.53	2.31	2.20	2.82	1.61	1.39
Supporting Institutions	1.63	2.54	2.31	2.97	1.95	2.15
Overall Score	**1.66**	**2.52**	**2.41**	**2.81**	**1.97**	**1.97**

Source: IREX, "Bosnia and Herzegovina," in Media Sustainability Index for the years 2001, 2004, 2005, 2009, 2012, 2016.

In this chapter, we investigate the results of the international intervention in the media sector in BiH, in light of the recent challenges to reforms. Special attention will be given to some of the major assistance efforts, characterized by the amount of funding disbursed, the scope of the assistance provided, or the significance of the assistance for the media sector reforms: Public service broadcasting (PSB), the Communication Regulatory Agency (CRA), and the independent TV network Open Broadcast Network (OBN). Although all three bodies received significant international assistance, they have had rather different development paths: whereas the CRA has been celebrated as one of the most successful cases of media assistance, the OBN has often been labeled as "the greatest failure—and the most expensive experiment,"[3] while the assistance to PSB is seen to have had only limited effects, with reform stalled for over a decade. This chapter's goal is to contribute to the understanding of the reasons behind such differences in outcomes of media assistance efforts in the country.

With respect to the three case studies, the chapter is particularly concerned with how strategic the approach of donors was in respect to conceptual coherence, consistence, and commitment, as it is understood that a strategic approach to media assistance is a core precondition for

[3] Hozić, "Democratizing Media," 149.

the sustainability of reforms.[4] Other important aspects include the level of cooperation and coordination among donors and the nature of their relationship with local stakeholders, as well as the implications the proposed reforms would have on established local power relations. Earlier studies have indicated that weak coordination among donors[5] and lack of cooperation with local stakeholders[6] that translates into lack of local support for the reforms might have a detrimental effect on assistance programs.

On a more general level, and considering findings from numerous studies that have pointed out difficulties in transposing institutional models from developed democracies into transitional countries,[7] we were concerned with the very nature of the proposed Western models of institutional reforms and the extent to which those can be "transplanted"[8] into the local context of a democratizing society.

The chapter first provides a brief overview of the political and media system in BiH and democratization efforts to date. Next, the outcomes of media assistance efforts and reform challenges are discussed with particular attention given to the three case studies mentioned. A summary of key findings is provided in the concluding section of the chapter.

The Political and Media System

The Dayton Peace Agreement (DPA)[9] officially ended the armed conflict in late 1995. The country was placed under an international semi-protectorate to ensure the implementation of the peace agreement: the Office of the High Representative (OHR) was given the mandate to facilitate implementation of the civilian aspects of the peace agreement; the Organization for Security and Co-operation in Europe (OSCE) was tasked with orga-

---

[4] See for example: Ballentine, "International Assistance"; Susman-Peña, "Making Media Development More Effective," 11–15.

[5] See, for example, Ross, "International Media Assistance"; Dean, "Working in Concert."

[6] Shirley, "Institutions and Development."

[7] Carothers, *Aiding Democracy Abroad,* 96–101; Evans, "Development as Institutional Change"; Jakubowicz and Sükösd, "Twelve Concepts"; Voltmer, "How Far Can Media Systems Travel?"

[8] Berkowitz, Pistor, and Richard, "The Transplant Effect."

[9] "The General Framework Agreement for Peace in Bosnia and Herzegovina" [Dayton Peace Agreement]. Dayton: December 14, 1995.

nizing the first postwar elections, establishing a Provisional Election Commission, and monitoring the condition of human rights in the country; and the international military Implementation Force (IFOR),[10] made up of 60,000 troops and led by NATO, was dispatched to ensure the implementation of the military aspects of the peace agreement.

Just before and during the war, many media outlets were a mouthpiece for war propaganda. In the aftermath of the conflict, the media worked in a hostile environment, exposed to political pressures, an absence of regulation, threats and attacks on journalists, and bleak financial prospects.[11] The media landscape was divided along ethnic and territorial lines between three dominant ethnic groups—Bosniaks, Croats and Serbs—and tightly controlled by ruling nationalist parties, preventing opposition voices from entering the mainstream political discourse and continuing ethnically charged propaganda that cemented war-time divisions. Consequently, a significant number of media outlets continued their war practices even after the peace agreement was signed, inciting hatred among ethnic groups and fostering distrust against international peace-implementation organizations. Only a handful of smaller, independent media outlets offered space for opposition voices. Moreover, from late 1995 on, BiH experienced chaotic growth in the number of media outlets due to the absence of a proper legal framework[12] and significant donor support.[13] Such a situation prompted the need for urgent reform.

However, even in 2015, the media system remains ethnically and politically divided. The governments at various administrative levels own or directly control almost 30% of broadcasters,[14] and provide, in a nontransparent manner, subsidies to public as well as private media outlets in exchange for positive coverage.[15] In addition, and similar to what Zielonka and Mancini have found to be common to Central and East European countries,[16] strong business parallelism is inherent to the system, where media outlets directly support the business and political interests of their owners.

---

[10] After 1997, IFOR was replaced by a much smaller Stabilization Force (SFOR), and finally the EU-led EUFOR mission.

[11] Human Rights Watch, *Human Rights Watch World Report 1998*, 241.

[12] CRA, "Annual Report ... 2010."

[13] UNDP, "Supporting Public Service Broadcasting," 16–17.

[14] CRA, "Annual Report ... 2010," 9.

[15] IREX, "Bosnia and Herzegovina" (2013).

[16] Zielonka and Mancini, "Executive Summary."

The problems are further exacerbated by an oversaturated, and in economic terms rather small media market. Advertising revenues are not viable to economically support today's media landscape, with forty-three TV and 144 radio channels,[17] accompanied by eighty-six weekly and monthly publications and eleven daily newspapers. According to some assessments, the total advertising revenue was around US$52.3 million in 2014, TV 69.34%, print 12.66%, out-of-home 9%, radio 5%, online 4%.[18] Such a small and fragmented market further contributes to the political and business parallelism in the media sector, as limited revenues force media to seek powerful patrons in order to survive.

Last but not least, the level of professionalization of journalism in BiH is rather low: it is characterized by weak autonomy and professional norms, and ineffective mechanisms of self-regulation.[19] As a consequence, the quality of journalism is low. This forms fertile ground for the instrumentalization of journalism and continuing political interference in the media sector.

Media assistance strategies and approaches

The scope and intensity of media assistance efforts in BiH were ambitious. A myriad of international organizations, donor countries, development agencies, and private foundations have been involved in democratization efforts.[20] An estimated €87 million were disbursed through media assistance programs in the country from 1996 until 2006,[21] and it can be safely assumed that by 2015, that number was probably over €100 million.[22] For example, USAID alone invested more than US$40 million between 1996 and 2013,[23] the European Commission spent over €20 million from 1996

---

[17] CRA, "Annual Report ... 2014."
[18] IREX, "Bosnia and Herzegovina" (2014).
[19] Hallin and Mancini, *Comparing Media Systems*, 33–37.
[20] This included USAID, the EU, the UK Department for International Development (DFID), Open Society Foundation, the Swiss Agency for Development and Cooperation (SDC), the Swedish International Development Cooperation Agency (SIDA), Press Now from the Netherlands, the Swedish Helsinki Committee (later renamed as Human Rights Defenders), and many others.
[21] Rhodes, "Ten Years of Media Support," 15.
[22] See for example: European Commission, "Mapping EU Media Support."
[23] Johnson, "Model Interventions," 102–103; USAID, "Bosnia-Herzegovina Democracy and Governance Assessment," 20.

to 2002 on media assistance in BiH,[24] while the Open Society Fund BiH disbursed over US$9 million from 1993 until 2009 to that end.[25]

Due to the "sheer weight of political interference in the sector,"[26] the OHR was assigned the central role in the implementation of the media assistance strategy. Its mandate concerning the media stemmed from its role in the oversight of the implementation of the peace agreement. Additionally, the OSCE had the mandate to observe media coverage of elections and through this mandate facilitated numerous media reform projects.[27]

BiH became a laboratory for developing and testing approaches for media assistance in a postconflict society, with a goal to contribute to its democratization and pacification. In particular, this involved: eliminating war propaganda and pacifying media discourse; supporting media pluralism and independent media as an alternative to nationalist and government-controlled media; introducing a legal and regulatory framework to foster the development of a media market and to discourage inflammatory propaganda; reforming government-controlled broadcasters into public service broad-casters; promoting professional and ethics standards through self-regulation and professional associations of journalists; and supporting the development of civil society organizations in the media sector, such as training, research, and investigative reporting centers, and media industry associations.

Donor Coordination or Competition

There were important conceptual differences in terms of approaches to media assistance, especially between European and American donors.[28] This resulted in a division in spheres of influence, with the former focusing on PSB reform and the latter emphasizing commercial media and freedom of expression.[29] More fundamental differences in their overall

---

[24] De Luce, "Assessment of USAID Media Assistance," 5–10.

[25] Official data from Open Society Fund Bosnia and Herzegovina, on file with author.

[26] Riley, "Painstaking Efforts," 4–5.

[27] Johnson, "Model Interventions," 96.

[28] Carothers, *Aiding Democracy Abroad*, 236–237; Hozić, "Democratizing Media," 145, 149; Bajraktari and Hsu, "Developing Media in Stabilization and Reconstruction Operations."

[29] Johnson, "Model Interventions," 106; Martin, "Media Reform and Development in Bosnia," 91; CIMA, "Empowering Independent Media," 60; Bajraktari and Hsu, "Developing Media in Stabilization and Reconstruction Operations," 6.

approaches to assistance sometimes resulted in "intense competition,"[30] so that "in some cases [the donors] put the promotion of their own projects, programmatic 'territory,' and reputations before the overall welfare of reconstruction."[31]

Many practitioners and politicians have cited the lack of donor cooperation and coordination[32] as one of the main reasons behind the ineffectiveness of their programs and initiatives in general. According to the UNDP, in the case of BiH "there was insufficient coordination at all levels including determining needs, developing a strategic plan and in the implementation."[33] On a formal level, donors tried to achieve consensus.[34] However, calls to simply "improve" coordination were not easy to implement,[35] even among donors from the same country. For example, in the case of United States, "an overarching strategy did not emerge until 1998 and was not consistently applied, partly because media assistance was not managed from a central point until 2000."[36] Similarly, very few EU-funded projects "have been designed and implemented in cooperation with member states or other donor agencies,"[37] and as such largely did not reflect media developments in the EU.[38]

Under such circumstances, the donors were rarely able to achieve cooperation synergies[39] and attempts to improve coordination often failed. For example, the OHR was tasked to coordinate international media support through regular biweekly roundtables with all major donors and a detailed database of donor projects,[40] but the results of this effort were weak.[41] When coordination did happen, it was when individual donors established ad hoc coalitions for implementation of more complex projects.[42]

---

[30] Martin, "Media Reform and Development in Bosnia," 92.
[31] Johnson, "Model Interventions," 109–110.
[32] See, for example, Ross, "International Media Assistance."
[33] UNDP, "Supporting Public Service Broadcasting," 21.
[34] Dean, "Working in Concert," 9.
[35] Martin, "Media Reform and Development in Bosnia," 95.
[36] De Luce, "Assessment of USAID Media Assistance," 5.
[37] European Commission, "Mapping EU Media Support," 47.
[38] Ibid.
[39] De Luce, "Assessment of USAID Media Assistance," 17.
[40] Martin, "Media Reform and Development in Bosnia."
[41] Johnson, "Model Interventions," 109–110.
[42] Price, Davis Noll, and De Luce, "Mapping Media Assistance"; De Luce, "Assessment of USAID Media Assistance," 17.

Phases and Areas of Engagement

Donors' approaches to media reforms depended on the political priorities and institutional preconditions at any given moment. Hence, one can identify three distinctive phases of media assistance in BiH.

The first phase (1996–1998) was characterized by a focus on the pacification of media discourse and the pluralization of the media sector. The goal was to sanitize media space that was polluted by ethnocentric, warmongering propaganda and to weaken the nationalists' grip on the main media outlets. Another goal was to give voice to moderates and to create basic preconditions for free and fair elections.[43] As Chris Riley, former head of the Media Development Office of the OHR put it, "[i]n 1996 and early 1997, there was little discussion of 'European standards' and 'self-sustainability.' Primary emphasis was placed upon breaking political control; creating alternative voices; promoting ethnic tolerance; fighting the rhetoric of hate . . . and developing pluralism."[44] The assumption was that the development of an independent media sector is of fundamental importance for the success of peace-building efforts and democratization of the country.[45]

As consensus among international actors gradually emerged,[46] the Peace Implementation Council (PIC)[47] extended the OHR's powers between 1995 and 1998, effectively establishing a semi-protectorate in BiH.[48] Since the DPA had no provisions regarding media, except in relation to the creation of the conditions for free and fair elections and freedom of expression,[49] the mandate of the OHR was expanded to include media reform as well (see table 3.2). Hence, this phase is characterized by a full-blown intervention into the media sector. For example, in late 1997,

---

[43] Hozić, "Democratizing Media," 149; Riley, "Painstaking Efforts," 2; UNDP, Supporting Public Service Broadcasting, 16–17.

[44] Riley, "Painstaking Efforts," 2.

[45] Hill, "Exploring USAID's Democracy Promotion," 107.

[46] Riley, "Painstaking Efforts," 2.

[47] The Peace Implementation Council was established to mobilize international support for the peace agreement. It consists of 55 countries and international agencies that provide support to the peace process.

[48] Peace Implementation Council, "PIC Bonn Conclusions."

[49] "The General Framework Agreement for Peace in Bosnia and Herzegovina," Annex 3, "Agreement on Elections," Art. 1.

NATO troops took control over the transmitters of the Republika Srpska public television network in order to prevent the spread of war-mongering propaganda.[50] The OSCE, in cooperation with other international actors and key local stakeholders, established the Provisional Electoral Commission in 1996, which issued the Electoral Code of Conduct,[51] defining, inter alia, rules for the media to follow during the electoral campaign. In April of the same year, the Media Experts Commission[52] was established, mandated to observe media coverage of elections and to ensure compliance with the Electoral Code of Conduct.[53] Furthermore, two countrywide, cross-ethnic broadcasters were created in 1996: the Free Elections Radio Network (FERN) and the Open Broadcast Network (OBN).

However, there was little strategic thinking and limited coordination concerning the implementation of actual projects and initiatives.[54] Media assistance policies were seen as reactive and contingent upon on-the-ground developments rather than proactive or based on coherent strategies.[55] In many instances, donors and international actors were simply forced to work with those willing to cooperate and did not have reliable ways of assessing the effectiveness of their approaches. Moreover, the key projects from this phase were rather provisional: some ceased to exist after several years, like the Media Experts Commission and FERN radio,[56] whereas others were abruptly abandoned by the donors, like the OBN. At the same time, the reforms faced strong opposition by local political elites.

---

[50] De Luce, "Assessment of USAID Media Assistance," 8.

[51] OSCE Mission in Bosnia and Herzegovina, "Rules and Regulations."

[52] The Media Experts Commission was headed by the OSCE senior advisor for media development, but it also included representatives and experts appointed by political parties, representatives of entity Ministries of the Interior, and representatives from the OHR, OSCE and IFOR. The Commission's mandate expired a few weeks after the second postwar election in 1998.

[53] Media Experts Commission, "Završni izvještaj," 10, 19.

[54] UNDP, "Supporting Public Service Broadcasting," 20; Ahmetašević, "A House of Cards."

[55] Johnson, "Model Interventions," 106.

[56] FERN continued to operate until funding stopped in 2001, whereupon it was merged with the PSB (De Luce, "Assessment of USAID Media Assistance," 11). See also Bajraktari and Hsu, "Developing Media in Stabilization and Reconstruction Operations," 11.

Table 3.2. Key PIC Decisions and Declarations Relevant to Media Reforms

Year	Title	Content
December 1995	London meeting	OHR called on to actively engage in media reform
April 1996	Broadcast Media Statement	Need to create "independent TV network" for the whole country mentioned
May 1997	Sintra Declaration	Extensive powers given to OHR, including power "to curtail or suspend" any media network or program found to undermine the peace agreement
December 1997	Bonn Declaration	OHR powers extended to include: • Power to remove public officials who obstruct the peace from their public office • Power to impose laws when BiH legislatures fail to do so • Power to act in respect to the media
June 1998	Luxemburg Declaration	Called for the creation of a single PSB system and prompted OHR to oversee complete transformation of existing public broadcasters
December 1998	Madrid Declaration	The Madrid Declaration called, inter alia, for: • The reform of state-controlled broadcasters and the establishment of an independent PSB system for the whole country • Continued support to the independent regulator for broadcasting • The introduction of a legislative framework on hate speech, libel and defamation • The establishment of a self-regulatory mechanism for the press • Donor governments to continue supporting OBN and FERN

Source: Office of the High Representative website.[57]

The frustrating experience of international actors during the first few years resulted in a relatively quick change in the overall approach to media reforms. It became clear that there was a need for more comprehensive and long-term reforms if efforts were to yield any substantial results. The second phase (1998–2002) was marked by structural reforms focused on the creation of a robust legal and regulatory framework,[58] public service

---

[57] For full insight into Peace Implementation Council, see OHR, "Peace Implementation Council Decisions and Communiqués."

[58] Hozić, "Democratizing Media," 149.

broadcasting reform, and "the creation of an independent, commercial alternative to the public broadcasting system."[59]

This phase was characterized by extensive use of OHR powers.[60] International actors coordinated the drafting of and imposed key media legislation. For example, the OHR suspended criminal prosecution of defamation and insult in 1999[61] and instructed political actors to adopt legislation on defamation.[62] The OHR also required[63] governments to adopt Freedom of Information Acts (FOIA), developed under the guidance of the OHR, the OSCE and international legal experts.[64] Moreover, after the Council of Ministers of BiH could not reach an agreement on the matter, the OHR imposed[65] the Law on Communications[66] in 2002, creating the legal basis for regulating the broadcasting and telecommunications sectors.

Apart from legal reforms, the OHR and other international actors concentrated on the creation of key institutions of the media system. In 1998, the OHR established the Independent Media Commission (IMC),[67] a regulatory body that was later transformed[68] into the CRA. The same year, a process of transformation of government-controlled broadcasters into the PSB system also started. Another important pillar of assistance was the creation of a self-regulation body for print media, the Press Council.[69]

Finally, the third phase (from 2002 onward) was characterized by a gradual decrease of direct international involvement in media reforms and a more significant role for local actors. For example, the CRA was fully transferred into local hands, while responsibility for PSB reform was given to local political leaders. The OHR stopped intervening in media legislation in line with the overall trend of reduced involvement of interna-

---

[59] Riley, "Painstaking Efforts," 4–5.
[60] Ibid., 3; De Luce, "Assessment of USAID Media Assistance," 8; UNDP, "Supporting Public Service Broadcasting," 20; Johnson, "Model Interventions," 108.
[61] OHR, "Decisions on the Restructuring."
[62] The defamation legislation was developed by an advisory body consisting of local and international experts (including the OSCE and the OHR), and in consultation with local actors. See IJNET, "Draft Defamation Legislation."
[63] OHR, "Decisions on the Restructuring."
[64] FOIA were adopted at state and entity levels between 2000 and 2002.
[65] OHR, "Decision Enacting the Law on Communications."
[66] "Zakon o komunikacijama BiH."
[67] OHR, "Decision on the Establishment."
[68] OHR, "Decision Combining."
[69] Chemonics International, *Giving Citizens a Voice*, 21.

tional actors in local policies.[70] This was coupled with a gradual decrease in available donor funds. Donors mostly continued focusing on commercial and independent media outlets, albeit with reduced intensity.[71] The improvement of business management and the development of supporting institutions and professional organizations were seen as important elements of donor exit strategies.[72] This coincided with the country's EU accession process and the emphasis that was placed by the EU on PSB reforms and on ensuring the independence of the CRA. The interventionist approach of the first two phases was replaced by conditionality mechanisms linked to EU accession.

However, it appeared that with the retreat of the OHR and reduced donations, the situation in the media sector started to deteriorate, especially after 2008,[73] while most recipients of donor support remained donor dependent.[74] Such a situation prompted some of the donors to focus on media reform again, most notably USAID.

In order to be able to better appreciate and understand the ambition, scope and complexity of media assistance efforts deployed, table 3.3 below attempts to provide a schematic account of media assistance programs in BiH between 1996 and 2013.

---

[70] Ibid., 25–26; USAID, "Bosnia-Herzegovina Democracy and Governance Assessment," 19.

[71] See, for example, USAID, "ProMedia II"; Hume, *The Media Missionaries*, 37–38; Henderson, Kilalic, and Kontic, "The Media Environment," 12–15.

[72] Chemonics, *Giving Citizens a Voice*, 21–22.

[73] IREX, "Bosnia and Herzegovina" (2013).

[74] Chemonics, *Giving Citizens a Voice*, 18–25; USAID, "Bosnia-Herzegovina Democracy and Governance Assessment"; Henderson, Kilalic, and Kontic, "The Media Environment," 14–15; also see Johnson, "Model Interventions," 130.

Table 3.3. Overview of Media Assistance Efforts in Bosnia and Herzegovina, 1996–2013

Assistance Goals	Type of Assistance According to Phases and Assistance Goals		
	Phase 1: 1996–1998 (Peace Building, Liberalization, and Pluralization of Media Sector)	Phase 2: 1998–2002 (Structural Reforms)	Phase 3: 2002–2013 (Stabilization Efforts)
Eliminating War-Mongering Propaganda and Pacifying the Media Discourse	• Establishing legal basis for media intervention • Using military power to stop war-mongering propaganda • Helping distribution of papers/magazines across ethnic lines	• Not relevant	• Not relevant
Supporting Media Pluralism and Independent Media	• Establishing new independent media • Capacity building of existing media • Enabling countrywide distribution and reach • Supporting production of programs/content • Extensive support to independent media • Tendency toward donor-dependence • Absence of coherent donor strategy • Creation of cross-ethnic broadcasters OBN, FERN	• Consolidation of broadcasting sector • Continuous support to independent outlets (purchasing equipment, production of programs, etc.) • Creation of commercial TV network Mreža plus • Support to NGOs linked to media industry	• Focus on business management • Reducing the number of aid recipients • Issue-specific support through funding of content production • Funding capacity building of media • Funding production of programming • Support to online media • Support to NGOs linked to media industry
Introduction of Legal and Regulatory Framework	• Ad hoc rules and institutions setup, linked to elections and crisis mitigation • Absence of coherent strategy • Creation of Rules and Regulations Regarding the Media Coverage of Elections • Media Experts Commission established	• Introduction of legal framework, number of key laws drafted and imposed by international community • Creation of IMC, later CRA • Enforcing CRA rules	• Continuing support to CRA • Direct intervention into legal framework stopped • EU conditionality takes prominence

	Type of Assistance According to Phases and Assistance Goals		
Assistance Goals	Phase 1: 1996–1998 (Peace Building, Liberalization, and Pluralization of Media Sector)	Phase 2: 1998–2002 (Structural Reforms)	Phase 3: 2002–2013 (Stabilization Efforts)
Reform of State-Controlled Broadcasters into Public Service Broadcasters	• Issue largely ignored • Attempts to prevent their negative impact and open them up to opposition voices • Antagonistic relationship between international actors and government-controlled broadcasters • Forceful start of reforms by use of military power (case of Republika Srpska broadcaster)	• Focus on PSB reform • Capacity building for PSB • Legislative reforms • Highly interventionist approach, top-down reforms imposed by OHR • External experts lead reforms	• Hands-off approach • Improving legal framework through EU conditionality
Supporting the Professionalization of Journalism	• Issue largely ignored • Primarily addressed through trainings of journalists • Support to independent associations of journalists	• Intensive focus on self-regulation and the creation of the Press Council • Supporting professional associations	• Continuous support to Press Council • Support to journalists' associations
Supporting Civil Society Organizations in the Media Sector	• Support to media-related NGOs • Support to media training centers	• Continuing support to media-related NGOs • Supporting investigative reporting centers and initiatives • Supporting training centers	• Focus on financial sustainability and management of NGOs • Local NGOs promoted to partners in media assistance programs

Local Resistance to Reforms

An important characteristic of media reforms in BiH is the continuous resistance of the local political elites to the media assistance efforts of international actors. Local elites were not willing to easily relinquish their control, systematically obstructing efforts of international actors aimed at the liberalization of the media sector.[75] As a result, reforms were slow and often disrupted. For example, the first postwar elections were not held in a free and fair environment due to the negative treatment of opposition parties by mainstream media,[76] as they ignored the Media Experts Commission during the 1996 election campaign.[77] At the same time, political elites obstructed the work of FERN and OBN, so that these broadcasters were able to begin broadcasting only a few days before the 1996 elections. It was only under the threat of OHR sanctions[78] that media and political actors started to respect the introduced rules.[79] However, resistance continued, so that in the early 2000s the OHR was forced to impose fundamental legal reforms, such as the previously mentioned Freedom of Access to Information Law in the Federation of Bosnia and Herzegovina, the Law on Communication at the state level, as well as the PSB legislation.[80]

To a certain extent international actors attempted to establish cooperation with local politicians and the media community, albeit with limited success. According to some local sources, consultation with the local media community took place only after the laws were already drafted by international experts.[81] Often, mutual distrust prevented more meaningful cooperation between international consultants and local media professionals.[82] In many cases, international consultants merely dismissed local journalists and media professionals as incompetent or politically biased.[83] In the case of PSB reform, cooperation among stakeholders was only partial as well. According to De Luce, "the OHR sought only limited consultation with the public, other official entities (including the United States), the CRA, and the private broadcasters' associations."[84]

---

[75] Riley, "Painstaking Efforts," 2.
[76] Wheeler, "Monitoring the Media."
[77] Open Society Institute, *Television across Europe*, 285.
[78] Chandler, *Bosnia*, 116.
[79] Popovic, "Covering Bosnia and Herzegovina."
[80] "Zakon o osnovama javnog radio-televizijskog sistema i o javnom radio-televizijskom servisu BiH," "Zakon o javnom radio-televizijskom sistemu BiH," "Zakon o Javnom radiotelevizijskom servisu Bosne i Hercegovine," "Zakon o Javnom servisu radio-televizije Federacije BiH," and "Zakon o Radio-Televiziji Republike Srpske."
[81] Ahmetašević, "A House of Cards."
[82] Boro Kontić, Director, Mediacentar Sarajevo, interview with the author, August 28, 2013.
[83] Hozić, "Democratizing Media," 149–150; Kurspahić, *Zločin u 19:30*.
[84] De Luce, "Assessment of USAID Media Assistance," 10–11.

In order to gain a deeper insight into the nature of media assistance efforts in BiH, the next section looks at assistance efforts directed at the following three institutions: the CRA; the PSB system; and the independent TV network OBN.

Communications Regulatory Agency (CRA)

The independent regulatory body for broadcasters in BiH was created after international actors realized that there was a need to have a strong regulator capable of enforcing broadcasting regulation. Consequently, the PIC called for the creation of such a body[85] and in June 1998 the OHR established the IMC,[86] partly modeled on the US Federal Communications Commission (FCC).[87] It was tasked to manage the frequency spectrum, issue broadcasting licenses, introduce and enforce rules for broadcasters, engage in policy setting and policy implementation, and deal with complaints. It was vested with significant powers and could request assistance of all law-enforcement agencies and of peace implementation troops, if necessary. In 2001, the IMC and the Telecommunications Regulatory Agency were merged by another OHR decision[88] into the CRA, in charge of both the broadcasting and telecommunications sectors.[89] Its enforcement measures include monitoring and information collection powers, oral and written warnings, inspections, financial penalties, and the revocation of a license.[90]

The CRA's legal status was formally defined by the Law on Communications, imposed by an OHR decision. The law, which complies with the highest international standards,[91] provides strong guarantees for the agency's formal independence from external interference in decision-making,

---

[85] Peace Implementation Council, "PIC Bonn Conclusions."

[86] OHR, "Decision on the Establishment."

[87] Ahmetašević, "A House of Cards."

[88] OHR, "Decision Combining."

[89] Open Society Institute, *Television across Europe*, 276; Hans Bredow Institute for Media Research et al., *INDIREG*, 176; Thompson and De Luce, "Escalating to Success?"

[90] "Law on Communications of BiH", Art. 46. Also see Open Society Institute, *Television across Europe*, 276; Hans Bredow Institute for Media Research et al., *INDIREG*, 176; Thompson and De Luce, "Escalating to Success?"; UNDP, "Supporting Public Service Broadcasting," 20.

[91] Council of Europe, "Recommendation Rec (2000) 23."

and ensures its financial sustainability.[92] The law was also supposed to create the formal precondition for CRA's transition from an internationally managed institution to a regulatory agency integrated in the local legal and institutional framework—a somewhat paradoxical situation since the law was externally imposed amid the local failure to adopt it.

The agency's creation and operations mandated approximately US$19 million in donor support between 1998 and 2003.[93] The EU was a major donor to the regulator, while USAID provided assistance targeting its "outreach capacity, financial viability, and independence."[94] In its initial phase, the agency was fully donor-dependent, but its financial sustainability was secured after 2003 and the introduction of the Law on Communication, ensuring its budget from fees collected by issuing telecommunications and broadcasting licenses.

Initially, the IMC was placed under interim international supervision. Its managing directors were internationals appointed by the OHR, while its executive bodies included local and international representatives.[95] In 2003, with the transformation of the IMC to the CRA, the first local managing director was appointed, while the agency's core units had been run by local staff for several years by then. Moreover, efforts were made to include external experts, relevant ministry representatives, the media industry, and other international organizations in the policy-making processes.[96]

Given the challenging context, a relatively high level of coordination among key international actors and donors in terms of both their financial and their political support to the agency was necessary. The support was quite comprehensive until the introduction of the Law on Communications in 2003 and the formal integration of the agency into the local institutional framework. Various forms of support continue even a decade later, albeit with significantly lower intensity.[97]

---

[92] "Zakon o komunikacijama BiH," Art. 44.
[93] De Luce, "Assessment of USAID Media Assistance," 8.
[94] Chemonics, *Giving Citizens a Voice*, 22.
[95] See, for example, Ahmetašević, "A House of Cards."
[96] Ibid.
[97] For example, in 2010 and 2011, the CRA received technical assistance in the amount of €960,000 in order to harmonize regulation in the field of communications with EU rules. See European Commission, "Mapping EU Media Support," 35.

The introduction of an independent regulatory body in BiH is widely believed to be "the international community's greatest achievement in media development efforts."[98] It successfully introduced a regulatory framework for broadcasting and established order into the communications sector by issuing licenses. Additionally, the agency was a key factor that contributed to the significant improvement in the overall quality of radio and TV programs in the country—the journalistic standards in broadcasting improved, the hate speech and war-mongering propaganda was eliminated, and the access to airwaves was granted to voices and organizations from across the political spectrum.

However, the introduction of an independent regulatory agency was not without resistance. At the beginning, the IMC was especially opposed by Republika Srpska authorities, who were against the introduction of any state-level institutions that would take away entity competences.[99] The CRA has continuously been exposed to pressure from various sides ever since. Pressures primarily come from governments and legislative bodies at state and entity levels, but occasionally also from media outlets affiliated with political parties. Threats to the agency's independence have a negative influence on its administrative and policy-making capacity.[100]

Given the fact that the Law on Communication was imposed,[101] it does not come as surprise that after the CRA was placed in local hands a number of legal initiatives eroded its formal independence.[102] New legal provisions are frequently in conflict with the Law on Communications. Such a situation is a typical example of what Zielonka and Mancini call "floating laws and procedures,"[103] with legal documents being changed frequently due to short-term political and other interests, often resulting in conflicting legal arrangements, legal uncertainty, and regulatory chaos. According to the former CRA director of broadcasting, Dunja Mijatović, pressures were continuous, and laws were changed or introduced overnight to place the agency under political control.[104]

---

[98] De Luce, "Assessment of USAID Media Assistance," 8; also see Johnson, "Model Interventions," 121.

[99] Topić, "Electronic Media."

[100] European Commission, "Bosnia and Herzegovina 2009 Progress Report"; Helena Mandić, interview with the author, September 13, 2013.

[101] For some of the limitations of the law, see Bukovska, "Bosnia and Herzegovina."

[102] Hans Bredow Institute for Media Research et al., *INDIREG*, 300–301.

[103] Zielonka and Mancini, "Executive Summary," 6.

[104] Dunja Mijatovic, former Director of Broadcasting at the Communication Regulatory Agency and the former (2010–2016) OSCE Representative on Free-

Moreover, existing legal procedures pertaining to the financial and decision-making independence of the agency are often undermined. For example, legal nomination and appointment procedures for the CRA Director General and Council members were largely ignored by the BiH government and parliament. The appointment of the top management in CRA became highly politicized. A director general has not been appointed since 2007 up until 2015, with the incumbent director general acting in a technical mandate. Similarly, after the statutory term of the CRA council members expired in 2009, the Council of Ministers and the parliament of BiH failed to appoint new members in due time. The CRA council continued to operate under a technical mandate for several years.[105] At the end of 2012, the Law on Communications was amended and an ad hoc body within the parliamentary assembly of BiH was introduced with the task to propose the candidates for the CRA council that were formally appointed in 2013. Finally, in 2015, the new director of the agency was also appointed.

Moreover, the agency has also faced significant financial pressures from the Council of Ministers. The OHR intervened in 2002, issuing a decision[106] to ensure that the agency had the necessary funds for its uninterrupted operation. However, the pressures continued, so that the CRA struggles to resist political and financial challenges to its independence.[107]

Given the difficult situation, the agency has benefited from international scrutiny in light of continuous attempts to limit its independence. The OHR has intervened several times to ensure its independence from government interference. However, in recent years not much has been done beyond issuing press releases and protest letters, and it seems that the CRA is not high on the agenda of key international actors any longer.[108]

To sum up, the case of the CRA demonstrates the importance of a strategic, long-term approach to institution building. It also shows the importance of a clear and realistic institutional mandate and expectations,

---

dom of the Media, interview for a PhD study by Nidžara Ahmetašević, March 13, 2012, Vienna. Ahmetašević, "A House of Cards"; also see Bukovska, "Bosnia and Herzegovina."

[105] Halilović, "Disciplining Independent Regulators"; Hans Bredow Institute for Media Research et al., *INDIREG*, 177–178; European Commission, "Bosnia and Herzegovina 2011 Progress Report."

[106] OHR, "Decision Amending the Structures."

[107] Johnson, "Model Interventions," 121.

[108] Helena Mandić, Director of Broadcasting, Communications Regulatory Agency of BiH, interview with the author, September 13, 2013.

coupled with adequate resources and the mechanisms necessary for its operation. We can also note how vital the role of prolonged international scrutiny can be in the face of local resistance. Another important aspect is the internal institutional support for the adoption of the institutional model, which might be linked to the strong "internal culture of independence" manifested in the professional integrity of the CRA staff, and the transparency and accountability of the agency in its decision-making.[109] However, this case also shows how difficult it is to impose an institutional model amid opposition from the local political elite and then to ensure its sustainable integration into the local institutional and political context in the long run.[110]

Public Service Broadcasting System

Between 1998 and 2002, under the pressure of the OHR, the two government-controlled entity broadcasters—Radio-Television of the Federation of Bosnia and Herzegovina (RTVFBiH) and Radio-Television of Republika Srpska (RTRS)—were transformed into public service broadcasters. A third, statewide, cross-ethnic public service broadcaster, Bosnia-Herzegovina Radio and Television (BHRT), was established. The three broadcasters were ambitiously supposed to establish a joint public service broadcasting system, to closely cooperate in the production of programs, to manage assets, share advertising revenues and collect the subscription fee through a joint corporation—a new organizational unit that would facilitate cooperation among the three broadcasters, coordinate the activities within the system, manage the equipment and the transmission network, and be in charge of sales and advertising (see figure 3.1).

This model was proposed by international consultants[111] and inspired by the BBC, which operates according to a similar concept: The system rests on an internal market among PSB units, where all the services would be purchased between the units, thus making the production more cost-

---

[109] Hans Bredow Institute for the Media et al., *INDIREG*.

[110] Helena Mandić, interview with the author, September 13, 2013.

[111] A BBC consultancy team was established in 2002 in order to facilitate the restructuring process, and was tasked to navigate the reform in cooperation with the management. The team was funded by DFID in the amount of £2 million. See De Luce, "Assessment of USAID Media Assistance," 10.

**Figure 3.1. The Organization of the Public Service Broadcasting System
in Bosnia and Herzegovina**

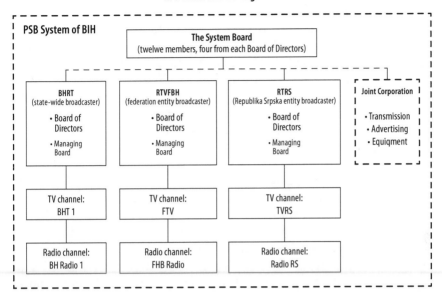

effective and the system more accountable.[112] The consultants produced a reconstruction plan which was adopted by the managing board of the PSB System in 2004. The plan was subsequently used as a blueprint for the future adjustments of the PSB legal framework.

The goal of the reform was to reduce the nationalist grip on government-controlled entity broadcasters—RTRS and RTVFBiH—and to create a third TV channel that would represent the country as a whole, thus performing a strong integrative function in the ethnically and territorially divided society. In the view of international actors, the state-wide broadcaster "would serve to bring together the two entities for the common good of the entire country"[113] and would thus "function as a national information source and thereby support the emergence of a Bosnian civic identity."[114] Another goal was to create a functional and sustainable PSB system that would serve all citizens, and would not be politically instrumentalized. Given the nature of these ambitious goals, it

---

[112] Lindvall, "Public Broadcasting Reform," 3–4.
[113] UNDP, "Supporting Public Service Broadcasting," 18.
[114] Johnson, "Model Interventions," 130–131.

is not surprising that a continuous feature of the PSB reform process was strong resistance by the local ruling political elite, which tried to maintain its grip on public broadcasters.[115]

The reform of public service broadcasters started by a rather dramatic act of direct international intervention with the help of NATO-led military forces: On October 1, 1997, under the instruction of the OHR, peacekeeping troops took control of the transmitters of the Republika Srpska entity broadcaster.[116] The broadcaster had increasingly taken an antagonistic stand toward the international community and labeled NATO-led peace implementation forces as an occupation army,[117] which triggered the intervention.

This demonstration of force opened up the path to the reform of government-controlled broadcasters and the creation of a public service broadcasting system. The "international community, particularly European donors and the European Commission as well as the OHR, was fervent in its support for the development of PSB, especially for the creation of a statewide public service broadcaster."[118] The OHR tried to obtain support for PSB reform from local political elites, albeit with limited success. In 1998, the OHR negotiated a memorandum of understanding with the members of the tripartite presidency of BiH, outlining the path for the creation of the statewide PSB system.[119] However, the memorandum was accepted by Bosniak and Croat parties in the Federation of Bosnia and Herzegovina while the Republika Srpska leadership refused to support it.[120] At the same time, under the supervision of the OHR, leading Bosniak and Croat parties established a transitional commission for the restructuring of the Federation of Bosnia and Herzegovina entity broadcaster, while international experts proposed draft laws for its transformation.[121]

Nevertheless, all efforts to obtain substantial local support for the introduction of a genuine PSB system were in vain, and no progress was possible. As a consequence, the OHR took an active role and issued a number

---

[115] Hozić, "Democratizing Media," 152–153.
[116] Associated Press, "US Sends Electronic Warfare Planes to Bosnia."
[117] Kurspahić, *Zločin u 19:30*, 164–173.
[118] Johnson, "Model Interventions," 130–131.
[119] Mediaonline, "Novosti u medijima."
[120] Thompson and De Luce, "Escalating to Success?," 220; Lindvall, "Public Broadcasting Reform," 2.
[121] "Federalna a ne državna," 5.

of decisions between 1999 and 2002 that effectively changed the legal status of existing entity broadcasters, and created the legal framework for a new public service broadcasting system amid local resistance (see table 3.4).

Moreover, an international supervisor was appointed for the Republika Srpska TV network. The supervisor was active until 1999, when the OHR imposed the amendments to the Law on Radio-Television of Republika Srpska.[122] The OHR also appointed an international transfer agent, later renamed the Broadcasting Agent of the High Representative,[123] tasked to oversee the process of the creation of the public service broadcasting system.[124]

Table 3.4. International Decision and Actions Regarding PSB Reform

Year	Action
October 1997	OHR and NATO take control over transmitters of Republika Srpska public broadcasting network
1998–1999	International supervisor appointed by OHR for the Republika Srpska network
July 30, 1999	OHR Decisions on the restructuring of the Public Broadcasting System in BiH and on freedom of information and decriminalization of libel and defamation[125]
September 1, 1999	OHR Decision amending the Law on Radio-Television of the RS[126]
December 6, 1999	OHR Decision on the implementation of the Law on Radio-Television of the Federation
2000	IMC suspends illegal operations of EROTEL[127]
March 3, 2000	OHR Decision amending the Law on Radio-Television of the RS
March 16, 2000	OHR Decision amending the decision on Public Radio-Television of BiH

[122] OHR, "Decision Amending"; also see Lindvall, "Public Broadcasting Reform," 1–2.
[123] OHR, "Second Decision"; also see Čengić, "Zemljotres u Sivom domu," 171; Ahmetašević, "A House of Cards," 146.
[124] OHR, "Decision on the Appointment."
[125] OHR, "Decision on the Restructuring."
[126] OHR, "Decision Amending."
[127] The nationalist Croat ruling party operated an illegal TV network EROTEL TV that rebroadcasted radio and television programs from neighboring Croatia to parts of the Federation with a majority Croat population. At the beginning of 2000, with the support of the OHR, the illegal operations of EROTEL were terminated. Lindvall, "Public Broadcasting Reform," 2.

Year	Action
April 15, 2000	OHR Decision on the appointment of the Transfer Agent and the Expert Team for the establishment of public service broadcasting
July 27, 2000	OHR Decision on the appointment of the Board of Governors of Radio-Television of the RS
October 23, 2000	OHR Second Decision on restructuring the Public Broadcasting System in BiH[128]
May 23, 2002	OHR Decision Imposing the Law on the Basis of the Public Broadcasting System and on the Public Broadcasting Service of Bosnia and Herzegovina[129]
May 24, 2002	OHR Decision Imposing the Law on Radio-Television of the Federation of Bosnia and Herzegovina
May 24, 2002	OHR Decision Imposing the Law on Radio-Television of Republika Srpska[130]
May 24, 2002	OHR Decision on the Liquidation Procedure to be Applied in the Winding-Up of the Public Enterprise Radio and Television of Bosnia and Herzegovina[131]
2002	BBC consultancy team established to facilitate the restructuring process
2003	The European Commission takes lead role in PSB reform, OHR retreats from the process; EU conditionality used as a strategy rather than direct intervention by OHR
April 2004	BBC consultancy team produces reconstruction plan, adopted by the management of the PSB system and used as blueprint for future adjustments of legal framework
2005	Changes to the PSB legal framework introduced as a condition for signing the Stabilization and Association Agreement (SAA) between the EU and BiH

From 2003 on, the European Commission began to play an increasingly important role in PSB reform, while the OHR's involvement was significantly reduced as the reform of the PSB system became one of the conditions in the EU integration process for BiH. As a result, "the BiH authorities had to take ownership of the reform and the High Representative would

---

[128] OHR, "Decision Imposing the Law on the Basis of the Public Broadcasting System"; "Zakon o osnovama javnog radio-televizijskog sistema."

[129] OHR, "Decision Imposing the Law on the Basis of the Public Broadcasting System"; "Zakon o osnovama javnog radio-televizijskog sistema."

[130] OHR, "Decision Imposing the Law on Radio-Television of Republika Srpska"; "Zakon o Radio-Televiziji Republike Srpske."

[131] OHR, "Decision on the Liquidation Procedure."

no longer be able to impose any decisions."[132] Consequently, in accordance with EU requirements,[133] the PSB legislation was adjusted, albeit with continuous resistance from local political elites and other stakeholders.

For example, the current model of PSB has continuously been opposed by main Croat parties, which demanded a separate Croatian-language channel.[134] In an act of defiance, leading Croat parties and large parts of the Croat population boycott the payment of the monthly subscription fee for PSB.[135] Similarly, ever since the introduction of the reforms Republika Srpska politicians have resisted the introduction of a new, shared umbrella entity—the joint corporation—that would integrate entity PSBs into a centrally coordinated, joint PSB system.[136] Official policy in Republika Srpska is not to support the introduction of additional central institutions, as it favors a maximum level of autonomy for the entity, including its PSB channel.

There has also been strong opposition to the proposed model of redistribution of commercial income from advertising among the three broadcasters,[137] according to which most of the funds are to be redirected to the state-level broadcaster, disregarding the commercial success of each broadcaster within the system. Such a model has resulted in resistance to the implementation of the legal framework by entity broadcasters, so that the redistribution formula has not been applied in practice.[138]

Moreover, there is strong internal resistance to change and the resulting lack of internal reforms, especially in terms of debt reduction, cost-cutting and the scaling down of the workforce.[139] As a consequence, "the broadcasters were not only unreformed, but heavily burdened in debts, threatened by strikes and all in all at very unequal positions."[140]

---

[132] Lindvall, "Public Broadcasting Reform," 3.

[133] The adoption of the legal framework was included as a condition for signing the Stabilization and Association Agreement (SAA) between the EU and BiH.

[134] Johnson, "Model Interventions," 131; Lindvall, "Public Broadcasting Reform," 7–8; Hozić, "Democratizing Media," 152–153.

[135] Johnson, "Model Interventions," 131.

[136] Lindvall, "Public Broadcasting Reform," 4; Udovičić, "Bosnia-Herzegovina," 46–47.

[137] "Law on the Public Broadcasting System," Art. 23.

[138] Lindvall, "Public Broadcasting Reform," 6–7; Hozić, "Democratizing Media," 153–154.

[139] Boro Kontić, interview with the author, August 28, 2013.

[140] Lindvall, "Public Broadcasting Reform," 5–6; also see Hozić, "Democratizing Media," 153.

Solutions proposed by the BBC team were fiercely opposed, especially the idea to reduce the number of redundant staff and to sell the large and useless building. Additional internal resistance came from politically affiliated journalists who opposed the efforts of international consultants to introduce principles of impartiality and objectivity in news reporting.[141]

Last but not least, there have been persistent attempts by ruling parties to exercise direct control over PSB through procedures of appointment of their supervisory and governing bodies.[142]

Consequently, the PSB system is as dysfunctional in 2016 as it was ten years ago, burdened by lack of funding, political interference and lack of cooperation between the three broadcasters, while its major component—a joint corporation—is still not established. Effectively, the reform process has been stalled for years. Although a new set of laws has been introduced as of 2005, and more than €5 million were invested during the initial phase,[143] the model failed to be implemented.

It is fair to say that the reforms have resulted in some positive changes at the level of individual broadcasters. Especially in respect to the quality of content and treatment of opposition parties the "public broadcasting [is] in an incomparably better condition that in the years that followed the war."[144] However, overall, the case of PSB reforms is an illustrative example how politically unfeasible solutions and unfounded assumptions about possibilities of transposition of models between societies undermine the transformation process. This case amply demonstrates how damaging the absence of true commitment to the reforms by local political elites can be. As no true ideational change has taken place among key local stakeholders, the externally imposed models have been systematically subverted. It seems that the proposed model, based on the BBC experience, did not take into consideration the particularities of the BiH context and has wrongly assumed that a technical solution would be sufficient to resolve a complex political issue[145] and to meet the political

---

[141] Dominic Medley, former International News Supervisor (OHR), based in the BHTV newsroom, Sarajevo (2000–2001), NATO Spokesman, Afghanistan (June 2010–June 2013), interview with the author, August 26, 2013.

[142] CRA, "Annual Report … 2010," 17; Gorinjac, "RAK mora dva puta raditi isti posao"; European Commission, "Bosnia and Herzegovina 2011 Progress Report," 16; Udovičić, "Bosnia-Herzegovina," 43–44.

[143] Rhodes, "Ten Years of Media Support," 25.

[144] Lindvall, "Public Broadcasting Reform," 3.

[145] Ibid.

ambitions of state building that were on the agenda of the international community.

More than anything, the proposed model largely failed to take into consideration the interests of dominant local stakeholders and ruling elites, or the business interests of broadcasters in the PSB system. In essence, there is a significant discrepancy between proposed reforms and the interests of key local stakeholders, who were expected to give up the privileges of control and funding that they possess for a political project without clear benefits for them.[146] The proposed model neglected the particularities of the local context, resulting in what Berkowitz et al.[147] call "the transplant effect"—a mismatch between a transplanted model taken from another context and specific local conditions.

Moreover, given the depth of resistance, and the ambition of the reforms, it appears that the OHR and other international actors pulled out of the PSB reform too early. According to De Luce, "the OHR and the European Commission have been criticized for taking the same top-down, short-term approach to reforming the public broadcasters, prompting comparisons to the OBN experience"[148] which is elaborated in detail in the next section of this chapter.

The Open Broadcast Network (OBN)

In 1996, the international community, instructed by the Peace Implementation Council[149] and led by the OHR, decided to establish an independent TV network that would cover the entire BiH territory. According to the Carl Bildt, the first High Representative in BiH, the purpose of this endeavor was to "provide equal time for all political parties and candidates, as well as news coverage free of political coloring"[150] and to "bring decency to the media and life to democracy in Bosnia."[151] As a result, the OBN was established and the attempt was "to get the television network

---

146 On the importance of the support of local elites, see, for example, Goetz, "Manoeuvring Past Clientelism," 404.
147 Berkowitz, Pistor, and Richard, "The Transplant Effect," 171.
148 De Luce, "Assessment of USAID Media Assistance," 18.
149 Peace Implementation Council Steering Board, "Broadcast Media Statement."
150 Hedges, "TV Station in Bosnia."
151 Bildt, *Peace Journey*, 260.

on the air in time for the September 1996 election."[152] Donors and peace implementation actors believed that the statewide, independent TV network would help to break the dominance of nationalist parties over the broadcasting sector in the country[153] and ensure that the first postwar elections were free and fair.

OBN was established around a network of small affiliate stations from across the country. The affiliates broadcast the OBN program in exchange for donations in equipment and funding, and the opportunity to air their own programs over the OBN network to a broader audience. Apart from the distribution of the signal through the affiliates, there was also a direct broadcast signal covering 30% of the country.[154]

From the very beginning, the network faced significant resistance from local political actors and governments at all administrative levels, as well as by some local media that were not part of the project. Authorities attempted to "block its legal registration, deny it frequencies and access to transmission sites."[155] In order to counteract the anticipated obstacles, the Peace Implementation Council decided to install the network without consulting the local actors and governments in BiH. Moreover, it made it clear that local authorities cannot impose any conditions on the creation of the network, and that "the full transmission of its programming must be permitted throughout Bosnia and Herzegovina, in both entities."[156] However, in order to be able to cover the whole country, and given the systematic obstruction by local authorities, the "OBN was forced to use costly satellite transmission between its stations."[157] As a consequence of the various delays and obstructions, OBN started broadcasting only eight days before the 1996 elections, which was far too late to be able to make any difference.[158]

The program went on air in September 1996, covering mainly the territory of the Federation of Bosnia and Herzegovina, but gradually broadened its reach through affiliate stations to cover some 80% of the

---

[152] De Luce, "Assessment of USAID Media Assistance," 4.
[153] Ibid.; Becker and Hollifield, "Market Forces, Media Assistance and Democratization," 12; Lindvall, "Public Broadcasting Reform," 1; UNDP, "Supporting Public Service Broadcasting," 18–19; Ranson, "International Intervention," 90–91; CIMA, "Empowering Independent Media," 59–60.
[154] Ranson, "International Intervention," 32.
[155] Ibid., 95.
[156] Peace Implementation Council Steering Board, "Broadcast Media Statement."
[157] Palmer, "Power-Sharing in Media," 35.
[158] De Luce, "Assessment of USAID Media Assistance," 4.

country. Although its primary purpose was to provide objective news, the program also included documentary, sports, children's programming and entertainment, in an attempt to broaden its audience appeal and attract revenues.[159]

A number of donor countries, development agencies and private foundations provided funding to OBN.[160] At least US$20 million was donated for the development of the network between 1996 and 2001, while an additional US$1.9 million was collected through advertising and sponsorship.[161]

Although attempts were made to have more local input in managing the network, it was administered by the OHR and run by international consultants[162] while the affiliate stations had "no say in the management or ownership of the venture."[163] OBN became a centrally run project without much grassroots credibility.[164]

Apart from political obstacles and the top-down approach, the project faced other problems as well. First, it was characterized by poor planning and unrealistic expectations in respect to its potential to attract revenues from advertising,[165] which can be linked to the fact that "no implementing organization with broadcast expertise was asked to carry out the project."[166] Its programming was considered unimpressive and irrelevant[167] and audience figures remained low.[168]

Moreover, the funding was often provided only after long delays. Donors frequently failed to fulfill their pledges, especially toward the last few years of their support, which completely stopped by 2002.[169] The problems in obtaining funding also indicate the lack of coordination

[159] Ranson, "International Intervention," 30–31; Rhodes, "Ten Years of Media Support," 25; Johnson, "Model Interventions," 103–104.

[160] Rhodes, "Ten Years of Media Support," 25; Ranson, "International Intervention," 30.

[161] UNDP, "Supporting Public Service Broadcasting," 18–19; Ranson, "International Intervention," 132.

[162] De Luce, "Assessment of USAID Media Assistance," 4–5.

[163] Hume, *The Media Missionaries*, 37–38; also see ICG, "Media in Bosnia and Herzegovina."

[164] Ibid.

[165] CIMA, "Empowering Independent Media," 59–60.

[166] De Luce, "Assessment of USAID Media Assistance," 4.

[167] Johnson, "Model Interventions," 104–105.

[168] De Luce, "Assessment of USAID Media Assistance," 4.

[169] Ranson, "International Intervention," 40–41, 133.

among donors[170] which, for example, sometimes resulted in the donations of equipment that was incompatible or unnecessary.[171] In addition, donors had different funding policies, reserving their donations for specific types of support such as training or equipment purchase that often prevented OBN from other investment or from pursuing any strategic plans.[172]

By the end of 1998, donors decided that OBN's sustainability would depend on its capacity to attract commercial revenues. A strategic business plan was developed in early 1999, aiming for OBN to achieve financial sustainability in five years.[173] However, the donors were not satisfied with the quality and appeal of OBN programs.[174] This soon resulted in the withdrawal of donor support and the collapse of the project. According to Jenny Ranson, OBN's former CEO, the network was closed down as a consequence of the changing priorities of the international community, which focused on the restructuring of a public service broadcasting system[175] and was not ready to commit to the long-term project of building a commercial statewide network.[176] For example, after donating €4.7 million to OBN, the European Commission stopped its support in order to be able to focus on the reform of PSB.[177]

As the donations ran out by 2002, managerial control was given to a liquidator, while the network continued operations with minimal staff.[178] In 2003, OBN was sold to a TV and advertising mogul from Croatia, but the details of the deal remained classified.[179] The network was rapidly transformed into a commercial entertainment TV channel.

Although the OBN project collapsed, the network had created initial access to airwaves for opposition parties and other groups that had been excluded from the mainstream media.[180] During its first two years, OBN

---

[170] Ibid., 37–38.
[171] Ibid., 40–41.
[172] Ibid., 32–34.
[173] Ibid., 32–34.
[174] UNDP, "Supporting Public Service Broadcasting," 19.
[175] Ranson, "International Intervention."
[176] Also see UNDP, "Supporting Public Service Broadcasting," 19; De Luce, "Assessment of USAID Media Assistance," 4.
[177] De Luce, "Assessment of USAID Media Assistance," 10.
[178] Ibid., 5.
[179] Hozić, "Democratizing Media," 155.
[180] Becker and Hollifield, "Market Forces, Media Assistance and Democratization," 12; Kurspahić, *Zločin u 19:30*, 176.

succeeded in broadcasting "balanced news and current affairs programming across ethnic boundaries."[181] Even today, some of the former OBN affiliate stations continue to function.[182] Several of them, such as ATV in Banja Luka and Hayat in Sarajevo, play an important role in today's media market.[183]

To sum up, the network was created in a rush, without much strategic planning.[184] The concerns of local media practitioners and experts, who suggested that the funds be directed toward the reform of PSB rather than establishing a new outlet from the scratch, were too easily dismissed by international consultants.[185] According to Ranson, three crucial factors were ignored, leading to the collapse of the network: the enormous costs necessary for setting up a statewide TV network; the time needed for such a start-up to build an audience; and the weak local media market that could not provide much-needed advertising revenues for the network.[186] In addition, the low ratings[187] of OBN demonstrated the difficulty of achieving relevant audience appeal with neutral, peace-oriented journalism in a context characterized by an ethnically polarized, fragmented and traumatized society.[188] The OBN case demonstrates how the absence of an implementation strategy can hurt such a project. It also shows how top-down change can be imposed at the institutional level, but cannot guarantee the acceptance of such institutions among audiences. This points to the underlying problem with the idea that a commercial outlet can perform a PSB function, especially given the limitations posed by an over-saturated market and ethnically fragmented audience. The case illustrates the need for a solid financial foundation, donor coordination, long-term donor commitment, and realistic expectations. The absence of these core elements in the donor approach had a detrimental effect on the chances of the project's success.[189]

---

[181] De Luce, "Assessment of USAID Media Assistance," 7.
[182] Ibid., 5; see UNDP, "Supporting Public Service Broadcasting," 19.
[183] Boro Kontić, interview with the author, August 28, 2013.
[184] Kurspahić, *Zločin u 19:30*, 174–175.
[185] Boro Kontić, interview with the author, August 28, 2013.
[186] Ranson, "International Intervention," 132.
[187] Udovičić, "Media in B-H," 203.
[188] Bratić, Ross, and Kang-Graham, "Bosnia's Open Broadcast Network."
[189] De Luce, "Assessment of USAID Media Assistance," 7; Ranson, "International Intervention," 40–41; Rhodes, "Ten Years of Media Support," 25.

Conclusions

The case of BiH demonstrates that media reform is a slow, time-consuming process,[190] which is closely related to the consolidation of democratic institutions that foster free media. The three case studies presented here amply demonstrate a deep tension between externally driven reform initiatives and the democratization agenda on one hand, and the complex set of contextual challenges to reforms on the other. Hence, our findings support Mcloughlin and Scott who claim that media reforms "can only produce results at the same pace as democratic evolution in a given country, and should be integrated into broader democratic governance reform."[191]

It appears that only a few donors and international actors considered whether and in what ways the local context in BiH would be able to absorb the transplanted institutional models and policies. The detrimental effects of the absence of an "enabling environment,"[192] an undeveloped market, and the persistence of old undemocratic practices of political elites were largely underestimated. In that respect, the case of BiH presents a set of important lessons for media assistance efforts that have broader relevance.

The process of introducing new media institutions and practices by "mimicking," and often transplanting, Western European media institutions and policy models into the BiH context has proven difficult, at best. Such "institutional monocropping"[193]—the process of transposing institutional blueprints from advanced democracies into recipient countries caught in the early stages of democratization—is likely to suffer from what Berkowitz et al. call the "transplant effect,"[194] and has limited chances of success. The models from Western democracies have been only partially transposed, and in the process of localization have been transformed to combine old and new institutional practices into "hybrid" institutional arrangements.[195] Those new institutional forms blend imported values and modes of operation with local legacies and practices, often with unpredictable results and unwanted consequences. What really emerged is similar

---

[190] Taylor and Kent, "Media Transitions," 362–365
[191] Mcloughlin and Scott, "Topic Guide," 22.
[192] Price and Krug, "The Enabling Environment" (2002).
[193] Evans, "Development as Institutional Change," 31.
[194] Berkowitz, Pistor, and Richard, "The Transplant Effect," 171.
[195] For more on hybrid media system see Voltmer, "How Far Can Media Systems Travel?"

to what Jakubowicz and Sükösd call an "atavistic" media system that is "colonized" by political parties—a phenomenon common for many post-communist societies, not just BiH. In such a context, the political elite formally and declaratively accepts the externally imposed reforms and the "mimetic" orientation, but does everything in its power to maintain its old system of control over the media. The democratic laws are only partially implemented, and new institutional arrangements suffer from undemocratic practices—they are often misused and misinterpreted in the narrow interests of political elites.[196]

Given all of the above, it is apparent that a strategic orientation, coordination of media assistance efforts and prolonged monitoring of government actions[197] are among the key preconditions for sustainable reforms. Early intervention in BiH was often based on ad hoc decisions and subject to a sudden changes in priorities, short-term and unreliable funding,[198] a lack of strategic orientation and longer-term commitment by donors, and an absence of coordination. All this contributed to the failure of reform efforts. Too often, media assistance is seen as a way to quickly influence the political climate[199] but is driven by the narrow interests of individual donors. All this has had a negative effect on the success of reforms, as is amply demonstrated by the analyzed cases.

Much attention has been given to the issue of donor dependence and the importance of the financial sustainability of recipient media outlets and institutions. It is argued that "although initial aid to media start-ups can be vital, donor engagement, especially long-term, may have the unintended effect of fostering 'a culture of dependency.'"[200] However, our analysis shows that the situation is much more complex: in order to achieve financial sustainability, public and private media institutions need sufficient time to conceive and implement robust financing models. For example, OBN suffered from the absence of long-term funding and commitment, which resulted in its collapse. Namely, an underdeveloped market simply could not sustain this institution.[201] Financial sustainability

---

[196] Jakubowicz and Sükösd. "Twelve Concepts," 17–23.

[197] Kumar, "International Assistance to Promote Independent Media," 162.

[198] Johnson, "Model Interventions," 109.

[199] De Luce, "Assessment of USAID Media Assistance," 11.

[200] CIMA, "Empowering Independent Media," 59–60; also see Kumar, "International Assistance to Promote Independent Media," 658.

[201] Bajraktari and Hsu, "Developing Media in Stabilization and Reconstruction Operations."

has much more to do with the existence of coherent, longer-term commitment, combined with a clear strategy of sustainability tailored to each institution. Donors often lack such an approach.[202]

Also, findings from relevant literature demonstrate that enduring institutional changes occurred where local elites welcomed external assistance efforts.[203] Goetz demonstrated that "reform involves considerable risk to leaders: risk that they will lose patronage resources (public sector jobs and rents), and also lose popular support."[204] In other words, radical institutional change that significantly modify the resources of elite patronage and the power equilibrium are more challenging to implement than incremental institutional change,[205] as is clearly demonstrated by all three cases studied here.

An ethnically divided, postconflict society that is undergoing slow democratic transition leaves a very limited window of opportunity for substantial cooperation with local decision-makers. Often, programs could not effectively be coordinated through local governing institutions due to pervasive ethnic divisions and a political capture of the state.[206] In some cases, consultation with the local media community took place only after the laws were already drafted by international experts, and mutual distrust prevented more meaningful cooperation between international consultants and local media professionals. Consequently, there is a lack of a sense of ownership of the reforms among local actors, which translates into weaker support for, or even outright opposition to, the proposed solutions.

To conclude, the media reforms in BiH have been the result of unprecedented external intervention in the face of relentless opposition from the side of a local political elite. The prospects of the externally introduced media institutions will depend on the development of the local democratic culture[207]—a process that will take time. This discrepancy between institutional reforms through the transposition of Western institutional models on one side, and a cultural change[208] on the other, is a core challenge for the sustainability of the media assistance efforts in BiH and in similar contexts elsewhere.

---

[202] UNDP, "Supporting Public Service Broadcasting," 21.
[203] Shirley, "Institutions and Development," 32–33.
[204] Goetz, "Manoeuvring Past Clientelism," 404.
[205] Ibid., 421.
[206] Martin, "Media Reform and Development in Bosnia," 92.
[207] Jakubowicz and Sükösd, "Twelve Concepts," 22–23.
[208] Ibid., 22–23.

CHAPTER 4

Starting from Scratch: The Role of Media Assistance in the Establishment of Independent Media Institutions in Kosovo

NASER MIFTARI

Introduction

For almost a decade Kosovo was governed by the United Nations Mission in Kosovo (UNMIK)—a governing structure introduced in Kosovo at the end of conflict in 1999 with the mandate to set up the institutions of self-government in Kosovo, based on UN Security Council Resolution 1244 (1999). The status of Kosovo as a de facto UN protectorate lasted until February 17, 2008, when Kosovo proclaimed itself an independent state.[1] When UNMIK deployed in Kosovo together with its military component—the NATO-led Kfor—its structure consisted of four pillars operating under the UNMIK umbrella.[2]

The third pillar of UNMIK—Democratization and Institution Building—was entrusted to the Organization for Security and Co-operation in Europe (OSCE). As part of its mandate, the OSCE helped establish a range of local media institutions including Radio Television of

---

[1] UNMIK continues to implement its mandate in a status neutral manner under Security Council Resolution 1244 (1999). The Special Representative (SRSG) ensures a coordinated approach with the OSCE—its pillar for institution building—and EULEX, which is deployed under S.C. Res. 1244 (1999) and operates under the authority of the United Nations.

[2] Pillar I was under UNHCR and addressed Humanitarian Assistance postconflict. Pillar II was the UNMIK Civil Administration led by the United Nations; and Pillar IV: Reconstruction and Economic Development, was led by the European Union (EU).

Kosovo[3] (RTK), the Temporary Media Commissioner[4] (TMC)—the predecessor to the Independent Media Commission (IMC)—and the Press Council of Kosovo (PCK). Starting in 2005, the management of these media institutions was handed over to the self-administration of Kosovo.

During the decade-long international management, the Kosovar media sector had been experiencing important transformations. Yet, a general perception persists that the media "underperforms" and the sector vacillates between a stable and a precarious state. The liberal media regime UNMIK introduced was indeed successful in liberalizing print and broadcasting media in Kosovo. However, the uncontrolled increase in media outlets has disrupted the sector, creating a saturated media market with declining sources of revenue.

The European Commission's (EC) progress reports and the IREX Media Sustainability Index (MSI) on Kosovo recognize that media pluralism and de-monopolization of information have been successfully addressed. However, the proliferation of media outlets also caused an overly saturated media market while sources of revenue started to decline. Other persisting challenges are ensuring freedom of expression and the independence of the media, protecting journalistic sources and raising the overall professionalization of the media and journalistic professions.

Between 2005 and 2007 the EC's annual progress reports on Kosovo recognize progress being made in guaranteeing freedom of expression and the implementation of audiovisual media policies as well as the adoption of the legal and self-regulatory framework for the media.[5] Starting in 2008, the EC repeatedly raised concerns in its reports about the uncertainty regarding funding, operations and the independence of media institutions.[6] In particular, the reports expose political interference in the appointment of board and management members in both RTK and the IMC and how RTK's editorial independence remains precarious due to its reliance on state funding. Another challenge that is identified in the

---

[3] Through an agreement with the OSCE Mission in Kosovo, UNMIK invited EBU to set up and manage RTK in 1999.

[4] In June 2000 UNMIK introduced Regulation 2000/36 on the Licensing and Regulation of the Broadcast Media and Regulation 2000/37 on the Conduct of Print Media and established the TMC, citing "special circumstances" until the introduction of an "effective self-regulation of the print media", making Kosovo a unique place where print was being regulated by authorities. See OSCE Mission in Kosovo, "Broadcast and Print Regulations."

[5] European Commission, "Kosovo Progress Reports" for 2005, 2006 and 2007.

[6] European Commission, "Kosovo Progress Reports" for 2008 to 2014.

EC reports is the continued pressure exerted on journalists and the media, including the dangers faced by journalists and partisan as well as ownership influence on the media.[7]

Between 2001 and 2015, the IREX MSI periodically assessed the structural conditions for free speech, the state of the journalism profession, the amount of pluralism in news sources, and the degree to which supporting institutions recognize progress in Kosovo. Similar to the EC progress reports, the MSI notes persisting obstacles, such as pressure on journalists, inadequate provisions for the independence of RTK, limited access to information and the impunity enjoyed by those who commit crimes against journalists.[8] Alarmingly, the 2015 IREX MSI sees the biggest decline of the conditions for media sustainability in Kosovo since it started measuring it, pointing to worsening conditions for media and journalists in Kosovo.

Table 4.1. IREX Media Sustainability Indicators for Kosovo, 2001–2015

Indicator	Year					
	2010	2011	2012	2013	2014	2015
Free Speech	2.53	2.70	2.46	2.52	2.65	2.25
Professional Journalism	2.63	2.54	2.20	2.38	2.32	2.13
Plurality of News Sources	2.77	2.78	2.51	2.64	2.90	2.57
Business Management	2.32	2.15	1.88	2.22	2.27	2.02
Supporting Institutions	2.76	2.50	2.63	2.53	2.58	2.36
Overall Score	2.60	2.53	2.33	2.46	2.54	2.27

Source: IREX, "Kosovo," in *Media Sustainability Index* for the years 2010 to 2015.

This chapter is concerned with the development of central media institutions in Kosovo as influenced by foreign assistance and funding. Tracing media institutions' evolution over time and in relation to international assistance and their embeddedness in a local political and media system is central to this research. The development of the IMC, RTK, and the

---

[7] Ibid.

[8] IREX, Media Sustainability Index (MSI) annual reports on Kosovo, 2001–2015, available at https://www.irex.org/resource/media-sustainability-index-msi#europe-eurasia.

PCK provide in-depth case studies in order to observe the conditions for their autonomy and functionality over time. As central pillars in Kosovo's media system their institutional independence and sustainability are important conditions for democracy and freedom of expression in Kosovo. Moreover, the conclusion of a Stabilization and Association Agreement (SAA) with the EU is also conditional upon demonstrating independent and functioning media institutions.[9]

The chapter builds on evaluations of media programs, progress reports and other research on Kosovo's media sector and its institutions. It also relies on primary data obtained from sixteen interviews with representatives of media institutions, journalists, civil society activists and academics that were conducted between December 2012 and March 2013.[10]

Incorporating the theoretical framework presented in the introduction to this volume, this chapter briefly covers the tenets of the political and media system in Kosovo before summarizing the main trends, strategies, and goals of foreign assistance to Kosovo media institutions. The chapter then investigates how three specific media institutions—the IMC, RTK, and the PCK—all established with considerable foreign media assistance, have evolved from their inception until 2015. The chapter concludes with a discussion of the findings and some final considerations on the current status of Kosovo's media institutions.

---

[9] European Commission, "Recommendation."

[10] Agron Bajrami, Editor in Chief of the *Koha Ditore* newspaper and Board Member of PCK, email message to author, 5 March 2013 (PCK) and March 7, 2013 (RTK); Agron Demi, Executive Director, Institute for Advanced Studies GAP, email message to author, January 9, 2013; Andrew Clayton, Chief of Party, IREX Kosovo, email message to author, January 28, 2013; Arben Hajredinaj, National Program Officer, OSCE Mission in Kosovo, email message to author, March 8, 2013; Ardita Zejnullahu, Executive Director of AMPEK, email message to author, January 29, 2013; Argjentina Grazhdani, former Media and Civil Society Advisor to USAID Kosovo Mission, email message to author, February 10, 2013; Avni Zogiani, Codirector of the Organization for Democracy, Anticorruption, and Dignity (COHU), email message to author, January 23, 2013; Baton Haxhiu, Director of Klan Kosova, a popular TV channel, and a former Executive Director of APJK, email message to author, January 27, 2013; Mentor Shala, Director General of RTK, email message to author, March 18, 2013; Milazim Krasniqi, Head of the Journalism Department, University of Pristina, email message to author, January 17, 2013; Naile Selimaj-Krasniqi, CEO of IMC, email message to author, February 23, 2013; Nehat Islami, Executive Director of PCK, email message to author, March 8, 2013; Remzie Shahini Hoxhaj, Professor of Journalism, University of Pristina, email message to author, January 29, 2013.

The Political and Media System

Kosovo is a parliamentary democracy with a multiparty proportional system. The 120-member unicameral National Assembly is the highest legislative, representative and oversight institution. The central decision-making powers are vested with the government and the prime minister. Kosovo's political system can be considered fragmented and relatively unstable. The two main parties are the Democratic Party of Kosovo (PDK) and Democratic League of Kosovo (LDK). Since the aftermath of the Kosovo conflict neither party has had a majority appeal; however, in joint coalition and/or in coalitions with other less-sizable parties, LDK and PDK have determined the outcomes of government formations.[11] Between 2005 and 2015 Kosovo has had five different prime ministers and as many governing coalitions.

This makes it difficult for governing coalitions to push forward relevant political or media agenda. The voting on relevant legislation, including media legislation, is often driven alongside political party lines, interests and calculations.[12] The postconflict democratic transition in Kosovo exhibits the characteristics of what is known as the "politicization of the state," namely a certain degree of business parallelism, direct or indirect government control, floating laws and fuzzy ownership.[13]

Concerning the phenomenon of "business parallelism," a 2012 report indicates that the resilience of Kosovo media outlets despite economic hardship is explained through business subsidization.[14] Another report points out to a number of Kosovo media outlets that are dependent on businesses that own them.[15]

---

[11] Since the end of the conflict Kosovo was governed through a broad-based coalion and the prime minister was chosen by consensus. From 2004 the prime minister has been proposed by the winning coalition and voted on in the assembly.

[12] When the laws on IMC (2005) and RTK (2006) were first passed Kosovo was ruled by a minority government, and both laws received a minimum threshold (fifty-plus votes) while the opposition voted against. When the modified laws on RTK and IMC came up for voting in 2012 they again received the votes of the new governing coalition but not the votes of the opposition. (The RTK law was passed with forty-two votes in favor, thirty-six against and four abstentions.)

[13] Zielonka and Mancini, "Executive Summary."

[14] Qavdarbasha, "The State of the Media in Kosovo."

[15] YIHR, "State of Constriction?" A number of interviewers have also pointed to cross-subsidization impact in the Kosovo media.

A number of incidents signify how different governments assert control over the media. For example, in 2009, the European Broadcasting Union (EBU), criticized Kosovo's prime minister for undue political and financial influence on the media.[16] The government's influence in diverting state advertising toward government-friendly media has been extensively documented.[17]

"Floating laws"[18] describe legal insecurity due to stalled reforms, too frequent changes of the legal framework and the presence of implementation deficits. Important examples from Kosovo are the laws on the IMC and RTK, introduced in 2005 and 2006, respectively, and amended in 2012.[19] The process of their amendment was dragged on for years leaving the boards of RTK and the IMC dysfunctional for several years. Once introduced in 2012, these laws narrowed the independence of RTK and the IMC, allowing the Kosovo Assembly greater scrutiny in the selection and appointment of their board members, respectively.[20]

There is no legal requirement that would require ownership transparency. Consequently media ownership in Kosovo is only partially transparent, contributing to what is known as "fuzzy ownership." In addition, problems with privatization are not yet fully resolved. For example, none of the three national television stations that operate in Kosovo today (including RTK) have legal clarity about the ownership of their premises. Instead, they have benefited from the legal uncertainty, making use of low-rent or even rent-free premises, while remaining vulnerable to government influence pending of how the latter will resolve ownership issues of formerly state-owned enterprises.[21]

---

[16] EBU, "EBU accuses PM."

[17] KIPRED, "Circulation and Politicization."

[18] Zielonka and Mancini, "Executive Summary," 4.

[19] "Law no. 02/L-15 for the Independent Media Commission and Broadcasting"; Law no. 04/L-044 on the Independent Media Commission"; "Law no. 02/L-047 on Radio Television of Kosovo"; "Law no. 04/L-046 on Radio Television of Kosovo."

[20] Based on the IMC law of 2005 the agency was in charge of inviting the applications for the boards of IMC and RTK and upon submission of the list the ad hoc committee could approve the candidates in a pro forma vote. The IMC law of 2012 took away such powers from IMC, leaving the selection process entirely in the hands of the ad hoc committee of the Kosovo Assembly.

[21] Representatives of the Kosovo Privatization Agency, email message. April 26, 2013.

In Kosovo mass media is still used to amplify political and/or business interests.[22] Media bias is nuanced across the larger spectrum of media outlets. It surfaces in the selection of news events, the tone of coverage, and the selection of sources of information in the media, in particular during election periods.[23] This was further exacerbated by media personnel taking positions in political parties and even as members of parliament or in the government.

On matters of media freedom, Kosovo civil society is not strong and vocal enough.[24] Based on the feedback from interviewees, over the last decade civil society has largely failed to tackle the issues relevant to media freedom.[25] Such claims have been echoed in the EC progress reports emphasizing civil society's continuous weak status, lack of ability to influence change and an overall absence of civil society legacy in Kosovo.[26]

Articles 40 and 42 of Kosovo's 2008 constitution guarantee the freedom of the press, media pluralism and ban state censorship. However, press freedom can be limited in cases where it would encourage violence and hostility linked to race, nationality, ethnicity or religion.[27] Kosovo has a dual media system that combines public service and commercial radio and television.

Currently, the number of licensed broadcasters in Kosovo is 186, with twenty TV stations, seventy-eight radio stations, thirty-four cable operators and fifty-four service providers that operate via cable. Broadcasters and cable operators with national coverage are mainly located in the capital Pristina and dominate the media market. Three TV stations have

---

[22] Some notable examples include *Koha Ditore* publisher Veton Surroi as the leader of the political initiative ORA represented in the Kosovo Assembly (2004–2007); Blerim Shala of the newspaper *Zeri. Lajm* newspaper (discontinued in 2012) owner Behxhet Pacolli, as the head of the Alliance for the New Kosovo represented with thirteen MPs in the assembly (2007–2010); and *Infopress* (discontinued in 2011), whose publisher, Rexhep Hoti, was an MP from the ranks of the PDK (2007–2010).

[23] KIPRED, "Monitoring of Media"; KIPRED, "Media Monitoring."

[24] An inefficient and corrupt judiciary system and the undue influence of politicians on the judiciary in Kosovo are regarded as the main obstacles to helping prosecute the crimes against journalists. See Basile, "Kosovo."

[25] A number of interviewers emphasized that civil society did not come to the defense of RTK's independence by pressuring the assembly to find a suitable alternative when KEK terminated its contract with RTK.

[26] For an analysis of the civil society impact, see European Commission, "Kosovo Progress Reports" for 2007–2010.

[27] "Constitution of the Republic of Kosovo," Art. 40 and 42.

Kosovo-wide coverage: RTK and the commercial broadcasters—Radio
Television 21 (RTV21) and Kohavision (KTV). The rest of the channels
provide regional (ten) and local (seven) coverage.

The recent census data shows that 90% of the 1.8 million Kosovar
inhabitants are Albanians.[28] Of the twenty television stations, fourteen
broadcast in Albanian, five in Serbian and one in Turkish. In addition,
there are four nationwide radio stations, out of which two are public
service radios (Radio Kosova and Radio Blue Sky), and another seventy-
four local radio stations throughout Kosovo broadcasting in the languages
of different ethnic communities.[29]

Turning to the press, there are seven daily (print) newspapers in
Kosovo: *Koha Ditore, Zëri, Kosova Sot, Tribuna, Bota Sot, Lajm,* and *Epoka
e Re.* Although there is no independent information on the exact number
of copies sold,[30] the circulation of printed newspapers continues to
decline. Some other publications, such as *Gazeta Express,* have switched
recently from print to electronic versions. New media, especially online
news portals, have witnessed a surge in recent years with the leading media
portals reaching between 200,000 and 400,000 visitors daily on average.[31]

In 2013 the IMC has prepared a research report which was presented to the Kosovo Assembly putting the size of the media market at
close to €30 million annually. Of this amount, 15% goes to newspapers
and Internet, 49% to national, cable and local TV, and 31% is shared by
national and local radio stations.[32]

Overview of International Democratization and Media Assistance

THE NEED FOR MEDIA ASSISTANCE IN KOSOVO

During the socialist Yugoslav period, citizens could only access state-
owned media channels and Communist Party press. When Slobodan
Milošević ascended into power in 1989 in Serbia, this led to an escala-
tion of the repression of the Albanian media in Kosovo. It culminated with
the suppression of the Albanian-language service of the then provincial

---

[28] Kosovo Agency of Statistics, "Kosovo Population and Housing Census 2011."
[29] IMC, "Annual Report Presented to the Kosovo Assembly."
[30] OSCE Mission in Kosovo, "Freedom of Media."
[31] Taylor, "Setting Media Standards."
[32] IMC, "Advertising Market Research and Analysis in Kosovo."

broadcaster Radio Television Pristina (RTP) and the termination of the only daily newspaper in Albanian.[33] Throughout the early 1990s, access to independent sources of information in the local Albanian language remained scarce.[34]

Toward the mid-1990s Kosovo witnessed the emergence of a few independent media outlets, such as the weeklies *KOHA* and *ZERI*, under the sponsorship of the Soros Foundation. After the end of the conflict in 1999, the few early media outlets restarted publishing, for example, the newspapers *Koha Ditore* and *Kosova Sot*, and the magazine *ZERI*. At this time dozens of new media outlets entered the market.[35]

Operating under UNMIK, Kfor was first in charge of issuing temporary broadcasting licenses and remained in charge of the frequency spectrum. Since 2000, the OSCE, through the TMC, was mandated to confirm the licenses to broadcasters in Kosovo.[36] UNMIK and the OSCE were not unified in their strategies and actions regarding the development of local media, adding a great deal of confusion and inconsistency.[37] This lack of trust and cooperation was visible in the procedure and timing of granting frequencies (i.e., UNMIK) and licenses (i.e., the OSCE) to broadcasters.[38]

The distrust ensued due to the persistence of the United States to determine the features of the postconflict media development in Kosovo. The US insisted on the introduction of commercial media, in particular two commercial broadcasters with national coverage. On the contrary, the OSCE wanted a public service broadcaster on air, namely RTK, and to increase its appeal before other broadcasters emerged. The OSCE feared that the introduction of powerful commercial broadcasters too soon after the conflict could interfere with the fragile peace and political agenda.[39]

---

[33] Berisha, "Kosovo/a."

[34] IREX, "Kosovo" (2002).

[35] Ibid.

[36] When the UN administration was deployed, it initially declared applicable all laws that existed before the conflict. Later, it declared applicable only laws that were effective until March 22, 1989, the time when Kosovo was stripped of its autonomy. However, relevant media laws from the communist period were also not seen as suitable to regulate the media in the post conflict Kosovo. Therefore, UNMIK had to introduce regulations from scratch. See Sullivan, "Restructuring the Media."

[37] Loewenberg, "United Nations Media Strategy."

[38] Ibid.

[39] Sullivan, "Restructuring the Media."

The pursuit of parallel media projects—the OSCE focusing on RTK on one side, and the Americans focusing on the commercial broadcasters KTV and RTV21 on the other side—polarized the media sector, shaped assistance programs, and affected the content of the draft broadcast legal framework.[40]

It is estimated that international media support provided between €60 to €80 million to Kosovo media. Rhodes[41] puts media assistance in Kosovo between 1999 and 2006 at €58.6 million, €45.6 million (more than 80%) given to media outlets, €6.1 million in professional training of journalists, and €6.9 million toward enabling a media environment. This does not take into account the support provided to the media prior to 1999 and an additional €15–20 million provided since 2006 on ongoing media support. Another report compiled for the OSCE estimated for the period between 1998 and 2004, €36 million of international media assistance was provided. The report notes that 50% of that amount has gone toward RTK and the Kosovo Terrestrial Telecommunications Network[42] (KTTN), 37% to the private broadcasters KTV and RTV21, and the rest (13%) to other activities, including support for print media, minority stations and programming, and development of a legal framework.[43] In later years (between 2007 and 2013) donors continued support for a range of projects which combined exceeded €15 million.[44]

---

[40] Kaufman, "Kosovo Media Assessment."

[41] Rhodes, "Ten Years of Media Support."

[42] KTTN was built as a part of the USAID-funded Kosova Independent Media Project (KIMP), implemented by IREX. Until 2004 it was financed up to 95% by USAID. Recently it became a shareholding enterprise of the three main broadcasters (RTK, KTV, RTV21) and a commercial radio station (Radio Dukagjini). KTV and RTV21 are the main shareholders of KTTN, holding 70%; RTK holds 25% and Radio Dukagjini holds 5%.

[43] Laue, "Local Electronic Media in Kosovo."

[44] IREX Kosovo's Strengthening Independent Minority Media (SIMM) is estimated at $5.5 million (€4.1 million) of which $462,000 (€320,000) was provided for equipment to minority media outlets in Kosovo between 2007 and 2011. The OSCE has downsized its commitments and it operates with a smaller annual budge, which in 2004 was estimated to be €400,000. The Foreign Ministry of Norway has disbursed €6.25 million for running the Kosovo Institute of Journalism and Communication (KIJAC). The Kosovo Media Institute (KMI) established by the OSCE received €1.3 million from the European Commission between 2006 and 2011, an estimated €500,000 from the Kosovo Foundation for Open Society and €500,000 from OSCE Kosovo. See Chetwynd and Chetwynd, "Mid-Term Evaluation." The IMC has received €1 million from EC for its equipment. The donors have also continuously supported the Press Council

PHASES OF MEDIA ASSISTANCE TO KOSOVO

International media assistance in Kosovo has undergone three phases. First, support to opposition media during Serbian rule (1990s). Second, postconflict media intervention (1999–2007). Third, limited media support (since 2007). There are four broad categories of initiatives: (1) human capital development, (2) directly supporting media outlets, (3) regulatory framework, (4) supporting media institutions.[45]

In the first phase throughout the 1990s international media assistance focused on establishing oppositional and alternative news media. The efforts consisted of direct support to Albanian media outlets and offering training abroad for journalists and editors of the emerging Kosovo media. Funding was provided to outlets such as the weekly political magazines *KOHA* and *ZERI* (and later to *Koha Ditore*), primarily from the Soros Foundation. Another major supporter during this period was the Swiss government, which enabled *KOHA* to purchase its printing house and hence gain full control over its production process.[46] In spring 1999, at the time when large-scale conflict broke out in Kosovo and more than a million Kosovo-Albanians were displaced, the embassies of France and Great Britain in Skopje financially supported the publication of *Koha Ditore* in Macedonia to be distributed to the refugees in the camps.[47]

International media assistance to Kosovo was the most intensive and comprehensive from 1999 through 2007. This second phase was characterized by a growing variety of international donors and a range of initiatives that were also funded and pursued. At least sixty-two different international NGOs, foundations, states and multilateral organizations were

---

of Kosovo (PCK) with running and operational costs, which averaged €50,000 to €60,000 annually over the last eight years. Another media outlet that received donor funding between 2006 and 2013 is the Balkan Investigative Reporting Network in Kosovo in support of a range of journalism and media projects. It is estimated that between 2006 and 2013 BIRN Kosovo has also received funding well in excess of €1 million, with about one-third of such funding provided from RBF. See BIRN, "BIRN."

[45] Ballantine (2002) categorizes media assistance into human capital development; direct support to media outlets; and regulatory framework. See Ballentine, "International Assistance." This research introduces the fourth category, supporting media institutions. Such institutions could be journalist clubs and associations, media research or media studies institutes and other institutions of a similar nature.

[46] Sullivan, "Restructuring the Media."

[47] Miftari and Surroi, *Koha Ditore*.

engaged during this phase, providing funds, equipment, training and expertise.[48] Initially, their efforts centered on supporting media outlets (with funding and technology), and extensive efforts in human capital development.[49] The support from European-based donors targeted primarily the operation of the public service broadcaster RTK. IREX, an organization primarily funded by USAID, concentrated its efforts toward the commercial broadcasters KTV and RTV21, aiding with the purchase of equipment and programming. The Soros Foundation meanwhile continued to match funds to IREX to this end. USAID and IREX were also instrumental in setting up the terrestrial broadcasting network operator KTTN, which was subsequently turned into a shareholding entity.[50] Other important donors include the Swiss Cooperation, the Swedish International Development Cooperation Agency (SIDA), and Press Now, which provided financial support and training. International media assistance to Kosovo media outlets peaked in 2001/2002 and has declined ever since.[51]

Human capital development, according to Rhodes, accounts for one-tenth of international media assistance to Kosovo.[52] It aimed at the professionalization of journalists and media personnel with the view to improving the sustainability of Kosovo's media and the overall standards of reporting. Another objective was to strengthen the role of the media as the fourth estate in democracy through the promotion of investigative skills in legal, political and economic reporting.[53]

The second phase of international media assistance to Kosovo saw efforts to set up a regulatory framework for the media and, in parallel to that, the establishment of media-supporting institutions. As early as 1999, UNMIK introduced rules to combat hate speech.[54] A year later the first regulatory authority (TMC) was set up and charged with monitoring the media under the international management of the OSCE.[55] Together

---

[48] Sorge, "Media in Kosovo."

[49] Kaufman, "Kosovo Media Assessment."

[50] Ibid.

[51] Ibid.

[52] Rhodes, "Ten Years of Media Support."

[53] Franqué, "The Other Frontier."

[54] UNMIK regulations put the emphasis primarily on ensuring the limitations to hate speech and intolerance. In February 2000 the SRSG promulgated the "Regulation on the Prohibition against Inciting to National, Racial, Religious or Ethnic Hatred, Discord or Intolerance."

[55] Broadcast and print regulations for Kosovo media issued by UNMIK include: "Regulation on the Conduct of Print Media in Kosovo," "Regulation on the

with IREX and the OSCE, the TMC was instrumental in the discussions leading to the introduction of the Code of Ethics for Kosovo media and later of the Law on Access to Information, Copyright Law, Law on Libel and Defamation, and so on. Other organizations, such as the International Federation of Journalists (IFJ) and Article 19, also lent their support to the development of the media regulatory framework in Kosovo, providing expertise and advocacy. EU media experts have been closely engaged to ensure that the constituting laws of key media institutions, the public service broadcaster RTK and the new media supervisory authority IMC were in line with the European best practices.[56]

The OSCE attempted to establish a journalist association in 2000, but it failed.[57] The OSCE helped to set up the Press Council of Kosovo (PCK) in 2005 (which is covered in more depth below). In 2002–2003, the IREX office in Kosovo helped establish the Association of Professional Journalists of Kosovo (APJK) to represent journalists and the Association of Independent Electronic Media of Kosovo (AMPEK) to represent the media industry.[58] Both of these associations failed to become self-sustainable over the course of the next decade.[59]

Other notable media projects established through US donor assistance included Internews Kosova, an organization active in training nonmainstream media members at different levels, minority media reporters,

---

Licensing and Regulation of Broadcast Media and on the Code of Conduct for Print Media in Kosovo," and "Regulation on the Prohibition against Inciting to National, Racial, Religious or Ethnic Hatred, Discord or Intolerance."

[56] In 2003 FES organized the first postconflict roundtables between Serbian and Albanian journalists.

[57] Berisha, "Kosovo/a," 220–247.

[58] Kaufman, "Kosovo Media Assessment." US assistance started in 1998 by the Office of Transition Initiatives (OTI), with approximately $2.25 million in media assistance (1998–2001). OTI support included broadcasting equipment for radio and television outlets and funds for the construction of KTTN. Subsequently the USAID Mission in Kosovo has undertaken two large projects which represent the bulk of involvement of USAID/IREX in the Kosovo media sector—Kosovo Independent Media Program (KIMP) 2001–2004 ($7.7 million) and 2004–2008 ($5 million). Most of the activities carried by IREX were focused on the building of media infrastructure, specifically, KTTN, KTV, TV21, and Kosova Live. In addition, efforts were made to increase professionalism by supporting the development of institutions, the legal and regulatory framework and efficient business-management practices.

[59] UNDP and USAID, "Action Paper."

and journalism students.[60] Internews was also instrumental in setting up the radio-network CerpiK.

In 2002, the EU funded the Kosovo Media Association (KOSMA) network with €260,000 in order to connect minority radio stations across Kosovo. This project helped the development of short news program produced by five core radio stations. Later, IREX also became involved in KOSMA and the European Centre for Broadcast Journalists, provided training for KOSMA network journalists.[61]

In 2005 the Kosovo Institute of Journalism and Communication (KIJAC), sponsored by the Norwegian Ministry of Foreign Affairs, was established, offering graduate-level studies in journalism. In 2010 KIJAC had to shut down following allegations of financial mismanagement (which subsequent audits did not confirm). An estimated €6.25 million were put into the project.[62]

The OSCE did not support KIJAC as it was seen as a duplication of the work of the Kosovo Media Institute (KMI) it had helped to set up, together with the EU and Soros Foundation funds. At the end of 2007 KMI began operating as a nonprofit training and media advocacy center for Kosovo in order to provide short-term and mid-career training for journalists. In recent years, the functioning of KMI has been marred by hardships due to uncertain financing.

The third and ongoing phase of international media assistance to Kosovo commenced in 2007. In this phase the intensity of media support across all activities was rapidly reduced and some major donor operations for mainstream Albanian media and minority media concluded. IREX Kosovo and the OSCE took the lead in such efforts beginning in 2007 with a program on Strengthening Independent Minority Media (SIMM).[63] The last stage of media assistance—aimed primarily at the minority media—has likewise intensified from human capital development to support for media outlets and the establishment of supporting institutions for minority media and journalists.

---

[60] Internews Kosovo: http://www.internewskosova.org. Accessed November 10, 2016.

[61] Kaufman, "Kosovo Media Assessment."

[62] Norway Ministry of Foreign Affairs response to Rrokum TV. See Rrokum Television, "Rrokum Television."

[63] IREX, "Strengthening Independent Minority Media (SIMM) in Kosovo, Factsheet."

APPROACHES TO MEDIA ASSISTANCE

While there was some coordination between donors regarding general principles, there was little coordination in relation to specific activities and projects. Following the violent events in Kosovo in March 2004,[64] the donors began to direct assistance more closely toward minority media. However, the lack of coordination among donors continued to persist. Petra Sorge notes that the development of minority or multiethnic media often mirrored the lack of coordination among donors in relation to the support for the Albanian-language media. The report further notes that projects were uncoordinated, the minority media market became even more congested and outlets that were set up were poor and underfunded, with donors supporting three similar, parallel radio networks linking minority communities. USAID/IREX supported private local TV channels in four Kosovo Serbian enclaves operating under TV Mreza in north Kosovo and the OSCE, remaining committed to the public broadcasting mission, was more in favor of introducing RTK2 in the Serbian language. According to Sorge, in the minority print media the concurring efforts seem to have yielded even more catastrophic results. Out of four former Serbian-language magazines—three of them founded with the help of donors—not one is still in existence.[65]

The specific projects pursued by the OSCE on the one side and IREX/USAID on the other have been all product oriented. The OSCE's support ensured that RTK could go on air and maintained a primary position. It pursued the same logic with the PCK, KMI, the IMC, and KOSMA. IREX, on the other side, tried the same thing—to ensure the setup and the self-reliance of KTV and RTV21. It continued the same strategy with APJK, AMPEK and KTTN in order to ensure these projects succeeded.

Meanwhile, smaller organizations and projects such as Medienhilfe and Press Now, albeit to a lesser degree, have been systematic in supporting the core mainstream newspapers—*Koha Ditore* and *Zeri* and their earlier predecessors, the weeklies *KOHA* and *ZERI*, as well as a few other alternative projects that emerged after the conflict.

---

[64] OSCE Representative on Freedom of the Media; see Haraszti, "The Role of the Media."

[65] Sorge, "Media in Kosovo."

What seems to be outside of the donors' control nonetheless are the environmental conditions in which such institutions were set up and the lack of better insight with regard to ensuring their sustainability once established. A number of authors who have analyzed the impact of media assistance in Kosovo note that donors either focused too little on the economic sustainability (market orientation) of the private media outlets or, if this was a matter of focus, the fragile economic and political conditions in Kosovo proved detrimental.[66] Furthermore, there seem to be a consensus that donors focused for too long on ad hoc training sessions as well as on supporting different competing media outlets. Thereby donors contributed to creating a congested media market and undermined the international media development strategy in Kosovo.[67]

INDEPENDENT MEDIA COMMISSION (IMC)

The IMC operates as an independent regulatory body based on Article 141 of the Kosovo constitution. Its operation is further defined by the Law on the IMC (2012).[68] The IMC is mandated to set guidelines and license public and private broadcasters, establish and implement policy and regulate broadcasting rights, obligations and responsibilities of individuals and entities who provide audiovisual media services in Kosovo.[69] It reports annually to the Kosovo Assembly and its budget comes from the Ministry of Finance.[70] In 2009, the IMC began to collect license fees but it cannot use such a budget on its own terms. Based on the amounts it collects annually for license fees it could support 20% to 25% of its annual budget. The current staff of the IMC is thirty-one, and its annual budget, provided by the government, has ranged between €350,000 and €1.4 million over the last decade.

Its highest decision-making bodies are the IMC Commission (formerly known as the IMC Council) and the Media Appeals Board (MAB). The Commission is supposed to consist of seven members, with a mandate of two to four years, but for most of its existence, until last year, it has had six or fewer members and had been dysfunctional for longer periods of time, an indicator of the informal functioning of the IMC. The

---

[66] Ibid.
[67] Ibid.
[68] "Law no. 04/L-044 on the Independent Media Commission."
[69] IMC, "About the IMC."
[70] "Law no. 04/L-044 on the Independent Media Commission," Art. 45.

Table 4.2. The Main Sources of Revenue for the IMC, 2006–2015

Year	Donors	License Fees	Kosovo Budget	Capital Investment	Salaries	Goods and Services	Municipal Costs	Collected Fines
2006	20,000	0	360,369	0	63,569	256,881	17,419	0
2007	0	0	358,478	0	68,765	247,027	13,914	0
2008		57,329,65	557,606	−150,000	82,787	289,216	10,327	n/a
2009	1,000,000	240,102 (130,730)	1,000,576	−450,000	139,673	254,170	13,343	44,883
2010	n/a	218,636 (188,344)	1,115,788	−460,000	202,171	241,887	15,093	12,800
2011	n/a	212000 (138,288)	1,147,939	−450000	224,456	237,142	18,495+8120	n/a
2012	n/a	221,290 (214,536)	977,651	−240,000	232,619	178,416	16,980	6785
2013	n/a	312,501	834,863	10,000	373,769	385,770	20,000	89,472
2014	n/a	291,330	1,415,174	694,000	367,769	336,405	17,000	33,831
2015	n/a	306,683	1,254,162	577,112	362,239	287,812	26,999	2,643

Source: IMC Annual Budgets, 2006–2015 (Euro amounts provided under Capital Investments are accounted for in the Kosovo Budget column).

IMC Commission must also reflect a multiethnic and gender balance.[71] At least two members of the IMC are required to have professional qualifications in the relevant fields. However, such criteria have not been fully met and in deciding on the appointments to the Commission, the Kosovo Assembly has primarily pursued a line of favoring political appointees. Furthermore, the former head of the IMC Commission was in breach of the IMC law clause as he was a political appointee when he was selected for the IMC Commission.[72]

The IMC also has third-party decision-making powers, on all broadcasters, as it sets the cap on the amounts of advertising on RTK and can impose sanctions—ranging from a warning to fines and/or suspension and revocation of license. However, such sanctions cannot be applied against RTK. Based on the 2005 law, the IMC can apply sanctions ranging from requiring RTK to broadcast a correction or apology to termination of license. The amended IMC law of 2012 allows the IMC the right to impose fines of up to €100,000 against RTK but no right to change the broadcaster's license conditions or terminate its license. Therefore, the IMC's powers over RTK were essentially removed in the 2012 law[73] and sanctions could not go through.[74]

INTERNATIONAL ASSISTANCE STRATEGIES AND THE EMERGENCE OF THE IMC

As its successor, the IMC inherited characteristics and routines from the TMC.[75] All staff members (including the current CEO) worked at the TMC before being hired by the IMC. Throughout its mandate the

---

[71] At least two members of the IMC must represent non-Albanian communities and two others must reflect gender balance.

[72] The former head of the IMC Commission, Shefki Ukaj, was considered in breach of the IMC law of 2012, Art. 12, para. 1.3, given that he was holding a public post at the time when he was elected as a member of the IMC Commission.

[73] The nomination process for appointments in the IMC Commission as well as the RTK board has shifted from IMC's ad hoc Civil Society Council into the hands of the Kosovo Assembly's ad hoc committee based on the IMC and RTK laws of 2012.

[74] IMC, "Komisioni i Pavarur per Media."

[75] Part of the expertise was based on the experience in Bosnia, where a number of TMC international experts were based prior to joining the UN mission in Kosovo. See Sullivan, "Restructuring the Media."

TMC was headed by foreign experts guided by diverse philosophies about how the media sector should be regulated in a postconflict society.[76] The primary goal of the TMC was to establish order in the chaotic media system in Kosovo, where numerous media outlets began operating without proper licenses. The TMC took an active role primarily in monitoring the print media to prevent hate speech[77] and limit the vitriolic political discourse in the postconflict Kosovo media.[78] It should also be noted that before 2004 the TMC had a limited focus in the broadcast media due to its lack of capacities. The fact that the TMC did not have the authority to introduce legislation of any kind left behind a legal vacuum, which was difficult to fill quickly by the IMC in subsequent years. The staff of the IMC was not qualified to tackle serious legal matters regarding the media environment, and their reliance on outside expertise further delayed efforts.

When the work on establishing the IMC began, the plan was welcomed by broadcasters.[79] However, the plan for the IMC was opposed by the Telecommunications Regulatory Agency (TRA) and the Committee on Media of the Kosovo Assembly, who were not in favor of a broadcast regulator that would also manage the frequency spectrum. The issue was later addressed in a memorandum between the IMC and TRA, recognizing the former as the sole authority in charge of broadcast service frequencies.[80]

The main international donors of the IMC were the OSCE, IREX/USAID and the European Commission. Donor approaches to the IMC consisted of legal reform, institution building, technical support (equipment/software and monitoring system), salaries, capacity building and

---

[76] Di Lellio, "Empire Lite as a Swamp."

[77] Van Zweeden, "The State of the Media in Kosovo."

[78] TMC has imposed fines for violating the electoral rules and the Print Code of Conduct on many occasions. Since its establishment in 2000, the TMC has addressed 115 complaints: in 2000 (two complaints), in 2001 (twenty-three), 2002 (forty-four), 2003 (forty-six). See Berisha, "Kosovo/a."

[79] A new broadcast regulation was drafted in 2002 to transform the TMC into a permanent agency, the Independent Media Commission (IMC). However, the IMC draft was kept in the Prime Minister's Office and was not sent to the Kosovo Assembly for review and debate until after the elections scheduled for fall 2004. The delay was allegedly caused by concerns that the IMC could be captured by certain political interests and be used to direct the media against their political rivals. See Kaufman, "Kosovo Media Assessment."

[80] "Memorandum of Understanding."

training (in-house or abroad), as well as awareness campaigns.[81] While
the interim period toward Kosovarization was partially supported by the
OSCE (i.e., salaries for international board members from 2006–2008),
the agency received only a €20,000 kick-off grant from the OSCE in 2006
as part of an awareness campaign. Since then the funding for the IMC has
come primarily from the Kosovo budget.[82]

According to Naile Selimaj-Krasniqi, the IMC's CEO, assistance of
the donors—IREX, the European Commission, the OSCE—after the Kosovarization was not based on an external assessment of needs or evaluations but was provided as a response to specific requests made by the
IMC.[83]

The assistance was aimed at the institutional level but it tried to
address both individual and policy levels and took thus a multilevel
approach. Although this has been coordinated assistance, interviewees
nevertheless found that the goals for the IMC were not realized. This
seems to have been the result of the lack of a clear insight about the IMC's
needs. In part, this should be attributed to the missing feedback from the
IMC, due to a dysfunctional IMC Commission for a long period of time
(thirty-one months). Under such conditions the IMC decisions remained

---

[81] The OSCE provided salaries for international members of the IMC until 2008.
In addition, through single activities the OSCE supported the IMC (2006–
2013) by hiring experts/consultants to draft the IMC bylaws, encourage the participation of IMC members to attend conferences, purchase software, support
training and study visits, and facilitate the organization of conferences, meetings
and workshops. IREX's support for the IMC was focused primarily on legal
reform and capacity building and training, including, for example, expertise
in drafting bylaws; regulation on cable operations (2007); the analysis of the
RRC-6 plan and the alternatives for a Kosovo plan for digitalization (2009);
training of media-monitoring staff; and amendments to the cable regulation
(2010).

[82] International donors continued to be instrumental in giving assistance to the
IMC. In 2009 the IMC received a grant from the European Commission (EC)
in the amount of €1 million to upgrade its monitoring system. The technical
equipment enabled the IMC to monitor and archive the services operated by
licensed operators and to assess their compliance with rules on quotas, advertising and the protection of minors. Before that, the IMC relied on alternative
sources to ensure broadcasters' compliance, an indicator of the ad hoc approach
that guided the IMC's work in exercising its supervisory powers toward broadcasters from 2005 until 2011.

[83] Naile Selimaj-Krasniqi, CEO of the IMC, email message to author, February
23, 2013.

pending (due to the lack of quorum in the IMC Commission) and the projects could not be taken forward.

CHALLENGES TO IMC FUNCTIONALITY AND INDEPENDENCE

In the first year of its operation, the IMC adopted an internal code of procedure, a code of ethics, a policy on public rulemaking, a broadcasting policy, and guidelines on sanctions. However, as it became Kosovarized it faced a number of challenges and difficulties, such as the lack of professionally trained staff, a shortage of funds, an insufficient amount of equipment and so on.

When Kosovo proclaimed its independence the need arose for laws to be amended to reflect the new constitutional reality. Therefore, the work on amending the IMC law started in 2008 and the amended law came into effect in 2012. The dragging of the legislative procedure effectively paralyzed the work of the IMC, diminished its transparency and decision-making and left the work on important legislation, such as the digitalization process, pending. Furthermore, the procedural delays led to increased politicization of the process of IMC Commission appointments.[84] Subsequently, the illegal dismissal of the IMC's CEO and her subsequent reinstatement, while the former chair of the Commission was himself considered in breach of the IMC law, speak volumes about the continued politicization of the IMC and are just another example of failure to follow the procedures within the IMC.[85]

The IMC was successful in addressing to a certain degree the issues of compliance of the cable broadcasters with copyright law clauses and was able to expand its authority throughout Kosovo to include minority broadcast media.[86] However, elsewhere the IMC faced numerous challenges that were also damaging to its reputation. In particular, the IMC

---

[84] The Kosovo Assembly requested three times over the course of two years (2010–2012) that the IMC's ad hoc Civil Society Committee submit and resubmit its list of nominations for the IMC board, but the assembly delayed making the appointments indefinitely. Naile Selimaj-Krasniqi, CEO of the IMC, email message to author, February 23, 2013.

[85] The dismissal of Selimaj-Krasniqi from the IMC based on Article 46 of the IMC law of 2012 was overturned by the Kosovo courts and she was reinstated in her position on the grounds that IMC board disregarded the Law on Civil Servants when it initiated the dismissal procedure against her.

[86] Van Zweeden, "The State of the Media in Kosovo."

has been challenged about RTK's advertising quota.[87] A few years ago, the process of granting extensions to broadcasting licenses once again put into question the IMC's independence.[88] It was anticipated that once the new law on the IMC was approved the existing broadcasting licenses issued by the TMC would expire and be renewed, according to the new procedure.[89] Yet after the law was adopted,[90] the IMC, through an internal decision, extended all the licenses without due review. The approach taken by the IMC in the case of licenses is indicative of the degree of informality with which the IMC has operated or been pressed to operate.

A USAID report in 2007 pointed out numerous shortcomings in the functioning of the IMC, such as the lack of quorum, the uncertain budget, the weakening role of the institution, the competences of board members, and its reactive approach to challenges.[91] Some of those shortcomings have persisted. In its 2013 annual progress report on Kosovo, the European Commission criticized the IMC for not being able to legislate on must-carry requirements for cable operators in a timely fashion, a matter that seriously limits the audience's right of access to terrestrial free-to-air channels. The IMC has recently weighed in on the issue. Last year the European Commission's progress report criticized the IMC for not having adopted on time the strategy for digitalization; issues of incompatibility of the digital switchover strategy with EU law and not providing a sufficient technical and financial framework for a transparent and open process of digitalization. It has further warned that the independence of the IMC is

---

[87] Ibid.

[88] Critics argue that in order to ensure the extension of licenses for the two commercial broadcasters, the IMC, through an internal decision (which according to IMC's CEO Naile Selimaj-Krasniqi, was taken to avoid complications due to the timing and costs associated with such a process), decided to prolong all licenses predating the IMC law of 2005. The critics argued that national resources (broadcasting frequencies and public space) were allocated to KTV and RTV21 without a competitive procedure after the conflict, and that they should have been up for reconsideration. A number of interviewees raised this matter, with one of them considering it as an "IMC gratuity" to KTV and RTV21.

[89] OSCE Mission in Kosovo, "Kosovo's Temporary."

[90] On April 21, 2005, the Kosovo Assembly passed Law no. 02/L-15 for the Independent Media Commission, ratified by the SRSG on June 8, 2005. It came into effect on September 8, 2005. See "Law no. 02/L-15 for the Independent Media Commission and Broadcasting."

[91] Chetwynd and Chetwynd, "Mid-Term Evaluation."

challenged by political interference and lack of resources and required the IMC to demonstrate that it can carry out its tasks.[92]

Whether the IMC can sustain its independence is a source of controversy. According to Argjentina Grazhdani, a Kosovo media expert, after the IMC was Kosovarized it remained chronically underfunded and undermined by all.[93] Grazhdani noted that whatever the IMC has been able to achieve should not be attributed to the donors' impact. Other interviewees were split on whether the support to the IMC has yielded sustainable results. What a number of interviewees seemed to agree on is that the IMC's independence exists on formal grounds, but its functional independence is difficult to exercise due to constant interference from political and business interests and the IMC's own preferences regarding certain broadcasters.

The agency's independence rests primarily with the members of the IMC Commission. Its CEO, Naile Selimaj-Krasniqi, affirms this delicate position, noting that: "Since members of the Commission are the decision-makers, they determine the extent of the IMC's independence in its work. Through the procedures that have changed in the new IMC law for the selection of members of Commission and Media Appeals Board the door has been opened to having a politicized IMC and for the loss of the quality of the work of the regulator."[94]

Andrew Clayton, Chief of Party, IREX Kosovo, also echoed those concerns, noting that in 2013 there was evidence that political parties were trying to identify their own supporters to be candidates for the IMC Commission. He further argued that "while in the past it was harder for political parties to recruit their candidates because there existed an ad hoc Council made up of civil society figures within the IMC, which used to screen and put forward the nominees for the IMC Council, now the list of candidates for the IMC Council is closely administered by the Kosovo Assembly's ad hoc committee."[95]

---

[92] European Commission, "Kosovo Progress Report 2014."

[93] Argjentina Grazhdani, former Media and Civil Society Advisor to USAID Kosovo Mission, email message to author, February 10, 2013.

[94] Naile Selimaj-Krasniqi, CEO of IMC, email message to author, February 23, 2013.

[95] Andrew Clayton, Chief of Party, IREX Kosovo, interview with author, January 28, 2013.

Radio Television of Kosovo

ASSISTANCE PROGRAMS LINKED TO THE ORIGIN OF RTK

Radio Television of Kosovo (RTK) is the public service broadcaster established in September 1999. It represents a unique case in the region, as the public broadcaster did not emerge as a continuation of the former state broadcaster. It consists of the television service made up of four channels (of which three are operational at this point) broadcasted via a terrestrial transmitter network, and carried via cable and digital satellite and two radio stations, Radio Kosovo and Radio Blue Sky.[96] Before RTK, the only broadcaster in Albanian in Kosovo was Radio Television Pristina (RTP), which formed part of the larger network of Yugoslavia's state broadcasting. Following the Serbian crackdown in 1990 in Kosovo, extraordinary measures were introduced against Albanian media and 1,200 Albanian employees of the then state broadcaster were expelled. Later, in 1993, with the support of the Kosovo government in exile, some of the former employees of RTP started a few hours of satellite broadcasting from neighboring Albania.

After the Kosovo conflict, in fall 1999, UNMIK invited the European Broadcasting Union (EBU) to set up and manage an independent public broadcaster in Kosovo, based on an agreement with the OSCE. A few months later RTK began transmitting two hours of program on analogue satellite.[97] While the main buildings of RTP remained intact during the Kosovo conflict in 1999, the terrestrial broadcast network had to be rebuilt. Thus, the assistance to RTK initially consisted in investing heavily in broadcast via satellite before the terrestrial network could be set up.

While it was expected that UNMIK would be staffed with former RTP personnel, this actually did not happen. The goal of UNMIK was to set up a multilingual public broadcasting service that would help toward peace and reconciliation in postconflict Kosovo.[98] So, when a large group of former employees of RTP tried to get inside the RTP premises in June 1999 with the goal to resume their work, a standoff ensued and ex-RTP staff members were prevented by UNMIK from entering the premises.[99]

---

[96] RTK, http://www.rtklive.com.
[97] Ibid.
[98] UNMIK, "UNMIK Sets out Plans."
[99] Thompson, "Slovenia, Croatia, Bosnia."

Despite the fact that the OSCE was entrusted with the task of setting up the broadcaster, the contractual negotiations were conducted between UNMIK and the EBU. Instead of a broadcaster designed to meet the needs of the Kosovo public, RTK emerged as an "emergency satellite TV service" that would serve both as UNMIK's public information program and as the nucleus of a future public service respecting the program needs and expectations of the entire population of Kosovo. UNMIK's daily news broadcasts on RTK continued for one and a half years.

In these circumstances RTK began operating from scratch. From the beginning, the EBU appointed the senior international managers at RTK in charge of executive and editorial policies, while the rest of the staff gradually became predominantly local. However, from the point when UNMIK decided to set up RTK (fall 1999) and the end point in 2001 where RTK was handed over to local ownership three international managers had run RTK. Richard Dill from ZDF in Germany was its first director. He helped set up RTK, followed by Erik Lehmann, who was a former president of the board of the Swiss Broadcasting Association. He in turn was succeeded by Richard Lucas from the BBC. During this transition period the EBU and the BBC provided staff training and equipment to RTK.[100]

A year after RTK started operating, technical facilities in television and in the two radio stations under its umbrella were upgraded, facilitated with a substantial donation from the Japanese government of $15.2 million.[101] It subsequently began expanding programming and broadcasting on the new Kosovo Terrestrial Transmission Network.[102]

In 2001 UNMIK Broadcasting Regulation 2001/13 formally established RTK as an independent public service broadcaster with a board of directors made up of local staff, and the EBU mandate ended. RTK retained the retiring international director general, Richard Lucas (a former BBC manager) for another six months as an advisor to the new director general, Agim Zatriqi, but once he left in 2002 there were no other consultant working with RTK except for two international members sitting on the RTK board.[103] At that point RTK received one year of

---

[100] Loewenberg, "United Nations Media Strategy."

[101] Kaufman, "Kosovo Media Assessment." Other donors included the EU (€4 million in direct support to RTK during 2001–2002) and the Swiss Cooperation (CHF5 million in support for RTK's radio stations between 1999–2005).

[102] RTK, http://www.rtklive.com.

[103] Loewenberg, "United Nations Media Strategy,"

bridging funds from the Kosovo budget, pending the introduction of a license fee in 2003. Next, UNMIK signed the directive on the implementation of a license fee, enabling RTK to launch its twenty-four-hour program schedule.[104]

The subsequent development of RTK was shaped according to the interests of multiple stakeholders (UNMIK, the OSCE, the Kosovo Assembly, the Kosovo government, and political party agendas). As noted by Baton Haxhiu, the process of transition in RTK "was accompanied with brutal faux pas."[105]

Following the March 2004 riots in Kosovo, when the professionalism of the people running RTK was seriously questioned, international direct monitors were imposed on RTK by the OSCE. They stayed on until 2006 to advise RTK on editorial issues. When the mandate of the monitors ended in spring 2006, RTK refused to accept a successor OSCE monitor.[106] Pursuant to the RTK law of 2006, RTK oversight was transferred from UNMIK to the Kosovo Assembly, with the Kosovo Ministry of Finance in control of its budget. RTK saw the continued international oversight as an intrusion of its independence. Nonetheless, two international members continued to sit on the RTK board past 2006 as consultants.

Only in the first few years of donor assistance to RTK was an effort made to coordinate the technical setup of facilities and securing quality programming for minorities. While in charge during 1999–2001, the EBU strived to set certain general standards and model RTK closer to the BBC example. However, once RTK was transferred to local management it evolved in its own ways. The media assistance in the case of RTK was short-term, but intensive. Laue has written that approximately €18 million in donor assistance went to RTK.[107]

FORMAL ARRANGEMENTS FOR RTK

RTK is governed and managed by its board and a director general as prescribed in the RTK law of 2012. The board is a collegial steering body composed of eleven members with mandates of two, three, or four years. The board is responsible for the general administration of RTK, and it

---

[104] RTK, http://www.rtklive.com.
[105] Baton Haxhiu, Director of Klan Kosova TV and ex-CEO of APJK, interview with the author, January 27, 2013.
[106] Van Zweeden, "The State of the Media in Kosovo."
[107] Laue, "Local Electronic Media in Kosovo."

reviews and approves its programs and their standards.[108] Just as in the case of the IMC, the board of RTK until recently had operated with nine members instead of eleven, indicative of governmental intervention in the composition of the board.

Most interviewees agree that the 2006 law on RTK marks a turning point after which RTK's editorial independence became more vulnerable to the dictates of politicians. At this time Kosovo was ruled by a minority government, and the law received just the minimum threshold of votes, while the opposition voted against it. RTK resisted the approval of the amended law.

The provisions contained in the amended RTK law of 2012 cemented the political control over RTK even further. The 2012 law recognizes RTK as the public broadcaster of Kosovo, a legal nonprofit entity with the status of an independent public institution of particular importance.[109] Hence, the Kosovo Assembly must ensure its institutional autonomy as well as financing adequate for the execution of RTK's public service mission. The RTK law of 2012 stipulates that the assembly must allocate 0.7% of the Kosovo budget for the next three years (until the end of 2015) to finance RTK. It granted the assembly one year from the date of the publication of the RTK law (April 27, 2012) to find a solution for the long-term funding. However, despite entertaining numerous possibilities to collect the license fee and a public hearing organized earlier in 2015, to date no sustainable solution has been found.

In terms of editorial independence, Article 18, paragraph 3, states that RTK shall lead, develop and cultivate editorial policy from a sound, positive, impartial, and creative perspective, and with civilizing, professional and humane content. A few years ago RTK produced its own house code of professional standards and ethical principles to guide the work of its journalists and editors. Yet, the code seems to have been disregarded in the past and it is lacking important clauses that would make it functionally applicable.[110] A number of interviewees emphasized that RTK's editorial independence is subject to great interferences by politicians and their protégés seeking airtime and positive coverage. According to some of the interviewees, such influence is possible due to the editors' close ties to politicians, and due to clientelist ties between journalists and politicians.

---

[108] "Law no. 04/L-046 on Radio Television of Kosovo."
[109] Ibid.
[110] KIPRED, "RTK Challenge."

Most of the interviewees agreed that the potential for such an increased influence of politicians has been multiplied by the fact that RTK does not have its own source of revenue (such as a license fee).

CHALLENGES FOR RTK FUNCTIONING AND INDEPENDENCE

Between 2002 and 2007 RTK strived to achieve financial independence from the Kosovo budget. To RTK a license fee would have been the best possible outcome.[111] Between 2003 and 2009 the Kosovo Electric Corporation (KEK) collected the license fee on behalf of RTK, a situation that ensured financial sustainability for RTK. However, the arrangement did not leave much space for political interference in RTK. A year before the expiry of the license collection contract with RTK, KEK, claiming that it was suffering losses under the arrangement, decided to unilaterally terminate the contract.[112] KEK allowed RTK six months to find an alternative collection method; however, the Kosovo Assembly delayed the matter further by not adopting the new law on RTK.

The Constitutional Court of Kosovo suspended RTK's license fee, considering its collection unconstitutional.[113] The then RTK management saw this development as an effort of politics to interfere with RTK in connection with the 2007 elections.[114] RTK also cited UNMIK's lack of support in continuing the collection of the license fee, despite the recommendations of the EBU to the contrary.[115] In the absence of a solution, in 2010, from a situation in which it was ensuring more than 80% of its income from the license fee (2007) and the rest from advertising, RTK moved to the point where it became 80% dependent on the Kosovo budget. Not long after, amid alleged political pressure, its director general resigned.[116]

---

[111] RTK, "Raport Vjetor" (2005).

[112] Gap Institute, "RTK's Financial Sustainability." The court required the assembly to review Article 20.1 of the RTK law of 2006 by December 1, 2009. On June 14, 2010, the court reiterated the temporary measure until January 1, 2011.

[113] Gap Institute, "RTK's Financial Sustainability"; Decision of the Constitutional Court on the temporary measure Case KI 11/09, *Tomë Krasniqi vs. RTK et al.*

[114] RTK, "Raport Vjetor" (2007); The RTK annual report cited a government spokesperson's remarks that "the reintroduction of the contract with RTK could be done if it changed its editorial policy toward the government" as a signal that politics was behind the termination of contract.

[115] Ibid., 7.

[116] KIPRED, "Monitorimi i Programit Informativ."

Table 4.3. The Main Sources of Revenue for RTK, 2001–2015

Year	Donors	License Fee	Marketing	Kosovo Budget	Other Sources	Total
2001	8,294,473	0	2,569,975	0	1,074,040	11,938,488
2002	4,827,398	0	n/a	0	4,813,870	9,641,268
2003	750,000	1,929,140	1,311,275	2,000,000	937,578	6,927,993
2004	0	4,800,000	1,387,969	1,000,000	713,625	7,901,594
2005	63,300	5,160,000	801,309	600,000	728,450	7,353,060
2006	0	7,080,000	1,432,654	0	325,334	8,837,988
2007	0	7,991,363	1,526,519	0	294,400	9,812,282
2008	0	8,652,000	1,493,000	0	244,000	10,389,000
2009	0	7,080,276	2,540,445	0	107,345	9,785,042
2010	0	0	1,733,817	10,464,000	107,345	12,305,162
2011	0	0	1,474,000	7,900,000	212,000	9,586,000
2012	0	0	1.900,000	8,900.000	0	10,800,000
2013	0	0	2,100,000	9,700,000	0	11,800,000
2014	0	0	2,072,000	9,348,000	256,000	11,676,000
2015	0	0	2,221,000	9,769,000	279,000	12,269,000

Source: RTK Annual Reports, 2001–2015 (amounts under 2001 in Deutschmarks in Euro for other years; revenues from marketing are not made available for 2002, but are reflected under Other Sources).

The new RTK management refrained from requesting the reintroduction of a license fee. Mentor Shala, the director general of RTK, claimed that "the current financing form is the most suitable." He argued that the potential political influence would continue even if RTK switched to a license fee, since RTK would still be obliged to report to the assembly. Therefore, direct funding from the assembly "is the most secure form of financing as it never leaves the public broadcaster without income." He further argued that the EBU's recommendations was that RTK should continue with the Kosovo budget financing suggesting even an increase to 0.9% of the Kosovo budget toward such a goal. Shala has argued that pending the increase in its budget, the advertising cap on RTK could be lowered.[117]

The issue of succession regarding the rights and obligations of the former state broadcaster, Radio Television Pristina (RTP), is one important challenge affecting RTK. Since RTK it is legally not the successor of RTP it cannot make permanent use of the premises in which it is located. Its future once again is depending on a decision by the Kosovo Assembly. This has implications with regards to the handling of the issue of some 1,200 former employees of RTP, who were expelled during the 1990s and who claimed their right to return to their jobs and collect benefits as ex-employees. In 2006 the Kosovo government prepared a draft law to transfer the ownership of RTP to RTK but the strategy was abandoned following a refusal from the union of the ex-RTP employees. Shala has noted that around 60% of RTK's staff (872 employees, of which 698 are permanent staff) is made up of either former employees of RTP or their immediate family members. Even though RTK has no obligations to hire them, this practice serves as an example of the informality that guides the work of the broadcaster due to the unresolved issue with the succession.

In terms of RTK content, a number of interviewees noted that between 2002 and 2006 (when RTK was still in the process of Kosovarization) it had a more balanced approach in its coverage and was less prone to being politicized. After its independence the content of RTK was perceived to be more uniform and the medium was increasingly regarded as politicized. According to Baton Haxhiu, the standard of neutrality that RTK strived to maintain started to break down after 2007, and this happened because all political parties started to recruit people inside RTK.

A number of interviewees pointed to the content of the news bulletins, debates and informative programs on RTK in recent years, as a sign of its increased subordination to the government's influence. The head of RTK, Mentor Shala, has played down such influence, noting that according to their internal analysis RTK offers considerable space to all. "It does not happen that one political party has an activity that is not reported, unless it doesn't meet the criteria to be reported." He attributes the greater coverage of the government to the fact that the government has more capacity to organize pseudo-events.[118]

---

[117] Mentor Shala, Director General of RTK, interview with the author, March 18, 2013.
[118] Ibid.

A NOT SO PROMISING PERSPECTIVE

In short, numerous changes in recent years have affected RTK's independence in one way or another. Informality in the functioning and management of the broadcaster and nepotism; the purchase of expensive programming from outside production companies with close ties to RTK; often excessive compensation for select hosts in charge of its in-house programs; politicization in the processes of appointments to the RTK board and editorial and managerial positions. These have all been negative developments that have impeded the functioning of RTK in recent years, based on the input from a number of interviewees.

Recently, RTK has taken steps to diminish the potential for mismanagement. It published an open bid on its website for the purchase of outside productions. It also makes annual reports and other relevant documents accessible on its website, a sign of a contextual effort to demonstrate transparency. However, such changes are regarded as superficial among its critics. Interviewed as part of this research, Avni Zogiani, codirector of the Organization for Democracy, Anticorruption, and Dignity (COHU), emphasized the efforts of his organization to obtain details about the allocation of contracts to outside production companies by RTK. He noted that "RTK has not been transparent at all about it. We had to seek alternative ways to secure such data." Zogiani also voiced concern about the transparency of the board of RTK and noted that not even basic information about the board (such as the times when it meets or what decisions it makes) are made available to the public.[119]

Undoubtedly, a major change impacting RTK and its independence is the termination of the license fee, which served to subject RTK to the whims of the Kosovo Assembly and, by default, under government control. Another notable change is the shift in the selection process of RTK board members from the IMC to the Kosovo Assembly's ad hoc committee, as per the amended RTK law of 2012, a clear-cut example of floating laws. Other shortcomings mentioned in the 2013 European Commission's progress report were incompletion of the board, and politically influenced board and management appointments within RTK. The following year, the European Commission's progress report warned that even though the RTK board was completed in 2014, political preferences were

---

[119] Avni Zogiani, Codirector of the Organization for Democracy, Anticorruption, and Dignity (COHU), interview with the author, January 23, 2013.

the main criteria applied during the assembly's selection process. Added to this is the problem of short-term provision of funding from the Kosovo Assembly, following the transfer of RTK's budget to the Kosovo treasury, which posed another challenge. Albeit committed on a three-year basis as per the RTK law of 2012, funding has been provided on a quarterly or semiannual basis, making RTK management more vulnerable to political influence. At the same time, this has had an impact on the financial situation of RTK, causing disruptions in its projections and in recent years it has led to RTK amassing a growing debt now standing at close to €4 million.

THE PRESS COUNCIL OF KOSOVO

The Press Council of Kosovo (PCK) is a self-regulatory body for the print media in Kosovo. Its mission is embedded in the Code of Conduct for print media in Kosovo. Its statute states that the PCK promotes and enforces the Code of Conduct, scrutinizes complaints about breaches of the code and decides on measures if a complaint is considered justified. One important procedure that allows the PCK greater independence is that in cases when it deals with media related to those sitting in its board, the representative of the print media whose case is being judged is not allowed to vote, which is a symbolic measure of formal independence.

Seventeen mainstream print media published in the languages of different Kosovo communities subscribe to the PCK. Their annual membership fees range from less than €50 (periodicals) to €800 (dailies), and if paid accordingly, such fees could defuse a part of the operational costs of the PCK.[120] In principle, its adjudications are taken into account unless the plaintiffs are not content with the decisions of the PCK and decide to address the courts. While the PCK does not intend to replace the courts, it serves as the primary address for complaints against print media in Kosovo.

When the PCK was set up, its structure was also based on lessons learned from Bosnia and Herzegovina. In Kosovo the goal was to empower the PCK with a mandate to impose fines and to cement its function in the law so that complaints against the print media could not bypass

---

[120] Editors-in-chief or their delegates sitting on the PCK meetings are paid €30 for each meeting, €60 to the deputy chairman and €100 to the chairman. It also reimburses members (from outside Pristina) for travel expenses.

the PCK and end up in the courts.[121] So, the OSCE proposed a mixed system, giving the PCK power to impose fines (up to €2,000) and force members to print adjudications.[122] Another important feature that makes the PCK distinct is that it is the editors in chief who enforce the Code of Conduct while sitting in the Council, and the publishers who finance it (at least partially), in order to avoid total dependence on donors.

ORIGINS OF THE PRESS COUNCIL OF KOSOVO AND ASSISTANCE EFFORTS

In 2004, the OSCE set out to establish a press council in Kosovo as a self-regulatory mechanism.[123] This press council was to be built on the principle that the existence and functioning of a self-regulatory body for print media that was entirely independent (politically and financially) of government structures is an important indicator of the level of media democracy in a society. The PCK was established in June 2005.

The establishment of the PCK was one of the standards Kosovo had to meet for the status talks to resume and a precondition for the TMC to revoke control over the print media. Prior to the establishment of the PCK, there was no self-regulating mechanism for print in Kosovo. While its establishment was pushed forward by the OSCE, Kosovo print media could not agree on more than signing up to a common Code of Conduct. Since the Code of Conduct was being enforced by the TMC (in the absence of a genuine print media mechanism) and the TMC used its powers on numerous occasions to issue hefty fines to print media, the print media (especially the vulnerable ones), saw the introduction of the PCK as an opportunity to avoid having to deal with such fines in the future. So the OSCE was able to push forward the PCK idea quickly. This was the shortest amount of time in which such an institution had ever been established. It took months and years before other institutions of a similar nature (e.g., the IMC) were established or transferred to Kosovars.[124]

The first head of the KPC was an international appointment. Willem Houwen, a Dutch national and a former OSCE employee with extensive insight and knowledge of the media situation in Kosovo. He was later

---

[121] Van Zweeden, "The State of the Media in Kosovo."
[122] Ibid.
[123] Stiglmayer, "OSCE-Supported Press Council."
[124] Van Zweeden, "The State of the Media in Kosovo."

in charge of the Kosovo Institute of Journalism and Communications (KIJAC) and resigned from his post in 2010. His appointment as the head of the PCK was a result of a consensus among the local editors sitting on the PCK board that they should make an international appointment rather than select one of themselves to be in charge.[125]

Since its establishment the PCK has been operating primarily through foreign donations and member dues. However, member dues are inconsistent and even in the ideal case of all members paying, the amount collected falls short of being sufficient to cover its annual operations. According to Nehat Islami, its executive director, 95% of the PCK budget is dependent on donors and only 5% comes from member dues.

Table 4.4. Revenue and Expenses of the PCK, 2009–2012 (in Euro)

Year	Donors	OSCE Direct Support of Activities of PCK	Member-ship	Salaries and Per Diems	Goods and Services	Office Rent	Total Expenses (Excluding OSCE Input)
2009	37,750	20,000	3,299	28,050	9,865	3,600	41,515
2010	39, 175	n/a	2,333	29,660	9,159	3,000	41,819
2011	49,000	n/a	2,033	30,620	20,644	3,420	54,684
2012	58,000	n/a	1,333	33,616	16,997	3,324	58,937

Source: PCK Secretariat.

Some of the main supporters of the PCK are the OSCE Mission in Kosovo, the Swedish Helsinki Committee, Free Press Unlimited, the Norwegian embassy in Pristina, the Kosovo Foundation for Open Society, the Swiss Cooperation Office, and the Civil Rights Defenders. Only the reports for the years 2009–2012 were made available for review.

Quite exceptionally, donor assistance to the PCK has been coordinated. The PCK management has made use of various projects to cover a number of costs, from operational costs and equipment, to ethics workshops, networking and the smooth continuation of its functions. The OSCE covered the PCK's operational costs for the first year and then continued to provide project assistance. The Swedish Helsinki Com-

---

[125] Stiglmayer, "OSCE-Supported Press Council."

mittee then moved in to cover the cost of the PCK's operations on an annual basis. The OSCE as the main sponsor has been and remains the primary contributor to the development of the PCK. The OSCE also provides annual technical project support to the PCK in order to increase its role and to promote professional journalism.[126] The purpose of the media assistance to the PCK both in the case of the OSCE as well as in the cases of other supporters has been a mix of system-wide support, environmental support, and institutional support.

Over the last decade, the core media assistance to the PCK has gone toward operational costs (salaries of the director and press complaints officer, to provide for an honorarium for a lawyer and a PR person engaged with the PCK, as well as to ensure the participation of the board members in its meetings). The funding projects of the PCK, according to Nehat Islami, its executive director, have been short-term (six months) to medium term (three years) and have always matched each other.[127] Various projects have gone toward supporting the basic activities of the PCK (decision-making regarding complaints, workshops on journalism ethics, and awareness campaigns of the PCK).

CHALLENGES TO THE FUNCTIONING OF THE PCK

It became obvious that the PCK was not capable of enforcing imposed fines. Notably, the PCK could not collect at least two maximum fines against one of its members in cases of severe violation of the Code of Conduct. As a result and, with the help of the OSCE, the PCK has revised its statute and abolished monetary penalties altogether.

The core problem of the PCK is that despite recommendations to encourage members to pay their dues, which are symbolic, most of the members fail to do so. Yet, the PCK board members receive a small attendance fee for each meeting. A USAID report on the work of different media institutions in Kosovo noted with regard to the PCK that some of the difficulties earlier in the process were that financial contributions by the affiliated papers remained late—or not at all—in coming, and attributed this to the failure of editors to also involve the owners of the papers in the work of the PCK.[128]

---

[126] Press Council of Kosovo, "OSCE Mission in Kosovo."

[127] Nehat Islami, Executive Director of PCK, email message to author, March 8, 2012.

[128] Van Zweeden, "The State of the Media in Kosovo."

To a certain degree, of the three institutions established in Kosovo in the aftermath of the conflict, the PCK reflects more closely the so-called "transplant effect"[129] since its strength relies on the belief that the ethical principles of the media and journalists will prevail. In states in flux, such as Kosovo, this might be too ambitious.

Agron Bajrami, the editor in chief of *Koha Ditore*, one of the champion members of the PCK, notes that while the initiative to establish the PCK came from the OSCE, it helped create a standard that never existed before in Kosovo. He describes the PCK as an institution "that was based in Western experience, but evolved over time into an entity that greater reflects local culture and environment."[130]

On a positive note, that the PCK continues to receive and adjudicate on complaints—more than eighty complaints between 2012 and 2014—is a sign that there is some need for its continued existence. In the words of Bajrami, a general improvement in the media environment has been noticed as a result of the work of the PCK. Newspapers are more open to publishing retractions and reactions, while editors are involved in quality discussion related to ethical and professional reporting. However, other interviewees were keen to note that media outlets often ignore the PCK's deliberations and fail to publish its adjudications, with one of them calling the PCK "a club of editors sitting around, not being harsh to each other."

Ever since its establishment the PCK has made sure to publish all its rulings on its website. Yet it is not clear how often the requests made by the PCK to member and nonmember media to issue public apologies or corrections have been taken into account or disregarded.

However, in some cases PCK rulings were considered controversial. In a 2007 report prepared for USAID it was noted that the PCK has to show its capability of handling difficult self-regulatory issues.[131] The report noted that it was challenged with such an issue in 2007 and proved unable to cope.[132] In 2010 it was again faced with another high-profile case when the

---

[129] Berkowitz, Pistor, and Richard, "The Transplant Effect."

[130] Agron Bajrami, Editor in Chief of *Koha Ditore*, Board Member of PCK, interview with the author, March 5, 2013.

[131] Chetwynd, Gjurgjeala, and Smith, "Kosovo Media Assistance Program."

[132] Ibid. The report refers to *Infopress* newspaper (no longer published). In 2007 the paper published the names of Serbs in one community who had joined the Territorial Defense organization in the late 1990s in Kosovo. The issue was referred to the Press Council, which found that *Infopress* had not broken the Code of Conduct. The chair of the Council and a number of others resigned as a result. The Council ceased operations for a few weeks, and only the mediation

ex-US ambassador to Kosovo accused several media outlets of breaching his privacy by making public his private texts. The PCK rejected the complaint, ruling in favor of the media outlets, which led to criticism of the PCK for being biased in its deliberations. Such cases have led some to challenge the role of the PCK in important ways brought it under increased scrutiny. However, its decision to relinquish its entitlement to impose monetary fines (of up to €2,000) has deprived it of a right to act as something more than a court of honor whose role (depending on the evolution of the courts in Kosovo) could either gain weight or be diminished in the future.

According to the data made available for this research, the PCK, since its establishment, had resolved more than 250 complaints by 2014, organized over fifty workshops throughout Kosovo and a number of institutes of journalism ethics, published a summary of all its decisions online, and provided open access to some 300 publications on journalism ethics and media in its library. Despite this, the role of the PCK seems to be situated in the sidelines of the public debate and the organization maintains a low profile, despite efforts from its sponsors to raise its public profile.

The fact that the PCK does not receive funding from the state budget makes it independent in certain ways. However, its board members have entertained the idea of also becoming a state-budget-supported agency in the future. At present, its continued and extensive reliance on international donors to cover its basic operational costs ten years after it was set up gives little hope regarding how it will ensure its financial independence in the future.

Discussion of Findings

This research study was built on primary data received from sixteen interviews with representatives of media institutions, journalists, civil society activists and academics in the period between December 2012 and March 2013, as well as on secondary data obtained via research reports, studies, and other materials. The research has built substantially on various evaluations of Kosovo media programs and analyses and reports on the Kosovo media situation.

---

effort by OSCE persuaded the chair and the Council to resume their work. The case of *Infopress* and a subsequent case led PCK to decide to remove the clause on fines from its statute. The report notes that the PCK learned from experience and successfully handled a number of less divisive complaints later.

The findings of the research have confirmed that international assistance was crucial for starting and moving the transformation process in Kosovo, in particular with reference to RTK, the IMC and the PCK. The research confirms that the issue of political interference in media institutions has intensified following "Kosovarization," and that the institutions, after their handover, quickly emulated the "Balkan context," as one of the interviewees observed.

A closer examination on the conditions of RTK, the IMC and the PCK points to a number of challenges faced by these media institutions on their path to consolidation. Funding remains a key issue for all three institutions. The politicization of the state, with its different shades, has played against the greater independence of the IMC and RTK and is reflected in the politicization of appointments, informality and floating laws that inhibit the proper functioning of both institutions. The high level of political parallelism in the media further diminishes the prospects of an independent media sector in Kosovo.

The amendments in the RTK and the IMC laws as well as the changes in the statute that guides the work of the PCK have altogether diminished the independence, functionality and the importance of all three institutions—and a number of interviewees have drawn a similar conclusion.

All three institutions remain either donor dependent or heavily reliant on the Kosovo budget. Such a financial dependence keeps them captured when it comes to projecting a formal and/or a functional independence. While the IMC had enjoyed some degree of formal independence its de facto independence has been compromised due to the political appointments and growing influence of politics in its function. Its continued dependence on the Kosovo budget makes it susceptible to interference. Furthermore, the digitalization process, which was tied to the phenomenon of increased politicization of appointments in the IMC Commission, was bound to make it an even more vulnerable institution.

It appears that the efforts to set up a public service broadcaster in Kosovo modeled upon the BBC produced a hybrid model broadcaster that still remains under relatively strong governmental influence. RTK might have an even harder time ensuring its autonomy if it does not reevaluate its goals and orientation—notably on the decision to reintroduce the license fee—that makes it most susceptible to political influence.

In the case of the PCK, the fact that the dues from media outlets have dwindled, with fewer outlets paying their dues, is a matter of concern, regarding how it might increase its funding appeal to the wider media sector in the future. Otherwise, it seems to have been reconfirmed that the absence of coordination among the donors below the general level (and sometimes even this was not the case) coupled with the failure to determine the strategic goals and orientation of the projects supported has caused confusion and polarization in the media sector. This, in turn, has served politicians as a lead to attempt to influence the media.

It appears that the quick donor withdrawal and failure to leave behind appropriate mechanisms to monitor more closely the content produced and the appointment processes used to hire managers and appoint board members (in the case of RTK and the IMC), as well as the quality of decision-making and the internal and external barriers to sustaining independence (in the cases of the IMC and the PCK) have taken their toll. In addition, the fact that media assistance programs have taken a copy-and-paste approach from other similar cases, notably Bosnia, is worrisome, keeping in mind the limited success of the international assistance in reforming the media sector in Bosnia and Herzegovina.

Considering that, as Rhodes[133] argued, political and social goals and media-specific objectives have guided the media support in the Western Balkans, the findings seem to point out that in cases where social and political goals overlapped with media-specific goals, the results were questionable or even negative. It appears that following Kosovarization all three media institutions, at different points in time, were left to handle the "hot potatoes"—in other words, meet objectives beyond their potential or capacities to address. Hence, all three institutions faced impediments to their functioning.

For example, the IMC challenges (such as licensing of broadcasters or ensuring compliance with copyright law) have been successfully addressed and the IMC's independence was sustained. Yet, when the IMC had to decide on extending broadcasting licenses or ensuring RTK's compliance with advertising quotas (both of them issues with political implications), it was unable to deliver on its mandate and its reputation suffered. The same thing seems to have happened with RTK. When it began in 1999 its central role was to achieve specific social-political goals (promoting peace, a multiethnic state and diversity). RTK not only met these goals but became their champion. Yet, in due time RTK also set out to achieve important media-specific objectives—such as the goal to have the best current affairs programs, thus competing with commercial

---

[133] Rhodes, "Ten Years of Media Support," 11.

broadcasters in the coverage of politics. This approach embroiled RTK in an unfair competition with commercial broadcasters, making RTK attractive to politicians as a medium for advancing their political agendas. Given RTK's unique potential to achieve this (due to its technical capacities and greater audience penetration, with its news bulletins reaching more than 500,000 viewers across Kosovo), its advantage as a medium became, in a sense, its own liability.

Kosovo as a postconflict society needs a public service media organization that is dedicated to a public service mission and independence. However, as long as RTK focuses on politics instead of political events in its agenda, politicians will likely continue to attempt to use and abuse it. The focus of RTK, instead of concentrating on day-to-day politics, should be on political events; in other words, to put aside the coverage of party politics and focus more on advancing the sociopolitical and cultural agenda of Kosovo as a new state. Given that Kosovo now has a diverse spectrum of media outlets, including cable channels in which political actors can compete successfully, RTK could leave them handle more politics and instead focus itself on political events and reorient more toward a broader sociocultural agenda on par with its focus on nurturing multi-ethnicity and diversity. After all, the RTK law of 2012 sets out such a role in great detail, and this could serve as a roadmap for a successful transformation. Lastly, the PCK has a similar challenge in regards to exercising its role in a fair manner when confronted with issues likely to cause political interference. It would have been in a better position if it had opted to avoid handling political hot button issues altogether and to refer them to the courts, rather than to attempt to deal with them, and end up with its reputation questioned.

When it comes to preserving their formal or de facto independence, institutions such as the IMC and RTK seem to be in better position, since both of them can partially subsidize their operations, based on the income they generate. Capital investments aside, the IMC might become financially independent in the future with some more serious efforts.

In 2011 it seemed that RTK had "temporarily solved" the issue of funding through 2015. Four years later, however, it was again at the same crossroad and its budget for 2016 was uncertain. RTK generates about one-seventh of its budget through income from advertising and other resources. In the absence of a reintroduction of the license fee its connection with the public as a public broadcaster will further diminish and its ratings and viewership will suffer further, making it ever less significant and less respected in the public eye.

The PCK continues to be heavily reliant, ten years after its establishment, on international donors to cover its operational costs. Although its operational costs are small (they ranged between €40,000–50,000 annually but have increased to €70,000 in recent years), the PCK still doesn't seem to be close to finding a long-term solution that would make it self-sustainable and economically independent in the future. The fees collected through its subscribing members and the level of membership are still too low. Furthermore, the fact that it has given up on its right to collect fees from penalties makes it even harder to figure out avenues toward self-reliance in the future. The independence of the PCK is not affected by politics at this point but its position is bound to become more politicized as the media landscape changes and new media and portals gain in popularity. Also, if it decides to pursue the approach of becoming another state-budget-dependent institution it might be faced with the challenges that independent agencies dependent on state budgets are faced with in this part of the world. Consequently, if Kosovo courts increase their efficiency down the road in addressing media matters with greater diligence, its importance is likely to be diminished.

In conclusion, it should be reiterated that the use of the Western liberal media models[134] as a guiding model for the media setup in Kosovo might have been too ambitious a goal. It gave too much credit to the cultural ethos at the time, assuming it to be an environment in which a liberal media sector could be firmly rooted. Obviously, Kosovo is a progress story, having moved from a point where it had no institutions to the point where, however imperfect, the media institutions continue to operate. Overall, however, its media institutions, based on their current condition, are still years away from achieving functional independence.

---

[134] Hallin and Mancini, *Comparing Media Systems.*

CHAPTER 5

Assisting Media Democratization after Low-Intensity Conflict: The Case of Macedonia

TAMARA DIMITRIJEVSKA-MARKOSKI AND ZHIDAS DASKALOVSKI

Introduction

Since its independence in 1991, Macedonia has undergone rapid democratization and liberalization throughout public and private sectors, including the media. However, according to the IREX Media Sustainability Index (MSI), the Macedonian media system progressed until 2005, and has since been in constant decline. In 2001 the overall MSI score was 1.73, which improved to 2.58 in 2005, only to fall to 1.52 in 2012 and slightly improve by 2015 to 1.72[1] which places it in the category of unsustainable mixed media systems. The reasons behind the deteriorating Macedonian scores are the consequences of the "long-term trend toward state control, politicization and economic deterioration."[2]

Similarly, the European Commission (EC) progress reports for Macedonia reflect this negative trend. The EC has repeatedly expressed concerns about the uneven implementation of the legal and regulatory framework,[3] the vulnerability of the Broadcasting Council (BC) and the Public Service Broadcaster Macedonian Radio Television (MRTV) to political

---

[1] IREX, "Macedonia" (2015), 79.
[2] Ibid., 76.
[3] European Commission, "The Former Yugoslav Republic of Macedonia: Progress Report 2010," 42.

Table 5.1. IREX Media Sustainability Index for the Republic of Macedonia, 2001–2015

Indicator	2001	2005	2009	2011	2015
Free Speech	1.72	2.49	1.65	1.66	1.66
Professional Journalism	1.89	2.48	1.66	1.69	1.62
Plurality of News Sources	2.17	2.67	1.93	1.70	1.77
Business Management	1.33	2.45	1.61	1.39	1.38
Supporting Institutions	1.55	2.83	1.71	1.79	2.19
Overall Country Average	1.73	2.58	1.71	1.65	1.72

Source: IREX, "Macedonia," in Media Sustainability Index for the years 2001, 2005, 2009, 2011, 2015.

interference,[4] the financial dependence of MRTV,[5] the inability of the regulator to monitor the media market effectively[6] and the disproportionately large share of governmental advertising in the overall advertising market.[7]

Given the importance of various media assistance programs and projects in Macedonia over the last two decades, which were aimed at developing democratic and sustainable media institutions, this chapter examines the complex interplay of factors that conditioned the success or failure of such media development efforts. We chart the international donors' media assistance with a particular emphasis on the nature of the assistance strategies deployed. The focus is placed on the following three institutions of the media system in Macedonia that benefited from media assistance programs: the Broadcasting Council, Macedonian Radio Television, and the independent, nonprofit organization Macedonian Institute for Media. The analysis is anchored within the theoretical framework outlined in the introduction to this volume.

The chapter is structured as follows: In the first section, a brief overview of the recent political history and system of Macedonia is provided,

---

[4] European Commission, "The Former Yugoslav Republic of Macedonia: Progress Report 2007," 13; European Commission, "The Former Yugoslav Republic of Macedonia: Progress Report 2009," 17.
[5] European Commission, "The Former Yugoslav Republic of Macedonia: Progress Report 2006," 13.
[6] European Commission, "The Former Yugoslav Republic of Macedonia: Progress Report 2010," 41.
[7] Ibid., 16.

followed by a summary of the defining elements of the local media system. The second section discusses international donor involvement in the media assistance projects and analyzes the nature and scope of assistance strategies. The chapter then proceeds with an analysis of the evolution of three cases that benefited from the media assistance programs: the Broadcasting Council, Macedonian Radio Television and the Macedonian Institute for Media. The chapter is concluded with a discussion of the findings about the current status of Macedonian media institutions in the context of two decades of media assistance programs implemented in the country.

Background: Political System and Media System

DEMOCRATIC TRANSITION AFTER YUGOSLAVIA

Modern Macedonia emerged in 1945 as one of the six constituent republics of the Socialist Federal Republic of Yugoslavia. When Yugoslavia disintegrated in the second half of 1991, Macedonia chose to assert its own independence rather than remain in a truncated Yugoslav state.

Macedonia, an EU candidate country, has just above 2 million inhabitants, the majority being Macedonians (64%) and ethnic Albanians (25%), and the rest (11%) belonging to other ethnic groups such as Roma, Turks, Serbs, Vlachs, Bosniaks, etc.[8] In international relations the country is referred to as the former Yugoslav Republic of Macedonia because of an unresolved dispute over the name with Greece, which has a region called Macedonia and negates the right of Macedonia to name itself as such. Macedonia was not affected by the armed conflicts in the early 1990s when Yugoslavia fell apart, yet the transformation of Macedonian society was characterized by an uneasy period of state building that culminated in the internal armed conflict in 2001 when the Albanian minority demanded greater rights and autonomy for Albanians in Macedonia.

The 2001 conflict quickly ended through an EU- and US-mediated agreement. The so-called Ohrid Framework Agreement (OFA) envisioned a series of political and constitutional reforms aiming to accommodate the grievances of the Albanian community, while at the same time preserving the unitary character of the state. The agreement introduced features of consociational power sharing, such as a system of double majorities

---

[8] State Statistical Office, *Census of Population*, 15.

requiring consent from minorities represented in parliament to key decisions of the parliament. A substantial degree of decentralization has also been implemented.[9]

When it comes to other impediments to democratization, Macedonia is not an exception to the regional trend of "state politicization." Although the legal framework was amended on numerous occasions, it still does not sufficiently protect journalists and fails to meet international standards.[10] In addition to this, there are restrictive and arbitrary procedures subject to political interference[11] while the media ownership structures remain elusive.[12]

Contrary to the belief that it is difficult for coalition governments to achieve direct control over the broadcasting system,[13] Macedonia proves the opposite is also possible. Since 2001 all of the governments have been coalition governments of ethnic Macedonian and ethnic Albanian political parties that applied a pedantic distribution of spheres of influence whereby the Macedonian party influenced the Macedonian-language media, and the Albanian political party exercised its influence in the Albanian-language media. The coalition partners were united in the aim to control the broadcasting system and assuage opposition voices.

LIBERALIZATION OF THE MEDIA SECTOR

There have been three stages of media development in Macedonia. The first stage (1991–1997) is characterized by demonopolization, decentralization, and internalization of television content. The second stage (1998–2005) was distinguished by the introduction of new legislation and initial efforts toward promotion of journalistic professionalization in the newly created commercial media. The third stage (2006–present) features legislative consolidation, continuing professionalization of journalism, and the beginning of media concentration processes.

In socialist Yugoslavia, the Macedonian media system was subject to strong state control and an absence of alternative media[14] and the only

---

[9] Daskalovski, *Walking on the Edge*, 144, 188.
[10] IREX, "Macedonia" (2013), 81.
[11] Ibid., 81.
[12] Freedom House, "Freedom of the Press."
[13] Hallin and Mancini, *Comparing Media Systems*, 52, 106.
[14] Macedonian Institute for Media, "Development of the Media," 3; Bennett, "How Yugoslavia's Destroyers Harnessed the Media."

existent broadcasting media was state-owned TV Skopje. As of 1991, liberalization and deregulation started with a new constitution, but media laws took another six years to be adopted.[15] Article 16 of the constitution guarantees "the freedom of personal conviction, conscience, thought and public expression of thought." Moreover, protection of sources is granted to mass media and censorship is explicitly banned.

Until the first Law on Broadcasting Activity[16] was adopted in 1997, there were more than 210 radio and/or television stations operating in the country.[17] A year after the adoption of the Law on Broadcasting Activity, the Law on the Establishment of the Public Enterprise Macedonian Radio Television[18] was also enacted. These laws set the basis for the transformation of MRTV into a public service broadcaster. However, the legal framework being inadequate, the two laws were consolidated in a new Law on Broadcasting Activity (LBA) from 2005[19] which was praised by almost all international organizations, namely the OSCE, the Council of Europe (CoE), and the EU.[20] Since then, the LBA has been amended on several occasions.[21] In parts, these amendments were criticized as a legal backslide with regard to the independence of the media regulatory agency and the slow transformation and dependency of MRTV on governmental funds[22]

Another problematic aspect in the legal framework was the criminalization of defamation and libel. This practice was finally changed in 2012 when the parliament adopted a new civil law regulating insult and defamation and removed sanctions for speech offences from the Criminal Code.[23] When libel and defamation were still criminal offenses, it was believed that they had a negative impact on the exercise of freedom of speech. As an illustration, in 2010 there were 170 defamation cases.[24] Following the legal

---

[15] Daskalovski, "A Study of the Legal Framework."

[16] "Zakon za radiodifuznata dejnost" (1997).

[17] Kolar-Panov, "Broadcasting in Macedonia."

[18] "Zakon za osnovanje na javno pretprijatie Makedonska Radiodifuzija."

[19] "Zakon za radiodifuznata dejnost" (2005).

[20] Jakubowicz and Directorate General, "Analysis and Review"; OSCE, "OSCE Media Freedom Representative Welcomes New Macedonian Broadcast Law."

[21] Amendments of the Law on Broadcasting Activity from: February 19, 2007; August 19, 2008; December 5, 2008; January 15, 2010; November 5, 2010; July 18, 2011; January 27, 2012; and December 26, 2013 (Law on Audio and Audiovisual Activities).

[22] Popovic, "The Former Yugoslav Republic of Macedonia."

[23] OSCE, "OSCE Media Freedom Representative Welcomes Skopje Authorities."

[24] International Media Freedom Mission, "Macedonia Report."

changes, the civil procedure corresponds with international best practices, but some experts argue that the envisioned fines are still very high.[25]

THE MEDIA MARKET

In the period between 1991 and 1997 privately owned TV and radio stations rapidly emerged throughout the country. In 1991 the first private radio station was opened and in 1993 the first private TV station (A1). By the beginning of 1994, there was uncoordinated market entry of new media and the estimation is that there were 191 broadcasters in Macedonia, the vast majority owned by private individuals or companies.[26]

Currently, there are ten TV stations and one public service broadcaster with three channels with national coverage; nine TV stations with regional coverage; and forty-eight TV stations with local coverage.[27] There are five radio stations with national coverage, three of which are private stations, and two national stations operated by MRTV. There are also seventeen regional, and sixty local radio stations.[28]

Significant foreign investments, with the exception of that of WAZ,[29] which bought a number of print media including the most influential, *Dnevnik*, have not been made in the media market. The "economic stability [of the media outlets] is shaky, as many of the media outlets are vulnerable and exposed to commercial and political pressures,"[30] and this is one of the most influential reasons behind the reluctance of foreign investors to enter the media market.

An additional problem is that the government is one of the biggest advertisers in the market.[31] In 2008 the government invested €12 million and ranked as the fifth largest advertiser. In the following year it bought advertising for €17 million, which rendered it the second largest advertiser in the country.[32] Also the government has been accused of a lack of transparency in the way it chooses media outlets for its advertisements.[33]

---

[25] Marusic, "Macedonian Journalists"; Marusic, "Libel Law."
[26] Daskalovski, "A Study of the Legal Framework."
[27] Broadcasting Council, "List of Registered TV Outlets."
[28] Broadcasting Council, "List of Registered Radio Stations."
[29] Handwerk and Willems, "WAZ and the Buy-out."
[30] Haraszti, "The State of Media Freedom," 2.
[31] Broadcasting Council, "Analiza na pazarot."
[32] Ibid.
[33] Brunwasser, "Concerns Grow"; IREX, "Macedonia" (2013), 94; and Manevski and Skerlev-Cakar, "Macedonia," 87.

That allows it to "arbitrarily disperse advertising funds to favorable media, or to openly bribe them to support their viewpoint."[34] There are no official public figures that would reveal how much the government spends on public advertisements per media outlet but the available information indicates that the biggest beneficiaries are those media with close links to the government. Contrary to logic, public advertising does not directly correlate with audience share, but with political ties.[35]

MEDIA AND POLITICS (POLITICAL PARALLELISM)

There are concerns about the high level of political parallelism in the media sector.[36] Even though media outlets do not openly and publicly support any political party or coalition, there are clear indicators of significant relations among media and political parties. This is directly discernible from media ownership. Quite a few television stations are considered politically influenced since the owners of these outlets are also political leaders. For instance, the most influential electronic outlet until 2010, A1 Television, was owned by Velija Ramkovski, a leader of the Party for Economic Renewal, who also owned two daily newspapers (*Vreme* and *Koha*) while Sitel TV is owned by Goran Ivanov, son of Ljubisav Ivanov, who is the president of the Socialist Party. Similarly, Kanal 5 is owned by Emil Stojmenov, son of Boris Stojmenov, who is the leader of the VMRO (Vistinska Party), the family of an ethnic-Albanian businessman, Vebi Velija, owns Alsat TV, while TV ALFA was owned by businessman Shterjo Nakov, close to the leader of the biggest opposition party, SDSM (Social Democratic Union of Macedonia).

Biased media output is another feature which points to political parallelism. For example, after the purchase of TV ALFA, the new owners that are allegedly close to the ruling VMRO-DPMNE (Internal Macedonian Revolutionary Organization–Democratic Party for Macedonian National Unity) cancelled political debate programs,[37] and there was a transfer of journalists from the progovernment media, such as MRTV, SITEL, Vecer and Dnevnik, to TV ALFA.[38] The biased reporting is also visible during

---

[34] IREX, "Macedonia" (2012), 94.
[35] Gadzovska Spasovska, "Sovet za radiodifuzija."
[36] Manevski and Skerlev-Cakar, "Macedonia," 85.
[37] These political programs were cancelled: *Win-Win* and *Word by Word*. The former show is now broadcast on ALSAT-M television station.
[38] Infocentar, "Media Mirror," 4.

election campaigns where equal [quantitative] allocation of time to all candidates and political parties is not followed.[39] During the last local and parliamentary elections, at MRTV and most of the other channels the governing coalition was allocated disproportionally more time than the opposition and smaller parties.[40] Furthermore, the government coalition is "represented in a disproportionally favorable light and the opposition in a disproportionally negative light."[41] Hence, as far as political coverage is concerned, the editorial and content bias in Macedonian media is widespread.[42]

Journalists in both electronic and print media outlets often mix news with commentaries; do not distinguish between facts and opinions, do not use multiple sources to verify the story, and present information in a sensationalist style.[43] Information is spun in order to serve broader political goals.[44] Working for progovernment media, journalists often misreport news and interpret events in a partisan way. The practices of journalists and editors employed in media linked with opposition parties are similar.[45]

ETHNICALLY DIVIDED MEDIA SECTOR

There is fragmentation of the audience based on their ethnic background and separate programming for different ethnic groups in separate languages. There is a significant number of TV and radio stations which are operating in languages other than Macedonian (see table 5.2). The majority of the newspapers and periodicals are written in the Macedonian language, but there are daily newspapers and periodicals in Albanian as well as in the Turkish language.[46] There are no newspapers and periodicals in other languages.[47]

---

[39] Jakimovski et al., *My Choice 2011*, 26.
[40] Broadcasting Council, "Izvestaj od Mediumsko Pokrivanje," 3–15.
[41] Jakimovski et al., *My Choice 2011*, 26.
[42] Trajanovski, "Što znači."
[43] Mihajloski, "VMRO-DPMNE."
[44] Ilić, "Recenzija."
[45] European Commission, "The Former Yugoslav Republic of Macedonia: Progress Report 2012."
[46] In the Albanian language: *Fakti, Lajm, Zurnal*; bilingual: *Tea Moderna, Kichevo Miror, Time-Out*; in the Turkish language: *Zaman* and *Yeni Balkan* (ibid.).
[47] Ibid.

Table 5.2. Electronic Media in Macedonia According to the Language of Broadcast

	Macedonian	Albanian	Albanian and Macedonian	Mixed*
RADIO				
National Public	1	0	0	1
National Commercial	3	0	0	0
Regional and Local Commercial	59	11	1	5
TV				
National Public	1	0	1	1
National Commercial	9	—	1	
Regional and Local Commercial	38	12	2	5
TOTAL	111	23	5	12

*Mixed includes Albanian, Macedonian, Bosnian, Turkish, Serbian
Source: Broadcasting Council of Republic of Macedonia.[48]

In Albanian-language media current events from neighboring Albania and Kosovo are covered in much more detail. On the other hand, the Macedonian-language media has a more balanced coverage of regional and international news, while domestically it offers little information on the activities of ethnic minority parties.[49]

PROFESSIONALIZATION OF JOURNALISM

There is a significant problem with the professionalization of journalism in Macedonia. First, journalists continue to be under strong pressure by media owners and editors who still exercise strong influence over journalists' level of autonomy and creativity. One recent case was made public after an editor of a newspaper resigned when a text that was to be published in the next issue of the paper was withdrawn from printing when

---

[48] Broadcasting Council of the Republic of Macedonia, List of Registered TV Outlets, and Broadcasting Council of the Republic of Macedonia, List of Registered Radio Stations.
[49] Šopar, "Macedonia," 152.

management ordered the printing house to do so.[50] In addition, most of the journalists are aware of the owners of the media and are cautious when writing about the owners' businesses or political interests.

Further, there is a lack of developed and respected professional norms and rules. The Code of the Journalists of Macedonia[51] it is not respected. Although a Council of Honor exists, its impact is limited due to the fact the media who were supposed to publish the decisions of the Court of Honor, did not publish them.[52]

Moreover, journalists and journalists' organizations are divided across party lines. The Association of Journalists of Macedonia (AJM) was founded in 1946,[53] but has not managed to incorporate all journalists. There is division among prominent journalists over the quality of the work and the management of AJM, resulting in many joining the Macedonian Association of Journalists (MAJ).[54]

CIVIL SOCIETY

There are a number of organizations that have played an active role in the process of development of new media laws[55] and act as watchdogs over the government, but their success rate varies. This sector has been successful in organizing training, but less successful in the process of development of laws and regulations, where their policy overviews have often been ignored.

NGOs have been included in the development of the LBA from 2005[56] but there are cases where their inclusion has been selective. For instance, the process of drafting the law on civic responsibility for defamation and libel was not inclusive as it only included the AJM. In addition, there are cases where NGOs believe that their inclusion in the process came at too late a stage, when their impact was irrelevant.

---

[50] Zoran Dimitrovski, Editor in Chief of *Nova Makedonija*, interview with the author, November 26, 2012.

[51] Association of Journalists of Macedonia, *Code of the Journalists of Macedonia*, 1–3.

[52] Mirche Adamcevski, President of the Macedonian Institute for Media, interview with the authors, December 19, 2012.

[53] Association of Journalists of Macedonia, *Code of the Journalists of Macedonia*, 1.

[54] Netpress, "ZNM."

[55] Such as the Media Development Center, the Macedonian Institute for Media, the Foundation Open Society Macedonia, and the NGO Infocentar.

[56] Šopar, "Republic of Macedonia," 326.

DEMOCRATIZATION AND MEDIA ASSISTANCE: AN OVERVIEW

International media assistance to Macedonia has been provided by: international organizations (e.g., the OSCE, the EU, the Council of Europe), foreign governments (e.g., USAID, embassies of the Netherlands, Sweden, Germany, Norway) and nongovernmental organizations (e.g., Article 19, the Open Society Institute, Friedrich Ebert Stiftung, the National Endowment for Democracy, IREX ProMedia, Press Now, Norwegian People's Aid, Medienhilfe and the Swedish Helsinki Committee). These organizations have provided support on an individual, institutional and policy level. Donor support has been provided mostly through direct support to media, training for media workers, consulting for agencies and outlets, monitoring and lobbying for legal amendments.

There is an absence of official and accurate information on the exact amount spent on media assistance. Estimates suggest that, in the period 1996–2006, approximately €23.8 million was spent on media development.[57] Most of the funding—€11.2 million—was spent on improving the media environment: €9.2 million as direct media support, and €3.4 million on media training.[58]

The Phases of Media Assistance

International media assistance can generally be divided into four phases: 1991–1999, 2000–2005, 2006–2010, and 2010–present, each with its specific scope and programmatic focus.

The first assistance period, 1991–1999, was characterized by a few media donors who were oriented toward increasing pluralism in the radio, television and printed media sectors by providing assistance on an individual and institutional level. Among the first donors that entered the country was the Foundation Open Society Macedonia (FOSM), which is also one of the biggest and most influential international donors still present in the country. In this assistance period FOSM and the CoE strived to demonopolize the work of the state TV and radio and of the print media outlet *Nova Makedonija*, and foster media pluralism. In order to do this, FOSM and CoE provided direct support to alternative media outlets

---

[57] Johnson, "Model Interventions," 214.
[58] Ibid.

Table 5.3. The Four Phases of Media Assistance in Macedonia

1991–1999	2000–2005	2006–2010	2010–IP
Low assistance	Intensive assistance	Withdrawal of donors	Signs of donors reentering
• Few donors • Direct support to media outlets • Aim: pluralism of views	• A lot of donors • Legal development • Capacity building of civil society organizations • Aim: broader social and political goals and reinforcing of peace	• Withdrawal of donors due to anticipation of EU funding	• Deterioration of the overall media sphere

and offered various training opportunities for journalists and other media workers such as editors and cameramen. Johnson estimates that FOSM supported six television and ten radio stations[59] and, according to the OSCE, more than fifty broadcasters benefited from OSI support. FOSM also assisted the printed media, helping launch the now major newspaper *Dnevnik* by subsidizing a private printing house, Europa 92, and the establishment of a distribution network independent of the government.

Besides direct financial assistance, donors also engaged in capacity building within institutions through training for election reporting, media monitoring, multilingual programming, and news exchange.

Creating an enabling environment through legal reforms was an important aspect of media assistance.[60] The Macedonian Broadcasting Law from 1997 "went through six drafts and was prepared with input from CoE and Article 19, a British-based NGO, in a process often used as an exemplary form of cooperation of international bodies [and donors] with the Macedonian authorities."[61]

During the second phase, in the period between 2000 and 2005, media assistance climbed higher on the donors' agenda. This was not part of a calculated or planned aid strategy but a spontaneous response to the 1999 Kosovo refugee crisis[62] and the internal armed conflict in 2001. The donors increasingly engaged in urgent media assistance to provide equipment when

---

[59] Ibid., 213.
[60] Thompson, "Slovenia, Croatia, Bosnia," 51, 58.
[61] Ibid.
[62] Johnson, "Model Interventions."

media transmitters were destroyed[63] and support for independent media outlets.[64] In this phase direct assistance was given quickly, following simplified procedures,[65] and most of the support came in the form of technical assistance to the outlets that broadcast programs in the northwestern part of the country, disproportionally affected by the refugee crisis and conflict.

Following the conflict and the signing of the OFA, the media assistance assumed a broader perspective, that is, to serve the broader goal of democratization. In this second stage, EU conditionality was effective in pushing for policy reforms and fostering changes in the media environment. The adoption of the LBA of 2005 and the decriminalization of defamation and libel from 2012 were also inspired by the potential EU membership.[66] However, once the laws were passed, the EU conditionality had a limited effect in the policy implementation phase.

During this stage not only media outlets, which were the main donor recipients in earlier stages, but also nongovernmental organizations started to be aid recipients. This shift in donors' strategies came as a result of the assumption that once donors leave, civil society organizations should assume the role of watchdog of the government. Therefore, in the second period, focus was placed on capacity building of nongovernmental organizations as well.

This second period seems to be the most intensive period of donor assistance. The OSCE budget alone for the period 2003–2006 was somewhat below €2 million[67] and the IREX ProMedia Program for five years, 2001–2005, had a budget of US$3.8 million.[68] Donor presence was massive up to 2006, when many international donors started to phase out.

The third phase, 2006–2010, was marked with the withdrawal of donors. Press Now, one of the major donors, left the country, followed by IREX ProMedia, Norwegian People's Aid, as well as the OSCE and the Stability Pact Media Task Force (Stability Pact for South Eastern

---

[63] Medienhilfe, "Crisis Assistance"; Brunner, "Urgent Media Assistance."
[64] Ibid.
[65] Rhodes, "Ten Years of Media Support," 21.
[66] Marusic, "Macedonian Journalists."
[67] Mihajlo Lahtov, Project Manager at Macedonian Institute for Media and Senior Public Information and Media Assistant at OSCE Mission to Skopje, interview with the author, December 18, 2012; Mirvete Islam, Senior Public Information and Media Assistant; OSCE Mission to Skopje, interview with the author, December 18, 2012.
[68] Sladjana Srbinovska, Project Manager, Civil Society Sector, USAID, interview with the author, February 11, 2013.

Europe). Both the OSCE and USAID discontinued their media programs in this phase. The decline of US resources for media programs in Macedonia was also a result of the anticipated increase of EU funding, as well the shift in this donor's priorities. Macedonia was perceived as a country where significant progress had been achieved, as evidenced by the rise of the IREX Media Sustainability Index and funds were allocated to needier places, such as the Middle East and North Africa.[69]

The fourth phase is characterized with initial signs of donors returning. After 2010 there is significant deterioration of the media sphere, which was duly noted in all international reports which monitor Macedonian media. One explanation about the return of US donors reflects also on the failed assumption that the EU candidacy and expected EU accession would serve the media democratization. Hence, in 2012 USAID launched a new three-year media program to target the nongovernmental sector and support the professionalization of journalists.

Coherence of Media Assistance: Coordination and Monitoring

Throughout the phases of international media assistance to Macedonia a number of donors became active and a need for coordination of their activities emerged. In 1998, the International Media Fund (IMF) for Macedonia was established as "a loose and informal association of international donor organizations." Furthermore, donors agreed that the pooling of funds served to lower costs and associated risks and also enabled donors to support a broad range of activities.[70] Pooled funds were especially useful during the 2001 conflict when fast reaction was needed. For example, during the conflict in the area of Tetovo, when the radio and TV transmitters were destroyed, the IMF replaced them and hence prevented a "media blackout." Similarly, in April 2001, the IMF created the Crisis Assistance Program (CAP). This program provided for improvement of the security of the journalists and assisted media to cover the higher expenses during the period of conflict, as well as to strengthen the self-regulatory mechanisms.[71] It was mainly emergency support in the form of quick, nonbureaucratic and targeted assistance.

---

[69] Cary and D'Amour, "U.S. Government Funding for Media," 7.
[70] Dean, "Working in Concert," 12.
[71] Medienhilfe, "International Media Fund."

Later on, the Media Task Force (MTF) of the Stability Pact for South Eastern Europe aimed to provide a forum for the coordination of the major media assistance programs in the period 2002–2006. The MTF and national working groups comprised of media professionals selected projects and proposed them for funding.[72]

Understandingly, with the phasing out of donor presence in Macedonia, in phase three there was not much coordination. Nowadays there are some donor meetings mainly to avoid overlapping, but there is not much coordination. The incentives for coordination are rather low since the available funds are quite limited although some argue that on the contrary, lower resources available for media assistance demand higher coordination.[73]

Monitoring and evaluation as a donor strategy has been implemented but has not been sufficient to correct policy deficiencies. The European Commission, Reporters without Borders, and Freedom House provide regular reports on the media sphere, and the MDC, MIM, and NGO Infocenter monitor media developments. Although criticism by the EU manages to attract the widest public attention, it has not been sufficient to alter some practices. In particular, repeated concerns in the EC reports over the financial dependence of the public service broadcasters and the politicization of national and private media outlets have proven to have little effect.

The following case studies analyze the development of the Broadcasting Council, Macedonian Radio Television and the Macedonian Institute for Media. Each case study briefly introduces the institutions, analyzes the approach of the foreign donors toward them and draws conclusions on their formal and de facto independence and functionality.

The Broadcasting Council

Newly independent Macedonia took a laissez-faire approach to the media, which resulted in a rapid proliferation of the number of outlets.[74] Regulation was minimal. Besides the constitution, there was no specific media

---

[72] Stability Pact for South Eastern Europe, "Media Task Force."
[73] Violeta Gligorovska, Program Coordinator, OSI Macedonia, interview with the author, February 4, 2012.
[74] Daskalovski, "A Study of the Legal Framework," 23, 36.

policy,[75] and there was no concession fee or frequency maintenance charge.[76] However, following the oversaturation of the media landscape there was a need for at least some kind of regulation and the Broadcasting Council (BC) was established.

An important role in the establishment and development of the BC was played by international organizations. The BC was established in 1997 as a regulatory body in charge of the regulation of the commercial electronic media sector as well as of the PSB. Although development of legal framework and regulation was not a priority of the international donors at the time, the chaotic market triggered the donors to foster the development of such a body.

The legal grounds for the establishment of the BC were developed with assistance from a number of international organizations such as Council of Europe and Article 19, and the process included the active engagement of the local authorities. After the legal framework itself was generally evaluated as good, the OSCE worked on improving the institution-building process by providing technical assistance and consultation to the BC.[77] For example, in 2008 the OSCE Mission to Skopje donated equipment to the BC to monitor the elections.[78] The BC also benefited from expert assistance where the Strategy for Development of Broadcasting Activity for the period 2007–2012 was developed with assistance from TAIEX (European Commission Programme) and in cooperation with the OSCE.

Donor strategies were aimed at the creation of an independent regulatory body which relies on local funds. The BC is financially independent from the government and the funds for its work are collected from the broadcasting fee and the fee for licenses for performing broadcasting activity (as provided in LBA, Art. 36). The parliament reviews but does not have to approve the annual financial plan of the BC. The BC is not accountable to the government or any ministry, except to the parliament to which it sends its annual report. According to Trajcevski, the BC is in principle financially independent from the government, as the government has no powers to interfere in its work or the distribution of the finances.[79]

---

[75] Kolar-Panov, "Broadcasting in Macedonia."

[76] Thompson, "Slovenia, Croatia, Bosnia," 50.

[77] Večer, "OBSE ke mu pomaga."

[78] Zoran Trajcevski, President of the Broadcasting Council, interview with author, February 1, 2013.

[79] Ibid.

In order to stimulate changes the EU employed a mechanism for conditionality and regular monitoring, and successfully managed to influence changes in the legislation. One example is the Law on Broadcasting Activity from 1997 which was amended in 2005, increasing the independence and powers of the BC. Namely, prior to 2005 the BC had powers only to give recommendations in the process of issuing broadcasting concessions (de facto licenses to operate) while the end decisions were made by the government.[80] The law from 2005 empowered the BC to make decisions in the process of allocating licenses independently.[81] In the policy debates over this law, not surprisingly, the European Commission and civil society organizations insisted on the exclusion of members of political parties from the structures of the BC.[82]

Notwithstanding the importance of the carrot—the prospects of EU accession of Macedonia—the monitoring system exercised by the EU proved to work as a potential stick in that process and encouraged the BC to work in a transparent manner.[83] Compliance with EU standards on the transparency of the BC meant that the EC in its annual progress reports on Macedonia could not criticize the work of the BC as an obstacle to the future EU accession of the country.

As a result, EU conditionality and monitoring have produced results. The work of the BC is now public, and its documents such as public calls, agendas, minutes of meetings, decisions, are made available through its webpage and the media reports. However, even though the information is available online, the minutes are rather poor and do not provide detailed information or the reasoning behind the decisions of the members of the BC.

Although the international donors have advanced the work of the BC by assisting the enabling of the legal environment, capacity building and technical assistance, there are still serious obstacles, the most notable being state politicization.[84] There is political interference in the appointment of the members of the Council, controversial financial assistance from the government to the BC, and lack of professional management of the BC.

---

[80] "Zakon za radiodifuznata dejnost" (1997), Art. 13.
[81] "Zakon za radiodifuznata dejnost" (2005), Art. 52.
[82] Šopar, "Republic of Macedonia," 319.
[83] Zoran Trajcevski, President of the Broadcasting Council, interview with the author, February 1, 2013.
[84] Zielonka and Mancini, "Executive Summary," 2.

Politicization is visible through the process of the appointment of the members of the BC. The LBA of 2005 was amended in 2011 and 2013, politicizing the appointment procedure. With these legal changes, the number of members of the BC was increased from nine to fifteen, two of which would be nominated by the president. There were strong reactions to the entitlement of the president to nominate members of the BC, notably with claims that as this is a regulatory body the president should have no role in the process.[85] Disappointment with the enlargement of the body was expressed by the Association of Journalists and MIM[86] as well as other organizations which believe that the proposed changes to the membership structure of the BC "will politicize this regulatory body, curtail media freedom, and reduce pluralism within the country."[87]

The safeguards inserted for assuring the independence of BC members have not been respected. Since 2005, the parliament has chosen candidates through so-called speedy procedures leaving no time for public reaction or debate over the quality of the nominees. The procedural aspects of the process are not respected and the names of the nominees for these positions are not published in newspapers.

The BC is not free from political interference. For example, one of the current members appointed to the BC is a brother of a member of the parliament, coming from the ruling DUI Party (Democratic Union for Integration).[88] A serious downturn was the fact that "in 2008, the government allocated 600,000 Euros from the State Budget as 'financial support to the BC for monitoring the election activities in 2009.'"[89] With the money the BC bought equipment to monitor the elections in Skopje only—not in the whole country. The funds for this purpose were paid to a BC subcontracting party that monitored the elections. However, the BC subcontractor was a company with little track experience; that project was its first, and only, project.[90] Additionally, of particular concern is the silence of the BC with regard to governmental advertising in the media. This silence causes distrust regarding the independence of the BC.

In their media assistance to Macedonia international donors aimed at creating an independent regulatory body which relies on local funds

---

[85] Spasovska, "Novinarite se bunat."
[86] Ibid.
[87] International Press Institute, "Proposed Changes."
[88] Dzamazovski, "Novi prepukuvanja."
[89] Hans Bredow Institute for Media Research et al., *INDIREG*, 22.
[90] Zoran Trajcevski, interview with the author, February 1, 2013.

and is independent from government influences. Although with some outstanding obstacles, most notably political interference in the appointment of the members of the Council, suspicious financial assistance of the government to the BC, and lack of professional management of the BC, the standards for the independence of the work of the BC have been established. Although further work needs to be done to anchor the independence of the BC from politics, international donor assistance has been pivotal in this process.

Public Service Broadcasting

Macedonian Radio Television went through a long transformation process. In the early stages of democratization in Macedonia, MRTV entered a period of constant decline both in content production and technical capabilities. While MRTV faced financial difficulties, lost some of its key anchors and entered a period of decline,[91] a number of private media outlets were founded. The idea of the government, at the time led by the Social Democrats, was not to control the programming of MRTV but to increase the viewership of private media.[92]

In the early 1990s MRTV was not on the donors' agenda. International organizations did not at first prioritize the transformation of MRTV as they believed priority should be given to the pluralization of the media sector in general. A few years later, international organizations realized the need for the transformation of state-controlled MRTV into a public service broadcaster.

The most important support that MRTV has received from donors is assistance for the creation of an enabling legal environment for its operation. The operation of MRTV was regulated in 1997 with the Law on Establishment of Public Enterprise Macedonian Radio Television, which in 2005 was consolidated with the Law on Establishing Broadcasting Enterprise in a new Law on Broadcasting Activity. Yet the results of the legal amendments have been evaluated as poor.[93]

---

[91] Dime Ratajkovski, Manager and Head Editor, MTV, interview with the author, March 12, 2013.
[92] Zoran Dimitrovski, Editor in Chief, *Nova Makedonija,* interview with the author, November 26, 2012.
[93] Thompson, "Slovenia, Croatia, Bosnia," 58.

Another component of donor-assistance programs included capacity-building training for journalists as well as some technical assistance and equipment. There is no precise information on the number of media workers from MRTV who have benefited from the training, but the information obtained by various donors indicates that almost all of their media training were open to MRTV representatives.

As a result, compared with the period of the socialist past, MRTV has achieved significant progress. However, like in the case of the BC, politicization is an important feature which significantly affects its operation. Frequent politically driven changes in the management illustrate this point. In 1998, the coalition government started to interfere at an even lower level, replacing editors and directors.[94] In 2006 and 2007, heads and editors were replaced more than once, which had negative effects on the output and the ratings.[95] The new 2013 MRTV management is striving to change the negative perception of the outlets, and is introducing program and staff changes.

Since 2008 the government coalition has been stable and there has not been a potential veto player able to produce drastic changes in the operation of MRTV. Although the government is a coalition government there is a pedantic distribution of the spheres of influence, whereby the Macedonian political party exercises influence over MRTV1 and the Albanian over MRTV2. Moreover, there is political influence on the ethnic makeup of the managing team of the public broadcaster. There is a system of balances in places, so that if the managing director of the public enterprise is Macedonian, the deputy would be an ethnic Albanian and vice versa. This is an informal practice between the Macedonian and Albanian parties in the ruling government coalition and not an official legal requirement.[96]

An explanation for the existent political parallelism of MRTV can be found in the low rate of collection of the broadcasting fee and its dependence on government transfers. The law stipulates that MRTV is to be financed from the broadcasting fee, advertising, sponsorships, donations, sales of programs and services, and from funds in the budget of the Republic of Macedonia for the current year. Until 2006, the average collection rate of the broadcasting fee was between 60% and 70%. "In 2006, the

---

[94] Ibid., 53.
[95] Šopar, "Republic of Macedonia," 320.
[96] Vesna Šopar, Professor at the School of Journalism and Public Relations in Skopje, interview with the author, February 8, 2013.

collection of the fee plummeted to 6 per cent amidst confusion caused by changing the mode of collection."[97] Collection has been transferred from the EVN Electrical Power Company to MRTV. Delinking the payment of the broadcasting fee from the payment of electricity bills meant that many households simply decided not to pay the fee. While the penalty for not paying the electricity bill would have meant no access to electricity, for not paying the fee households only risked a prolonged court case.

At times when MRTV's financial situation became bleak, "the government provided cash injection by transferring money from the Public Enterprise for Airport Services."[98] According to Article 178 of the LBA the state budget was supposed to allocate 80% of the total license fee for the first six months following the change in the collection mechanism. But even after that in 2007, MRTV was unable to collect the fees, with the collection rate dropping to 0.5%.[99] The crisis continued, even though when in "2009 MRTV managed to collect three times more than in 2008, the total amount of collected fees [was] only 922,784 Euros."[100] Currently, the mechanism for collection of the broadcasting fee still does not function well. Many households received more than one bill for the broadcasting fee, which left many people frustrated and nervous.[101] The funding from the government and the state budget "damages the station's independence."[102] In the last financial report for 2011, the majority of the funds for the operation of MRTV came from the state budget; the total income for 2011 was approximately MKD1.2 billion out of which some MKD305 million (24%) was secured from the government.[103]

Hence, although donors have somewhat affected the development of the MRTV law, offered a limited number of trainings to journalists and donated some equipment, they have not been able to eliminate the biggest threat to the development of MRTV—political influence; neither did they manage to influence the achievement of financial independence for PSB. Frequent politically driven changes in the management illustrate this point. Moreover, there is a pedantic distribution of the spheres of influ-

---

[97] Šopar, "Republic of Macedonia," 347.
[98] Ibid.
[99] Ibid., 349.
[100] Broughton Micova, "Finding a Niche," 2.
[101] Alfa, "MRTV naplaka radiodifuzna taksa."
[102] Šopar, "Republic of Macedonia," 320.
[103] Macedonian Radio Television, "Godišen izveštaj."

ence on the work of MRTV among the Macedonian and ethnic Albanian governing coalition partners. The key problem unsolved since independence has been the financial independence of MRTV, which suffers from the low rate of collection of the broadcasting fee, making it dependent on government transfers.

Macedonian Institute for Media

In the 1990s civil society in Macedonia was weak and there were no independent organizations that would act as media watchdogs or be able to offer hands-on training to media professionals. However, the expansion of the overall civil society sector happened in the late 1990s and early 2000s as a result of the rapid democratization, donors' response to the spillover effect from the Kosovo crisis, and the internal conflict in 2001.

Within such a context, the Macedonian Institute for Media (MIM) was founded in 2001. It was established as a "nonprofit organization that promotes excellence in media and public communication through policy initiatives, research, training, publication and production."[104] Its main goal was to provide practical training and contribute toward the maintenance of professional standards in the media sector. As such, it was the first training center for journalist and media personnel in Macedonia,[105] offering training, workshops, and roundtables that dealt with issues such as investigative journalism, conflict reporting, management or reporting on minorities, to name only few.

MIM was founded thanks to foreign aid although the initiative for its establishment came from local media professionals.[106] It was founded by IREX ProMedia, the Danish School of Journalism and the Macedonian Press Centre.[107] These organizations provided the initial bulk of funding and other forms of capacity-building support but the organization has also cooperated with a number of other donors, through various grants for projects.[108] Among the other donors were the British embassy, the OSI

---

[104] Macedonian Institute for Media, "Development of the Media," 7.
[105] Ibid.
[106] Ibid.
[107] Macedonian Institute for Media, "About Us."
[108] Biljana Petkovska, Executive Director, Macedonian Institute for Media, interview with the authors, December 25, 2012.

Media Program, the OSI Roma Support Program, the Balkan Trust for Democracy, the Swedish Human Rights Defenders, the Helsinki Committee, and Norwegian People's Aid.

Although initial assistance programs, such as those of the Danish School of Journalism and IREX ProMedia, have ended, this has not affected the continuation of the work of MIM. The mentioned donors changed the priorities of their support in the region and discontinued their funding of MIM, but the organization has been able to continue operations and even expand its scope of activities.

Namely, notwithstanding the dependency of MIM on donor-assistance programs and funds, the development of the organization was strategically guided in order to ensure its sustainability. The first years of its existence were focused toward the development of capacities and building of the institution and later toward the training of journalists and other media workers. The need for diversification of sources of income lead to the creation of a nonprofit educational institution, the School for Journalism and Public Relations, which is accredited by the Ministry of Education and Science and offers graduate and postgraduate programs in journalism and communication science. At the same time, the scope of other activities also expanded, and the organization was continuously adjusting to the contextual challenges in order to continue its operations.

Today, fifteen year after its creation, MIM remains a prominent organization contributing to the democratization and development of the media sector in Macedonia. It has managed to expand its activities, while at the same time preserving its financial independence—thanks to the diversification of activities and financial sources it does not depend on single large donor and it has never received government funds.

In spite of this challenging context—one characterized by political polarization, changing donor preferences, and grave economic circumstances (especially since 2008)—MIM continues to play an important role in the Macedonian media sector. Such an outcome is the result of a combination of two key factors: the long-term, strategic orientation of the organization and a reliance on local talent to populate the management of the organization. Throughout its years of operation MIM has been able to gather a team of professionals who have successfully competed for international tenders, grants, and projects dealing with the media sector. Thus, MIM is a good example of how international donors in cooperation with local professionals and organizations can create a self-sustainable institution which is politically independent, enjoys public credibility, and contributes toward the development of the journalistic profession.

Conclusions

Bearing in mind the political and economic circumstances in the early stages of development of a democratic Macedonia, international donors played an important role in fostering a vibrant media landscape, including establishing a legal framework and the relevant institutions. Donors engaged in a number of media assistance projects, producing mixed results.

First, the liberal model, characterized by strong professionalization, a market-dominated sector and neutral reporting, which was fostered in the early 1990s, failed to develop. Instead, Macedonia suffered from the "opaque imitation"[109] of external practices. Instead of information-oriented journalism and a market-oriented media system, there is high political parallelism, partisan polyvalence, a distorted media market, and biased reporting.

Second, most of the donors that engaged in the country deployed short-term and mid-term media projects, which ceased to produce results soon after the donors' withdrawal. Although assistance to the public service broadcaster and the BC were policy oriented, they failed to prevent governmental abuse and the dependence of these organizations on domestic funds.

Third, most of the reforms were completed prior to 2005, when the incentives for EU integration were the highest. Not surprisingly, as the country is currently stuck in the EU integration process (due to a Greek blockade of the start of membership negotiations), the EU is losing its importance.

Fourth, the intensity of donor assistance was highest in turbulent times when Macedonia was either neighbor to a conflict or had internal violent disturbances. A few years following the Macedonian peace settlement in 2001, donors started to withdraw their resources but failed to anticipate the upcoming political usurpation of the media landscape. Today, there are signs of donor reentry into the country.

Fifth, donors' achievements were most significant at policy level and less sustainable when they were focused on the individual level of specific media organizations and institutions. Various agencies and individual donors had the biggest impact in the development of the legal framework and supporting the professionalization of journalism but were less successful in abating political influence over private and public media and the

---

[109] Zielonka and Mancini, "Executive Summary," 6.

media regulator, the BC. Even though many independent media outlets were supported in the early 1990s, very few of them survived, while others fell victim to the intense politicization that dominates the country.

The reasons behind the donors' limited success can be explained through Berkowicz's "transplant effect."[110] In particular, the reforms in the Macedonian media sector were conducted according to the model of the liberal media system, underestimating the potential dangers of the local context. In that light, the local context of high state politicization, strong business and political parallelism and ethnic segregation were to a great extent overlooked.

In addition to the lack of understanding of the local context, there was an absence of a coherent donor-assistance strategy. This has contributed toward the overall limited success of the assistance efforts. With several notable exceptions, most of the media assistance in Macedonia was of short- and mid-term orientation, which finally resulted in short-lived results. The absence of a strategic approach on the part of the international donors and the ad hoc nature of their assistance were additional factors contributing to the donors' failure to produce long-lasting results. The lack of coordination among donors was also a problem that could not be overcome. After 2006, the decline of resources available from donor assistance, followed by a decline of donor coordination, ultimately led to the weakening of their influence on the media sector and increasing political interference.

All in all, donors were successful in contributing toward the increase of the sheer number of media outlets in the nation, providing professional journalist training, improving the legal environment at the policy level, and increasing the transparency of the BC. However, establishing a sound legal environment is only one step toward achieving high media standards. Donors have little influence over the implementation of laws which primarily depend on contextual factors that are largely beyond the reach of external actors. Hence, since most of the reforms were completed prior to 2005 when the incentives for EU integration were the highest, once media laws were passed the EU conditionality had limited effect in the policy implementation phase as extensive politicization of the media system, the high level of informality, and financial dependence exerted a detrimental influence on newly introduced legal solutions, institutions, and media organizations.

---

[110] Berkowitz, Pistor, and Richard, "The Transplant Effect."

CHAPTER 6

Media Reforms in Turbulent Times: The Role of Media Assistance in the Establishment of Independent Media Institutions in Serbia

Davor Marko

Introduction

The media system of Serbia passed through several development phases in the country's recent history. When the socialist era ended, at the beginning of the 1990s, the Socialistic Party of Slobodan Milošević managed to consolidate control over a large portion of the media space. This period was marked by a strong etatization of the media, the adoption of undemocratic laws, and an increasing number of local and private electronic media A handful of independent or oppositional media that existed were mainly supported by international donors. After 2000, successive governments in post-Milošević era established a new legal framework led by the ideals of a free press and a dual broadcasting system in which the transformed PSB would play an important democratizing role.[1]

Throughout the last two decades a significant role in the development of the media system in Serbia can be attributed to international assistance. During the 1990s, the assistance primarily focused on supporting independent media with the aim to provide an alternative voice for the public in Serbia and ensure its survival. After the fall of Milošević, international media assistance expanded in scope, trying to address the adoption of an adequate legal framework, the establishment of regulatory bodies, the transformation of the state TV into a public service broadcaster, and the empowerment of journalists and media managers to cope within the market conditions.

---

[1] Matić, "Servis građana ili servis vlasti," 156.

Nevertheless, significant media assistance efforts have not resulted in the development of the truly democratic media sector. According to the International Research & Exchanges Board (IREX) Media Sustainability Index 2015, Serbia has an unsustainable mixed media system.[2] Compared to previous years, there is a drastic drop in rankings in each of the categories, primarily due to economic and political downturn. Following the elections of March 2014, at which the leading Serbian Progressive Party won a majority of seats in the National Assembly, the media landscape in Serbia was affected "with an extension of control and censorship, including an increase in self-censorship, which pervades the media industry."[3]

Table 6.1. IREX Media Sustainability Indicators for Serbia, 2001–2015

Indicator	Year			
	2001	2005	2009	2015
Free Speech	1.72	2.39	2.21	1.94
Professional Journalism	1.43	1.75	1.89	1.50
Plurality of News Sources	2.21	2.71	2.64	1.79
Business Management	1.73	2.86	2.45	1.60
Supporting Institutions	2.21	2.79	2.58	2.17
Overall Score	1.86	2.39	2.06	1.80

Source: IREX, "Serbia," Media Sustainability Index for the years 2001, 2005, 2009, 2015.

EU progress reports on Serbia for recent years have indicated some progress in the sphere of media, but qualified it as slow and inadequate.[4] The report from 2014 emphasized limited capacities of the regulatory body for electronic media—the Republic Agency for Electronic Media—to apply the regulation. The report indicated that the agency's "independence as well as the transparency" must be ensured.[5]

---

[2] IREX, "Serbia" (2015).
[3] Ibid.
[4] European Commission, "Serbia 2012 Progress Report."
[5] European Commission, "Serbia [2014] Progress Report."

Given the importance of international support to the media reforms, this chapter attempts to shed some light on the underlying factors that led to unsatisfactory results when it comes to the development of democratic media system in Serbia. To that end, the chapter offers a general overview of media assistance efforts over the last two decades, accompanied with an in-depth analysis of the international assistance to some of the most prominent media institutions in the country: the Republic Agency for Electronic Media (RAEM), Radio-Television of Serbia (RTS) as the principal public service broadcaster, and the television and radio broadcaster B92. The chapter takes a systematic look at the nature of media assistance approaches in relation to the political and media system of the country, in order to understand the conditions for creation of sustainable media institutions through international aid.

Building from the theoretical framework outlined in the introduction to this volume, the chapter relies on the broad review of reports, papers, and other secondary sources on the media sector in Serbia. Additionally, it incorporates insights obtained through twelve interviews with media professionals, analysts, civil society representatives, and other relevant actors that were conducted during late 2012 and early 2013. The chapter initially provides an analysis of the link between the political context and the media, followed by an overview of media assistance to the Serbian media during last two decades. In order to obtain more thorough insights, three case studies are presented, addressing RAEM, RTS, and B92. The chapter concludes with a discussion of key findings and their implications for the contemporary development of media institutions in Serbia.

The Political and Media System

Taking into account its transitional path, socialistic legacy, cultural heritage, and political and economic development, Serbia could be classified as a "hybrid" regime.[6] It combines various characteristics of preceding regimes—socialistic while it was part of Yugoslavia, autocratic during the 1990s, democratic (at least in part) after 2000 when democratic institutions began to be introduced. As a consequence, Serbia seems to be somewhere in-between—it is no longer an autocracy, but neither is it a fully developed democracy.

---

[6] Voltmer, "How Far Can Media Systems Travel?," 240–241.

Serbia resembles what Almond and Verba in their *Civic Culture*
(1963) call the "subject political culture"[7] that is inherited from the
socialistic period and amplified through the rise of authoritarianism
under Milošević during late 1980s and early 1990s.[8] It is characterized
by a "hegemonic public sphere in which the ruling party's interpretation of the political situation prevails while oppositional views are marginalized and even delegitimized."[9] Consequently, the regime of Milošević
controlled the major part of the media space, spreading propaganda
and excluding oppositional voices.[10] This period was also characterized
by the adoption of undemocratic laws, an increased number of media
outlets within highly unregulated market, and the birth of an independent
media.[11]

Seeking to establish an alternative voice, foreign donors supported
the development of independent media during the Milošević era. In the
1990s, reflecting the increasing polarization in political realm, the Serbian
media scene was sharply divided into two camps: progovernmental and
counterregime. Independent media were among the most active in the
preparation of the October revolution in 2000 when Milošević was over-
thrown. Following the political changes in 2000, links between the government and the leading media in Serbia gradually weakened and the content
and the manner of reporting became more pluralized.

In practice, post-Milošević governments—declaratively of pro-Euro-
pean and democratic orientation—continue to misuse and exert control
over the media in a more subtle way. Notably, elected politicians have
obstructed necessary structural changes to the media system.[12] Although
most media laws in this period were adopted in order to meet precondi-

---

[7] A "subject political culture," as defined by Almond and Verba in their *Civic
Culture* (1963), can be detected when citizens are aware of the central govern-
ment and are heavily subjected to its decisions with little scope for dissent. See
Almond and Verba, *The Civic Culture*.

[8] Golubović, Kuzmanović, and Vasović, *Društveni karakter*.

[9] This is actually not only Voltmer's claim but can be traced back to Humphreys,
Mass Media and Media Policy, and Hallin and Mancini, *Comparing Media Sys-
tems*. In total we call this "systemic parallelism." See Voltmer, "How Far Can
Media Systems Travel?," 236.

[10] Thompson and Article 19, *Kovanje rata*; Reljić, "Killing Screens"; Kurspahić,
Zločin u 19:30.

[11] Veljanovski, *Medijski sistem Srbije*, 24.

[12] The most important laws adopted in this period were the "Zakon o radiodifuziji," "Zakon o javnom informisanju," "Zakon o slobodnom pristupu informacijama od javnog značaja," and "Zakon o oglašavanju."

tions for membership in the Council of Europe and the EU, they have been drafted and subsequently implemented in a way that neglects professionalism and favors political loyalty.

Financial constraints create additional incentives for the media to seek powerful patrons and limit the space for independent journalism. Namely, the Serbian media market is too small to be able to meet the needs of all the media: there are 744 print outlets, 344 radio stations, 116 televisions, and 277 Internet news portals.[13] Following the global financial crisis, advertising revenues dropped by 22% in 2009, putting further pressure on what was already a relatively poor market. The advertising revenues in recent years were somewhere between €155–175 million. Out of that, 54% goes to TV, 21% to print, 11% to outdoor advertising, 9% to Internet, and 5% to radio.[14] Overall, such a situation leaves little maneuvering space for running a sustainable and independent media operation, let alone producing quality reporting.[15]

Table 6.2. Media Revenues, 2001–2013

Year	Revenues	Year	Revenues	Year	Revenues
2001	30[16]	2006	115	2011	175
2002	50	2007	175	2012	172
2003	65	2008	206	2013	155
2004	80	2009	161		
2005	95	2010	175		

Sources: IREX, "Serbia," *Media Sustainability Index* for 2001 through 2013; AGB Nielsen (in million Euro).

Dire financial circumstances make the media vulnerable and easy to manipulate by the state as well as political and business interest groups. Based on the analysis from 2010, approximately one-quarter of media income comes from state institutions[17] and there is no reason to believe that situation is much different today although exact data are not available. The state exercises its influence through funds that local-level governments regularly spend on media as well as through contracts for the

---

[13] IREX, "Serbia" (2015), 116.
[14] Nielsen Srbija.
[15] See, for example, the chapter by Ršumović in this volume.
[16] This amount is in US $.
[17] Anti-Corruption Council, "Report on Pressures," 3–4.

provision of specialized services between government institutions and media outlets (such as, for example, organizing different events like public debates and conferences, conducting research, etc.). In recent years the questionable practice of "allocating state-owned company advertising to individual media outlets along clientelistic lines"[18] continued. As a consequence, the media that are financed in this way are likely to provide a positive coverage of the incumbent politicians and parties[19] and disadvantage opposition voices.

The Serbian media system largely confirms the findings of previous studies of transition countries in Central and Eastern Europe[20] and the contemporary literature on media systems in non-Western countries.[21] It is characterized by a high level of state politicization, political parallelism, and weak professionalization of journalism. When analyzing Serbia against the parameters of Hallin and Mancini's concept of media systems, it meets most of the characteristics of the polarized-pluralist model[22] with particularly strong hegemonic role of the state over nonstate actors and, the increased role of political parties (developed into a "partitocracy").

Besides external pluralism, what characterizes journalism practices in Serbia are commentary-oriented journalism, the lack of professional standards in reporting, relatively biased reporting and reliance on unilateral sources.[23] The trend of tabloidization represents a new means for various groups to spread and promote their particular interests. Short-lived tabloids are regularly used in campaigns against individual persons, companies and organizations. One media researcher and analyst observes that "their editorial policies are characterized by conservatism, nationalistic ideology, hate speech, and disregard of professional and ethical norms."[24]

---

[18] Zielonka and Mancini, "Executive Summary," 5.

[19] Interview with Dr. Jovanka Matić, media researcher and analyst, Institute for Social Sciences Belgrade, January 25, 2013.

[20] Zielonka and Mancini, "Executive Summary"; Voltmer, "How Far Can Media Systems Travel?"; Voltmer, The Media in Transitional Democracies.

[21] Hallin and Mancini eds., Comparing Media Systems beyond the Western World.

[22] Hallin and Mancini, Comparing Media Systems, 46–65.

[23] Interview with Dr. Jovanka Matić, media researcher and analyst, Institute for Social Sciences Belgrade, January 25, 2013.

[24] Ibid.

Democratization and Media Assistance

Media assistance in Serbia started in early 1990s and can be divided into five phases in terms of the overall approach and objectives. Each phase is outlined in table 6.3 and further elaborated in the subsequent text.

The first phase covers the period of severely restricted access to international aid, from the 1990s until 1995. Due to international isolation and sanctions, the access of international donors to Serbian media was limited. Direct involvement of Western governments was not welcomed by Milošević's regime. The help given to local media outlets was categorized

Table 6.3. Media Assistance in Serbia: Phases and Main Characteristics

Phase	Main Characteristics/ Contextual	Media Assistance	
		Main Characteristics	Main Actors
Severely Restricted Access (1990–1995)	• Strong and authoritarian rule of the Milošević regime • Restricted access for donors • Independent media in "survival mode"	• Directed mostly to individual media outlets (through trainings and technical support) • No focus on broader policy issues • No coordination • The help to local media was classified as humanitarian assistance	• Open Society Fund (OSF) • EU (through the International Federation of Journalists) • US government (through International Media Fund) • Swedish Helsinki Committee (SHC)
Post-Dayton Phase (1995–1998)	• End of the war in BiH and Croatia (1995) • Opposition won elections in local communities all across Serbia (1996) • Proactive role of independent media	• Liberalized access of donors to independent media • Politically driven support (independent media as a means of political change) • Coordination among donors • Creation of ANEM as a joint platform for local media	• OSF • USAID • IREX • EU (through SHC) • British embassy

Phase	Main Characteristics/ Contextual	Media Assistance	
		Main Characteristics	Main Actors
Kosovo Crisis and a New Repression (1998–1999)	• Armed conflict in Kosovo (1998, 1999) • NATO bombing over Serbia (1999) • Independent media became stronger and more influential • Adoption of the "draconian" Public Information Law	• US officials were not allowed to work in Serbia • Politically driven support (independent media as a means of political change) • Strong and institutionalized coordination among donors	• US-based donors (including US embassy, USAID, IREX, OSF) • The Swedish Helsinki Committee • Norwegian People's Aid • EU
Democratic Changes and Building Enabling Environment (2000–2008)	• Democratic changes on October 5, 2000; overthrow of Milošević • Adoption of new laws and regulations in the domain of the media • Setting the EU enlargement agenda as the main goal • Clash between government and independent media over their mission	• International donors flooded Serbia with money • Policy-oriented assistance (building an enabling environment) • Focus on contextual changes; legislative reform, institution building, and trainings in the field of media management and marketing	• This period brought a new shift in donor strategies: • US-based donors were moving to other regions • USAID, IREX, and NED remained • The EU (through EAR, CARDS, IPA, Stability Pact, and EIDHR)
Economic Crisis, and "Partitocracy" (2008–present)	• Economic crisis • Decline in market revenues in 2009 • New forms of dependence on state money • No more substantial support from the donors • Adoption of media strategy	• International donors decreased their investment and provided support for project-based initiatives (for example, EU promotional projects) • There is no strategically oriented and direct financial support for media development	• The EU (through EAR, CARDS, IPA, Stability Pact, and EIDHR) • USAID, IREX, NED • Civil Rights Defenders • KAS Media Program

as humanitarian assistance.[25] The Open Society Fund, the EU (through the International Federation of Journalists), the US government (through the International Media Fund), and the Swedish Helsinki Committee (SHC), were the main donors. External support was directed mostly to individual media outlets while there was no focus on broader policy issues. In terms of strategy, media assistance in this phase was characterized by high levels of external funding dependence, nonsystemic support to particular media outlets and organizations (such as the TV station Studio B, Radio B92, the magazine *Vreme*, the daily newspaper *Danas*, the Independent Association of Journalists of Serbia (NUNS), and the Media Center Belgrade). It was externally designed and developed, and it was of a rather disruptive character in respect to the local context due to the lack of an enabling environment.[26]

The second phase relates to the period after the Dayton Peace Agreement in Bosnia and Herzegovina that was signed in late 1995 (Serbia being one of the signatories) until 1998. This period is characterized by a gradual opening of Serbia to international donors although the regime continued to use repression and authoritarian means to influence the media.[27] Following the political changes at the local level in 1996/1997,[28] local media in some of the larger cities and towns were liberalized from direct political influence and repression. This was the period when the independent stations Radio B92 and Radio Index gained over a million weekly listeners each.[29] In June 1997, the ANEM[30] (Association of Inde-

---

[25] Price, Davis Noll, and De Luce, "Mapping Media Assistance," 1.

[26] Ibid., 57.

[27] In the form of a ban (in December 1996, the Serbian Government shut down Radio Boom 93 in Požarevac) or a takeover (in 1996, the regime installed new management in the independent RTV Studio B in Belgrade).

[28] Antiregime protests in Serbia took place during the winter of 1996–1997, when the oppositional coalition Zajedno (Together) and students reacted to the electoral fraud after local elections held in 1996. Protests lasted until February 1997 when Milošević signed the "lex specialis" that confirmed the victory of the opposition in several Serbian cities and enabled them to establish local governments. See Balkan Peace Team, "Protests in Belgrade and throughout Yugoslavia—1996/1997."

[29] BeoMedia, "Radio Listening Report."

[30] ANEM was founded in 1993 and its initial goal was to unite existing isolated media as the first step toward breaking the state-controlled media monopoly. In 1997, ANEM was formally registered by its founders (Radio B92, Radio Boom, and Radio Cetinje). Source: Saša Mirković, (former) ANEM president, email message to author, April 18, 2013.

pendent Electronic Media) launched a network consisting of nineteen affiliate independent local radio and TV stations. The network grew rapidly to more than a hundred radio and TV stations by 2000. This network, supported by various donors, developed into a useful platform that empowered local media. In this period, the activities of international actors became more focused, coherent, coordinated, and strategically oriented, aiming to influence political changes in Serbia. Besides direct financing, technical support and training, international actors offered their assistance in awareness rising.[31] The most active in media assistance programs were OSF, EU (through Swedish Helsinki Committee) and USAID. This was the period when donors started to coordinate their activities regarding the assistance to media sector.[32]

From February 1998 until June 1999 the armed conflict over Kosovo[33] took place, introducing the third phase in the development of the media sector in Serbia. In 1998, the regime attempted to impose strict control over the media with a draconian Public Information Law[34] that gave Serbian authorities a legal basis to control and interfere with the work of media outlets in the country. The US officials were not allowed to work in Serbia, and US-based donors continued to support independent media from the outside.

After the "October revolution" in 2000 that brought about the fall of Milošević's regime and rapid liberalization of the country, as Presnall observes, the "international donors virtually flooded Serbia with money to seize a perceived window of opportunity to boost efforts at democratization of the new order."[35] In this fourth phase, the media assistance was focused on building an enabling environment for the media, with donor activities becoming more policy oriented, focusing on legislative reform, institution building, and training in the field of media management. The focus shifted from supporting the "survival mode" of operation toward creation of the conditions for sustainability of an independent and profes-

---

[31] McClear, McClear, and Graves, "US Media Assistance Programs in Serbia," 11.

[32] For example, in 1998, Open Society together with USAID and the EU organized a donor conference, pledging $2.5 million each to support ANEM.

[33] For more on the Kosovo conflict see Bacevich and Cohen, *War over Kosovo*; Malcolm, *Kosovo*; Nigel, *The Yugoslav Wars (2)*.

[34] This law, usually labeled as "Vučić's law," was enacted when the current first deputy prime minister in the Serbian government, Aleksandar Vučić (in office from July 2012), served as minister for information (1998–2000) in the Milošević regime.

[35] Presnall, "Which Way the Wind Blows," 662.

sional media sector. External actors provided substantial assistance to that end: significant financial assistance was given to RTS, B92, and ANEM. For example, the BBC provided an extensive training program for RTS staff and numerous other training and educational activities have been offered by various donors; expertise and consultancy for policy reforms was also provided, where a prominent role was played by the Council of Europe (CoE) and the Organization for Security and Co-operation in Europe (OSCE). US organizations that work with media paid less attention to Serbia after the 2001 terrorist attacks on 9/11, following the shift in US international policy toward the Middle East. The leading role in the democratization and further development of Serbia was taken by the EU through the Stability Pact (2002–2006),[36] the CARDS assistance program (European Agency for Reconstruction, 2001–2008[37]), and IPA funds (from 2006). Examples of systemic approaches could be found in direct support to the transformation of public media, the establishment of TV B92 (which will be dealt with in more detail below), and efforts to empower local actors to survive new market conditions.

As stated earlier, the economic crisis of 2008 caused the Serbian media market to experience a drastic decline in advertising revenues, triggering the start of the fifth phase of media development in the country. The government, state agencies, and public companies became the most important advertisers. Buying influence by providing financial support was conducted in the form of subscriptions, campaigns, and advertising paid for by public institutions and companies under political control as well as engaging media outlets to provide research services.[38]

At the same time, international donors decreased their investment and provided support on a project basis rather then through longer-term support initiatives. This was the case, among others, with the OSF, the National Endowment for Democracy (NED), Civil Rights Defenders, the French government, and the Konrad Adenauer Stiftung (KAS) Media Program. With the exception of the EU there was no strategically oriented financial support for media development. Support was primarily aimed at assisting Serbia to adjust the current laws and improve their practice, and to adopt new strategic documents with regard to media development and digitalization, such as the 2011 Media strategy[39] adopted by the Min-

---

[36] Media Task Force, "Stability Pact."
[37] EAR, "Serbia."
[38] Anti-Corruption Council, "Report on Pressures."
[39] OSCE Mission to Serbia, "Draft Strategy."

istry for Culture. Leading media associations, gathered around the Media Coalition, took an active part in preparing and drafting the text of the strategy. The entire process was an externally supported initiative by IREX ProMedia and the EU.

An Overview of Media Assistance Funding

There is no precise data on the amount of funds directed to the Serbian media. As Rhodes estimates in his 2007 study, from the overall amount of €269.2 million of recorded support for the media in Western Balkans between 1996 and 2006, Serbia received €44.9 million (or 17%). Rhodes breaks down the distribution of this sum, as €26.4 million (58%) for direct support to media outlets, €13.1 million (or 29%) for the media environment and the remaining €5.4 million for training.[40] If all recorded and estimated support to Serbian media from 1991 to 2012 is taken into account, one can assume that roughly more than €100 million was spent on media development.[41]

From 1990 to 1995, USAID donated $600,000 to a few media outlets. This support was directed to the International Media Fund to provide equipment to Studio B, the magazine *Vreme*, Vin (an independent production), the newspaper *Borba*, the television and radio broadcaster B92, Media Centre, and some regional media.[42] The US intensified its support for the media during the period from 1997 to 2002, and its projects were mainly implemented by the National Endowment for Democracy (NED), the National Democratic Institute (NDI) and the International Republican Institute (IRI). NED became an increasingly important actor from 2005 to 2011, supporting various project-based media initiatives in Serbia with around $2 million.[43] Instead of the Media Fund, IREX

---

[40] Rhodes, "Ten Years of Media Support," 15.

[41] This is an estimated amount based on an analysis of available and published data; for example, USAID published that they spent around $38 million from 1997–2012; the OSF supported Serbian media with $28,5 million in the 1990s; the EU supported media with €1.7 million in the 1990s and with more than €20 million from 2000 to 2012, plus €8 million planned for digitalization. Additional support was provided by NED (around $2 million between 2006 and 2012), and other donors such as Norwegian People's Aid, the Balkan Trust for Democracy, Konrad Adenauer and its media program, Friedrich Ebert Stiftung, etc.

[42] Ibid., 5.

[43] *National Endowment for Democracy*, "Annual Reports 1984–2004."

was the main contractor through which USAID invested more than $38 million between 1997 and 2012.[44]

The EU- and US-based donors matched their efforts in 1999 and directed aid to the independent media. As part of this coordinated effort IREX provided "survival grants" to media outlets. The US spent $1 million through thirteen emergency grants, and the EU spent €1 million on media support.[45]

OSF Serbia substantially increased its democracy-promotion funding assistance in 1999–2000, from roughly $3.9 million to $4.45 million. In 1999 its priority in Serbia was the mass media, to which it donated $1.34 million.[46]

While US-based donors were crucial during the 1990s, after 2000 the EU funding for media development exceeded US sources of grants and donations. In the period from 1993 to 1998, the EU supported media projects in Serbia with €1.7 million, and this aid was administered by the IFJ.[47] After 2000, the EU support to the Serbian media amounted to around €20 million through the CARDS assistance program. Its main focus was to advance journalism training, development of quality media production, investigative reporting skills and enforcement of media legislation, but most of this money was spent on its own promotion. Since 2001 various contractors such as the Swedish Helsinki Committee, Press Now, and the Media Center Belgrade implemented media assistance programs funded by the EU. Most of this money has been administered through the European Agency for Reconstruction (EAR) that invested, based on available data, €18.5 million from 2000 to 2007. Half of this amount (€9.64 million) has been spent on technical and logistical support, mainly to RTS.[48]

Other areas of EU support include the 2007 IPA Multi-beneficiary Media Program (focused on production) and €3.3 million aimed at enhancing public participation in debate and raising awareness in Serbia on European Integration. In 2009, the Delegation of the European Commission to Serbia launched the European Integration Media Fund project through the IPA 2008 instrument, with the total value of €3 million. The goal of the project was to boost the capacity of local, regional and

---

[44] IREX, "Serbia: Building Independent Media—Documentary."
[45] McClear, McClear, and Graves, "US Media Assistance Programs in Serbia," 8.
[46] Presnall, "Which Way the Wind Blows," 667–668.
[47] Ibid., 664.
[48] See EAR, "Contract List."

national media for reporting about all aspects of the European integration process.[49]

★ ★ ★

In the following sections the three case studies are analyzed with the aim of offering deeper understanding of the relevance of the media assistance approaches to the development of sustainable media institutions in a transitional context of contemporary Serbia. The cases analyzed are the Regulatory Agency for Electronic Media (RAEM), Radio-Television of Serbia, and the private TV station B92. All of the three institutions have significantly benefited from international aid, albeit in different forms and at a different scale. What the results of the assistance offered are in terms of functioning and sustainability of these institutions will be discussed in the following sections.

The Regulatory Authority for Electronic Media (RAEM)

Mandated in the 2002 Broadcasting Act, the Regulatory Broadcasting Agency (RBA) was established in 2003. Following the Law on Electronic Media from 2014, RBA was renamed as the Regulatory Authority for Electronic Media (RAEM) and was provided with a broader jurisdictional domain, including spectrum management, licensing, and implementing broadcasting laws and regulations.[50]

Prior to the establishment of the regulator, the state tolerated a great number of media outlets operating without licenses.[51] This resulted in an oversaturated and unsustainable broadcasting sector. In the absence of a developed media market, media were highly dependent on the state and donors. According to the 2002 Broadcasting Act, RBA was responsible for "determining which of the estimated 1,200 broadcast outlets that jam Serbia's radio and television dials would survive."[52]

---

[49] The complete list of grantees is available online. See "Rezultati konkursa."
[50] Irion, K., Ledger, M., Svensson, S. and Rsumovic, N., 2017. *The Independence and Functioning of the Regulatory Authority for Electronic Media in Serbia.* Study commissioned by the Council of Europe, Amsterdam/Brussels/Budapest/Belgrade, August, 2017.
[51] Veljanovski, *Medijski sistem Srbije,* 66–67.
[52] IREX, "Serbia" (2003), 91.

BACKGROUND

RAEM is not a converged regulator: it is responsible for audio-visual content matters, frequencies, license allocations and monitoring of broadcasters' activities. Responsibility for issuing licenses is shared with the Regulatory Agency for Electronic Communications and Postal Services (RATEL), the regulator in the field of telecoms. RAEM has a range of powers and sanctions at its disposal, from reprimands, warnings, the power to impose fines, the publication of decisions in the official journal, and suspension and revocation of licenses.

The highest decision-making organ of the regulator is the Council, which has the power to make decisions on all regulatory matters within its area of responsibility. The regulator has adopted documents regulating its internal relations and functioning and it is subject to annual financial auditing in regard to its spending. However, so far this audit has never been performed by the state, but it was carried out by private agencies in 2007 and 2008.[53]

POLITICAL SALIENCY OF THE REGULATOR

According to the Anti-Corruption Council, the regulator is greatly responsible for the present situation in the media sector in Serbia, which is characterized by combined economic and political pressures, a large number of media outlets, and unreliable public service broadcasting.[54] Namely, since its formation, this body has failed to establish itself as an institution of authority and credibility,[55] starting from the first appointment of the members of the RBA Council in 2003, considered to be a result of a deal among ruling parties rather than adherence to the procedures and criteria prescribed by the law.[56]

Continuous revisions of the provisions on election and composition of the RBA Council (in 2004, 2005, 2006, and 2009) progressively increased the possibility of political influence. The most contentious issue in regard to the state pressures on the independence of RBA has been linked to how the members of its Council are to be elected. The initial

---

[53] Hans Bredow Institute for Media Research et al., *INDIREG*, 186
[54] Anti-Corruption Council, "Report on Pressures," 37–38.
[55] Ibid., 37.
[56] Interview with Ljiljana Breberina i Sanja Stanković, OSCE Media Department, Serbia, February 12, 2013.

Table 6.4. RBA Annual Budget, 2007–2014

Year	Annual Budget (approx.)	Overall Revenues Transferred to the State Budget
2014	3.69	0.513 (13.9%)
2013	3.3	0.57 (17.4%)
2012	3.69	1.14 (30.8%)
2011	3.84	0.5 (13%)
2010	3.98	0,78 (19,.5%)
2009	4.78	1.46 (30.4%)
2008	4.65	2.67 (57%)
2007	5.79	2.984 (51%)

Note: All figures in million EUR.
Source: Republička agencija za elektronske medije, *Izvještaji o radu*, (http://www.rem.org.rs/).

draft of the Broadcast Act proposed that the Council should consist of fifteen members, of which twelve would be nominated by civil society organizations. This number was reduced to nine, with only four to be nominated by civil society actors. This was a unilateral decision made by the government without a public debate. Amendments to the Broadcasting Act in 2005 stipulated three different lengths of term for Council members on the basis of a political decision instead of by drawing lots. In accordance with this change, the longest service (six years) was awarded to the Council members nominated by the parliament, while the shortest term was reserved for the nominees of the civil society organizations.[57] According to the amendments in 2009, the Committee for Culture and Information of the parliament is authorized to make a preselection of the candidates (which are nominated by civil society, professional associations, media, artists, etc.). This enables political parties to eliminate undesirable candidates for the regulator's Council.

Initial finances for the regulator's work were provided by the Serbian government, but from 2007, the agency has received income only from broadcasting fees in line with the Broadcasting Act (Article 66). The same act defines that the agency should transfer all extra incomes to the state

---

[57] Ibid.

budget (Article 34), which is then earmarked in equal parts for improving and developing culture, healthcare, education and social security.[58]

Assessment in the Light of International Assistance

European actors played the main role in setting the ground for establishing a functional regulatory body. In a strategic sense, their approach was intensive, coordinated (EU, OSCE, CoE), and of a short-term nature. At the beginning of the 2000s, the Serbian democratic government accepted the creation of the agency as a part of its "homework"—pursuing media transformation in line with European standards, the creation of independent, autonomous, and transparent[59] regulatory body was considered as crucial.[60] The creation of RBA was both a necessary step in the process of regulating the local media scene and a condition in the EU preaccession procedure,[61] meaning that EU conditionality played the crucial role in facilitating the establishment of the regulatory agency.

The external assistance for RBA's establishment was desirable due to the lack of experience in regulating broadcasting media. However, the initial role of international actors in the creation of RBA was more consultative and logistical. Experts from the CoE and the OSCE assisted local working groups in drafting the first edition of the Public Broadcasting Act of 2002, while regulatory bodies of various European states were used as models to create one that would fit the Serbian conditions.[62] The actual working group relied primarily on the efforts of the local experts, who transposed the best practices and principles of the European tradition into the Serbian context.

---

[58] Republic Agency for Electronic Media: http://www.rem.org.rs/. Accessed on October 16, 2015.

[59] IREX, "Federal Republic of Yugoslavia" (2001), 206–207.

[60] Indicators for Media in a Democracy, 8.15: "Regulatory authorities for the broadcasting media must function in an unbiased and effective manner, for instance when granting licenses. Print media and Internet-based media should not be required to hold a state license which goes beyond a mere business or tax registration" (Council of Europe, "Resolution 1636 (2008)"). Also see Council of Europe, "Recommendation 1848."

[61] European Union, "The Future of European Regulatory Audiovisual Policy."

[62] Interview with Mirjana Milošević, Head of Media Development, WAN, February 14, 2013.

As a candidate for EU membership, Serbia and its regulatory bodies are part of permanent, yet not very thorough monitoring. The monitoring only provides general requirements or recommendations.[63] As an illustration, the 2010 report states that "concerning administrative capacity, both the Regulatory Agency and the related ministry need to be strengthened." A year before, the Report highlighted the inadequate institutional and regulatory capacity that "needs further progress." Additionally, "the Regulatory Agency is in operation and financially autonomous, but its independence needs to be strengthened and it lacks sufficient expertise to regulate a liberalized market."[64] When it comes to local organizations, ANEM is implementing its legal monitoring of the Serbian media scene, which is a continuous effort to monitor and evaluate different aspects of the development of the Serbian media scene, including regulatory bodies and their independence. This project was initially supported by USAID and IREX Serbia, while now it is supported by the Open Society Fund, the Norwegian embassy, and the Dutch embassy.[65] Overall, although monitoring mechanisms do exist, their effects on actual practices are rather limited.

All in all, the most important achievement of media assistance was the establishment of RBA. Introducing the regime of licenses and the permanent monitoring of media with national coverage resulted in a certain order on the broadcasting sector. However, due to the untransparent and politicized elections for the RBA Council in May 2003, a number of international organizations discontinued their support for the further development of RBA.[66] Most of the international organizations, such as the OSCE, the CoE and the EU, expressed serious concern regarding the procedure for awarding licenses, which was assessed as biased, without appropriate application of the rules and criteria. The EU specifically indicated the lack of transparency in the process of decision-making by RBA[67] and the same concerns remain relevant today, in regard to the operations of RAEM.

---

[63] European Commission, "Serbia 2012 Progress Report."
[64] Ibid.
[65] More on the project is available on ANEM's website: http://www.anem.rs/en/aktivnostiAnema/monitoring.html. Accessed on March 20, 2013.
[66] IREX, "Serbia" (2003).
[67] Anti-Corruption Council, "Report on Pressures," 40

Radio Television of Serbia

Radio Television of Serbia (RTS) is the public service broadcaster in Serbia. It broadcasts five TV and four radio programs and it currently employs around 3,300 people.[68]

BACKGROUND AND CREATION OF RTS

RTS was created in 1992, when, under the Law on Radio-Television (1991), RTV Belgrade, RTV Novi Sad and RTV Priština[69] were merged. During the 1990s RTS played an instrumental role in supporting the Milošević regime. Until the end of the 1990s, RTS—often labeled as "TV Bastilla"—was used for political and war propaganda. In 1999, when the Kosovo crisis took place, NATO defined the broadcaster's headquarters as a legitimate target. In what is considered by many to be a violation of the Geneva Conventions, the main RTS building was bombed on April 23, 1999, resulting in the death of sixteen employees and estimated damages of around €530 million.[70]

The process of transforming the state radio-television service into a public broadcasting service started in 2000, when the building of an enabling environment took place. However, the actual transformation of RTS was delayed until 2006 when its management board was appointed. It was a big task for the new RTS management, as it had lost its reputation during the 1990s, its premises were severely damaged, and much of its audience was lost to other media outlets.

THE POLITICAL SALIENCY OF RTS'S OPERATION

The principal organ of RTS is its steering board. Board members can be appointed and dismissed by the regulator under conditions prescribed by the 2014 Law on Public Media Services. Steering board members' mandates last five years and the same person may be appointed for two con-

---

[68] N1, "Bujošević."
[69] RTV Novi Sad and RTV Priština were launched in 1975 and named after the capital of the Autonomous Province of Vojvodina and Kosovo and Metohija, as equal members of the public broadcasting system Yugoslav Radio Television (JRT).
[70] Andersen, "Serbia after Milošević."

secutive terms. The general manager serves a four-year term, which can be renewed once.

Formal arrangements, important for securing RTS's independence in terms of decision-making and finances, were set up in the 2014 law. RTS's decision-making structure is protected on two levels. The general manager is appointed among qualifying applicants in a public competition by the RTS steering board, which again is formally protected from political influence. Responsibility for the appointment of other managers is shared between the general manager (proposals) and the board (appointments).

While 2002 Broadcasting Act stipulated financial independence from the state, prescribing revenues from license fees and commercial advertising, the 2014 law abolished the license fee, replacing it with the budgetary funding as a temporary solution until the beginning of 2016, when an obligatory tax will be introduced. In line with international principles,[71] Serbian legislation underlines the editorial independence and the duty of PSB to ensure that the programs, particularly the news, are protected from any influence that may be exerted by authorities, political organizations or economic centers of power.

Despite formal changes, the operation of RTS from its establishment until 2013 was not transparent. Mechanisms for the public responsibility of RTS were missing and it often seemed to be a one-man operation, led by its omnipotent general manager. The Anti-Corruption Council issued a report identifying the problems with RTS as highly significant, pointing out that the broadcaster puts the interests of political parties and ruling elites before the public interest.[72]

Reporting, as a mechanism of public and transparent control, has not being sufficiently developed and respected by RTS officials. In many occasions, RTS management refused to comply with the Law on Free Access to Information of Public Importance and enable the public to see how public funds are spent. According to the Anti-Corruption Council report, this "puts into doubt its [RTS's] ability to fulfill the most important tasks of this public service, one of which is the fight against corruption."[73]

The financial stability of RTS has not been ensured so far. License fee collection for RTS has not been successful. Due to the dramatic economic situation as well as many other reasons (including politically motivated

---

[71] Council of Europe, "Recommendation CM/Rec (2012) 1."
[72] Anti-Corruption Council, "Report on Pressures," 3.
[73] Ibid., 37.

obstructions), the collection rate dropped considerably—in 2011 it was between 35% and 40%. This led to the abolishment of the RTS license fee in 2014, in spite of the fact that organizations such as the OSCE and the EU opposed any permanent solution in which RTS would receive its funding directly from the state budget. Turning to the state as a source of funding could and did make public service broadcasting exposed and vulnerable to political pressure.

The programming schedule of RTS differs only a little from other commercial broadcasters. RTS1 competes with commercial stations for better ratings by providing a considerable number of entertainment programs. In 2009, research on the program diversity of the leading six TV stations in Serbia indicated that the second channel of RTS, showing the highest level of genre diversity, is much more devoted to fulfilling the role of public broadcaster. Results also indicated a high degree of similarity between the programs of RTS 1 and B92.[74]

ASSESSMENT IN THE LIGHT OF INTERNATIONAL MEDIA ASSISTANCE

It is against this political backdrop that one can best understand the nature and effects of the international assistance provided to RTS. Technically devastated, with a bad professional reputation, overstaffed, and with no development strategy, at the beginning of the 2000s RTS needed a shock to the system. According to the Broadcasting Act, it was supposed to be transformed into a public service broadcasting organization by February 1, 2003. While the state was passive at the beginning, international actors invested much more effort to foster this process.

Significant leverage for international donors and development agencies came from the conditionality mechanisms related to the EU accession process, which included the transformation of RTS into a public service broadcaster.[75] Eventually, Serbia signed the Stabilization and Association Agreement (SAA) in 2008[76] and was finally granted EU candidate status in 2012.

---

[74] Matić, "Raznovrsnost."

[75] In order "to secure provision of accurate information to the public by publicly funded broadcasters, the EU assisted the restructuring of state-run Radio-Television Serbia into a public service broadcaster." See EAR, "Serbia: Civil Society."

[76] European Commission, "Stabilization and Association Agreement."

Within such a framework, the international assistance to reform RTS was important for many reasons: Experts appointed by international organizations played a key role in drafting the legal framework and helping in the implementation of proposed reforms. For example, consultants from the EU, the CoE, and the OSCE assisted local ministries and working groups when drafting new media laws to meet international and European standards.[77] Moreover, since its establishment in Serbia in 2001, the OSCE Mission has been acting as an implementing agent of the project assisting the transformation of RTS into a public service broadcaster. A year later, an OSCE office was opened inside the RTS premises and the organization concentrated heavily on RTS in its political lobbying and financial requests.[78]

In addition, grants from the EU, through various programs (CARDS, IPA), have been used for improving overall organizational capacity of RTS, through purchasing modern equipment and provision of training to its staff. Hence, from 2001 to 2008, the European Agency for Reconstruction (EAR) supported RTS with €3.5 million in technical assistance. The support included, for example, an external audit of RTS (€495,960) in 2001–2002, acquisition of production equipment (€1.1 million) in 2003, and around €2 million for equipment and technical assistance in 2004.

In order to implement the named programs, the EU cooperated with a number of international agencies and organizations involved in media development, such as the BBC World Service Trust, IREX ProMedia, the CoE and the OSCE. Consequently, implementing assistance programs in cooperation with a number of international organizations required a fair degree of coordination of media assistance activities.

For example, in 2007 a technical assistance program was implemented through the BBC World Service Trust, providing an extensive training program for RTS employees. Its aim was to assist the transition of RTS through consulting on financial management, sales and marketing strategies, as well as professional development opportunities for journalists. As a project partner, IREX Europe was responsible for organizing training in several areas, including financial management, on-air branding and promotions, program scheduling, and audience research. More than 730 trainees participated in the thirty-month lifespan of the project,

---

[77] Interview with Ljiljana Breberina i Sanja Stanković, OSCE Mission to Serbia, February 12, 2013.
[78] OSCE Mission to Serbia, "OSCE Opens Office."

including more than a hundred journalists across TV and radio and more than a hundred production and technical staff.[79] Nevertheless, the results of the training provided are questionable: While some RTS staff argue that the training by the BBC World Service Trust resulted in improved journalistic skills and better programs,[80] others claim that the training was not applicable due to specific circumstances and the institutional nature of RTS.[81]

However, as we seen from the previous section, the results of the assistance efforts have been rather mixed. Although the relevant legal framework has been introduced at a formal level, and RTS entered a new phase of its development, trying to adjust to the standards associated with the new role of the public service broadcaster thrusted upon it, in many instances the intended objectives of the transformation of the broadcaster have not been achieved: it is financially dependent on the revenues from the budget and the new tax introduced in 2016, with dubious political links to the government, a shrinking audience, and rapid commercialization of its content. At the same time, it is characterized by the lack of adherence to the legal provisions when it comes to operative and financial transparency and a limited level of accountability of its management to the citizens.

B92: A Private Broadcaster

B92 is a private television broadcaster and a former radio broadcaster with national coverage in Serbia. It is important to distinguish the role and support provided for Radio B92[82] during the 1990s, and for TV B92, which was established in 2000 as a part of the same company. During the 1990s Radio B92 was a symbol of resistance against Milošević's regime. It managed to remain independent from political influence, including by the opposition. As one of the founders of B92 recalls: "I remember when the oppositional leader, Zoran Đinđić, proposed that donations should be channeled through them. We resisted this idea of being exclusively opposi-

---

[79] Knežević, "Uloga programa obuke BBC-ja."
[80] Ibid., 123–142.
[81] Ibid., 135.
[82] As result of the privatization process, Radio B92 stopped broadcasting its programming in July 2015 and fired its journalists, later renaming itself Play Radio. See Balkan Insight, "Belgrade's Radio B92 Axes Most Remaining Staff."

tional media. We stood strongly for the profession, trying to be as objective as was possible in those times."[83]

In the 1990s Radio B92 existed thanks to international assistance programs and projects. During this period various donors supported its survival, considering Radio B92 as the pioneer of independent and professional journalism in Serbia. The Milošević regime tried to suppress its work on a number of occasions: the station was closed several times and the accusation of being "foreign mercenaries" has often been invoked to discredit the work of B92.[84]

The idea for the establishment of TV B92 came from the management of Radio B92. The goal was to establish a TV station that would perform a public role similar to Channel 4 in the UK.[85] In domain of informative program, B92 introduced new professional standards, especially when it comes to production of their own informative program. However, the international assistance was fundamental for the establishment of TV B92, including technical and financial assistance provided by USAID and the EU.

Nevertheless, from the very beginning TV B92 found itself in an unfair position compared to other TV stations. For example, RTS was privileged to be financed both through public money and commercial activities while a commercial competitor, TV Pink, had the advantage of an early start.[86] Moreover, both of these TV stations already had developed technical infrastructure. The situation was further complicated as a result of legal uncertainty because the Broadcasting Act had not yet been adopted and broadcasting licenses were not issued.

---

[83] Interview with Saša Mirković, President of the Trust of B92 Ltd. and President of ANEM, February 6, 2013.

[84] In December 2012, the right-wing movement SNP NAŠI called on the competent authorities to revoke the national frequency of TV B92, accusing them of "demonizing their own people in the last twenty years through crafty media manipulation and portraying Serbs as a genocidal and criminal nation, responsible for the wars of the 1990s, for which there is plenty of evidence to back such claims and that is why the general public considers these media as stooges of international power players." See SNP NAŠI, "Tražimo gašenje antisrpskih medija."

[85] Matic, "Media Cannot Survive on Donations Alone."

[86] Since its creation in 1994 TV Pink was oriented toward entertainment programs. The close relationship between TV Pink's owner with the Milošević regime was key to the success of TV Pink. After the political changes in 2000, it established good relations with the newly elected government and this lead his media to survive. See Luković, "Nemam problema sa svojom prošlošti."

Therefore, external assistance was particularly important to support the creation of an environment in which the new channel could operate. Above all, that required an adequate legal framework and a regulatory regime for the management of broadcasting licenses.

With the USAID support through IREX, B92 built a new broadcast center, and through training and consultancy improved its professionalism. While Radio B92 remained the top-rated station in Belgrade two years after the fall of Milošević, TV B92 has not become profitable, even though its audience has increased significantly, and the television station increased its revenue dramatically in the first quarter of 2002.[87] In the terms of infrastructure, in 2003 IREX supported the construction and renovation of B92's premises with $1.2 million. This provided B92 with a new television and radio studio complex, along with a modern newsroom and office space.[88]

In addition, European-based organizations also provided assistance to B92. In 2003, €1.96 million grant was provided by EAR for education and training delivered through the European Centre for Broadcast Journalism and the BBC World Service Trust.[89] This support lasted for two years and encompassed all the employees of B92.

The TV station additionally benefited from the support aimed at improving its managing capacity. Hence, the assistance of international donors—the EU, USAID and IREX—was of the outmost importance when it comes to the establishment and managing of TV B92 in its early years. As one of the managers of TV B92 stated, "IREX was his right hand in managing the new television," and its help was crucial for the success of the initiative.[90]

In comparison to Radio B92, TV B92 was complex and expensive project, with almost 500 employees. Therefore, ensuring the financial sustainability of TV B92 required the diversification of sources as it could not become sustainable while depending only on donor support. As a consequence, a key strategic goal of the management was to transform B92 from a mission-oriented media outlet to a commercial media company, while

---

[87] McClear, McClear, and Graves, "US Media Assistance Programs in Serbia," 14–15.
[88] IREX ProMedia/Serbia, *Quarterly Report*, April 1, 2003–June 30, 2003, 8.
[89] EAR, "Serbia."
[90] IREX, "Serbia: Building Independent Media—Documentary."

retaining high professional standards.[91] Such a move required a shift in the editorial policy toward more commercial programs, which have been met with some serious criticism, especially when the reality shows were introduced in its program scheme.

The shift toward commercialization also required the ownership structure that would ensure both its commercial viability as well as its programming quality and independence. Hence, when seeking to ensure a financially sustainable business model for B92, the first task was to prevent the state from becoming the majority shareholder. In this situation, obtaining assistance from the Media Development Loan Fund[92] was crucial for enabling the B92 Trust to be positioned as a co-owner of the company[93] in order to ensure the independence of editorial policy through controlling shares which are an inseparable part of the new ownership structure. As a result, today B92 is registered as a closed shareholding company, owned by Astonko DOO (84.99%),[94] B92 Trust Ltd (11.35%), and small shareholders (3.66%), former and current employees.[95] Under its statutory provisions, "the owners of the B92 Trust are not permitted to sell or transfer their shares in the B92 Trust, nor to receive any profit or dividend from B92 on the basis of their equity in the B92 Trust."[96] In this way, the latest shareholder agreement (established in 2010) stipulated that the editorial policy would remain under the control of the B92 founder.[97]

Those who were active in the programs of external support to B92 would say that its transformation was partial. As former chief of the party for USAID assistance programs observed, "B92 had a split personality,

---

[91] B92 was the only media reporting on controversial business activities. As a consequence, companies under state control and many private companies did not advertise on B92.

[92] The Media Development Loan Fund (MDLF) is a mission-driven investment fund for independent news outlets in countries with a history of media oppression. It provides low-cost capital as well as loans and technical know-how to help journalists in challenging environments build sustainable businesses around professional, responsible, and quality journalism. (It has a new name now: Media Development Investment Fund.) See Soros Files, "Media Development Loan Fund."

[93] Matic, "Media Cannot Survive on Donations Alone."

[94] Astonko DOO, a joint company founded by the Swedish investment fund East Capital and a Greek investor Stefanos Papadopuolos, became the major owner in 2010.

[95] B92, "Vlasnička struktura."

[96] Ibid.

[97] Mastilović Jasnić, "Matić."

part surrogate public service broadcaster, part commercial, market driven media house. It never really reconciled this conflict in business models. It tried to reconcile *Big Brother* with *Insider*."[98]

It is very hard to predict the future development of B92 but from what has happened so far there are not many indicators that support an optimistic outlook. Competitive market conditions have forced the broadcaster to adapt its programming scheme toward commercial content which is not well received by the traditional B92 audience. Many high-profiled journalist left and some of the earlier flagship TV shows, such as *Insider* and *Impression of the Week*, are not on air anymore. However, in spite of the rapid commercialization of its programs, TV B92 today largely lags behind RTS and TV Pink when it comes to audience share.[99] At the same time, Radio B92 stopped the broadcasting of informative program in July 2015, fired its journalists, and was renamed Play Radio.[100]

Radical switch in donor priorities,[101] and sudden decrease in support to individual media outlets forced many to cease their operations. For those that survive, the reduction in donor support almost inevitably leads to commercialization—B92 being case in point. Being established as result of intensive and direct donor support, once left to operate on its own B92 failed to preserve its primary mission and has been transformed into a just another local, commercial, TV station. In 2015, B92 was subsequently sold by its owners to a business group based in Cyprus. Editorial standards are widely considered to have plummeted under the new ownership.

Conclusions

Serbian case is particularly interesting as it offers a rare possibility to analyze media assistance efforts in the three distinct phases—in the pre-democratization phase (1990–1995), during a period of political turmoil (1995–2000), and in the context of transition and democratic consolidation (after 2000). Each phase required different approaches to media assistance: focusing on pluralization and ensuring the survival of a few independent voices in the first period; building capacity of independent media

---

[98] Interview with Rich McClear, former Chief of Party of USAID media assistance programs, February 11, 2013.
[99] IREX. "Serbia" (2013), 116; IREX. "Serbia" (2015), 116.
[100] See Balkan Insight, "Belgrade's Radio B92 Axes Most Remaining Staff."
[101] CIMA, "Empowering Independent Media," 59–60.

to act as agents of social change during these second phase; and focusing on creating a broader enabling environment for the media system in the third phase.

The shifting contours of media assistance from one phase to another indicate several dimensions deserving special attention and elaboration. The first is related to the nature of the local context and the associated character of media assistance. The second dimension is the models of media institutions established once the local actors and environment embraced the reforms. The third is related to the nature of donor support and activities, including their interests and agendas. Finally, the fourth is the issue of sustainability and functionality of supported outlets and institutions.

When it comes to local conditions, the Serbian case demonstrated that the more disruptive the local context was (this refers to the period of the 1990s), the more direct media assistance was and the more focused it was on supporting individual media outlets and organizations. Also, a disruptive context combined with a limited scope of support produced a polarized media scene (proregime vs. independent media). Once the local political climate had changed, the space for more comprehensive media support was opened and ownership over the process of media development was partly transferred to local actors. However, although political actors declaratively accepted the principles and norms of democratic media reforms, in practice newly established institutions continued to suffer from strong politicization, resulting in the emergence of an "atavistic"[102] or "hybrid"[103] media system—a system that blended together old and new institutional forms and practices.

The process of mere copying of legal solutions and institutions from developed countries in the new context which is in the early stage of democratization resulted in what Berkowitz et al. call the "transplant effect."[104] Even laws are cognitive categories[105] and they cannot be imposed or transplanted, but should contain elements of local tradition and context in order to be accepted and functional. A mismatch between local conditions and culture and transplanted solutions and models "inevitably weakens the effectiveness of the imported institutional solutions."[106]

---

[102] Jakubowicz and Sükösd, "Twelve Concepts," 17–23.
[103] Voltmer. "How Far Can Media Systems Travel?," 224–245.
[104] Berkowitz, Pistor, and Richard, "The Transplant Effect."
[105] Ibid., 171.
[106] Ibid.

According to Jakubowicz,[107] such institutions are often "empty shells" stuck between a formal liberal framework and ideals, imported forms from developed countries, and politicized, semiauthoritarian local political culture and practices. The case of Serbia shows how in the long run, the media system and individual institutions and media outlets undergo a recalibration in order to adjust to contextual factors, as international assistance weakens and local political forces take control, once again.

---

[107] Jakubowicz, "Social and Media Change."

CHAPTER 7

Looking for Shortcuts? Assistance to— and Development of—Public Service Broadcasting in Bosnia-Herzegovina, Serbia, Kosovo, Macedonia, and Albania

MARK THOMPSON

The Value of Public Service Broadcasting

It is worth remembering at the outset why public service broadcasting has been—and, despite everything, remains today—a central objective of media development in Europe's new democracies.

The immediate reason for this is that public service broadcasting features in European intergovernmental treaties and other documents as a pillar of democracy, "directly related to the democratic, social and cultural needs of each society," and to the need to preserve media pluralism, "an element of social cohesion, a reflection of cultural diversity and an essential factor for pluralistic communication accessible to all."[1] All the member states of the European Union, the Council of Europe, and the Organization for Security and Co-operation in Europe (OSCE) have undertaken to support public service broadcasting and ensure that it can operate with financial autonomy and editorial independence. It follows that the governments of the countries in the region that the EU calls the "Western Balkans" have made commitments that they should respect, and to which they should be held accountable.[2]

---

[1] The quotations are from the Protocol on the System of Public Broadcasting, attached to the EU Treaty of Amsterdam (1997), and the Council of Europe's Seventh Ministerial Conference on Mass Media Policy (Kiev), 2005. See Bašić-Hrvatin and Thompson, "Public Service Broadcasting."

[2] In the EU's definition, the Western Balkans comprise Albania, Bosnia and Herzegovina, the former Yugoslav Republic of Macedonia (i.e., the Republic of Macedonia), Montenegro, Serbia, and Kosovo. (Before Croatia acceded to the EU

However, given the antagonistic and sometimes aggressive nature of the discussion around public service broadcasting today, when even the most respected and influential PSBs are cornered and defensive in the face of claims or mere assumptions that they constitute an unwarranted burden on the public, a hindrance to private sector dynamism, a hangover from the era of analogue bandwidth scarcity, even an obsolescent form of communications welfarism—given all this, it is easy to forget that the European emphasis on public service broadcasting is much more than a "politically correct" ritual, divorced from measurable benefits. For PSB can be shown to bring public goods to society at large. Onora O'Neill, a philosopher of political rights and justice, has listed some of the "public goods" to which PSB "can make significant contributions": "a shared sense of the public space; communication with others who are not already like-minded; access to a wide and varied pool of information; access to critical standards that enable intelligent engagement with other views; understanding, awareness and toleration of the diversity of lives and views among fellow citizens and others; a shared enjoyment of cultural and sporting occasions that would otherwise be the preserve of the few or the privileged."[3]

These are not abstract values, and comparative analysis of broadcast output indicates that public service broadcasters do help to advance them.[4] For example, PSBs show more of certain important categories of content—news and current affairs, arts, culture, education—than commercial broadcasters; and the more public money a PSB receives, the more output it shows in these categories. Moreover, the news and current affairs output of PSBs is more likely than commercial news and current affairs to be "hard" rather than "soft."

Public service broadcasters show more domestic content than commercial broadcasters, and contribute more to local or national production. There is likewise evidence that PSBs do (in certain circumstances) drive up the standards of quality across an entire media system. When he was chief executive at Channel 4, Michael Grade used to say, "It's the BBC that keeps us honest."[5] This benefit to the wider public should be felt wherever public service broadcasting is in a healthy condition.

---

in July 2013, it too was counted in the Western Balkans.) Montenegro was not included in the research project behind this book.

[3] O'Neill, "What Is Public," 5.

[4] The following points are adapted from Hanretty, "Public Service Broadcasting's."

[5] Grade, "Building Public Value."

Perhaps less predictable is that good public service broadcasting appears to boost voter turnout in elections. A 2009 study of seventy-four countries found that each percentage increase in the audience share of the PSB correlated with an increase of 0.15% in turnout, after accounting for a host of other variables (including compulsory voting, party funding, and the electoral system in use). Comparative research into levels of political knowledge across Europe, during two waves of European Parliament elections (measured in terms of respondents' ability to identify political parties' allegiances on the political spectrum), found, moreover, that exposure to PSB news broadcasts increased political knowledge among all sections of the population—even those with low levels of expressed interest in politics.

The latest research issued by the European Broadcasting Union confirms these positive correlations between public service broadcasting and democratic standards; countries with strong PSB enjoy better press freedom, higher voter turnout, lower levels of "right-wing extremism," and also "better control of corruption" than countries with weak PSB.[6] Yet correlation is not causation, and these findings cannot explain how a country might move toward the healthier end of the spectrum and turn a vicious circle into a virtuous cycle. Just like the challenge of reducing corruption or improving press freedom, the challenge of establishing strong PSB is daunting. The potential is immense.

The Toughest Challenge in Media Reform

If we were asked to invent a form of external assistance to media which combined the maximum number of challenges, it would be hard to conceive anything more formidable than the task of establishing public service broadcasters in transitional (newly democratic) states. When those states are recovering from profound trauma and systemic breakdown, the odds against significant achievement become even greater. And when the trauma involved interethnic bloodletting on a vast scale, in which neighboring countries were deeply complicit, and which was ended by armed intervention by yet other countries, the chances of decisive success become incalculably small.

---

[6] EBU, "PSM Correlations."

Let me list some challenges—with no certainty that the list is complete. A public service broadcaster produces, commissions, and disseminates a range of content to a universal (non-niche) audience. It has to be enabled and supported by an appropriate legal and regulatory framework, one which entrusts it with a public service mission, establishes suitable mechanisms for funding and accountability while protecting its editorial independence against parliament and government.

A public service broadcaster needs to provide a range of programs that "inform, educate and entertain"—the famous mantra that originated with the BBC nearly a century ago. It has to provide this for all sectors of the population, aiming for excellence in all strands, skillful enough to blend more rarefied output with popular material, juggling the schedule to reach large audiences with high-quality news and information. The broadcaster needs to be funded by a mechanism that engages the public (such as the license fee), on a generous scale and with a stability that allows it to fulfill its mission and to invest for the future. Also, it needs to be technically well-equipped and resourced. If it cannot deliver excellent content to the entire population through broadcasting and also online, the public is unlikely to wish to sustain it, and politicians will be quick to exploit such disaffection.

From all this, it follows that the providers of such assistance need to be prepared to engage on many fronts—journalistic, technical, institution building, political—and to spend lavishly, with no expectation that they will obtain rapid results. They need to have the stamina for a prolonged political and diplomatic struggle with local elites who will be reluctant to support a project that threatens to subtract an important lever of political influence; and with a media industry that will likewise resent and probably resist this noncommercial intruder. They will need to be ready to persuade media professionals and the wider public why they should support a kind of media output which may be unknown in their own language. In order to do this, they may have to leave their own "comfort zone" and replace their mild-mannered, roundabout communication with some blunt speech.

These providers will also need to invest in costly institution building and professionalization: training journalists, editors and managers to fulfill their distinctive mandates in a PSB. They need to provide technical assistance at a high level for producing and disseminating content on several platforms. The preparation and adoption of a suitable legal and regulatory framework—one that provides political and public accountability on one hand, and constrains the opportunities for political manipulation on the other—requires appropriate international expertise, sensitively offered, and also for dialogue with lawmakers, media professionals, and civil society groups.

Finally, the suppliers of such assistance must be prepared for a long and patient (but also vigilant) engagement which may fail even after the actual steps have been taken. Journalists can be trained only to find they are unable or disinclined to exercise their new skills in the given conditions. Media outlets can be brought into existence but then fail to find a loyal audience. Codes of ethics and self-regulatory mechanisms can be introduced and then roundly fail to make an impact on actual practice.

The Timing and Limits of International Engagement

By the standard of Europe's half-dozen best public service broadcasters, in the north and west of the continent, those in the Western Balkans fulfill their mandate or mission weakly, by and large. They are more or less politically captured, underfunded, demoralized and held, for the most part, in middling to low esteem by the public. Other challenges to democratic governance and economic development across the region have taken priority and mopped up whatever reformist energies are available. Retaining control of the media has mattered more to local elites than media independence has mattered to outside powers. Moreover, public broadcasting sits in a blind spot of policy making at the European level: hugely important for democracy, it is devolved (subsidiarized) to the care of national governments. The prerogative of national sovereignty is respected, almost regardless of how abusively governments treat their public broadcasters. Diplomats posted to the Western Balkans and visiting dignitaries who robustly criticized poor governance in other sectors have usually tiptoed around the media: a form of discretion with obvious costs and benefits.

The chief exception to this rule has been Bosnia and Herzegovina, which is also the country that most glaringly lacks essential conditions to establish viable public service broadcasting. The country's postcommunist transition had scarcely begun when the country was plunged into violence in 1992. Europe's worst conflict since 1945 was ended by international intervention in autumn 1995. The resulting peace agreement established a constitutional and governance system which allotted very extensive powers to three nationalities or ethnicities: Bosniak, Croat, and Serb. The political leaders of these groups continue to compete jealously, locked in zero-sum rivalry over state assets, maintaining their respective power bases at whatever cost to the viability of state bodies and the welfare of their communities alike, often preferring to obstruct progressive moves when they cannot control them for their own benefit.

The international community has sometimes succeeded in overcoming a deadlock in a strategic area of Bosnian public policy by imposing a solution. One of these areas is public service broadcasting: between 1998 and 2002, the international "viceroy" in Sarajevo, the High Representative, imposed a statewide PSB on the two self-governing "entities." Hence the country has three PSBs: one for each "entity" and another for the state as a whole: Radio-Television of the Federation of Bosnia-Herzegovina (RTVFBiH), Radio-Television of Republika Srpska (RTRS), and Radio-Television of Bosnia-Herzegovina (BHRT). These systems overlap and compete in wasteful and mutually harmful ways.

Divided ethnically, by political party loyalties, and ultimately by family or clan bonds, public space in Bosnia and Herzegovina is cleft in so many antagonistic ways that politically neutral institutions can hardly emerge; if they succeed in doing so, they are not willingly tolerated. Civil society is by and large demoralized and disoriented while the ethnic leaders are adept at justifying their self-interested obstructionism with reference to the embattled national causes of the 1990s. Since the European Union succeeded the Office of the High Representative in 2011 as the leading international organ in Bosnia and Herzegovina, nothing much has changed in respect of public service broadcasting. Tarik Jusić and Nidžara Ahmetašević suggest that the international community abdicated prematurely from the task of ensuring that Bosnia has a sustainable public service broadcaster.

The other country where international actors have been most involved with public service broadcasting is Kosovo. The opportunity—unique in the region—to make a public service broadcaster from scratch was created in summer 1999, when the forces of the North Atlantic Treaty Organization (NATO) wrested control of Kosovo from Serbia, and the United Nations provided transitional authority until a local government could be constituted.

According to Naser Miftari's report, Radio Television of Kosovo (RTK) "represents a unique case in the region, as the public broadcaster did not emerge as a continuation of the former state broadcaster."[7] The present writer was a member of a small team sent to Kosovo by the OSCE shortly after NATO's arrival, in order to meet with interested parties

---

[7] Miftari, in this volume.

and define goals for media development that would inspire international support and also extensive (if not unanimous) local support. To my recollection, nobody argued against the proposal that a public service broadcaster should be the centerpiece of a liberalized media system. However, it may be true that not all local stakeholders would have spontaneously agreed to this. It may also be true that our team was a little intoxicated by a sense of new possibility that resulted from Kosovo's liberation. Furthermore, the development of RTK during its formative years was indeed "shaped according to the interests of multiple stakeholders (UNMIK, OSCE, Kosovo Assembly, Kosovo Government, political parties)."[8]

The international authorities were able to build a regulatory and institutional framework for RTK that conformed to international best practice, in terms of defending the PSB against direct political manipulation. More than this, international donors oversaw the PSB content in its entirety. The European Broadcasting Union, the BBC, Fondation Hirondelle and other outside institutions were brought in to help start radio and then television services. Japanese money rebuilt the transmitter network and equipped the studio. The scale of support was large: some €18 million had been spent on RTK by 2005, when external subsidies more or less ended. Direct international involvement in the broadcaster's output had already been withdrawn; after August 2002, there were no internationals at RTK except for two international members of the RTK board. When RTK faced its first major editorial challenge, in 2004, it lacked the balance of outside expertise that might have stopped it from providing "indefensibly one-sided and inflammatory" coverage of ethnic violence.[9]

In Bosnia, international diffidence has allowed local leaders to block the development of PSB. In Kosovo, international abdication (as I would call it) left the way open for local actors to determine what kind of broadcaster RTK would be. Miftari's account of RTK makes melancholy reading, for it shows how Kosovo's political class pushed out the international organizations that were more or less committed to RTK's operations as a PSB and then laid siege to the broadcaster, determined to capture this important locus of political influence and social power. And the international organizations let it happen.

---

[8] Ibid., 37.
[9] This phrase is taken from the executive summary and recommendations in ICG, "Collapse in Kosovo," ii.

The story of international engagement in Macedonia has been different again. There too, however, the timing and scale of assistance have been determined not by political opportunities for durable reform, but by the pressure to end violence and then to address its causes, as these were defined by the local power elites. In 2001, the stability and even, it appeared at the time, the here survival of Macedonia were threatened by an Albanian grouping that used violence in the pursuit, supposedly, of improving the status of Macedonia's Albanian minority. Until this crisis, external assistance to media in Macedonia had followed no strategy, unless the demonopolization of the broadcast sector amounted to a strategy. As elsewhere in postcommunist Europe, donors concentrated on multiplying the number of outlets, as if mere numerical plurality equaled pluralism. The country—one of Europe's poorest and smallest—was flooded with far more media outlets than it could possibly sustain. Nominally independent broadcasters and newspapers proliferated, and most of them were dependent on donor funding.

Macedonian Radio and Television (MRTV), meanwhile, remained under close control of successive governments: all coalitions formed by ethnic Macedonian with ethnic Albanian parties. MTV1 focuses on news, culture, education and entertainment in the Macedonian language, whereas the second channel, MTV2, broadcasts similar material in the languages of the national minorities, principally Albanian.[10] (At the international conference "20 Years of Media Assistance in Western Balkans" that was held in Sarajevo on September 27, 2013, Daskalovski called this arrangement the "ethnic division of the spoils" at MRTV.) The language split within MRTV is replicated throughout the media landscape; a few outlets that use both languages—sometimes at the encouragement of international donors—are exceptions which prove the rule.

Successive governments let MRTV decline during the 1990s, while building up new private outlets under their direct influence. During these years, Macedonia was eager for international approval, and broadly compliant with European expectations. But the pace and level of those expectations were a hostage to Greece's unreasonable insistence that Macedonia must not be recognized under its constitutional name, the Republic of Macedonia. MRTV was left to fester until the European Union joined the diplomatic search for a solution to the Albanian insurgency of 2001. The

---

[10] Dimitrijevska-Markoski and Daskalovski, in this volume.

solution entailed Macedonia's fast-tracked acceptance as a potential candidate in 2003, and as a full candidate at the end of 2005.

This accelerated (and, many would say, premature) progress had a mixed impact on media assistance: EU candidacy added to the pressure on the authorities to respect Council of Europe standards in the field of media, but it also led to an exodus of donors who believed the EU would now take care of the remaining problems. The worsening situation of the media since 2010 has seen a slow and partial return by donors.

By the time that external assistance focused on the public service broadcaster, MRTV was in a desperate condition. According to Tamara Dimitrijevska-Markoski and Zhidas Daskalovski, international efforts prioritized "enabling the legal environment, capacity building and technical assistance."[11] None of this made much difference to the broadcaster's plight. For the combination of political control and poor quality had wrecked MTV's ratings. By 2010, its audience share had fallen under 7%. The crisis of quality in the news performance is profound. The Broadcasting Council (BC) has criticized MRTV for lacking open debate on important topics "due to inconsistent editorial policy,"[12] with the result that its output "is not a reference point for the public."[13] Equally damning was the conclusion that "MRT is not a service that actively contributes in the production of audiovisual works and for promotion . . . of the national and European cultural heritage . . . and does not support the creation of domestic audiovisual works."[14]

The experience of Macedonia also illustrates that assistance to public service media reform needs to be offered on a generous scale. Support was not provided on a scale that could fundamentally change MRTV's performance. It scratched the surface. Computerizing the newsroom, developing MTV's website, and organizing television archives were valuable contributions, but they did not reach to the central problems: abysmal professional standards, rock-bottom morale, and incessant political interference (visible in, for example, the high turnover of senior managers).

Another reason was that the reform agenda in postcrisis Macedonia was so extensive—addressing the civil service, the police, local government, and education—that it was hard to win political attention for MRTV, and even harder for civil society organizations (CSOs) to per-

---

[11] Ibid.
[12] Ibid.
[13] Ibid.
[14] Quoted in Belicanec and Ricliev, "Mapping Digital Media," 30.

suade international organizations that Macedonia's leaders should be pressured over media reform. A third reason was that donor coordination over MRTV was lacking. The United States was not interested in public service broadcasting and continued to prioritize private outlets. The United States remains hugely important as a diplomatic player in Macedonia and the region; its indifference to MRTV may have encouraged the government to reject European advice about how best to fund the PSB. Above all, this assistance had no impact on political influence ("the biggest threat to the development of MRTV")[15] or on its dysfunctional funding mechanism.

Outside engagement with public service media in Serbia was likewise belated. In this case, however, the reason was not neglect (as with Macedonia) but the impossibility of helping with structural reform while the belligerent regime of Slobodan Milošević was in power (1987–2000). Under Milošević, there was no such thing as public service broadcasting; Radio-Television of Serbia (Radio-televizija Srbije, RTS) was a state broadcaster, fully controlled by government, and it played an infamous role before and during the wars of the 1990s.[16] Unlike the public service broadcasters in Bosnia and Herzegovina, Albania and Macedonia, RTS had not lacked basic resources during the 1990s, when the Milošević regime ensured that it had the means to dominate Serbia's audiovisual landscape with its propagandist output. Even so, the station was badly run down by the time of NATO's bombing campaign against Serbia in 1999, which devastated the RTS infrastructure. (The campaign included a highly controversial air attack on RTS headquarters in Belgrade, which left sixteen staff members dead.)

After October 2000, it became possible for the international community to engage with the Serbian authorities on media reform. Until then, international assistance to Serbian media was limited to supporting independent outlets which struggled to counteract the influence of RTS and to uphold public service values in the media.[17] Assistance took the form of

---

[15] Dimitrijevska-Markoski and Daskalovski, in this volume, 155.

[16] This role is documented in Thompson, *Forging War*, 51–133.

[17] The best known of the private beneficiaries in Serbia was Radio B92. In October 2000 (the month of Milošević's fall) TV B92 started broadcasting. It modeled itself on Channel 4 in the UK, and became famous; a British journalist wrote an admiring book about it. Veran Matić, B92's director and figurehead, used to say that B92 was the *real* public service broadcaster in Serbia, providing honest and reliable information to citizens. Yet B92 was subsequently sold by its owners in mysterious circumstances to a business group based in Cyprus. Editorial standards are widely considered to have plummeted under the new ownership.

direct support to a range of independent (in reality, oppositional) outlets. Paper was supplied to printing presses, journalists received training and bursaries for travel, technical support was provided. In the late 1990s, this support was lavish in scale, reflecting the international community's wish to weaken public support for the regime. After 2000, those outlets saw the tide of external funding turn away from them and toward the very institution that symbolized the previous regime at its worst.

In the context of the new government's strategic ambition to move toward international respectability, and eventual membership of the European Union, Serbia commenced the intergovernmental dialogue over media reform that neighboring countries had begun years before. The OSCE Mission to Serbia, established in 2001, became an influential partner in this dialogue, along with the Council of Europe. International experts came to Belgrade to help design new legislation. On the local side, civil society organizations got involved with proposals and initiatives of their own.

The transformation from state to public broadcasting was stipulated as an aim of EU engagement with Serbia. RTS was converted by law into a public service broadcaster in 2006. More precisely, it became two PSBs: one for Serbia, and the other for the northern province of Vojvodina. International support took the form of external audits, technical assistance, training in journalism and management, various kinds of expertise, sales and marketing. This input has improved journalism and production standards. Content monitoring has not been continuous or systematic, so it is hard to say whether RTS's output fulfills its public service mission.

What is clear, is that international engagement with reform or RTS has not been sufficiently intrusive to achieve the results that were possible when this engagement began. The question of the prerogatives and limits of structural intervention is always difficult to resolve to the

---

B92's value at sale would have reflected the "invisible assets" that derived from its international reputation. This value may even—who knows?—have included tangible assets bestowed by foreign donors. To be sure, donors to B92 did not intend to create a private-sector public service broadcaster; they wanted to strengthen a producer and disseminator of good quality information. And, of course, counterexamples could also be cited to show the lasting benefit of supporting private media. Yet the subsequent sharp decline of B92 cannot but illustrate the highly uncertain outcome of attempts to raise the level of journalism through piecemeal support to one or another outlet, while ignoring underlying structural problems.

satisfaction of all stakeholders. In a sovereign state, the nature of public service media is for the society itself to determine as it sees fit. (This may not be the case when sovereignty is qualified, as in postwar Bosnia and Herzegovina and postwar Kosovo.) Yet it is also true that when the state has made international commitments to provide public service media, the international community has a collective responsibility to ensure that this commitment is respected. This responsibility should be inalienable when the state is in course of establishing its institutions and its democratic credentials.

Where should this commitment end? Is it simply in the legal, nominal establishment of a PSB? Or should there be a more far-reaching requirement to ensure the delivery of accurate, comprehensive, high-quality news and current affairs—in other words, the kind of output by which any PSB should be judged? In the Serbian case, as elsewhere, the international community has settled for the first (minimal) answer. Again, the prospect of EU accession holds out the opportunity for a more exigent assessment. This opportunity should not be missed.

In Albania, a dire shortage of reliable data makes it difficult to analyze the media sector. External assistance to media development was smaller in scale, less intrusive, and probably less coordinated than those in the former Yugoslavia. PSB reform is, however, categorically dependent on large-scale, coordinated approaches to structural reform. As a result, these initiatives had less impact on the PSB than they should otherwise have had. The viewing figures of the state or public broadcaster, Radio Televizioni Shqiptar (RTSH), are unknown. No research has, it seems, been conducted into public opinion about TVSH. Nevertheless, assistance to RTSH appears to have "been less substantial" than the help given to commercial media. This support has consisted of training, program exchange (through the EBU), and legal expertise. Ilda Londo identifies the key omission in this approach: "Long-term efforts toward reforming RTSH daily practice have been absent."[18] Her report speaks of lip service to reform without real will on either the local or the international side. In sum, "A clear, long-term, and all-encompassing vision and strategy on how to reform RTSH has been lacking, both from foreign donors and from local actors."[19] In her report for the OSF's Mapping Digital Media

---

[18] Londo, "Limited Assistance for Limited Impact," 29.
[19] Ibid., 43.

project, Ilda Londo cites evidence that TVSH output is still biased in favor of the governing party, especially during election campaigns.[20] In its 2012 progress report on Albania, the European Commission found that "the editorial independence of the public service broadcaster has not been strengthened."[21]

This having been said, Albania may be the country in the region that has benefited most from external support to media. In part, this is because journalism started at a much lower point than in the rest of the Western Balkans. For Albania under communism was a full-blown dictatorship, ruling the most closed society in Europe, with no margin for the public expression of at least somewhat independent news or views. Furnished by a range of intergovernmental, international and nongovernmental organizations, assistance to media has, writes Ilda Londo, helped journalism to change "entirely."[22] The lion's share of aid was spent on improving professional standards. This included the promotion of self-regulatory mechanisms as well as training. There was no formal coordination of aid until 2005. Since 2008, the EU has been the main donor to media and civil society.

On the negative side, the "problematic triangle of business, politics and the media"[23] remains in place. Many outlets still serve as "loudspeakers for political parties." In the terms popularized by Hallin and Mancini, Albanian media "exhibit high political parallelism and external pluralism."[24] Internal pluralism—"defined as pluralism achieved within each individual media outlet or organization"—is, by contrast, "hard to detect." What Londo calls the "transplantation" of laws from other European countries has reflected a box-ticking approach to structural reform—one in which the international side is, of course, complicit.[25] The report also diagnoses a "stagnant quality" in Albanian reporting. And, with very few exceptions, media remain unprofitable; they are cross-subsidized by their owners from other lines of business.[26]

---

[20] Londo, "Mapping Digital Media," 30, 48.
[21] European Commission, "Albania 2012 Progress Report," 40.
[22] Londo, "Limited Assistance for Limited Impact," 8.
[23] Ibid.
[24] Ibid.
[25] Ibid.
[26] Ibid.

Implementing Laws and Regulations

In the 1990s, efforts were made in the region to improve the legal and regulatory framework around media and journalism. (Serbia—which then included Kosovo—was the key exception.) Over time, the investment of pressure and expertise brought good results. Laws and regulations were brought into line with international standards as these were defined by the Council of Europe and others. Yet laws are more easily enacted than they are implemented. Shortfalls in the implementation of basically sound legislation have become normal across the region.

In Serbia, the independence of the PSB is upheld in law but not safeguarded in practice. An assessment of Serbia's media landscape, prepared in 2012 for several civil society organizations, found that no institution or office is responsible for ensuring RTS's independence from political interference.[27] (The institution which could be charged with this responsibility, the Public Broadcasting Agency, has no such competence.) A separate concern is that RTS has refused to comply with access to information legislation. At the same time, the framework is still deficient in some ways. Public accountability mechanisms, report author Davor Marko says, "are still missing" in Serbia, with the result that RTS "often appears as a one-man company, led by its director general."[28]

In implementation, as in other respects, Bosnia and Herzegovina is an extreme case. The political class does not even pretend to want to implement laws and regulations in good faith. International support has been decisive in sustaining the converged media and telecoms regulator, but even this support has not induced the elected political leaders to appoint a new director for years—an obligation they have refused to fulfill from 2007 until 2015! Perhaps the most important obstacle in the development of public service broadcasting since 1995 has been the impossibility of establishing the Corporation which was intended—under legislation adopted in 2005—to coordinate the three distinct PSBs, as well as to "manage the equipment and the transmission network, and be in charge of sales and advertising."[29] Eleven years on, this corporation has not been

---

[27] Matić, "Serbian Media Scene vs. European Standards," 62–65.
[28] Marko, "Media Reforms in Turbulent Times" (2013), 37.
[29] Jusić and Ahmetašević, in this volume, 76.

established, due to successful resistance by the two "entity" PSBs as well as to the usual political hostility to unifying, state-building measures of almost any kind. It appears that ethnic leaders—especially in the Serb-controlled "entity," the Republika Srpska—who resent the establishment and survival of a converged communications regulator are determined to forestall the construction of an equivalent institution for public service broadcasting.

Following the Money

Even if a public service broadcaster enjoys strong political support, it needs sufficient and assured funding to perform well. Traditionally, PSBs have been provided with guaranteed income in exchange for delivering quality content with a high public interest to the whole society. For their part, governments are easily tempted to use funding as leverage with broadcasters, to obtain favors of one kind or another.

The record over PSB funding mechanisms has been mixed. The countries where postconflict mandates gave international actors the widest scope to influence the shape of these mechanisms were Bosnia and Kosovo. In Kosovo, license fees were collected by Kosovo's electricity utility, under a mechanism that was put in place as international funds dried up. In 2007, however, the utility cancelled the contract and the Constitutional Court found that the collection of a license fee in this way was unconstitutional. Both acts provoked suspicion of political interference, in the heightened atmosphere before parliamentary elections. An impression was given that RTK's precarious autonomy was being systematically undermined.

By 2010, the PSB was wholly dependent on the state budget. Under new direction, RTK no longer seeks the restitution of the license fee. Given that, as Miftari writes, "RTK has increasingly become a focus of overlapping political, economic and other interests of multiple stakeholders who see RTK as a strategically important asset," and that the broadcaster is constantly pressured "by politicians and their protégés seeking airtime and positive coverage,"[30] the lack of secure funding poses an acute danger to the prospect of editorial independence.

---

[30] Miftari, in this volume, 119.

In terms of content, Miftari reports third-party assessments that changes in funding since around 2004 coincided with changes in editorial policy. "A number of interviewees noted that between 2002—2006 when RTK was still in the process of Kosovarization it had a more balanced approach in its coverage and was less prone to being politicized. After independence the content of RTK became more uniform and the medium increasingly regarded as politicized."[31] The real break with the principle of neutrality probably came in 2007.

In Bosnia, the license fee has become a focus of political rivalry, with ethnic leaderships vying to control an important public resource. Džihana, Ćendić, and Tahmaz argue that the entire development of PSB in Bosnia is determined above all

> by questions of what each ethnic community will get. . . . In practical terms, Serbs in BiH seem the most reluctant to pay when it comes to the idea of an all-Bosnian public service. . . . On the other hand, the Croats in BiH largely refuse to pay the fee because they believe that the existing channels are not theirs. Eventually, as the statistics for 2010 show, Bosniaks also started to evade paying license fees. . . . The Serbian side does not seem interested in the existence of a broadcaster and the Corporation at state level, the Croatian side insists on the establishment of an exclusively Croatian broadcaster, and the Bosniak side is resistant to change as it fears that this would lower the income of the Federal Television, over which they have control.[32]

The license fee has been presented by Serb and Croat leaders as a means of depriving their electors of their rightful separate share of information resources, and imposing a media agenda that opposes their essential (national) interests. Bosniak leaders have not done enough to disprove this fear-mongering. All this has brought the PSB system to the brink of financial collapse in 2016.

Stable funding for PSB remains a huge problem in Serbia. RTS is permanently overdrawn; it appeared to have a shortfall of €25 million in 2011 (gap between operating budget and revenue).[33] Even though RTS

---

[31] Ibid., 41.
[32] Džihana, Ćendić, and Tahmaz, "Mapping Digital Media." (The author of this chapter, Mark Thompson, was involved in designing, commissioning, and publishing the Mapping Digital Media research.)
[33] Matić, "Serbian Media Scene vs. European Standards," 59.

news is the most watched in the country, and RTS has usually been the most watched broadcaster over recent years (averaging 25% to 35% of the national audience), half the population refuses to pay the license fee. Following adoption of the 2014 Law on Public Media Services,[34] the license fee was abolished and replaced by a tax that entered into force at the beginning of 2016.[35]

In Macedonia, the crisis of funding is absolute. As elsewhere in the region, the license fee has ceased to be a viable means of supporting PSB. MRTV depends on allocations from the government budget. Likewise in Albania, no durable funding model has been found to ensure that RTSH can fulfill its mission. The public broadcaster became "even more dependent on funding from [the] state in order to complete" the switchover to digital broadcasting.[36]

Public, Ratings, and Relevance

A public is more than an agglomeration of individuals. Its members compose an entity that is capable of articulation in plural and representative ways. One reason why media independence matters is that it allows communication between different segments of society. When media are captured by powerful groups with political agendas and economic interests, their role as intermediaries is harmed; the wider public can be marginalized and substantially excluded from the "national conversation" about matters of general concern.

Across the Western Balkans, the public has often not been able to articulate its interests with accuracy and nuance. The underdevelopment of public service media both reflects and perpetuates this deficiency. The linkage is well expressed in Davor Marko's report on Serbia, where "there are still some topics and issues that should not be reported" by the public service broadcaster—for political reasons. "It seems that the limited editorial independence of RTS is a result of strong clientelistic ties between the management and the political and business elites," Marko states. "Consequently, those elites . . . define what public interest is."[37]

---

[34] "Zakon o javnim medijskim servisima."
[35] "Zakon o izmenama i dopunama zakona o javnim medijskim servisima."
[36] Londo, "Limited Assistance for Limited Impact," 43.
[37] Marko, "Media Reforms in Turbulent Times" (2013), 51.

In their analysis of Bosnia, Džihana, Ćendić and Tahmaz trace the resistance to public service broadcasting in Bosnia back to the ethnicization of the very conception of the public interest. "Ethnic divides in BiH have strongly affected the very concept of the public interest," they suggest, "redefining it along ethnic lines." There is no agreement between politicians—or across society, either in its ethnic segments or as a notional whole—about the desirability of public service broadcasting as such, let alone about what sort of PSB should be constructed. Yet it would be premature to conclude that Bosnia's experience since 1995 proves the powerlessness of PSB to assist the cohesion of a radically divided society. For Bosnia has not experienced public service broadcasting worth the name. Rather, what has been proven is the refusal of the political class to *allow* Bosnia's citizens to get close to proper public service broadcasting. The story of PSB failure in Bosnia and Herzegovina has been told many times; it is, by this stage, wearily familiar. Deadlock has become a way of life. Nothing would be more shocking, today, than a declaration by the three national or ethnic leaderships that they agreed to respect the law of the land by letting the state-level broadcaster and corporation operate efficiently, in the public interest.

Like public service broadcasters everywhere else, those in the Western Balkans struggle to keep existing audience and win new ones in the teeth of ever-multiplying alternatives and more or less incessant political pressures. Of course, this pressure would be less if the broadcasters reached fewer people. For the fact is that most of them still reach a big public. In Albania, RTSH is the only terrestrial broadcaster in the country that achieves anything close to national coverage; it reaches 80.5% of the territory. It has *access* to a full national audience, whether or not it is able to exploit this advantage.

In their report on Bosnia for the Mapping Digital Media project of the Open Society Foundations (OSF), Amer Džihana, Kristina Ćendić and Meliha Tahmaz made the following observations about the public service broadcasting system:

> Only the national public broadcaster . . . covers most of the country [among terrestrial broadcasters], reaching about 89.3% of the population. Radio-Television of Republika Srpska (Radio Televizija Republike Srpske, RTRS) in Republika Srpska and Radio-Television of Federation of Bosnia-Herzegovina (Radio Televizija Federacije Bosne i Hercegovine, RTVFBiH) in the Federation of BiH are aimed primarily at their respective entities,

where RTVFBiH covers 89% of the population of the Federation, while RTRS reaches 94% of the population of the Republika Srpska.[38]

In Bosnia and Herzegovina, the best hard news output on any of the three PSBs is on BHRT, the statewide broadcaster; but this output also includes much old-fashioned "protocolary" news items, which do not help its ratings. This is an example of a PSB struggling to fulfill a public service mission in a rather unimaginative way, and not winning audiences— though of course there are other (very political) reasons why BHRT is not more popular.

In Republika Srpska, the PSB had the best coverage of serious news issues until—in the words of Džihana, Ćendić, and Tahmaz—it became "increasingly perceived as a mouthpiece of the president." This makes RTRS a particularly clear example of politicization harming the news output of a PSB. Federation TV, in the other entity of Bosnia and Herzegovina, is an example of a different but equally harmful trend: the commercialization of news going hand in hand with politicization. This approach seems to help the ratings: Federation TV is the only PSB that is among the three most watched stations in Bosnia and Herzegovina. But even its audience share fell by nearly two-thirds in the decade after 2001, "with commercial television stations picking up the spoils."[39]

In Serbia, RTS1 (the first channel, which carries the main news and current affairs programs) increased its ratings significantly from 2005 to 2009. "RTS1 news is the most watched output of its kind in Serbia and *Dnevnik 2*, the mid-evening bulletin, is the most watched news program in the country."[40] RTS is widely considered to have the best quality news of any Serbian television station. Despite some concerns about the harmful effects of commercialization on RTS output, the broadcaster retains substantial public trust as a news provider.

In Macedonia, the slump in ratings has been alarming. By 2010, MRT's audience share stood at under 7%. The crisis of quality in the news is profound. The Broadcasting Council (BC) criticized MRT for lacking open debate on important topics "due to inconsistent editorial policy," with the result that public service output "is not a reference

---

[38] Džihana, Ćendić, and Tahmaz, "Mapping Digital Media."
[39] Ibid., 24.
[40] Surčulija, Pavlović, and Jovanović Padejski, "Mapping Digital Media."

point for the public."[41] Yet, by 2012, even though Macedonia's citizens had been very badly served by their PSB, public opinion appeared not to have become hostile to public service media as such. Rather, it was dissatisfied with the quality achieved, and with the failure to deliver quality output across the different strands of production. This remarkable finding gave ground for hope that passive civic support for PSB might one day become an active demand, if an encouraging lead could be given. But there is no sign of such a lead. In 2015, the so-called "phone-tapping scandal"[42] revived debate about the status and operation of MRT, questioning the independence of its journalists and its role in defending the public interest.[43]

Currently, however, there is nobody to give such a lead. Consider the case of Kosovo, which is extreme but not unrepresentative in the region. The history of RTK to date confirms that public service broadcasting may—under extraordinary conditions—be installed very rapidly, without a background of consultation with society (not that public service broadcasting has ever been established on a basis of general demand); but that a genuine PSB is sustainable in a society only with a domestic environment that is politically, financially, and culturally supportive. With hindsight, Kosovo's new leadership was always going to obstruct the survival of a strong, competent, confident, independent PSB. And journalists and citizens were never going to rally in significant numbers to defend PSB against the political takeover that began around 2007. The population of Kosovo had no experience of PSB, and no way of imagining that nonpartisan, high-quality media were possible in their society—let alone, that they were as citizens entitled to such media. Beset with the practical challenges of living in one of Europe's poorest countries, Kosovo's citizens would surely have remained immune to appeals on behalf of RTK, even if those appeals had been made. The best prospect for improving PSB in

---

[41] Belicanec and Ricliev, "Mapping Digital Media," 30.

[42] On 9 February 2015, the main opposition party, the Social Democratic Union of Macedonia (SDSM), began to publish recorded conversations among government officials and others, featuring a widespread abuse of authority, election fraud, corruption scandals, controlled appointment of main judicial office positions, instrumentalization of the police, direct control of the media, etc. The scandal marked the tipping point of a lengthy political crisis.

[43] A comprehensive assessment of the Macedonian media system's capacity to deliver public service is provided by Trpevska and Micevski, "Macedonia."

Kosovo probably lies in modest attempts to raise the quality of important strands of production on old and new platforms.

Looking Back, Looking Ahead

"An international strategy [for media development in the Western Balkans in the 1990s] emerged piecemeal, without quite being articulated. It envisaged the creation of a mixed public-private media sphere with public service broadcasting as the hub or axis, balanced by a strong private sector, and protected by liberal laws and regulations. This normative model is something new in the region."[44]

State broadcasting under one-party political control was a defining feature of the authoritarian regimes in central and eastern Europe before 1989. When Europe's postcommunist states set themselves the target of introducing democratic norms in all sectors of governance and society, they had no choice but to undertake the conversion of their state broadcasters into public service broadcasters. Given the prominence of these institutions in the daily lives of their citizens, their real or assumed influence over public opinion, and their role as symbols of unaccountable (if state) or accountable (if public service) power, these expectations of reform were likely to be endorsed by liberal leaders and championed by prodemocracy activists.

Why, then, were these expectations not better fulfilled? First, they were not codified, or specified, or timetabled. This was because the structure and operations of public service broadcasting are decided by each country. (This "subsidiarized" approach to PSB is statutory in European Union law.) It was also because authority over media systems is a jealously guarded prerogative of sovereignty. Second, the sources of resistance to PSB in the new democracies were multiple and strong. Resistance was active—though rarely overt—on the part of politicians who were reluctant to lose a traditional lever of influence, and of senior journalists who could hardly imagine not working as the clients of politicians; for their sense of themselves as professionals was premised on their close, often dependent relationship with political figures. Resistance was passive, however, on the part of journalists and others in public life who did not understand what PSB meant or why they should take risks on its behalf. And it was abetted by the indifference of citizens, to whom PSB meant nothing at all, and

---

[44] Thompson, "Slovenia, Croatia, Bosnia," 77.

who faced a daunting range of more pressing challenges as their societies wrestled with the transition to democracy.

The Council of Europe had resources to guide and advise the transitional states on their path to PSB. A range of donors offered training and technical assistance. The needs of state-to-public transition far outstripped the help that was given, however. Indeed, it is impossible to imagine any program of support that could have met the challenge of completing the root-and-branch reform of institutions with thousands of employees, entangled in very close (formal and informal) relationships with power.

Having said this much, an assessment of international assistance to public service media in southeastern Europe depends on one's expectations. Judged by the editorial standard of the state broadcasters which they supplanted, the record of public service broadcasting in the Western Balkans looks better; not acceptable, nor perhaps even respectable, but—better. PSBs are profoundly cultural institutions, rooted in the customs and values of their societies, shaped by local traditions (which include public expectations) of political power and bureaucracy, as well as those of journalism and of civil society. Given this, it would be unrealistic to expect a swift transformation, in the way that an electoral system, for example, can be transformed. (Political behavior during election campaigns is more resistant to change, however, and provides a more accurate guide to the nature and democratic health of political life.)

In the aftermath of the historic changes that followed the breaching of the Berlin Wall and the end of one-party regimes, hopes ran high that democratic transformation in many sectors of state and social life would follow almost automatically. Media reform initiatives shared these hopes, which did not feel unrealistic because those changes had been heralded and driven and symbolized by the free speech of anticommunist leaders and movements across central Europe. Media freedom appeared to be an undeniable demand, an unstoppable trend.

What followed was disillusioning and also educational. Among the lessons learned was that the total transformation of a state into a public service broadcaster in a single process, over a period of a few years, should never have been an objective. While the structural reforms might in some countries be made with relative ease, the reform of managerial, editorial and journalistic practices proved doggedly resistant to change. (This is why many training programs were a waste of money and time.)

This lesson was actually learned a long while ago. Evidence that the "heroic" phase of international assistance to PSBs ended more than a decade ago is not hard to find. "Ten Years of Media Support to the

Balkans: An Assessment," a report prepared for the Stability Pact by Aaron Rhodes and published in June 2007, made no mention at all of public service broadcasting in its conclusions and recommendations, beyond the evasive exhortation that "[d]onors should emphasize the 'public service' function of media." This omission in a document for a European body was striking; perhaps it reflected a sense that the scale of the challenge was so great, and the fruits of assistance were so small, that remedies were not worth proposing.

More recently, a report from BBC Media Action is decidedly modest about international aspirations to improve PSB around the globe. "Fragile States: The Role of Media and Communication," by James Deane, reveals how the language of media intervention has changed since the 1990s, becoming more sensitive to local prerogatives, and more attentive to consultation and debate. "More creative strategies and external support will be required if national public service broadcasting systems are to be more successful in providing such platforms in the future," Deane writes. The overall aim, in his view, is to help PSBs to build "shared identity" and "support national public conversations in fragile states." Also this: "Supporting models built on public service broadcasting values to encourage a greater sense of shared identity can emerge from work with a single broadcaster or highly connected networks of private or community broadcast media."

Deane's approach shows how the debate about PSB assistance has been bruised by the recent (and ongoing) failures in Afghanistan and Iraq: environments where traditional models of PSB were doomed to fail. But it also shows how the debate about PSB as such has evolved in its northern and western European heartland. Under the pressures of digitization and the emergence of new platforms for media consumption, PSBs face challenges at every level, and have been forced to rethink every aspect of their mission. *Creative* is a watchword of the new approach. "A sustained and creative debate on how to transform state broadcasters into public service broadcasters, or develop alternative models of national public service broadcasting, is especially necessary in fragile states." Structural transformation is no longer the game: "Public service broadcasting can work very effectively from the ground up," Deane observes—a conclusion that might surprise anyone who has worked only in southeastern Europe, but that makes sense against the experiences in Angola, Libya, Nepal, Sierra Leone, Tanzania, Tunisia, Zambia and elsewhere.[45]

---

[45] See Deane, "Fragile States."

The key focus now is on "support for programming that is characterized by public service broadcasting values: putting the audience first, being impartial, insisting on editorial independence, building trust and being creative."[46] Good-quality public service content can be inserted into a PSB schedule regardless of the general quality of output, and without seeking to reform the host institution.[47] It is not clear whether this approach has been tested in the Western Balkans; an experiment in Macedonia with funding public service output by commercial producers was not effective.

An objective examination of the results of PSB across the region might well encourage the view that genuine support for public service principles would entail the closure of the existing public service broadcasters. A more likely scenario is that these institutions will follow the dismal example set in Macedonia and decline into a vegetative state, unable to be reformed or abolished. Unless, one has to add, the European Union should decide that the proper performance of public service media is a condition for candidate countries to accede to membership. For EU membership is the only incentive in view that could induce these governments to release their national broadcasters from political control and put them on a sustainable footing to they can fulfill their remit. The European Commission seems somewhat aware that the accession negotiations leading to the enlargements of 2004 and 2007 did not go far enough in leveraging structural reform in the media sector. (Presumably the national authorities pretended they were committed to public service broadcasting, and the European Commission officials pretended to believe them.) But there are no signs that the EU is yet ready to go far enough beyond a box-ticking exercise to ensure that ongoing and future accession negotiations will have a different outcome. And this is probably as it must be, given than Italy, Hungary, Greece, Bulgaria, Romania and other public service broadcasting abusers are EU members.

---

[46] Ibid., 22.

[47] Another indication of this changed—diminished but, undeniably, more realistic—approach is found in Kalathil, *Developing Independent Media*. Referring *en passant* to "reforming the state broadcaster into a public service broadcaster" as one possible aim of media development, Kalathil notes coolly—and correctly—that this activity does not "produce lots of outputs" (59). The report omits, however, to explore the effect of that lack of output on donor decisions, to critique efforts to date, or to propose more effective approaches.

In summer 2013, the European Commission's DG Enlargement convened a consultative conference called "Speak Up!," which agreed a number of broad aims including this:

Renewing the Reform Commitment of Public Service Broadcasters

> The partnership established between the European Commission and European Broadcasting Union (in 2012) in an attempt to help Public Media in the Enlargement region should be supported by a strong national commitment to the needed reform of Public Service Broadcasters. Achieving their political independence, financial autonomy and sustainability, as well as defining the tasks under the public service remit, should be orientations of this reform.

If this statement was an accurate measure of international commitment to PSB in candidate states, then the political elites in southeastern Europe still have little to worry about. The partnership with the EBU can only encourage foreboding; for the EBU has been prevented by its own multilateral structure and bureaucratic outlook from confronting in any adequate way the crisis of public service media in Central and Eastern Europe.

There are, then, no shortcuts. If public service media ever take root, it will be as the result of society's own determination. The fostering of this determination among journalists and citizens should be the chief priority of further initiatives in this area.

CHAPTER 8

The Uncertain Future: Centers for Investigative Journalism in Bosnia and Herzegovina and Serbia

Nevena Ršumović

Introduction

In the past decade, independent nonprofit centers devoted to the production of investigative journalism according to the highest standards were established in the Western Balkans, joining a worldwide trend of investigative journalism migrating from mainstream media into specialized organizations. This chapter focuses on two such centers in Serbia and BiH, dedicated to the production of investigative stories of the highest standards of Western journalism: the Center for Investigative Journalism Serbia (CINS), based in Belgrade, and the Center for Investigative Reporting (CIN), based in Sarajevo. It aims to understand how such a model of an organization, successful primarily in the US, but also in several other places, can operate in the specific conditions of the media markets of the two countries or are we, possibly, witnessing what Zielonka and Mancini dub "the opaque imitation of external models" referring to imported models that "have been put in practice in very different environments from those in which they originated"?[1] Additionally, the study examines the role and the impact of donor assistance in the Western Balkans on the operation and future of these two centers.

While there are many definitions of investigative journalism, there is a broad understanding among professionals that its components are "systematic, in-depth, and original research and reporting, often involving the

---

[1] Zielonka and Mancini, "Executive Summary," 6.

unearthing of secrets."[2] We could add that it covers issues which are in the public interest. It often entails heavy use of public records and data-driven journalism, and focuses on social justice and accountability.[3] While some claim that all good reporting should be investigative, the reality is that methods of investigative reporting can take years to master.[4] Kaplan warns that investigative journalism "should not be confused with what has been dubbed "leak journalism"– quick-hit scoops gained by the leaking of documents or tips, typically by those in political power,"[5] which is a common case in the Western Balkans.

Donors recognized the contribution of investigative journalism to accountability, development and democracy and included it in programs aimed at strengthening independent media, fighting corruption and promoting accountability, good governance and democracy.[6] In the Western Balkans, donors have used three main approaches aimed at fostering development of investigative reporting: provision of training, grants for investigative reporters, and the creation of nonprofit centers that specialize in producing investigative reporting as a response to various impediments to practicing it in the mainstream media.

The development of investigative journalism nonprofits in the former communist countries of Central and Eastern Europe, including the region of the Western Balkans, was not only due to the lack of funding in the mainstream media, but "can also be seen as investigative journalism trying to deflect pressure from political, commercial or other special interests."[7] These independent, often nonprofit centers are almost entirely dependent on donor funding. They use cutting-edge research methods, such as data-driven journalism, publish mainly on the Internet, foster cross-border investigations, and seem to fill the void created among the traditional media.[8] The question is, however, whether such centers in the Western Balkans are able to follow in the footsteps of successful examples abroad.

This chapter first provides an overview of the trend of investigative journalism nonprofits and a brief analysis of the centers that CIN and CINS used as their role models. Second, it outlines the problems in the

---

[2] Kaplan, "Global Investigative Journalism," 10.
[3] Ibid.
[4] Ibid.
[5] Ibid.
[6] Kaplan, *Empowering Independent Media*, 84.
[7] Smit et al., *Deterrence of Fraud*, 54.
[8] Ibid., 32.

media landscapes of BiH and Serbia which have an impact on investigative journalism. What follows is an overview of the assistance to investigative reporting in the two countries, and in-depth case studies of the two selected centers, based on interviews with their managers, funders and independent media experts. Finally, it provides a conclusion of the findings pertaining to the success in transposing the models upon which the centers were established, discussing their perspectives for sustainability.

The Model: Nonprofit Investigative Journalism Organizations

The model of nonprofit investigative journalism organizations is a global trend. It began in the US in the 1970s[9] and 1980s with only a small number of such organizations, as it has always been a challenge to obtain support for investigative journalism in commercial media.[10] Scaling back of investigative reporting in traditional media was triggered by the widespread availability of free-of-charge news due to technological advancements, declining news budgets and shrinking audiences.[11]

There are now more than a hundred nonprofit organizations devoted to investigative journalism around the world.[12] They include reporting centers, training institutes, professional associations, grant-making bodies (which typically allocate small grants to journalists to do investigative stories), and regional and global online networks. The majority of these organizations are based in the US, while a quarter are located in Eastern Europe and the former Soviet states.[13] There are considerable differences among them in terms of their staff and budget, from very small organiza-

---

[9] Starting with the Berkeley-based Center for Investigative Reporting in 1977. See Kaplan, "Global Investigative Journalism," 29.

[10] Ibid., 15–16.

[11] Smit et al., *Deterrence of Fraud*, 31; Kaplan, "Global Investigative Journalism," 16.

[12] "The number of nonprofit investigative reporting groups has jumped from only three in the late 1980s to more than 100 today, with vibrant centers in such diverse places as Romania, the Philippines, Jordan, and South Africa," notes Kaplan ("Global Investigative Journalism," 11). "When CIMA surveyed nonprofit investigative journalism centers in 2007, it found 39 in 26 countries, with more than half of those appearing since 2000. A follow-up 2012 survey shows that this rapid growth has continued, with 106 nonprofits in 47 countries" (ibid., 28).

[13] Kaplan, "Global Investigative Journalism," 26–33.

tions in developing countries, to powerful ones, such as ProPublica[14] in the US, which relies on multi-million-dollar funds.[15]

Despite the growth of nonprofit organizations dedicated to producing investigative journalism, the dominant models will not be successful in every context.[16] Several organizations around the world are dormant or defunct due to different reasons, such as the lack of funding, managerial problems, small and uncompetitive markets or poor editorial standards.[17] However, they have proven to be "viable organizations that can provide unique training and reporting, serve as models of excellence that help to professionalize the local journalism community, and produce stories with social and political impact" observes Kaplan.[18] Sullivan notes that "sometimes these are the only independent news organizations in a country, and many have become important locally as a unique source of investigative news."[19] Although supporting investigative centers is expensive, it is a good approach where the independent media are underdeveloped or nonexistent.[20]

The investigative journalism nonprofit sector worldwide is heavily dependent on donors. Some 84% of such organizations cited grants and donations as their major source of income,[21] while in a survey by the Center for International Media Assistance (CIMA) only 53% stated that they have a developed sustainability plan.[22] The development of investigative reporting globally has attracted millions of media development dollars from international donors, especially from the US and northern Europe, and some private foundations—notably the Open Society Foundation.[23] However, this type of aid has been recognized as "a major gap in international media assistance" as the funding is "largely episodic" and constitutes a small part of the overall funding targeting media development,

---

[14] ProPublica is the first ranking nonprofit among the largest investigative journalism nonprofits in the US with the 2011 annual budget of $10,100,000. The second one is the Center for Investigative Reporting with $5,200,000 and the third one is the Center for Public Integrity with $5,100,000, according to data by Investigative Reporting Workshop and CIMA (Kaplan, "Global Investigative Journalism," 31).

[15] Ibid., 25.

[16] Ibid., 25.

[17] Ibid., 37.

[18] Ibid., 7.

[19] Sullivan, "Investigative Reporting," 24.

[20] Ibid., 32.

[21] Ibid., 38.

[22] Ibid.

[23] Ibid., 11.

according to CIMA.[24] Investigative reporting programs are estimated to attract about 2% of the nearly $500 million provided for international media assistance annually: in 2007, only $2.6 million went to investigative reporting nonprofits in developing and democratizing countries.[25]

One of the main challenges for investigative journalism nonprofits around the world is sustainability. Many are trying to find solutions to the issue as few working models for it exist.[26] "Even in the United States, organizations that have many donors available to them are struggling with this issue. It is a problem that the journalism industry as a whole must confront," notes Sullivan.[27] Investigative reporting is never sustainable even in the West as it is expensive and generates few stories.[28] For instance, the thirty-five-year-old Center for Investigative Reporting based in Emeryville, California, has been donor supported for all its life.[29] Ninety percent of its US$10.5 million budget comes from donations.[30]

The growing US nonprofit investigative sector benefits from a strong tradition of philanthropy and a large domestic market from which to solicit support relying on the wealth of the nation.[31] In the US the funding is coming from "local philanthropists, community and family foundations, and national foundations with interest in media and public policy."[32] Also, the US tax law is favorable for the development of nonprofits—it prescribes a tax exemption for nonprofits and a 100% tax deduction for contributions by donors.[33] A survey of sixty-four nonprofits that produce investigative and public interest journalism shows that foundations and philanthropists are the source of 70% of their funding, while only a small amount comes from other sources: membership (7%), distribution (10%) and training, events and advertising (13%).[34]

---

[24] Ibid., 12.

[25] Ibid., 22.

[26] Drew Sullivan, former Director of the Center for Investigative Reporting (CIN) in Sarajevo, BiH, former President of CIN's board and an editor with the Organized Crime and Corruption Project, interviews with the author, July 8, 2013, and August 18, 2013.

[27] Sullivan, "Investigative Reporting," 20.

[28] Drew Sullivan, interviews with the author, July 8, 2013, and August 18, 2013.

[29] Ibid.

[30] Enda, "Staying Alive."

[31] Kaplan, "Global Investigative Journalism," 27.

[32] Ibid., 16.

[33] Ibid., 34.

[34] Enda, "Staying Alive."

A look at the largest and best-known investigative journalism non-profits in the US shows that they rely on donations to produce stories with great effects. The Center for Public Integrity receives support from foundations and individuals and does not accept contributions from governments.[35] In 2012, the organization attracted close to US$9 million in tax-deductible grants and contributions, while other sources constituted only some 2% of the total revenue.[36] Many of its stories have had an impact on the entities investigated, either by making them change their behavior or by precipitating a swift reaction by the responsible authorities.[37] Pulitzer Prize-winning ProPublica has annual operating costs of around $10 million.[38] It is dependent on contributions and grants from institutions and individuals,[39] diversifying its donor base with the aim to be increasingly less dependent on one benefactor—the Sandler Foundation—which has been providing a significant part of the funding and made the establishment of ProPublica possible in 2008.[40] The center mostly does not sell its stories, but allows their republishing for free,[41] forging partnerships with dozens of news organizations for increased visibility and impact.[42] The center's stories have a great impact in triggering investigations, changes in regulation and other actions by responsible authorities.[43] Earnings of both centers from commercial sources, such as selling e-books, are minimal.

A look outside of the US, on the renowned Philippine Center for Investigative Journalism, which has persisted for more than twenty-five years owing to context-specific factors, also reveals dependence on donor funding. The small, but very important endowment from the Ford Foundation accounts for 30% of the center's annual budget and provides it with basic financial flexibility and security.[44] Although the center attracts about 20% of income from journalism training services and selling stories

---

[35] Center for Public Integrity, "Frequently Asked Questions."

[36] Center for Public Integrity, "Worldwide Watchdog."

[37] Ibid.

[38] ProPublica had the largest annual 2011 budget of US$10,100,000 among largest investigative journalism nonprofits in the US. See Kaplan, "Global Investigative Journalism," 31.

[39] Center for Public Integrity, "Return of Organization."

[40] Enda, "Staying Alive."

[41] ProPublica, "Steal Our Stories"; Goodman, "ProPublica."

[42] Ellis, "ProPublica at Five."

[43] ProPublica, "Annual Report 2012."

[44] Kaplan, "Global Investigative Journalism," 17.

to other media, international grants have been a major support to the center's work.[45]

Investigative Reporting and Contextual Challenges

Investigative journalism in the mainstream media is rare in Serbia[46] and BiH,[47] with some notable exceptions. In Serbia, there are sporadic, scattered examples of investigative journalism stories, difficult to catalogue as investigative journalism is far from being a continuous practice in the media. It is a result of enthusiasm of individuals and not a strategic decision by the specific media outlets in both countries.[48] Media do not have funds or human resources for investigative feats. Investigative journalism is not rewarded as it does not increase the audience or advertising income[49] and it is thus difficult to get support from owners and publishers for it.[50] However, the key problem seems to be controlled media where even the best editors do not have freedom and therefore cannot do much.[51] Also, there is a lack of adequate expertise among editors and journalists.[52] Furthermore, journalists often tend to label as investigative journalism stories that do not satisfy adequate criteria.[53] Such stories are often politically biased, descriptive rather than based on facts—in a word, unprofessional.[54] Pseudo-investigative texts "scream" from front pages in Serbia—stories that are a result of pushing documents to journalists and media from

---

[45] Ibid., 18.
[46] Jovanka Matić, PhD, media researcher, the Institute of Social Sciences in Belgrade, interview with the author, August 16, 2013; Milorad Ivanović, Editor, weekly *Newsweek* (Serbian edition), interview with the author, August 21, 2013.
[47] Mehmed Halilović, Legal Adviser for Media Issues, Internews in BiH, interview with the author, August 16, 2013; Boro Kontić, Director, Mediacentar Sarajevo, interview with the author, August 19, 2013; Amer Džihana, Director of Media Policy and Research, Internews in BiH, interview with the author, August 23, 2013.
[48] Milorad Ivanović, interview with the author, August 21, 2013; IREX, "Bosnia and Herzegovina" (2013), 26.
[49] Jovanka Matić, interview with the author, August 16, 2013.
[50] Mehmed Halilović, interview with the author, August 16, 2013.
[51] Boro Kontić, interview with the author, August 19, 2013.
[52] Ibid.
[53] Mehmed Halilović, interview with the author, August 16, 2013.
[54] Boro Kontić, interview with the author, August 19, 2013.

power centers. Therefore, the public cannot discern the real from pseudo-investigative journalism.[55]

Worthy examples of investigative work in Serbia surface on the occasion of the annual award for investigative reporting administered since 2006 by the Independent Association of Journalists of Serbia (NUNS) and the US embassy, the recipients of which are often young reporters. Notable but rare examples of high quality investigative journalism in Serbia are the national B92 TV's series *Insider*, renowned among the general public and known for complex and dangerous investigations, and the work of the nonprofit Center for Investigative Journalism of Serbia (CINS) which is republished in Serbian media. The most prominent example of investigative journalism provider in BiH is the nonprofit Center for Investigative Reporting (CIN), whose content is republished in other BiH media filling the investigative void. While some stories of the weeklies *Slobodna Bosna* and *Dani* are often labeled investigative, it is highly dubious if they conform to the widely accepted criteria for what constitutes investigative reporting.

A part of the reasons for such a situation lies in the specifics of the media landscapes of the two countries, burdened with a host of problems which have a negative impact on the practicing of investigative journalism.

The state still exercises significant influence over media in both countries. Although the privatization of all media with state ownership in Serbia was mandatory by July 1, 2015, the state continues to exercise its influence on the media via advertising. It was estimated in 2011 that almost 25% of the total income of the Serbian media[56] comes through advertising from the state budget.[57] Although more recent data is not available, the problem of state advertising persists, as noted by the Anti-Corruption Council of the Republic of Serbia, which called on the responsible authorities in 2015

---

[55] Milorad Ivanović, interview with the author, August 21, 2013.

[56] This spending from the state budget, which enables "personal and party promotions in the media," is estimated by the Anti-Corruption Council (2011) to exceed €15 million annually, in addition to which media receive estimated €21–25 million through public tenders. Compared to the total amount of advertising in the media market, which is estimated at approximately €160 million, it can be concluded that the state institutions are a source of almost one-quarter of the total income of the Serbian media. See Anti-Corruption Council, "Report on Pressures," 4.

[57] For instance, through campaigns aimed at promoting activities of various ministries. See more in the Anti-Corruption Council, "Report on Pressures," 16–17.

to regulate it.[58] In BiH, a large number of the media are financially dependent on state financing, be it through advertising of public companies or direct state subsidies. For example, the Republika Srpska government entity exerted pressure on a selection of media by providing them with direct budgetary incentives for the sixth consecutive year in 2014.[59] In BiH, some 30% of TV stations and almost 50% of radio stations depend on financing by the authorities at various administrative levels.[60] The 2014 European Commission (EC) progress report on BiH expressed concern over government financing of media and lack of transparency and clear criteria in the distribution of subsidies.

There are also political and economic pressures influencing editorial policies in both countries. The 2014 EC progress report on Serbia warned about deteriorating conditions for the full exercise of freedom of expression and a tendency to self-censorship in the media due to continued lack of transparency over media ownership and sources of media advertising and funding.[61] Self-censorship by journalists and editors is stressed as a problem also by the Anti-Corruption Council of the Republic of Serbia in 2015.[62] The Anti-Corruption Council noted in 2015 that the public perception of censorship in the media is based on undisputable facts as several important political talk shows were taken off the air.[63] Also, there are "neither legal nor institutional guarantees of public service broadcasters' editorial autonomy."[64] In the case of BiH, the EC warned in a 2014 progress report that political and financial pressure on the media has increased.[65] The report warns that the advertising practices of public companies controlled by political parties also affect media integrity.[66] It also noted that the independence of the three public broadcasters remains to be ensured and that the two entity broadcasters were exposed to further

---

[58] Anti-Corruption Council, "Izveštaj o vlasničkoj strukturi," 168.

[59] United States Department of State, Bureau of Democracy, Human Rights and Labor, "Bosnia and Herzegovina 2012 Human Rights Report," 12; Udovičić, "Bosnia and Herzegovina," 17; United States Department of State, Bureau of Democracy, Human Rights and Labor, "Bosnia and Herzegovina."

[60] Zurovac and Rudić, "Shadow Report," 36.

[61] European Commission, "Serbia [2014] Progress Report."

[62] Anti-Corruption Council, "Izveštaj o vlasničkoj strukturi," 165.

[63] Ibid., 164.

[64] Matić, "Serbian Media Scene vs. European Standards," 66.

[65] European Commission, "Bosnia and Herzegovina 2014 Progress Report," 17–18.

[66] Ibid.

political influence. Overall, there is strong political parallelism[67] in the media in both countries.[68]

The political and financial pressures go hand in hand with oversaturated and poor media markets,[69] small advertising revenues and a "fierce" battle for audiences.[70] In Serbia, there is an excessive number of issued broadcast licenses relative to the size of the advertising market[71] causing a lack of media diversity and pluralism as the media are fighting for ratings by producing cheap programs likely to attract an audience.[72] Similarly, in BiH media there is a proliferation of entertainment content due to fast commercialization in the highly saturated media market.[73]

Also, there are problems in the application of legislation relevant for journalists' work,[74] while threats against journalists remain a concern in both countries.[75] Although libel was decriminalized in BiH, there are doubts about the impartiality of the judiciary, particularly where the plaintiffs are in a position of power.[76] In Serbia, defamation was decriminalized only in 2012[77] and prison sentences for libel were abolished in 2005.[78] The EC reminded Serbian authorities in 2014 that they have an important responsibility to create an enabling environment for freedom

---

[67] Hallin and Mancini, *Comparing Media Systems.*

[68] See the chapters by Marko and by Jusić and Ahmetašević in this volume; also see European Commission, "Bosnia and Herzegovina 2012 Progress Report," 16; Johnson, "Model Interventions," 154.

[69] Hozić, "Democratizing Media," 159; Johnson, "Model Interventions," 128; Matić and Ranković, "Serbia"; Kremenjak and Živković, "Serbia," 126.

[70] Hozić, "Democratizing Media," 159.

[71] Matić and Ranković, "Serbia."

[72] Kremenjak and Živković, "Serbia," 126.

[73] Hozić, "Democratizing Media," 159.

[74] European Commission, "Bosnia and Herzegovina 2011 Progress Report," 16; European Commission, "Bosnia and Herzegovina 2012 Progress Report," 17; European Commission, "Commission Staff Working Paper," 25; IREX, "Bosnia and Herzegovina" (2013), 22; Matić, "Serbian Media Scene vs. European Standards," 11–12; Zurovac and Rudić, "Shadow Report," 19.

[75] European Commission, "Commission Staff Working Paper," 25; European Commission, "Serbia 2012 Progress Report," 14; IREX, "Serbia" (2013), 119, 122; Kremenjak and Živković, "Serbia," 126; European Commission, "Bosnia and Herzegovina 2010 Progress Report," 16; European Commission, "Bosnia and Herzegovina 2011 Progress Report," 16.

[76] IREX, "Bosnia and Herzegovina" (2013), 22.

[77] "Zakon o izmenama i dopunama krivičnog zakonika," Art. 14.

[78] European Commission, "Commission Staff Working Paper," 25.

of expression, "including by reacting to and publicly condemning threats, physical assaults and cases of incitement to violence and hate speech from extremist groups" against journalists.[79] The inefficiency of the court system in prosecuting attacks on journalists and threats against them, which are often left unsolved,[80] contributes to self-censorship.[81] The EC has been warning in consecutive annual reports, including in 2014, that intimidation and threats against journalists and editors in BiH are of serious concern and that the follow-up by the authorities has been insufficient.[82]

And last but not least, there is a general low quality of reporting[83] and a notable pressure from PR departments on media to publish their content.[84] This has to do with the fact that newsrooms are understaffed, with journalists forced to be general-assignment reporters, pressured to fast production of content, often several stories a day.[85] Largely outdated and theoretical curricula of university-level journalism programs do not help the quality of journalism.[86] The IREX Media Sustainability Index (MSI) shows a decline in the score for professional journalism in BiH from 2.12 in 2010 to 1.77 in 2015, while the score for plurality of news sources dropped from 2.77 in 2010 to 2.23 in 2015.[87] The score for professional journalism in Serbia declined between 2010, when it was 1.74, and 2015, when it was 1.50. The score for plurality of news sources in Serbia dropped from 2.28 in 2010 to 1.79 in 2015.[88]

---

[79] European Commission, "Serbia [2014] Progress Report," 13.

[80] In the past eighteen years three journalists have been killed (Dada Vujasinović in 1994, Slavko Ćuruvija in 1999, and Milan Pantić in 2011) and there was a bomb attack on a journalist (Dejan Anastasijević in 2007). The perpetrators of these deeds have not been found to date. Three journalists are under police protection. See Matić, "Serbian Media Scene vs. European Standards," 44.

[81] Kremenjak and Živković, "Serbia," 126.

[82] European Commission, "Bosnia and Herzegovina 2014 Progress Report," 17; European Commission, "Bosnia and Herzegovina 2010 Progress Report," 17; European Commission, "Bosnia and Herzegovina 2011 Progress Report," 16.

[83] IREX, "Serbia" (2013), 124.

[84] Ibid., 121.

[85] IREX, "Bosnia and Herzegovina" (2013), 24, 26.

[86] USAID, "Bosnia-Herzegovina Democracy and Governance Assessment," 58.

[87] IREX, "Bosnia and Herzegovina" (2015), 16.

[88] IREX, "Serbia" (2015), 116.

Supporting the Development of Investigative Reporting in Bosnia and Herzegovina and Serbia

There is an absence of data on foreign assistance aimed at the development of investigative journalism in BiH and Serbia[89] and only partial data on foreign assistance to media in general in the two countries is available.[90] Still, it is estimated that BiH received a minimum of US$131 million for media assistance from 1996 to 2006, although the figure may be significantly higher as information from many organizations and government agencies is not available.[91] Similarly, it is difficult to piece together an estimate for the amount of foreign media aid to Serbia due to scattered, partial and unavailable data, but it is likely that in the period 1997–2012 the Serbian media sector received at least €55 million or US$73 million,[92] while Marko[93] provides an estimate of €90 million spent on media development in Serbia from 1991 to 2012. Within the media assis-

---

[89] For example, numerous investigative journalism projects were built into larger assistance initiatives, such as in the case of the support of close to $2 million to Serbia and Montenegro by USAID's Office of Transition Initiatives (OTI) between 2000 and 2002, and hundreds of small material assistance grants, including to investigative journalists, disbursed by OTI from 1997 to 2000. Cook and Spalatin, "Final Evaluation of OTI's Program."

[90] Rhodes notes the absence of reliable data on media interventions in the Western Balkans until 2005, both for the region and individual countries, and only a partial availability of data after 2005, see Rhodes "Ten Years of Media Support."

[91] Johnson, "Model Interventions," 102; also, for an estimate for BiH, see the Jusić and Ahmetašević chapter in this book. Over four years, between 1996 and 1999, the US government, solely through USAID, injected $38 million toward media-related programs in the country. See Johnson, "Model Interventions," 102.

[92] Between 1997 and 2002 the US government donated close to $13 million to Serbian media development. See McClear, McClear, and Graves, "US Media Assistance in Serbia." The EU supported more than eighty media and communications projects between 2000 and 2010 with €17.7 million, see European Commission, "Mapping EU Media Support," 26. In the period from 2007 to 2011 Serbian media received more than €20 million in foreign donor assistance. See European Union and A.R.S. Progetti S.P.A., "Technical Assistance," 5. Between 2005 and 2006, the European Agency for Reconstruction (EAR) allocated €2.8 million to media development, including for projects fostering investigative reporting. See Medija centar, "EAR Media Fund." The USAID-funded media development project in Serbia, implemented by IREX between 2008 and 2012, had a four-year budget of $8.8 million.

[93] See the chapter by Marko in this volume.

tance programs, some funds were allocated for the support of investigative reporting.

Although there is an absence of literature which would systematically document forms of media assistance efforts toward the development of investigative reporting in BiH and Serbia, evidence points to three main avenues of donor assistance, sometimes overlapping: training and mentoring, funding investigatory journalism, and supporting the development investigative reporting centers.

TRAINING AND MENTORING

Rhodes notes that in the Balkans "the greatest share of media support was devoted to training and education."[94] The leaders in investigative journalism training provision in Serbia have been the Independent Association of Journalists of Serbia (NUNS) and the Center for Investigative Journalism of Serbia (CINS), as well the Serbian chapter of the Balkan Investigative Reporting Network (BIRN), a network of hubs which act as news media and training centers, relying on donor funding. In BiH, the most notable training program in the past decade was provided for several consecutive years by Mediacentar Sarajevo, a local media development operation, based on the blended-learning method and six-month cycles. The participants produced investigative stories under the mentorship of trainers, some of which were featured in the media of the region and won awards. The key challenge, however, was publishing the stories, considering the various pressures and influences that the media operate under. The effective blended-learning approach has also been used by NUNS and CINS in their joint annual investigative reporting school (2007–2012, funded by NED), as well as by BIRN. NUNS and BIRN also have experience with in-house investigative training.

Among many other feats in investigating reporting training in Serbia and BiH, one could single out several as original for the region. In the early 2000s, Mediacentar Sarajevo ran a series of donor-funded trainings on computer-assisted reporting with local trainers. Since 2003 Mediacentar Sarajevo has been operating a popular website for media professionals (Media.ba), featuring a significant number of educational articles on investigative journalism among a vast array of material about various

---

[94] Rhodes, "Ten Years of Media Support," 12.

aspects of journalism.[95] The annual BIRN Summer School in investigative reporting targeting journalists from the Western Balkans was organized for the sixth time in 2015 with renowned international and local trainers.

FUNDING INVESTIGATIVE PROJECTS

While commercial media have been known to receive funding for investigative projects, there is no information that could help us understand the scope of such activities in BiH and Serbia. Rhodes notes that there have been numerous grants for investigative content in the Balkans.[96] For instance, the weekly newsmagazine *Dani* in BiH received substantial financial and technical support.[97] One organization based in Denmark, SCOOP, allocated small grants to individual journalists in the Western Balkans to work on investigative stories from 2003 to 2012 when it ran out of funds for the region. A dozen SCOOP-financed stories from the Balkans received various national, regional, and international awards.[98] Between 2004 and 2006, USAID supported more than 340 investigative and in-depth reports made by print, radio, and TV outlets in BiH. Several of these reports resulted in action aimed to address the problems which the stories exposed.[99] Internews in BiH, funded by USAID, had a media-support program between 2010 and 2015, a component of which was strengthening investigative reporting. The program was worth some US$200,000, implemented mainly through small grants awarded to media outlets and individual journalists for the production of investigative stories.[100]

SUPPORTING INVESTIGATIVE REPORTING CENTERS

Support to the nonprofits can be in the form of a fund which kick-starts it,[101] such as in the case of CIN in BiH, or more usually as funding for investigative projects. Both CIN in BiH and CINS in Serbia have been

---

[95] The website won the 2006 Transparency International BiH award for the advancement of investigative reporting.

[96] Rhodes, "Ten Years of Media Support," 24.

[97] Johnson, "Model Interventions," 139.

[98] For more information on the awards, see the website of SCOOP: Supporting Investigative Journalism, http://i-scoop.org/scoop/balkans/category/awards/. Accessed on October 31, 2015.

[99] USAID, "Giving Citizens a Voice," 11.

[100] Amer Džihana, interview with the author, August 23, 2013.

[101] Kaplan, *Empowering Independent Media*, 93.

running mainly on funding for investigative projects. In Serbia, a non-profit center, Pištaljka,[102] established in 2010 and funded by international donor organizations, publishes stories on corruption, including investigative ones, on its website, while 50% of its funding is aimed at advocacy activities regarding the protection of whistleblowers.[103] All of its funding is ad hoc, project-based and short-term.[104] Although BIRN Serbia has diversified its portfolio in the areas of good governance and public finance to capture more donor support, it still produces donor-funded investigative stories. The Crime and Corruption Reporting Network (KRIK) is a recently founded nonprofit devoted to production of investigative journalism in Serbia, started by former CINS journalists and supported by the Organized Crime and Corruption Reporting Project (OCCRP).[105] While Mediacentar Sarajevo conducted investigative reporting training for years, it has not managed to obtain continuous funding for these activities and thus it did not sustain investigative reporting as one of its core activities.

Other initiatives indirectly contributed to the development of investigative reporting. Most notably, the introduction of an adequate legal framework in the form of freedom of access to information laws in both countries and the decriminalization of libel and defamation were necessary preconditions for the development of investigative reporting.[106]

Despite efforts aimed at developing investigative journalism in BiH and Serbia, their effects and results are challenged by contextual factors. Although there were numerous grants for investigative content production, the long-term results of many such grants are not yet visible as much investigative journalism which is not subsidized by grants stops and, with some important exceptions, support for content has typically not resulted in continued practice "mainly because of owner and editorial decisions and market realities."[107] Numerous short-term training sessions, lasting several days, without work on stories with mentoring, are of dubious effect, considering the complexity of investigative methods and practices.

---

[102] https://pistaljka.rs/.

[103] Vladimir Radomirović, Editor-in-Chief, Pištaljka.rs, interview with the author, September 17, 2013.

[104] Ibid.

[105] KRIK, "About Us."

[106] On donor efforts in respect to legal reforms, see chapters in this book by Marko and Jusić and Ahmetašević.

[107] Rhodes, "Ten Years of Media Support," 24.

Although long-term training, involving story production, yielded investigative-savvy individuals, it is questionable whether they could continue to produce demanding investigative work in their newsrooms for various reasons, most notably lack of support from editors, lack of funding and the political affiliations of the media. Also, former participants of investigative training programs do not have in their newsrooms the quality mentoring and strict scrutiny over their stories which would guarantee that the media would not be sued. Therefore, legal insecurity and disrespect of laws by public institutions limit the effects of investigative reporting training programs in the long run. Additionally, it has become increasingly difficult to obtain funding for general investigative journalism training, which are thus nowadays rare to find.

In sum, it seems that nonprofit centers devoted to the production of investigative journalism which is republished by other media are the answer to ensuring a continuous supply of investigative journalism in the media sphere of both countries. As a founder of CIN noted, the large international development programs have insisted on the approach that the media in BiH just needs to be trained better, which had little effect.[108]

The following two case studies analyze two nonprofit investigative journalism centers in the Western Balkans dedicated exclusively to the production of investigative stories in accordance with the highest international standards—the Center for Investigative Reporting (CIN), based in Sarajevo, Bosnia and Herzegovina, and the Center for Investigative Journalism of Serbia (CINS), based in Belgrade. The case studies outline how the centers were founded and what foreign organizations their founders used as role models, as well as how they operate at present; they also explore the type of donor assistance the centers receive and show the achievements and the challenges to the operation of the centers, including the issue of the centers' sustainability.

---

[108] Drew Sullivan, interviews with the author, July 8, 2013, and August 18, 2013.

The Center for Investigative Reporting (CIN)[109]

THE ESTABLISHMENT OF CIN

CIN was established in 2004 as an initiative by New York University (NYU) and its subcontractor, Journalism Development Group (JDG), a limited liability company based in the US and founded by two US journalists. CIN was launched with a three-year, $1.7 million grant to NYU[110] by USAID, which was key to the center's early success. The center was officially registered as a nonprofit local organization in 2005. As of 2006 it operated independently of JDG. The board of directors, which includes one foreigner, oversees CIN's local management. CIN's activity is the production of investigative stories in accordance with the highest international standards.

The initial CIN expertise was international. NYU provided training curricula used by its journalism school, while experts from the US conducted intensive on-the-job training for the journalists for three years. The international editors guided the entire development of each story as the editorial expertise needed for the center could not be found in the BiH market.

CIN's average yearly budget (as recorded in 2015) is €380,000 to €450,000. In 2011, CIN had the sixth-largest annual budget among non-US nonprofits devoted to investigative journalism, totaling $468,000.[111]

In 2015 the center had a staff of fifteen, including ten reporters as an optimum number for its organizational structure and work processes. Reporters used to work on a contract basis, as freelancers would. The reason for this is the fact that organizations need to pay high contributions to the state for fully employed staff. However, as of 2014 all the reporters were fully employed as CIN has acquired enough funding to cover the cost. Still, depending on the available funding, it is possible that the employment status of the center staff could revert to the previous state since the reporters' contracts were tied to the length of individual project funding as the salaries are paid only from donor funds.

---

[109] Unless otherwise indicated, the information on CIN was mainly collected from the interview with its director, Leila Bičakčić, conducted on June 10, 2013.

[110] USAID, "Bosnia-Herzegovina Democracy and Governance Assessment."

[111] Kaplan, "Global Investigative Journalism," 31.

CIN produces forty to fifty complex investigative stories a year, with no fixed monthly output. Additionally, there is a large number of smaller feature or news stories, sometimes as a follow up to big projects. Owing to the introduction of additional media products (documentaries, short video story summaries, infographics, databases of documents), traffic to the CIN website increased more than twofold in one year (between 2013 and 2014).

THE MODEL

Despite hefty media assistance to BiH by 2003, the media was failing to meet international standards, with the basic problem being a visible lack of expertise.[112] The standards could not be improved by in-classroom training, neither could the media be changed from within due to political and financial interests.[113] Therefore, CIN's founders believed that an independent operation devoted exclusively to upholding the highest standards in investigative journalism is the answer to the lack of such journalism in the country.[114] Despite CIN being a foreign initiative, over time the CIN local staff took ownership of the center, which was crucial to its survival.[115]

The center's founders looked to foreign models of investigative nonprofits. The concept came from JDG, based mainly on two models—the Philippine Center for Investigative Journalism in Manila and the Center for Investigative Reporting based in Emeryville, California—but modified to meet the needs of BiH. The two foreign centers served more as an inspiration than blueprints.[116]

There is a series of differences that CIN's founders were aware of when basing their project on the role model centers. On the financial side, there was no robust market in BiH for selling the content. The belief that income could come from BiH television proved to be mistaken because of "corruption in local TV media."[117] Also, as BiH did not have a lucrative news industry and advertising was more political in the Balkans than in the countries of CIN's role models, the center's model did not include a plan to rely on advertising, although there is a plan to monetize the

---

[112] Drew Sullivan, interviews with the author, July 8, 2013, and August 18, 2013.
[113] Ibid.
[114] Ibid.
[115] Ibid.
[116] Ibid.
[117] Ibid.

website, drawing on the diaspora. Additionally, as there is no tradition of fund-raising through small contributions from individuals in BiH, that source could not be counted on. Considering the political influences on the media in BiH, CIN's founders knew they would have to spend much more time than their role models in protecting the center from political interference. Also, they knew that journalism standards would be lower than in San Francisco or Manila.[118] "We expected to spend more time training and we designed the copy flow and news-gathering process to be much more structured than they would have been in other centers. Journalism ethics are also different and we had to set strict rules on ethics to protect the center's reputation. Consequently, early on, things were very structured, there were more rules and we moved slowly making sure we didn't take on too many new tasks," one of the founders of CIN, Andrew Sullivan, comments.[119]

The CIN founders were aware of some advantages the center would have as well.[120] For example, the investigative product offered by the center would be unique in BiH and the region. Moreover, media were not interested in producing corruption and organized crime reporting as it is dangerous, difficult and expensive. Also, given the low standards in BiH media, it was to be expected that the public would appreciate the "good, fair and independent journalism" to be offered by CIN.[121] Knowing that corruption would remain a problem in BiH, and at the same time high on donors' agenda, it was to be expected that such a situation would translate into funding for CIN—eventually EU funds—available for a long time. Furthermore, it was also expected that the international community would remain engaged in BiH with likely a decade or more of heavy funding until BiH was well on its way to EU. The founders of CIN also hoped to generate income from regional and international media with the assumption that news from BiH was of interest to Europe and that CIN could produce the highest quality journalism. Knowing that BiH has a large diaspora, they hoped to leverage their interest. Also, as the Organized Crime and Corruption Project (OCCRP), a not-for-profit, joint program of a number of regional nonprofit investigative centers and for-profit independent

---

[118] Ibid.
[119] Ibid.
[120] Ibid.
[121] Ibid.

media stretching from Eastern Europe to Central Asia,[122] was planned as soon as CIN was set up, the costs for all regional member centers, including CIN, could be lowered by splitting them among OCCRP members, such as those for commercial databases, media insurance and international editors.

DONOR ASSISTANCE TO THE CENTER

CIN relies only on donor assistance and has a rather broad donor base. Apart from the hefty kick-start grant from USAID, its single largest donor is the Swedish International Development Cooperation Agency (SIDA), which has supported CIN since 2007, first with a three-year project, and then with a four-year core support grant aimed at raising CIN's capacities to help its sustainability. Such an institution-building grant is a true rarity. This one helped CIN produce business and marketing plans, and improve administration and newsroom efficiency. Some other donors provide project-by-project funding, while some have a continuous cooperation with CIN. The organization has also received EU funding. To a smaller extent it gets assistance through the OCCRP network's funders and the network, which provided some capacity-building support to CIN, covers the costs of the investigations and of the journalists who take part in the investigative work of OCCRP. Hence, the center manages to have relatively stable funding by establishing long-term cooperation with donors, and by diversifying the donor base.

CIN has never obtained a grant dedicated specifically to media development. Most of the grants that CIN acquires are tied to civil society projects as dedicated media funding was significantly reduced even before CIN began fund-raising in 2007, after the initial three-year USAID grant had expired. For instance, as the Open Society Fund BiH does not have a media program, it supports CIN through its other divisions: its legal program and its transparency and accountability program.

Although there have been some occasional communication among donors in order to avoid overlap,[123] in spite of their longer-term engage-

---

[122] OCCRP, "About Us." The umbrella group OCCRP, based in Sarajevo, was established in 2006. It helps its member centers achieve sustainability and improve standards (Sullivan, "Investigative Reporting," 14).

[123] Ivana Cvetković Bajrović, Senior Program Officer for Europe, National Endowment for Democracy, interview with the author, June 10, 2013; Mervan Miraščija, interview with the author, July 10, 2013.

ment with the center, there has been little systematic coordination among donors (although CIN has been trying to initiate a formal form of donor coordination for years).

EFFECTS OF CIN STORIES

Research that CIN conducts periodically shows that an increasing number of citizens recognize the name of the center and not only its stories. Assessing the impacts of the foreign media assistance in the period 2007–2011, the EU draft report notes that CIN's production had an impact on the media which republished its content, and on the public, as well as, very recently, on the government.[124]

Many of CIN's stories made an impact on the responsible authorities. A prominent case initiated by a CIN story in 2006 resulted in the removal of the prime minister of the Federation of Bosnia and Herzegovina from office. Some other outcomes of CIN stories were: the BiH Chamber of Lawyers initiating a change in the system of choosing pro bono lawyers; the indictment of a former director of the Indirect Taxation Authority of BiH; the resignation of a judge from the War Crimes Chamber in the State Court of BiH; the resignation of a State Court judge; the closure of a university; and the indictment of a police officer for vehicular manslaughter.[125] Hence, it seems that the authorities recognized CIN findings as firmly corroborated, so that the do not ignore them and even follow up with appropriate actions.[126]

REPUTATION AND COOPERATION WITH LOCAL MEDIA

It is important that media organizations in BiH accept CIN as an equal partner considering that it operates as a media agency offering its stories to the media and has no other way to publish its work except on its website. Not surprisingly, the relationship between CIN and the media outlets in BiH has been both fruitful and challenging, while its reputation among media outlets and journalists has been slowly but steadily growing.[127]

---

[124] European Union and A.R.S. Progetti S.P.A, "Technical Assistance," 30.

[125] Drew Sullivan, interviews with the author, July 8, 2013, and August 18, 2013.

[126] Mehmed Halilović, interview with the author, August 16, 2013.

[127] Boro Kontić, interview with the author, August 19, 2013; Amer Džihana, interview with the author, August 23, 2013; Mehmed Hailović, interview with the author, August 16, 2013.

Many media outlets carry CIN stories more or less regularly. In 2015 each CIN story was published in about fifteen different print and online news media. However, the publishing of CIN content by media in BiH is influenced by the specifics of the local media market and the media culture. The media market in BiH is split among the three ethnic groups, but the situation is favorable for CIN—it can publish the same story in two or three dailies simultaneously because the papers are not competing as they cater to different audiences. However, BiH media carry CIN stories selectively, depending on their political affiliations, ownership, and other ties, as they are divided along party, ethnic, and other lines. For example, CIN decided not to offer its stories to the daily *Nezavisne Novine*, which caters to Republika Srpska, due to the paper's strong political associations. Also, some media in BiH perceive CIN as competition and are thus reluctant to publish its stories.

Despite the interest of BiH media in publishing CIN's stories, the center has never sold a story in the local market. This is because current prices for content are far below what a CIN investigative story costs and the BiH media are in a dire financial situation.[128] Consequently, the center does not have contracts with the media which publish its stories. CIN has not offered syndication contracts to BiH media because they would entail exclusivity clauses and the center's stance is that exclusivity can be guaranteed only to the media that pay for stories. Therefore, the center opted to offer its stories to whichever media organization is interested.

Inevitably, CIN has faced a lot of criticism among local media, especially in the beginning, and there were instances of negative stories written about CIN, dismissing its concept and predicting its closure.[129] There were various reasons for this—from professional envy and a misunderstanding of CIN's organizational concept, to the political interests of those media that criticized the work of CIN. For example, a Montenegrin daily which is a mouthpiece of a high-profile politician investigated by CIN, wrote negatively about the center in order to diminish the impact of its findings.[130]

---

[128] Mehmed Halilović, interview with the author, August 16, 2013.

[129] Drew Sullivan, interviews with the author, July 8, 2013, and August 18, 2013; Mehmed Halilović, interview with the author, August 16, 2013; Boro Kontić, interview with the author, August 19, 2013.

[130] Boro Kontić, interview with the author, August 19, 2013.

PRESSURES AND THREATS

There have been pressures on and threats against CIN journalists. The more recognized CIN is as a source of information which conveys a different picture to that which politics would like to present, the more it is exposed to pressure. For example, after CIN published a series of award-winning stories, the lawyers of the story's focus sent a letter to CIN's funders urging them to stop funding the organization that, allegedly, spread lies. However, the donors were united in their stance of not intervening in CIN's editorial policy. There was also one instance of a death threat to a CIN journalist. There have been threats of lawsuits and one actual lawsuit that was dismissed during the prehearing. Other pressures include the withholding of documents, threats of sending various inspectors to the center and using politically aligned media to publish negative stories about CIN. However, CIN has successfully dealt with all these challenges and has maintained its independence.

LEGAL INSECURITY

A significant challenge to CIN's work comes from disrespect for the Freedom of Access to Information (FOI) law by the authorities and the instance of "floating laws"[131]—laws that are often changed. For example, changes proposed to the FOI law in 2013 would have severely impeded access to information and thus the core tool of CIN's work.[132] Luckily, they were not introduced owing to a coordinated effort of civil society sector, but the government is still determined to change the law.

Moreover, inadequate implementation of existing FOI legislation often creates obstacles for the center as the authorities are not used to the openness that the legislation requires.[133] Consequently, CIN was forced to go to the court in order to obtain information that was withheld by state institutions, and won the first court cases against the authorities for withholding information.[134]

---

[131] Zielonka and Mancini, "Executive Summary," 6.
[132] Leila Bičakčić, interview with the author, June 10, 2013; Mehmed Halilović, interview with the author, August 16, 2013.
[133] Mehmed Halilović, interview with the author, August 16, 2013. For information on the implementation of FOI laws in BiH, see European Commission, "Bosnia and Herzegovina Progress Reports."
[134] Mehmed Halilović, interview with the author, August 16, 2013.

SUSTAINABILITY OF CIN

Financial sustainability remains a great challenge for CIN. The projection that the center would cover 50% of its financial needs from commercial contracts in five years proved overly optimistic as CIN's commercial income, gained through CIN journalists delivering training and presentations, is negligible. Given the circumstances, CIN is not likely to become a fully self-supporting media organization, bearing in mind that similar organizations in much more developed media markets of the West are struggling to find a formula for generating income beyond donations.

Unlike in the cases of similar centers in other countries, such as the Philippines, earning interest from an endowment is not an option for helping the sustainability of CIN due to the unfavorable conditions for securing a deposit in BiH. A property endowment where CIN would be given a building and would lease a part of it is also not the way forward as a legal assessment done by SIDA and CIN could not devise a model to protect the property in the case of CIN being sued and losing in court.

It seems that the sustainability of the center will depend on its capacity to do substantial fund-raising in the foreseeable future, proven very strong so far. In order to continue with successful fund-raising in the long run, CIN has to become fully integrated into the local media market, so that it can demonstrate to donors that there is a need for its stories, and that the stories can have a significant reach and impact. However, so far the integration of the center into the local media landscape is only partial at best. Namely, civil society considers CIN a media organization and media organizations consider them a member of civil society.[135] Furthermore, it is possible that the media do not perceive CIN as a part of their community mainly because of its funding sources, as CIN is independent of the media market in BiH and does not share all the problems of other media which are struggling to survive.[136]

These limitations of integration into the local media sphere combine with a weak market which prevents the commercialization of the center's services and with relatively unpredictable donor funding (mainly accessible in an ad hoc manner), along with the unavailability of funding targeting media development specifically, ensuring the center's sustainability remains a tough call for the foreseeable future.

---

[135] Leila Bičakčić, interview with the author, June 10, 2013.
[136] Amer Džihana, interview with the author, August 23, 2013.

The Center for Investigative Journalism Serbia (CINS)[137]

THE ESTABLISHMENT OF CINS

CINS was established in 2007 as a section of the Independent Association of Journalists of Serbia (NUNS). It became an independent legal entity in 2012, registered as a nonprofit foundation[138] established by NUNS. CINS currently operates in the premises of NUNS. Its goals are the production of investigative stories and an increase in such content in the Serbian media.

The organization was a product of conversations between several entities: the NUNS leadership, the leadership of the investigative journalism school—organized at the time within NUNS and funded by the National Endowment for Democracy (NED), NED representatives and OCCRP.[139] OCCRP wished to see investigative centers spring up in the Balkans and helped this process. NED and OCCRP thought that a home was necessary for those trainees of the NUNS school who excel so they could continue their good work. CIN in Sarajevo also played a role in nudging NUNS toward establishing CINS.[140] There was no kick-start grant for CINS, but it has been applying for mainly small grants from different donors since its inception.

The center operates with a relatively small team considering the complexity of its investigations. There were ten people at the center in 2016, including an editor-in-chief and six investigative journalists. The number of journalists increases by one or two depending on the available funding and scope of work the projects entail. They produced twenty-six stories in 2014 and thirty-eight stories since (as of August 2016), most of them investigative, as well as two searchable online databases. As these stories and databases require complex investigations that last for months, CINS director Branko Čečen thinks that it is an excellent output for such a small team, but also considering difficulties in funding the center. Also, the

---

[137] Unless otherwise indicated, the information on CINS was mainly collected from the interview with its director Branko, Čečen.

[138] There are two types of nongovernmental nonprofits in Serbia: citizens' association and foundations. Citizens' association are established by individuals, while foundations can be established by legal entities.

[139] Ivana Cvetković Barjović, interview with the author, May 31, 2013.

[140] Ibid.

traffic to the CINS website has increased almost ten times in the past three years.

CINS has acquired a good reputation among media in Serbia and internationally.[141] For example, CINS journalists received six times the yearly award for investigative journalism in Serbia "Freedom Day," awarded by NUNS and the US embassy, twice in cooperation with other organizations (BIRN Serbia and the Sarajevo-based CIN). CINS is a member not only of OCCRP, but also of the Global Investigative Journalism Network, and various informal networks.

CINS is also a provider of training. It delivered a range of donor-funded training for Serbian NGOs and international organizations. However, the funding for general investigative training targeting journalists is increasingly less available. To keep training going and to draft new journalists for its team, CINS organizes and delivers investigative journalism training without funding from time to time. For a training it organized in 2015, there were eight application for each trainee position, which testifies to the excellent reputation of the center with young journalists.

THE MODEL

Several role models influenced CINS, including US investigative non-profits. When the current CINS director was appointed in 2010, he was guided by the success of different investigative journalism operations. The achievements of CIN in Sarajevo showed that such an organizational model could work in the Balkans. A positive example from Serbia was the investigative series *Insider* of the national TV broadcaster B92, with high international standards and excellent impact. Important influences were two US investigative nonprofits—the Center for Public Integrity and later ProPublica (after it commenced to operate in 2008)—although the US model of nonprofits was used in a flexible manner, considering the different circumstances in which CINS operates.

There are important differences when these foreign models are implemented in Serbia. First, relying on donor assistance only, CINS often has to adapt to donors' goals, project themes and deadlines. The center's director believes that is not the case with the largest US nonprofits as they have secure funding for years ahead which enables them to choose freely the topics of investigation. Second, as the personnel and other resources

---

[141] Milorad Ivanović, interview with the author, August 21, 2013.

of CINS and its production are still very limited, the models the center looks up to could only be transposed to an extent. Third, CINS operates in a small, poor and very controlled media market, and in a general environment with incomparably less money to support investigative journalism than is the case in the West. Therefore, some modes of income, such as the purchase of CINS stories or citizens' donations, cannot be counted on. Furthermore, CINS stories, offered for free to Serbian media, are sometimes rejected with no explanation, because the media have to consider their political and other ties, including sources of funding. In addition, as the level of political culture in Serbia is very low, the work of CINS lacks impact in the form of tangible consequences. Regardless of the significance of CINS discoveries, there is usually no follow up by the state in holding the perpetrators accountable. Neither is there follow up by the media after the initial publication of a CINS story. Finally, the availability of educated and professional journalists is significantly larger in countries with more developed media, while CINS has to create quality investigative journalists from scratch, educating and coaching young journalists.

DONOR ASSISTANCE TO THE CENTER

Relying entirely on donor assistance, CINS developed into an independent organization with permanent staff and a broadened funding base.[142] It attracts on average about US$150,000 in donations annually; the amount of donations has increased by more than 50% since 2010, although the center would need approximately US$250,000 in its annual budget to reach its full potential—with the given newsroom staff, but with strengthened management capacities and its own premises. The single biggest donor to the center used to be NED, while other significant donors have been the US embassy (which stopped offering support to the media), IREX Serbia (now closed) and the Balkan Trust for Democracy. In 2016, the biggest donor to the center was the EU Delegation to Serbia, while US donors have generally withdrawn funds from Serbia. The center's operation is challenged by fairly fast diminishing donor support and donors having increasingly fewer funds. Also, the pool of donors that cater to Serbia seems to be smaller than those available to CIN in Bosnia, such as direct funding from the Swedish SIDA, which is of great help to CIN. All

---

[142] Janet Rabin Satter, Assistant Program Officer for Europe, National Endowment for Democracy (NED), interview with the author, May 31, 2013.

of this creates a significant and a very realistic risk of gaps between spells of donor funding, jeopardizing the center's financial ability to pay the journalists and costs of investigations.

Although OCCRP does not operate as a donor organization, there is a spillover of OCCRP funds to CINS. For instance, some dozen investigative projects were carried out in cooperation with OCCRP. An international editor, paid by OCCRP, worked at CINS for two and a half years, taking on the additional roles as advisor and educator. A local editor-in-chief used to be kept on a retainer by the OCCRP as all the stories he did individually were within the scope of the cooperation between CINS and this network. OCCRP also engages CINS journalists on a story basis, in which case the stories belong to both organizations.

In 2015 CINS received a much-needed institution-building grant from the Rockefeller Brothers Fund. The term of the grant was a year with the possibility of an extra year extension. The grant covered the salaries of the director, a fund-raiser/project manager, and an editor-in-chief to enable them to focus on fund-raising and developing projects. A fund-raiser/project manager could be hired only owing to this grant as other grants target production of stories and do not provide institutional support. The role was an important addition to the team as the director could not handle intensive fund-raising with all the other duties and thus the center had spells when the journalists were not paid and the center was effectively dormant without funding.

While most of CINS's funding has been short-term and ad hoc, NED is an example of a donor that preferred a long-term approach to the center (that was training and product oriented).[143] The first four years of NED support (2007–2012) went through NUNS as projects on a yearly basis for the investigative journalism school, which yielded all but one member of the CINS staff. When CINS registered as a separate entity in 2012, NED began supporting it directly with funding for investigative projects. Although NED representatives are aware that continuous multiyear support would be better than project-by-project funding, NED can only disburse year-long grants due to administrative constraints.[144]

There is no formal donor coordination for CINS. Nevertheless, NED representatives routinely communicated with other US donors of their

---

[143] Branko Čečen, Director, CINS, interview with the author, May 29, 2013; Janet Rabin Satter and Ivana Cvetković Bajrović, interview with the author, May 31, 2013.

[144] Ivana Cvetković Bajrović, interview with the author, May 31, 2013.

grantees in order to avoid overlapping and combine efforts to the best possible effect.[145] However, this has been the only instance of donor communication known to CINS.

COOPERATION WITH LOCAL MEDIA

One of the key preconditions for the successful work of a nonprofit investigative reporting center such as CINS is the depth and scope of its cooperation with the media. CINS needs the Serbian media outlets to carry its stories in order for the stories to be relevant and effective. When offering a more exclusive story for publishing, CINS allows weeklies to publish it two days ahead of the story appearing on the CINS website, and half a day for dailies. In some cases, the deal is that the stories appear on the CINS website when the print media arrive on newsstands. So far, that relationship has been rather ambiguous.

It seems that not many Serbian media republish CINS stories except for the are dailies and online media. Several media outlets carried CINS stories relatively regularly, most notably nontabloid media, such as the daily *Blic* and the quality daily *Danas*. The quality daily *Politika* published CINS stories on organized crime. The newsweekly *Novi Magazin* and the Serbian edition of *Newsweek* (which closed down in 2016) carried CINS stories on a regular basis. However, only one TV station aired CINS findings—TV B92 (a cable channel without national coverage). TV Pink and *Politika* launched attacks on CINS in 2016, mainly accusing it of receiving funds from foreign donors. Stifling of the media by the new government, led by the Serbian Progressive Party, became increasingly obvious in 2016 and the result is that few independent mainstream media outlets continued to carry CINS stories regularly: a CNN affiliate, TV N1, and its website, and the liberal daily *Danas* (print and online edition). Other mainstream media republish CINS stories when these do not conflict with their political and advertising affiliations.

Although CINS has recorded that 75% of its stories in a one-year period between 2014 and 2015 were carried by other media, the relationships and cooperation with media outlets in Serbia is an unpredictable affair. For example, CINS had a deal with the weekly news magazine *NIN* to publish a CINS story in more or less every issue, but with the change of

---

[145] Janet Rabin Satter and Ivana Cvetković Bajrović, interview with the author, May 31, 2013.

NIN's editor, the weekly became more selective regarding CINS stories it is prepared to publish.

Moreover, the experience of CINS is that the media carefully choose the stories they publish due to the various affiliations and pressures they are under. Therefore, it is rather difficult to forge long-term deals with Serbian media to publish CINS stories.

Many media do not carry CINS investigations and are reluctant to cite them except when it is politically opportune for them, which is a manifestation of the position of the media as clients to external political and business interests.[146] There are examples of CINS stories cited in other media two years after they were published by the center because the parties in power and thus political circumstances changed. There is also resistance among media managers to publish sensitive stories. For instance, CINS could not publish stories about a prominent Serbian tycoon in other media until he was arrested. Tabloids, in particular, carry CINS stories opportunistically, when the stories become useful for their political and business interests. Tabloids carry CINS stories a lot as there is a very developed tabloid market in Serbia and the papers are in a fierce competition for unknown and important information. However, they often provide inadequate or no attribution to CINS and selectively publish CINS findings, in combination with their own information, giving an inappropriate context to the center's stories.[147]

Ultimately, the center has not succeeded in selling its stories to the Serbian media. The media are not financially capable of paying the actual cost of elaborate investigations, which is far beyond the market price of a story. Also, forging longer-term syndication deals with media pressured by various influences is not possible because they pick and choose the stories to be published according to their vested interests.

All in all, the center has not fully integrated into the Serbian media sector mainly because the media are serving the interests of political and business groups. "CINS is still somehow on the outside, as a self-sufficient body, and there is no effort by the media or by CINS to create a symbiotic relationship," comments Jovanka Matić, a media researcher.[148]

---

[146] Jovanka Matić, interview with the author, August 16, 2013.

[147] Branko Čečen, Director, CINS, interview with the author, May 29, 2013; Jovanka Matić, interview with the author, August 16, 2013.

[148] Jovanka Matić, interview with the author, August 16, 2013.

COOPERATION WITH THE CIVIL SECTOR

CINS has realized the strength of cooperation between investigative journalism organizations and civil society sector—investigative journalism supplies the civil sector with new, unknown facts, while it relies heavily in its investigations on the wealth of the expertise that various NGOs have. Also, investigative discoveries increase the visibility of problems that the NGOs deal with. Therefore, CINS is a member of an informal coalition of NGOs (PrEUgovor) that provides alternative monitoring of the implementation of policies in the EU accession process pertaining to two negotiation chapters—Chapter 23 (judiciary and fundamental rights) and Chapter 24 (justice, freedom and security). The findings of CINS investigations have been incorporated into the coalition's reports on an ad hoc basis, but grants have been obtained and new ones are sought to enable CINS to direct its investigations to the topics relevant to the areas of expertise of the coalition members. Additionally, recognizing the topic of energy management in Serbia as a very important, yet unexplored one, CINS is making first steps toward establishing a coalition of NGOs with significant expertise in this domain and hoping to attract donor funding for the work of the coalition and its own within it. CINS sees cooperation within NGO coalitions as a new avenue of potential success in approaching donors and is determined to explore it to the fullest.

INTERACTION WITH POLITICS AND BUSINESSES

It seems that the center has a rather delicate relationship with the spheres of politics and business. According to its director, the center has an influence on the political and business scene in Serbia, judging by the pressures it faces, such as attempts to stall the publishing of a story or pressure to stop an investigation by persons from an official's entourage. CINS has also received warnings to withdraw an already published story lest it be involved in a political conflict, with grave consequences for the center. There have also been instances of various sources telling CINS that there is an intention to cause them physical harm or to compromise them. Although there are many threats to sue CINS, it was sued only once and won in court. Additionally, sources sometimes refuse to talk to CINS. For instance, due to repressive attitude of the government toward nonprofit media, the Ministry of the Interior has completely shut out CINS by refusing to provide it with any information or contacts. Companies belonging to the most powerful tycoons and those dependent on their business networks demonstrate their resistance to CINS through a refusal to talk to the organization and their attempts to influence media not to publish the work of CINS. The latest pressures came from a government-controlled tabloid, *Informer*, which is leading a smear campaign against nonprofit media funded by foreign donors, CINS being among them.

REACTIONS OF STATE INSTITUTIONS

Sometimes CINS stories have surprisingly positive effects, notwithstanding the lack of satisfactory follow up by the responsible state institutions. After a series of CINS texts about a case of fraud, a large number of individuals, companies and institutions who were victims of the fraud joined forces and thus increased their chances of winning in court. However, action by the responsible state institutions, such as the prosecutor, is usually not taken following CINS stories. Most likely, this is a result of the party state and the lack of rule of law in Serbia[149] where the prosecutor and other bodies react only when they get a signal from the top—and the signal is usually not forthcoming.[150] The center's director is of opinion that the prosecutor and other bodies adjust their work to the expectations of executive government and are in a constant process of assessing political interests. Nonetheless, the director of CINS singles out the Anti-Corruption Council, as it follows up on the center's stories with appropriate procedures.

SUSTAINABILITY OF CINS

At this stage it is rather difficult to predict the chances of CINS becoming a sustainable organization with steady and relatively predictable sources of income and a developed market for its services and products. First of all, the financial security of the center is an issue due to donor dependence. The only alternative to donor dependence is finding a model for diversification and commercialization of services,[151] which is a tough call given the

---

[149] Ibid.

[150] Milorad Ivanović, interview with the author, August 21, 2013.

[151] Forms of financing other than donations require capacities and investment, which CINS is working on. The center plans to establish independent media projects, registered as separate legal entities, that could thus implement for-profit projects without jeopardizing the center's independence. The plan is to diversify sources of income. One avenue is TV production, where the products could be sold in the international market, the donor base could be broadened to interna-

poor and oversaturated market, the high costs of CINS operations and the investment these activities would require. So far, the center has no commercial sources of revenues.

Such a difficult situation has a rather negative effect on the center's capacity to reward the staff properly and focus on long-term development. For example, none of the staff are fully employed, but are engaged on temporary contracts as external associates, and their salaries are generally low—close to the country's average, but significantly smaller than they should be considering the long work hours and the stress the journalists are exposed to, their expertise and specific skills they keep developing. The salaries of journalists are ensured only on a project-by-project basis and they change depending on the success in winning projects.

The situation is further complicated due to the difficult relationship with local media, continuous political pressure on the media and nonresponsive state institutions, all of which limits the effectiveness and impact of CINS. Other restrictions such as undeveloped commercial potential and the limited prospects for it, as well as financial insecurity stemming from dependence on short-term donor funding significantly limit the capacity of the center to reach sustainability. It was thus caught in a vicious circle of lack of financial resources and human resources with management skills, primarily fund-raising; the two factors reinforced each other, and prevented or slowed down the center's development. The addition of the fund-raiser/project manager to the team is now breaking this circle with the hope of dwindling donor support arriving to the center to support this position and the operation of the center. However, in order to achieve this, a continuous stream of sufficient donor funds must be ensured, which is a tough call in Serbia nowadays.

Final Remarks

Having conducted an analysis of donors' efforts aimed at supporting investigative reporting projects and organizations in BiH and Serbia, one has to ask again the underlying research question of this study: Is it possible

tional calls for proposals pertaining to TV production, and people and equipment could be leased. The plan is for the new website to feature new content daily so as to attract more users and feature international ads, while also serving as a marketing tool for the TV production and commercial news web projects. See Branko Čečen, director, CINS, interview with the author, May 29, 2013.

to introduce, in a sustainable manner, investigative reporting practices and nonprofit centers into media contexts that lack the basic preconditions necessary for the development of investigative reporting? The answer seems rather multifaceted and far from obvious or definite.

For example, the effects of investigative journalism training programs and assistance for story production are questionable. The direct results of the numerous donor projects and programs aimed at improving the skills and knowledge of local journalists and the media about high-quality journalism are not readily apparent as the participants of such programs have had to return to media outlets that lack the basic resources to put the skills and knowledge they gained into practice and, more importantly, lack the will to publish stories that negatively affect the authorities and large advertisers. However, the potential cumulative impact of such initiatives should not be dismissed, as knowledge and skills spread through newsrooms, NGOs, and journalism schools. The long-term impact of such efforts remains a worthy subject for future studies. Similarly, the effects of the assistance toward the production of investigative content by media and individuals are unclear as the practice rarely continues beyond donor support due to unsupportive newsrooms and lack of funding.

When looking into the effects of the two nonprofit investigative reporting centers that were the focus of this chapter, the situation becomes much clearer. It is safe to say that CIN and CINS are functional media organizations, which fulfill a need in media markets with a serious lack of professional investigative reporting and a lack of independent media. However, their influence is hampered by a rather delicate relationship with media outlets that should carry their stories, most notably due to the political and business interests of the media, consequently limiting the reach and impact of the stories. Although offered for free, the stories are sometimes not published because of political parallelism, business parallelism[152] and the influence of state politicization on the media.[153] Hence, although many stories of the two centers are published by local media, still many are not and only rarely, if at all, do local media follow up on them. Even more problematically, in many instances the centers' stories are used opportunistically by media which cater to the interests of their political and business patrons, in order to bash political and business opponents. Moreover, the impact of the stories is further limited by virtually non-

---

[152] Zielonka and Mancini, "Executive Summary," 4.
[153] Ibid., 2.

existent follow-up by responsible state institutions in the case of CINS, although the situation is better for CIN as the examples provided earlier demonstrate.

Both centers are faced with various political pressures, threats, and some legal insecurity. As Voltmer notes, political elites operate in continuity, even after autocratic regimes have ended; they are used to subservient media and find it difficult to accept media which act as their opponent rather than as their mouthpiece, so they continue with "pressure, threats and editorial interference."[154] Nevertheless, the centers are successful in dealing with these challenges and maintaining their independence. However, it seems that the most significant threat so far to their sustainability is total dependence on donor support, and their inability to commercialize any services or products. The primary reason for such a situation are very controlled media markets in which the centers operate, which are also small and financially weak. This is combined with the high costs of investigative stories production.

In effect, the sustainability of the analyzed centers in BiH and Serbia will depend for the foreseeable future on their capacity to successfully raise funds from donors. Here, the main challenge for the continuous development of the centers has to do with the nature of donor aid. The funding that the centers depend on is mainly ad hoc and short-term, which impacts their financial security. A potentially more significant positive impact of donor funding is further limited by the absence of systematic and strategic cooperation and coordination of donor efforts toward the centers. Rhodes states that "*Donor coordination* is considered a *conditio sine qua non* of media aid, which also establishes a common ideal in difficult situations: increasing impact."[155]

Finally, considering diminishing donor support and the lack of funding alternatives, the centers are in a precarious position. While the donor dependence of the two centers examined in this study is not an exception, as even the most reputable nonprofit investigative journalism centers in the world are heavily reliant on donor assistance, such a position is problematic in the local circumstances, with dwindling donor support and infinitely fewer possibilities for financial assistance than their role models have—primarily those in the liberal media system[156] of the US.

---

[154] Voltmer, "How Far Can Media Systems Travel?," 235.
[155] Rhodes, "Ten Years of Media Support," 10.
[156] Hallin and Mancini, *Comparing Media Systems*.

Additionally, they are faced with solving the puzzle of commercializing some of their income in hostile market conditions in order to reach partial sustainability, which at present seems to be an impossible aim. Unless donor organizations assume a strategic and coordinated approach toward the two functional centers, which perform an important societal role by providing much needed investigative journalism in countries which suffer from a serious lack of it, the centers seem to be facing an entirely uncertain future.

CHAPTER 9

Building Media Systems in the Western Balkans: Lost between Models and Realities

Katrin Voltmer

Introduction

When dictators fall, the rhetoric of "revolution," "liberalization" or "new era" often disguises the enormous difficulties that lie ahead. Beginning with the fall of the Berlin Wall that marked the end of the Cold War, democracy has spread around the world in breathtaking speed. However, as the "third wave"[1] comes of age, it becomes ever more evident that bringing down dictatorships is one thing, but building sustainable democratic institutions and media systems is quite another.

The chapters in this book provide vivid evidence of the many obstacles, errors and setbacks—but also of the achievements—that accompany the attempt of transforming media systems that hitherto have served the needs of an authoritarian regime into democratic institutions. Each of the chapters describes in much detail the policies that have been implemented in the five countries of the Western Balkans to rebuild media institutions and journalistic practices in an environment that is marred not only by the legacy of communism, but also by the trauma of war, deep societal divisions and economic decline. Given the importance of the Western Balkans for the stability and prosperity of Europe, considerable efforts have been made by the international community to build democracy in the region. Thus, besides describing the problems of transforming media systems in postauthoritarian countries, the chapters of this book also provide unique insights into the mechanisms and consequences of international media

---

[1] Huntington, *The Third Wave.*

assistance in emerging democracies. In spite of the undeniable progress that has been made, the accounts given here are also rather sobering. The policies pursued by international donors often lack long-term sustainability and in some cases exacerbate rather than ameliorate existing problems.

Taken together, the significance of this book goes far beyond the region of the Western Balkans. The outstanding scholarship and in-depth knowledge brought together in this volume also help us to better understand the dynamics of media transformation in other emerging democracies around the globe. While some of the problems the media in the countries under study are struggling with are unique for the region—for example, the extremely small media markets of countries whose populations range between less than two million (Kosovo) and some seven million (Serbia)—many others show striking similarities with developments in other new democracies. For example, issues of persistent political interference into journalistic decision-making, low levels of journalistic professionalism, political parallelism and sharp polarization of public communication are common features around the globe. Moreover, the emphasis on the work of media assistance organizations described in this book further highlights the difficulties that arise when transplanting the institutions and norms of democracy as practiced in established (mainly Western) countries to contexts that either do not have any, or only little, experience with democratic governance or are part of cultural and historical traditions that have little in common with Western traditions. These apparent discrepancies between the established democracies of the West and the fledgling semi-, partial or defective democracies of the "third wave"[2] have provoked the question whether democracy and its essential ingredient of a free press can be exported to other contexts.

As elsewhere in the postcommunist world of Eastern Europe, policy makers in the countries of former Yugoslavia and Albania have looked out for role models in established democracies as guidance for the reconstruction of their media systems. Hallin and Mancini's[3] models of media systems have become an influential framework not only for academic research, but also for policy choices to design media systems in emerging democracies. The three models proposed by Hallin and Mancini iden-

---

[2] Bernhagen, "Measuring Democracy and Democratization"; Croissant and Merkel, *Consolidation and Defective Democracy?*

[3] Hallin and Mancini, *Comparing Media Systems.*

tify the key dimensions of media systems with regard to the regulatory arrangements and behavioral patterns that organize state-media relationships, media markets, journalistic professionalism and the relationship between the media and the main cleavages in a society ("political parallelism"). The resulting "ideal types"[4] are the "liberal model" that is characterized by low levels of state regulation, commercialism and objectivity and neutrality as key journalistic norm; the "democratic corporatist model" that includes a strong public service element and the attempt to accommodate different interest and groups; and the "polarized pluralist model" that is dominated by partisan journalism and a close relationship between politics and the media. Hallin and Mancini's analysis, which focuses exclusively on Western media systems, reveals that the "liberal model" is predominant in Anglo-Saxon countries, the "democratic corporatist model" can be mainly found in the welfare states of Northern Europe and the "polarized pluralist model" covers mainly the Mediterranean countries.

Even though Hallin and Mancini emphasize that these models are empirical descriptions that do not imply any evaluation of the quality and adequacy of the kind of public communication each of the models provides, the "polarized pluralist" model is widely seen as deficient and least desirable. Recent studies that have applied Hallin and Mancini's models to non-Western countries and in particular the new democracies of the "third wave" have come to the conclusion that it is the "polarized pluralist" model that best characterizes cases outside the Western world.[5] However, it appears implausible that eighteen Western media systems are diversified across three different models, whereas the rest of the world is lumped together into just one.[6] Besides the conceptual problems this lack of variance throws up, the classification as "polarized pluralist" usually also implies a normative judgment that marks these non-Western and emerging media systems as immature and flawed.

In this concluding chapter I want to explore in some more detail the normative underpinnings of democratic media systems, in particular the "polarized pluralist" model. The chapter aims to address some of the the-

---

[4] The term "ideal types" is used here according to Max Weber's definition as the aggregation of characteristics of a class of cases, rather than normative desirable features.

[5] See Hallin and Mancini, *Comparing Media Systems*; see also Dobek-Ostrowska et al., *Comparative Media Systems*.

[6] See Voltmer, "How Far Can Media Systems Travel?"

oretical and normative issues involved in transforming postauthoritarian media systems, which have been described and analyzed in the country chapters of this volume. The discussion starts by introducing the concept of "social constructivism" as an effective theoretical tool to understand processes of institutional change in processes of democratic transition. Two key elements of media systems serve as examples to demonstrate the "social construction" of norms and practices in different social and political contexts: partisanship and pluralism. While partisanship is seen as a deficiency of media systems, albeit widely practiced, pluralism is valued as an indispensible norm of democratic media, yet difficult to achieve. Both elements denote to principles of how diverse voices are represented in a media system and play an important role in media policy formation and the regulation of media markets.

The Divergence of Democracy and the Social Construction of Media Institutions

More than a decade ago, Diamond and Plattner[7] observed that instead of "third wave" democracies becoming more similar to their established counterparts, they were actually on a course of "divergence," leaving a growing gap between the liberal democracies of the West and postauthoritarian forms of democracy. While the emerging democracies successfully adopted some elements of democratic governance from Western role models, many other aspects appeared to be rather resistant to change, thus bringing about a hybrid blend of new and old institutional forms, orientations and practices. Similar observations can be made with regard to the media systems in new democracies. They incorporate structural elements and behavioral patterns of the regimes from which they emerged alongside forms of journalism that are associated with democratic public communication.[8]

Especially in postcommunist countries huge efforts have been made to privatize the media, assuming that the need to attract large audiences in a competitive market would force the media to distance themselves from their traditional bonds with the state and adopt a more professional approach to journalism. This rarely happened, as the chapters of this

---

[7] Diamond and Plattner, *The Global Divergence of Democracy.*
[8] See Voltmer, *The Media in Transitional Democracies,* 115–128.

volume demonstrate the many obstacles and unintended consequences of this policy. The alternative model, public service broadcasting, was not much more successful either. Even though the institutional structures of established public service broadcasting organization, such as supervisory bodies and license fee funding schemes, were implemented the resulting organizational forms resemble more the old system of state broadcasting than, for example, the BBC.

In order to understand media transitions in emerging democracies, it is important to keep in mind that neither the key concepts of democratic media, such as independence, pluralism and public interest, nor the norms of journalism, such as objectivity, investigation and factuality, are as unanimous as textbook knowledge might imply. Instead, the way in which they are understood and practiced is highly contingent on the particular historical and cultural context in which journalists work. Existing meanings and practices are carried over to newly established institutions, thus altering the forms and performance of institutions. Milton[9] argues that the democratization of existing institutions, which have their roots in the old regime, like the media, is more difficult and usually yields more fuzzy results than the creation of entirely new institutions, such as the electoral system or the central bank. According to Milton, it is almost impossible to eliminate the "institutional traces"[10] inherited from the past when transforming institutions that have already served the old regime. These "institutional traces" are not only imprinted in the procedures and rules that regulate institutional procedures; they also shape the expectations and behavior of both the members of the institution and outside stakeholders.

The persistence of "institutional traces" implies that democratic institutions like the media cannot be transplanted in a one-to-one fashion. Rather, the emerging forms and practices always constitute a complex juxtaposition of the old and the new, a compromise between an ideal vision and what is possible in a given situation, a unique conjunction between the trajectory of the past and the immediate constraints of the transition itself. Early democratization research and democracy assistance was based on the assumption that democracy can be "crafted"[11] or "designed,"[12] assuming that a functioning democracy—and with it a func-

---

[9] Milton, *The Rational Politician*, 23.
[10] Ibid.
[11] Di Palma, *To Craft Democracies*.
[12] Lijphart and Waisman, *Institutional Design*.

tioning media system—can be achieved if the right models are adopted and implemented.

The belief that democratic institutions and media systems can be "exported"[13] has often led to a tick-box approach that attempts to transfer institutional packages to countries that are reconstructing their media systems after the collapse of the authoritarian regime. Inevitably, in most cases the results were disappointing. Differences between the outcomes and the model that served as blueprint for the transformation are usually seen as deviances, flaws and shortcomings. This is not to deny that many emerging democracies and their media systems are imperfect and in some cases fail to observe the most basic rules of democratic governance. However, rather than regarding the emerging hybrid forms of democracy and media as indicators for incomplete and even failed transitions, a more nuanced view is necessary for evaluating the new "fuzzy" manifestations of democratic practice.

It is worth noting that in the literature on globalization hybridity is regarded as cultural forms in their own right that often represent creative and innovative ways of coping with the challenges of change.[14] In contrast, in the literature on democratization, hybridity usually denotes the many forms of "democracy with adjectives" that political scientists are reluctant to classify straightforwardly as "democracy."[15] What is often overlooked is the fact that for new institutions and norms to become legitimate, they have to be "domesticated" through a process of adaptation and integration into local value systems and customs. Far from undermining democratic ideals, the domestic anchoring of norms is a precondition, rather than an obstacle, for the consolidation of a sustainable media system that is able to play its part in the democratic life of its country. Thus, the resulting hybridity of journalistic practices extends beyond the dichotomy of democratic versus authoritarian, free versus unfree, professional versus unprofessional.[16]

Democratization research has only recently begun to acknowledge the large variety of pathways democratic transitions take, and the role that indigenous cultures play for the outcome of the process. The social constructivist approach provides a conceptual framework that helps to understand why "exported" democracies and their media systems differ signifi-

---

13 LaMay, *Exporting Press Freedom.*
14 See Chadwick, *The Hybrid Media System.*
15 Collier and Levitsky, "Democracy with Adjectives."
16 Voltmer and Wasserman, "Journalistic Norms."

cantly from their role models. According to this perspective, institutions emerge from, and are continuously recreated through collective discourses and social interactions.[17] Thus, the performance of institutions not only depends on their formal rules and hierarchical structures, but equally on the way in which they are interpreted by those who are applying these rules in their everyday actions. Consequently, even though institutions such as elections or a free press are signified by the same word, they mean different things in different cultural contexts. The dramatic consequences of different interpretations of what democracy means became evident when on July 3, 2013, the military in Egypt removed President Morsi from power following massive street protests against his leadership. Even though Egypt adopted elections as part of its transition to democracy, the country is deeply divided over the interpretation of these elections. One camp insists on the primacy of elections as binding mechanism for selecting a country's government; others believe that democracy expresses itself through the voice of the people on the street. The future face of Egypt's democracy depends on which interpretation of democracy prevails.

Adopting a constructivist approach, democratization scholar Laurence Whitehead[18] proposes an "interpretavist" understanding of democratic transitions. His argument can be equally applied to the institutionalization of independent media in emerging democracies: If "democracy" and "independent media" are "viewed as a contested and to some extent unstable concept, anchored through the invocation of practical knowledge and a deliberative filter of collective deliberation, then democratization [and the creation of independent media] can only come about through a lengthy process of social construction that is bound to be relatively open ended."[19]

This view emphasizes the ambiguous nature of democracy, which has its roots much less in philosophical arguments rather than in "practical knowledge." Even though democratic institutions and media systems have to be implemented at some point, they come into existence through practice. Building democratic media is therefore a long-term, often frustrating process of trial and error. Moreover, the practice of "constructing" democratic media is embedded in "collective deliberations." Without this rooting in public discourse institutions remain isolated, without legitimacy and ultimately unprotected. This seems to have happened in several of the

---

[17] Berger and Luckmann, *The Social Construction of Reality*; Searle, *The Construction of Social Reality*.

[18] Whitehead, *Democratization*, 6–35.

[19] Ibid., 30.

countries described in this volume. As soon as foreign donors withdrew their (financial and practical) support the newly implemented institutions dwindle or are being hijacked by particularistic interests. Apparently, the new institutions have not grown strong enough roots in their own soil to be able to survive without external support. From Whitehead's "interpretavist" point of view an important element of sustainable transition is missing: "collective deliberation." In many emerging democracies institution building is primarily regarded as an elite project in which the citizens are reduced to consumers of services and products, but not as "constructors" and active participants in their own right. Several democracy-promotion agencies, including the EU, have become increasingly aware of this deficiency and have begun to reach out to civil society organizations as partners in the transition process. However, civil society organizations often do not exist in these countries or do not have the structures and expertise that are necessary to participate in an elite-driven transition process. What should be a "collective deliberation" process is therefore often reduced to a behind-the-doors bargaining between different interests that can hardly claim to speak in the public interest.

Understanding the democratization of media institutions and journalism as social construction, that is, as a process of collective (re)interpretation and continuous practice, might sound like an esoteric academic discussion, but it has far-reaching consequences for the policy choices that are made and the evaluation of outcomes. One conclusion that can be drawn from the social constructivist approach is that the emerging media systems in new democracies are bound to deviate from Western models. For even if the new institutional structures are an exact adaptation of the Western model, they will ultimately function differently because of the way in which they are interpreted and used by individuals in the new environment.

The other conclusion is that the "models" of media institutions— usually the "liberal" one with some elements of "democratic corporatism"—which media assistance organizations try to export to new democracies do not exist, neither does the journalism that is taught in textbooks and many journalism training programs. The "real existing"[20]

---

[20] The term alludes to the expression "real existing socialism" which was widely used to describe the socialist countries in Eastern Europe (Sakwa, *Postcommunism*). The term was somewhat ambiguous: political leaders used it proudly to refer to the attempts of establishing socialism in their countries; but the term often opened up ironical, even critical connotations, as it pointed to the gap between the promises of ideal communism and what existed in reality.

media systems in established Western democracies deviate from these models and their underlying ideals in many ways—maybe as much as the new media systems in emerging democracies. In fact, the institutions and practices of Western media systems are themselves social constructions that have evolved in a historical process and are shaped by the specific cultural, political and economic conditions in which this process took place. Yet they are often seen as "natural," "objective" facts to which, apparently, there is no plausible alternative. Berger and Luckmann describe this tendency of taking for granted what is in fact contingent as "reification," that is, a false assumption that confuses specific social forms with universal norms that could claim validity across cultural boundaries. As Berger and Luckmann maintain, "man is capable of forgetting his own authorship of the human world, that the dialectic between man, the producer, and his products is lost to consciousness."[21]

★ ★ ★

In the following, the historical roots and contextuality of media institutions will be discussed by taking a closer look at two features of emerging media systems, including those in the Western Balkans, that are often regarded as evidence for the failure of exporting the Western model in postauthoritarian countries: partisanship and (external) pluralism.

Partisanship, Collective Identities, and Social Divisions

One of the key characteristics of the "polarized pluralist" model of Hallin and Mancini's[22] typology is "political parallelism." The notion draws on the concept of "press-party parallelism" introduced by Colin Seymour-Ure[23] to describe the pattern and degree to which the press system mirrors the party system in European history since the nineteenth century.[24] Seymour-Ure[25] emphasized the interdependency of political parties and the

---

[21] Berger and Luckmann, *The Social Construction of Reality*, 89.

[22] Hallin and Mancini, *Comparing Media Systems*, 26–33.

[23] Seymour-Ure, *The Political Impact of Mass Media*, 173–174.

[24] Hallin and Mancini prefer the more general term "political parallelism" to indicate that the media might associate with political organizations or groupings other than just political parties.

[25] Seymour-Ure, *The Political Impact of Mass Media*, 157.

rise of the mass-circulation press: "The growth of competing political parties in nineteenth-century Europe was widely paralleled by the rise of newspapers supporting them."

Conversely, newspapers depended on sponsors like political parties because other forms of revenues, such as advertising and the related economy of mass consumption, were still in their infancy. Seymour-Ure's argument resembles Benedict Anderson's[26] assumption of the role the printed press played in the rise of national identities. By creating narratives of current events, historical experiences and images of "us" and "them," the media contribute to the emergence of "imagined communities"[27] by enabling individuals to form emotional bonds with other individuals without sharing the same physical space. These bonds could be based on ideological beliefs, class, ethnicity or nationality.

Scholars of media history argue that neutrality and objectivity as a journalistic norm only emerged in response to changing economic conditions, especially in the US.[28] The rise of the so-called yellow press—that is, cheap, easy-to-read newspapers with mass appeal—made it imperative for media owners to produce content that would be attractive to mass audiences regardless of their particular political worldviews. The newly established news agencies also contributed to a less partisan style of journalism, as news became a commodity that was sold to a large number of different customers.[29] Even though the norm of objectivity and neutrality has become a widely accepted part of journalistic professionalism, in reality partisan-based political parallelism remains the dominant pattern of media pluralism—not only in new democracies, but also in established democracies. It is important to note that partisanship and quality journalism are not mutually exclusive, as the leading national newspapers in Europe demonstrate: from *The Guardian* to *Le Monde*, and from *La Repubblica* to the *Frankfurter Allgemeine Zeitung*; these national newspapers have clear and outspoken political preferences, but are at the same time widely praised for journalistic excellence. The most partisan media, and thus the strongest political parallelism, can be found in Britain, the country that Hallin and Mancini classified as representing the "liberal model."

With the spread of balance and objectivity as journalistic norms alongside a journalism of advocacy and partisanship, the foundations of

[26] Anderson, *Imagined Communities*, 37–46.
[27] Ibid.
[28] See Schudson, *Discovering the News*.
[29] Boyd-Barrett and Rantanen, *The Globalization of News*, 1–14.

the relationship between media outlets and their audiences also changed. Waisbord[30] distinguishes between a "journalism of information" and a "journalism of opinion," each of which makes different credibility claims. "While one says 'trust me, I'm an expert,' the other says 'trust me, I'm one of us.'"[31] Waisbord argues that for trusting the media people consume, partisanship is much more important than objectivity and balance. When trying to make sense of the political conflicts of the day, most people regard a source of information that supports their own political views as more trustworthy than a media outlet that challenges their beliefs. In an environment of information abundance "journalism of opinion" provides an important guide through an otherwise overcomplex and confusing political environment.

Biased information not only helps to make sense of political issues without investing an unreasonable amount of time into comparing and evaluating different sources of information; it also encourages political involvement and participation.[32] Martin Wattenberg[33] is another scholar who emphasizes the benefits of partisan media. Writing from the perspective of US politics, he argues that the neutral reporting style of modern media is, at least in parts, responsible for the decline of American political parties. As voters no longer find clear partisan cues in the media, party identification is eroding giving way to candidate-centered politics and an increasingly vacuous political discourse.

These positive views of media partisanship seem to be surprising given the widespread concern about political parallelism. And indeed, political parallelism is a double-edged sword. If media partisanship involves stirring hostility and disrespect for anybody who disagrees with one's own favored view, then it poses a serious threat to the viability of a democratic public sphere. Political parallelism can polarize a country up to a point where it becomes difficult to agree on any policy or definition of a situation or even the outcome of an election. In their comparative study on political attitudes in postcommunist countries, Anderson et al.[34] found that the political culture in these countries lack what they call "losers' consent," that is, the ability to accept the validity of opposing views. However, the legitimacy of elections not only requires that they have been conducted according to the

---

[30] Waisbord, "In Journalism We Trust?"
[31] Ibid., 84.
[32] Mutz, *Hearing the Other Side.*
[33] Wattenberg, *The Decline,* 90–112.
[34] Anderson et al., *Losers' Consent.*

rules, but also that whoever loses the election acknowledges that fellow citizens who voted for the winning side have made their decision on reasonable grounds. However, the reality in many new democracies looks very different. Elections are widely seen as a zero-sum game where the winner takes all and the loser loses everything. Hungary under Orbán is only one—admittedly extreme—example for the deep polarization of a society where the opposite political camp is regarded as enemies. In all countries where it has become impossible to reconcile the divisions between different camps, partisan media have played a central role. Many have made hostility against the other side and smear campaigns a kind of business model which secures them revenues from the political groups or individuals in whose services they have put themselves. However, in an atmosphere of hostile antagonism, moderation and compromise are becoming virtually impossible, thus keeping in motion a vicious circle of hatred. Given the ambiguity of media partisanship as a source of political identities on the one hand and social divisions on the other, it can be argued that the crucial characteristic of Hallin and Mancini's "polarized pluralist" model is not the existence of political parallelism, but a degree of polarization that leads to a dominance of centrifugal forces over the ability to maintain common grounds for a shared sense of citizenship.

Ironically, at a time when Western democracy promotion agencies invest considerable resources into exporting the "liberal" model of media systems and journalism to the emerging democracies of the "third wave," this model seems to be in decline in the very countries that serve as role models for objectivity, balance and factual news reporting. Britain has always had a strong—and at times aggressive—partisan press, which, however, is counterbalanced by a strong public service sector and the dominant role of the BBC. Recent empirical findings show that partisanship and polarization have even intensified over the past decades.[35] Arguably even more surprising is the recent rise of partisan media in the US. The proliferation of transmission capacities has allowed cable channels like Fox News to establish themselves alongside the big three national television networks. Fox News pursues a distinctly partisan editorial policy that caters for the right-wing sectors of the population and has supported the disputed foreign policy of the Bush administration.[36] In their comparative analysis of US, British, German, Swiss, French and Italian newspapers,

---

[35] Umbricht and Esser, "Changing Political News?"
[36] Aday, "Chasing the Bad News."

Esser and Umbricht conclude that "the ideal of Anglo-American journalism as a coherent benchmark . . . turned out to be a category of limited and at most historical value."[37]

Evidently, "real existing" media systems are shaped along partisan lines. Rather than converging toward the liberal model, as Hallin and Mancini[38] imply, they seem to converge to the model of "polarized pluralism" that is often regarded as less fit for the purpose of democratic public communication. The examples from the US and Britain demonstrate that the spread of the "polarized pluralist" model is not just due to the large number of new democracies which, one might argue, are still going through a process of developing mature democratic media systems. Instead, many established democracies reveal similar developments. It would be too easy to put the trends toward partisan media down to ruthless political instrumentalization by the ruling power elites or the market strategies of media owners who are looking for profitable niches in an overcrowded market. While these factors are undoubtedly playing an important role, it cannot be denied that there is a genuine need among audiences for a kind of information that helps citizens to find their place in the world.

The paradox is that democratic life—in particular in emerging democracies—needs both: vivid partisanship and detached and factual reporting. On the one hand, partisanship provides orientation in the complex and often chaotic circumstances of transition. It also helps to establish political loyalties that are important for the growth of civil society and a stable party system. On the other hand, objective journalism and unbiased information are crucial for developing a public sphere where different voices can be heard and listened to, and where compromises and shared visions can be forged.

Pluralism, Polarization and the Search for Unity

The normative principle of pluralism is often seen as the opposite of partisanship because it implies inclusion of different views rather than exclusion. However, pluralism is in fact the flipside of partisanship and it can be argued that the two develop in tandem.

---

[37] Esser and Umbricht, "Competing Models of Journalism?," 1003.
[38] Hallin and Mancini, "Americanization."

One of the main policy objectives of postauthoritarian media reconstruction is the creation of pluralism in the public sphere. The normative vision underlying this policy is the notion of a "marketplace of ideas," which goes back to John Stuart Mill's treatise *On Liberty*[39] in which he uses the metaphor as an argument to defend press freedom against the common practice of censorship of his time. In Mill's view it is through competition of different ideas and the confrontation of arguments and counterarguments that "the truth" will eventually emerge. Being one of the leading proponents of the nineteenth-century philosophical school of utilitarianism, Mill's justification of press freedom derives from the assumed beneficial consequences of competition between different ideas. In his view "the truth" is most likely to emerge from the free play of market forces rather than through state regulation. While Mill's notion of a "marketplace of ideas" is a metaphorical description of a space of human exchange and interaction, liberal media theorists and policy makers have adopted a literal understanding of the term to denote media as commodities that are offered and bought on a market of goods. The economic interpretation of the "marketplace of ideas" metaphor has led to the assumption that the plurality of channels equals the plurality of ideas that are expressed in the public realm.[40] It is therefore not surprising that privatization and increasing the number of media outlets figured high on the agenda of media assistance agencies that were engaged in rebuilding the media systems of the countries in the Western Balkans.

However, the experience not only in the countries of the Western Balkans, but also in emerging democracies elsewhere in the world, shows that the results of this policy are often counterproductive to the sustainability of the emerging media system and even detrimental to the consolidation of the young democratic order. Apparently, the scope of pluralism matters. Here, Downs's "economic theory of democracy"[41] can help to understand the dynamics of pluralism in a competitive environment. Downs developed his theory to explain the behavior of political parties in different constellations, but his argument can be equally applied to pluralist media systems. Downs argues that in a system with two competing players—parties, media—whose survival depends on the mobilization of mass support, these players will move toward the center of the space of

---

[39] Mill, *On Liberty*, 15–54.

[40] See Napoli, "The Marketplace of Ideas."

[41] Downs, *An Economic Theory of Democracy*.

competition in order to capture the "median voter"—or "median reader/viewer." As a result, the profile of the two players will become neutralized and almost indistinguishable, bringing about "catch-all parties"[42] which dominated postwar Western European politics, and—as described in the previous sections—neutral news media that adopt objectivity as a guiding journalistic norm.[43] Even though both arrangements seem to incorporate and balance different viewpoints, the spectrum of opinions that are represented is rather centralized and mainstreamed. As the number of players increases, the need to occupy the middle ground relaxes and actors—parties, media—seek to adopt a clearer profile that attracts particular voters or audiences, thus giving alternative and nonmajority positions a higher chance to be represented in the system.[44] A further increase of players usually leads to growing fragmentations with a strong pull toward polarization whereby individual actors adopt extreme positions in order to secure loyal followers, even though they might count for only small portions of the market.[45] Symbolic politics and political parallelism that draws on particular identities—ethnic, religious, regional or tribal—is a way of forging strong ties with particular groups of the population.

Thus, there is a point where pluralism turns into a destructive force. Where exactly this point is depends on the kind of divisions and how they are played out in the competitive game. To decrease the risks of fragmentation and polarization, many constitutions include mechanisms to limit pluralism in the party systems, for example, through electoral hurdles that require a minimum of votes in order to claim seats in parliament. However, similar considerations are rarely applied when rebuilding postauthoritarian media systems. Here, the principle of "the more, the better" seems to dominate—with detrimental consequences, as the case studies in this volume, but also other experiences from new democracies demonstrate. In some cases, the policy of encouraging the launch of new media outlets has led to an oversupply in very small markets. Newspapers with circulation

---

[42] Kirchheimer, "The Transformation."

[43] It has to be noted that neutrality is a rather superficial understanding of objectivity. Tuchman describes it as a mere "ritual" whose main objective is to avoid risks, such as accusations of bias or libel suits, but which fails to bring about "truth." See Tuchman, "Objectivity as Strategic Ritual."

[44] In party systems the key mechanism that affects the number of players is the electoral system. In media systems anticoncentration regulation of ownership exerts a similar function.

[45] See Lijphart, *Democracy in Plural Societies*.

rates of hardly more than 30,000 copies are not only unsustainable in the long run; they also lack the resources that are necessary to produce high-quality information. Unable to afford professional journalists, these newspapers often have to resort to "cheap" partisanship, which is hardly rooted in a coherent editorial or ideological program, but uses opinion journalism and ethnic or nationalist rhetoric to fill the daily news hole.

In postconflict societies the perils of unbridled pluralism are particularly evident. New democracies that emerge from war not only have to cope with the challenges of building functioning institutions; they also have to overcome the trauma of the past and the divisions that have triggered the conflict. Thus, achieving "democratic peace"[46] in postconflict societies requires more than a formal settlement on the future distribution of power and resources; it also involves creating conditions that make it possible for the antagonistic groups to live together in one nation. However, democratic politics and the liberalization of the media have not always brought about "democratic peace." The unsettling truth is that in many instances elections and uncensored public speech have exacerbated the already fragile situation in postconflict societies.[47] The reason is that the space opened up by liberalization and privatization is often immediately occupied by those who aim to manipulate public opinion. Especially where political parties campaign on a sectarian agenda, the media usually follow suit resulting in deeply polarized pluralism. The competition between claims for domination by different ethnic, religious, etc. groups fought out in media that put themselves into the service of these particularistic interests is worlds apart from Mill's "marketplace of ideas" where different truth claims compete for recognition through the force of the best argument. In their analysis of the policies of Western media development organizations in postconflict and crisis states, Putzel and Van der Zwan[48] criticize what they call the "unsophisticated liberalization of the media" that is not sufficiently aware of the complexities of deeply divided societies.

What could be alternative ways of building media institutions that are conducive for the consolidation of new democracies? Allen and Stremlau[49] suggest that in some circumstances a certain degree of censorship might be

---

[46] The term "democratic peace" usually denotes interstate relations between democracies, but can equally applied to the social order within states. See Huth and Allee, *The Democratic Peace.*

[47] See Voltmer, *The Media in Transitional Democracies,* 188–196.

[48] Putzel and Van der Zwan, "Why Templates."

[49] Allen and Stremlau, "Media Policy."

necessary in order to stabilize the fragile situation of transitional and post-conflict reconstruction. This might be an extreme measure that bears its own risks, most notably that of political instrumentalization when power-hungry elites try to exploit the call for security and peace as a pretext for self-interested censorship. Nevertheless, it cannot be denied that a pluralism of hate speech has little value for the emergence of a democratic political communication culture.

A different way of addressing the perils and virtues of media pluralism is to rethink what pluralism in public communication is about and what it is for. Most policy makers and scholars of normative media theory alike[50] understand pluralism primarily as a means for the representation of different views in the public sphere. However, a solely expressive form of pluralism would hardly yield the kind of public exchange that Mill had in mind when stressing the virtues of a "marketplace of ideas." Equally important as the opportunity to express views is therefore the opportunity to encounter and listen to divergent voices. As the philosopher Onora O'Neill[51] maintains, public communication and the freedom that underpins it involves both communicators and audiences, speaking and listening. It is only when citizens have the opportunity to encounter the viewpoints, experiences and worldviews of fellow citizens that divisions can be bridged. Voltmer and Lalljee[52] point out that in democratic life it will never be possible to reach agreement on divergent positions, as theorists of deliberative democracy imply. Rather, what is crucial for a viable democracy is respect for the other side and toleration for diversity which, as empirical evidence suggests, is fostered by exposure to different viewpoints in the media.[53] Voltmer and Lalljee's study also shows that exposure to opposing views and respect for political opponents ultimately increases the legitimacy of democracy because citizens are able to acknowledge that others might have good reasons for their views, even though they themselves do not agree with them.

Obviously, partisan media do not provide opportunities for listening that are much needed particularly in unconsolidated and divided democracies, like most of the countries of the Western Balkans are. However, partisan media, besides fulfilling an important function in their own right, will be with us for the foreseeable future, as shown in the previous section.

---

[50] See McQuail, *Media Performance.*
[51] O'Neill, "Practices of Toleration."
[52] Voltmer and Lalljee, "Agree to Disagree."
[53] See also Mutz and Martin, "Facilitating Communication."

Building democratic media systems therefore requires provisions for "forum media" where people and groups with different beliefs and identities can meet. Curran[54] emphasizes the importance of media systems being composed of different forms, formats and principles rather than being dominated by one particular "model." The institutional form that is most likely to serve the purpose of enabling listening across lines of division is public service broadcasting, provided it is committed to open pluralism and the public interest. In all successor states of former Yugoslavia building democratic media systems included creating public service broadcasters, usually by transforming the former state broadcaster into a public institution. Given the importance of communicating across lines of divisions, the decision to implement three different broadcasters in Bosnia and Herzegovina each serving one of the ethnic groups of the country would probably be a gross mistake. In countries such as Switzerland segmented public service broadcasters that serve the different language communities of the country might be a workable federal solution because there is a widely shared sense of national unity that binds different communities together. But in countries that emerge from ethnic conflict the separation of communication channels will only further divide and polarize the society.

Creating a forum media that is capable of bringing together different discourses requires political and civic will. It does not emerge naturally. It might also require new forms of journalism that does not indulge in playing out and exaggerating differences, but one that enables dialogue and listening. One of the main problems with establishing public service broadcasting is its vulnerability to political interference. In many new democracies of postcommunist Eastern Europe, public service has been hijacked by political elites to serve their needs of controlling the public agenda. In many cases, a majoritarian approach to appointing the editorial and supervisory bodies of public service broadcasters have been an invitation to the government in power to manipulate the operation and performance of the institution.[55]

Besides flaws in institutional design and political dependency, there is yet another danger for public service broadcasting that might even be more perilous to the survival of public service broadcasting and its underlying philosophy. This risk comes from a more universal paradigm shift in public policy that regards market forces and deregulation as the ubiquitous

---

[54] Curran, "Mass Media and Democracy."
[55] See Jakubowicz and Sükösd, *Finding the Right Place.*

solution to whatever problem is at hand; from education, housing, health-care to public communication. The technological innovations during the 1980s that made it possible to overcome the transmission scarcity that had dominated broadcasting policy since its beginning, coincided with the rise of neo-liberalism to global dominance. Both developments have pushed public service broadcasting to the margins of media policy across Europe where it originated and subsequently dominated national media systems for decades. Even though policy makers continue to pay lip service to public service broadcasting, most public broadcasters see themselves in a precarious situation between market forces and increased political pressure. In 1987, France sold its main channel (TV1) to the private sector, while the remaining public channel has been reduced to an, albeit high-quality, niche enterprise.[56] Meanwhile, the BBC, arguably the "mother of all public service broadcasting" worldwide, finds itself constantly under threat by voices that challenge the legitimacy of the license fee as "ineffective and unethical."[57]

These are only two prominent examples to demonstrate the decline of the institution of public service broadcasting. Thus, like with the "liberal" model, the reality and philosophical pillars of the "democratic corporatist" model are disappearing in the very moment when emerging democracies like the countries in the Western Balkans are setting out to implement them.

Conclusions

The underlying concern that guided this chapter is the question whether "models" of media systems that have developed in the West can be exported to other countries where democracy is less consolidated. Essentially, this is a question that—explicitly or implicitly—runs through all chapters of this volume. While the country case studies are addressing this question through a thorough account of the attempts of building democratic media systems in particular political and economic environments, this chapter approached the issues mainly from a theoretical perspective by exploring some of the key concepts that guide media policy decisions in processes of democratic transition.

---

[56] See Kelly, Mazzoleni, and McQuail, *The Media in Europe.*
[57] Elstein, "The Licence Fee"; see also Peacock, *Public Service Broadcasting.*

Since the publication of Hallin and Mancini's seminal book *Comparing Media Systems*,[58] the notion of "models" of media systems has been widely used to understand the distinct features of both established and emerging media systems. However, as this chapter argued, the term "model" is in itself ambiguous, as it refers to both empirical manifestations of media institutions and practices and normative role models, that is, how media systems are and how they (ideally) should be. Even though Hallin and Mancini present their models as empirical descriptions, the models they suggest are rooted in normative assumptions that have guided the development of Western media systems, such as political independence, competitive pluralism and journalistic professionalism related to standards of balance and objectivity. On a very abstract level these principles seem to be indisputable for a democratic media system. However, unpacking these norms in more detail reveals a more complex picture. In this chapter the ambiguity of general media norms was demonstrated with regard to media partisanship, a media practice that ostensibly violates the objectivity norm, and pluralism, a norm that is valued as a central principle of representing the diversity of opinions in democratic media systems.

Even though media partisanship is tolerated as a form of public communication that is protected by freedom of speech, most media assistance practitioners who are involved in reconstructing media systems and journalism in new democracies will aim to limit the level of partisanship in the media. However, politics is not a neutral enterprise and partisanship is an essential ingredient that makes political involvement and participation meaningful. This chapter argued that partisan communication helps to develop party support, which in turn is important for a stable electoral process. Yet, at the same time, the potentially destructive forces of media partisanship are irrefutable in situations when the promotion of particular beliefs and identities turns against outsider groups and political opponents. Since media partisanship is an inevitable, even indispensible, yet problematic part of a democratic public sphere, media development programs should initiate public debates about quality standards of partisan and advocacy journalism to ensure its benefits for a viable democracy. These standards should include, for example, fairness of critique, respect for the integrity of the opponent and moderation in the promotion of particular worldviews.

---

[58] Hallin and Mancini, *Comparing Media Systems*.

In contrast to partisanship, pluralism is an unequivocally positive norm—at least so it seems. Pluralism, or the diversity of voices that have access to the public sphere, constitutes the "marketplace of ideas" which fosters the expansion of knowledge and innovation; or, as Mill would put it: the truth. However, there is a dark side to pluralism. An expansion of plurality inevitably leads to fragmentation and, in the worst case, polarization. The idealized vision of a "marketplace of ideas" where people come together to exchange views is offset by the centrifugal forces of difference. Especially in divided societies, like in the Western Balkans, the plurality of voices has to be counterbalanced by shared narratives and opportunities to communicate across the lines of difference. Forum media, as embodied in the ideals underpinning public service broadcasting, can provide common spaces where public debates on the big issues that concern the nation as a whole can take place. However, with the rise of the Internet to soon become the dominant means of communication and the decline of traditional media, future media development has to think beyond existing models of "media systems" in search for new opportunities and forms for public communication.

CHAPTER 10

Conclusions: A Cross-National Comparison of International Assistance and Media Democratization in the Western Balkans

KRISTINA IRION AND TARIK JUSIĆ

Introduction

Western Balkan countries have been beneficiaries of international media assistance programs to varying degrees. Because of the intensity of media reforms and institution building, Bosnia and Herzegovina and Kosovo are the two postconflict countries that exemplify international media interventions.[1] International media assistance programs did also target Albania, Macedonia and Serbia but to a lesser degree. Even within this group, there are significant differences in the scope and the nature of media assistance, with much more extensive support to Serbia compared to fairly moderate assistance programs in Albania.[2]

The chapters in this edited volume with country-level studies provide accounts of the range and intensity of media reforms these countries undertook in order to conform with accession requirements of the European Union (EU) and the standards of the Council of Europe, among others.[3] From today's vantage point, when assessing the media assistance programs, the results are varied, both among countries, and among different media subsystems within all of the countries studied. Some of the internationally backed efforts produced fairly sustainable media institutions, while others ended in failure or are—to say the least—vulnerable to systemic and business parallelism. Yet, other projects and programs wit-

---

[1] Thompson and De Luce, "Escalating to Success?," 201.
[2] Rhodes, "Ten Years of Media Support," 15.
[3] See the contributions of Londo, Jusić and Ahmetašević, Miftari, Dimitrijevska-Markoski and Daskalovski, and Marko in this volume.

nessed initial progress followed by later stagnation or even return to earlier authoritarian practices and norms.

This concluding chapter explores the nexus between the democratic transformation of the media and international media assistance as constrained by the local political conditions in the five countries of the Western Balkans. This chapter ties in with chapter 1 in this edited volume,[4] where the research framework is set out, on which the cross-national comparison rests. Such a cross-national comparison is possible because of the variations in international media assistance between Western Balkan countries with similar political and economic context factors present. It aims to enhance the understanding of conditions and factors that influence media institution building in the region and evaluates the role of international assistance programs and conditionality mechanisms herein.

The cross-national analysis concludes that the effects of international media assistance are highly constrained by the local context. A decade of international media assistance of varying intensity is not sufficient to construct media institutions when, in order to function properly, they have to outperform their local context. From today's vantage point it becomes obvious, that in the short-term scaling-up international media assistance does not necessarily improve outcomes. The experiences in the region suggest that imported solutions have not been sufficiently cognitive of all aspects of local conditions and international strategies have tended to be rather schematic and have lacked strategic approaches to promote media policy stability, credible media reform and implementation.[5] To a certain extent, the loss of international media assistance's effectiveness is also self-inflicted due to a lack of coordination, contextualization and sustainability.

This chapter first discusses how the Western Balkan countries in the focus of this research benefitted and experienced international media assistance, including a critique of its overall consistency. The next section compares the achievements and pitfalls of international media assistance which can be explained against the backdrop of the local context. After the conclusions, this chapter proposes a set of policy recommendations, which address policies in support of democratic media transition and international media assistance, respectively.

---

[4] Irion and Jusić, in this volume.

[5] Berkowitz, Pistor, and Richard, "The Transplant Effect," 163f.; Irion and Jusić, "International Assistance and Media Democratization" (2014), 22.

International Media Assistance to the Western Balkan Countries

This research operates with a broad view on what is to be considered international media assistance. It incorporates all externally induced interventions, initiatives and incentives to reform media institutions in the countries of the Western Balkans. International media assistance can thus take very different forms and strategies, including but not limited to financial support, standard setting, transfer of legislative and operational expertise as well as capacity building. Our broad view of international media assistance would thus also include EU conditionality which is defined in the literature as "a bargaining strategy of reinforcement by reward, under which the EU provides external incentives for a target government to comply with its conditions."[6]

Between the early 1990s and today, international media assistance can be classified in three phases, which show some overlap:

Phase 1: Supporting independent media (throughout the 1990s and early 2000s) with the aim of overcoming information monopolies, such as in Serbia during the Milošević regime, and to contribute to reconciliation after the conflict in Bosnia and Herzegovina and Kosovo.

Phase 2: Media reforms and institution building (1998 until 2005) throughout the Western Balkans, with different intensity however, focusing on the provision of assistance in the context of media legislation, the introduction of a media supervisory body and the transition from state to public service broadcaster, in addition to support for self-regulatory bodies, advocacy organizations and industry associations in the media.

Phase 3: Phasing out international media assistance (2005 until today) is characterized by a significant roll-back of international media assistance across the region, often relying on the role of the EU and respective EU accession procedures in which conditionality is believed to be the new engine for democratic media transition. This goes hand-in-hand with the ultimate handover of ownership of and responsibility for media institu-

---

[6] Schimmelfennig and Sedelmeier, "Governance by Conditionality," 670.

tions to local stakeholders—a process of domestication. In Kosovo and Macedonia, scaled-back media assistance focuses almost exclusively on support to minority media.

International Actors

International actors can be broadly distinguished by their respective functions and put into two groups: those organizations that influence local media policy and institution building, and others that provide operational support targeting media in the Western Balkans. This does not preclude some actors being active on both levels.

From the first group, the most prominent international actors are those equipped with an international mandate, such as the Office of the High Representative (OHR) in Bosnia and Herzegovina and the United Nations Mission in Kosovo (UNMIK). Other significant actors in democratic media transition throughout the Western Balkans are the US, the EU, the OSCE, and the Council of Europe. Their relationships were more closely-knit, including delegating specific media mandates to the OSCE in Bosnia and Herzegovina and Kosovo. Nonetheless, even among the top-tier organizations approaches differed considerably, reflecting different values and priorities.

The second group of international actors is much more diverse, comprising of other countries, development and nongovernmental organizations as well as a plethora of implementing agencies. Their contributions have been significant but disparate, lacking overarching strategies and coordination.

Goals and Approaches of International Media Assistance

According to Rhodes there are two main and interrelated categories of goals and objectives of media support in Western Balkans: on one level, there are political and social goals, on the other are media-specific objectives.[7] Assistance programs that aimed to achieve political and social goals looked to the media as a tool for changing society at large—for example, by helping remove authoritarian regimes, by protecting human rights, by reinforcing

---

[7] Rhodes, "Ten Years of Media Support," 11.

peace agreements, by easing ethnic tensions, by promoting democratization, by helping state and nation building, and by supporting European integration. Programs with media-specific objectives were intended to help the development of a free and professional media sector based on Western models of professional and responsible media. Inevitably, these two levels of goals and objectives were intrinsically linked: political and social goals, by definition, created the demand for media-specific objectives, while media-specific objectives worked toward achieving political and social goals.[8]

The approach to media assistance was based on several core assumptions about the roles and the values associated with the function of the media in a democratic system according to the idealized model of a "developed Western democracy."[9] Hence, the media assistance efforts were aimed at developing "professional" and "objective" journalists and "independent" and "impartial" media outlets,[10] that would be financially sustainable and would offer a "plurality" of different views when covering political issues and current events. An adequate legal and regulatory framework is seen as one of the key elements of a functional democracy, for conflict mitigation, and toward Europeanization. However, the differences between the sociocultural and political contexts of Western Balkan countries compared to those in Western democracies manifest as contingencies in local media institutions and practices that differ in many respects from the Western-democratic models according to which local media systems were modeled.[11]

This shall not be interpreted in such a way to suggest that international media assistance promoted the wrong values of media in the Western Balkan region. In these countries, the constitutional protection of freedom of expression and media freedoms is necessary to counter state encroachments on such rights. Local media policy and legislation that corresponds to European best practices has been instrumental in opening up media markets, combating hate speech, decriminalizing defamation and introducing elementary journalistic privileges, such as source protection.[12] Where they exist, high formal standards lay the foundations for professional and plural media. Most country-level chapters conclude that the local fragmented media sphere holds external pluralism but that this does

---

[8] Ibid.
[9] Voltmer, in this volume.
[10] Johnson, "Model Interventions," 40.
[11] Ibid., 30f.; Voltmer, in this volume.
[12] Rhodes, "Ten Years of Media Support," 28.

not compound to a nationwide, interethnic or cross-political public discourse. The local organizations, alone when it comes to public service media, fail to live up to their remit to cater for objective reporting and the coverage of diverse viewpoints.

Absence of Coordination

The literature on international media assistance stresses that donor coordination is a *conditio sine qua non* for the development of the whole media sector.[13] Especially when many diverse organizations and programs operate in parallel, effective donor coordination is key to creating synergies, to dividing labor corresponding to the capacities and to preventing duplication.[14]

In some Western Balkan countries, there were attempts to improve the transparency and coordination of international media assistance. In 2005, the Albanian government created the Department of Strategy and Donor Coordination, which inter alia also gathered data on international media assistance. In Bosnia and Herzegovina, during the early period of media assistance efforts, the OHR convened regular biweekly roundtables with all major donors and maintained a database of donor projects. In the high phase of international media assistance to Kosovo, the chapter notes some donor coordination at the policy level regarding general principles, but at the operational level, concerned with specific activities and projects, coordination was barely perceptible.

The impact of these endeavors was, however, very limited, not least because donor organizations' decision-making preceded transparency and coordination, which essentially precludes a common strategy. Taken together, the mention of parallel efforts noted in the country studies amounts to an impressive testimony to the symptomatic absence of meaningful coordination mechanisms during the crucial face of media reforms and institution building in the Western Balkans.

More frequently, implicit coordination occurred when an international actor launched an initiative which factually demarcated its lead on the issue. Issue-based coordination occurred, for example, during the early support

---

[13] Price, Davis Noll, and De Luce, "Mapping Media Assistance," 53; Rhodes, "Ten Years of Media Support," 10.
[14] Rhodes, "Ten Years of Media Support," 10.

of the independent media network ANEM in Serbia and as a by-product of the involvement of the same international organizations in the construction of an independent media supervisory authority in Albania. What is of concern are accounts of donor competition that were noted in the chapters on Bosnia and Herzegovina and Kosovo. In the latter case, donors supported three concurring radio networks linking minority communities.[15]

If there is a lesson to be learned, it is that international organizations which provide media assistance should adopt and adhere to a code of conduct that formulates best practices, such as transparency and a coordinated approach, in addition to locally contextualized commitments to specific hallmarks of the emerging local media system. Consequent media assistance has to interlace the policy and the operational levels with an aim to create system-wide synergies and actions that reinforce local media institutions.

Conditionality Mechanisms

In international development and democratization, conditionality describes a mechanism by which states implement measures of their own accord in order to conform with international obligations or standards that are prerequisite for memberships in international organizations and in order to qualify for international aid. Contrary to measures being imposed externally, conditionality holds the advantage that legislation is passed by local authorities, which would seem to guarantee local ownership and deliberation from the outset.[16]

As a practice of international media assistance, the chapters with country-level case studies identify conditionality as an important driver to instigate media reforms in the countries of the Western Balkans in order to accede to the Council of Europe and ultimately the EU. The country-level chapters are illustrative of the outstanding leverage the stabilization and association process that governs EU relations with Western Balkan countries has had. For Bosnia and Herzegovina and Kosovo, which had been governed under international protectorate, the role of the EU has increased proportionately with the diminishing role of the OHR and UNMIK, respectively.

---

[15] Reflecting earlier findings, cf. Martin, "Media Reform and Development in Bosnia," 92.

[16] Schimmelfennig and Sedelmeier, "Governance by Conditionality," 670f.

In this context, the five Western Balkan countries under study have to fulfill a range of media specific commitments in their pursuit to guarantee freedom of expression and to bring local legislation in line with the EU *acquis*. This entails issuing an EU-compliant legal framework for the media sector and constituting legislation for key media institutions, that is, the independent national media supervisory authority and the public service media organization.

As a democratic quality, media and regulatory independence has to be assured and protected. The annual progress reports highlight fairly concordant issues with the independence of the local media supervisory authority and the public service organization. As a representative for the Western Balkans, the chapter on Albania holds that conditionality mechanisms failed to ensure absence of political and financial pressures on the media.[17] Notwithstanding its success in transposing European values and EU-compliant normative frameworks in the countries of the Western Balkans, EU conditionality has had limited effect on their implementation and on converging formal arrangements with local practices.

Another caveat is that EU conditionality is most prescriptive when it comes to the transposition of the EU *acquis*, that is, media-specific legislation by the EU. Yet, the competences of the EU in the media sphere are heavily curtailed and consequently EU media legislation primarily focuses on the freedom to provide services within the internal market. The EU *acquis* is mute when it comes to the organization of public service broadcasting, that is, a prerogative of the member states, and remains superficial at best regarding the independence of media supervisory authorities.

The central piece of EU media legislation, the 2008 Audiovisual Media Services Directive,[18] addresses issues of media convergence that may be more pressing in the old member states but less meaningful and rather distracting for Western Balkan accession and candidate countries, which have to absolve democratic media transition and media institution building first. As a result, EU conditionality in the media sector often does not set the right priorities for local media systems, such as promoting transparency of media funding and ownership or safeguarding the independence of the local media supervisory authority and the public service media organization, among others. By contrast, the need to issue EU-compliant legislation has been used to introduce new control mechanisms, for

[17] Londo, in this volume.
[18] European Parliament and the European Council, "Directive 2010/13/EU."

example, in relation to new and online media, or has provided the pretext for yet another reform of the media supervisory authority.

While conditionality is widely used to influence public policy at the normative level, it seems that international media assistance in Western Balkan countries at the operational level did not effectively condition funds to nonstate actors by, for example, requiring beneficiaries to demonstrate compliance with media self-regulation as well as to contribute to media-supporting institutions, such as professional associations. Harnessing conditionality in the private sector can develop into a promising vehicle to achieve media system-wide effects beyond the single beneficiary and "cultivate" media professionalism.

Grappling with Local Media Economics

Local media economics, which are described above as particularly challenging, turned out to severely affect the efforts invested into the democratic transformation of Western Balkan local media systems. For a variety of reasons international media assistance to the Western Balkan countries failed to reduce the overreliance of local media on (potentially compromising) subsidies and more broadly to adequately address the economic sustainability of media outlets in print and broadcasting, as well as self-regulatory bodies and supporting institutions.

There are several reasons for this, notably the disregard for local media economics and economic sustainability; the dismissal of measures to structure media markets; and the fact that aid can also provoke artificial demand locally.

The first and most obvious reason for this is an initial total disregard for the fact that in many situations local media markets are too weak to sustain conventional media business models that rely on selling advertising and/or subscriptions in order to take foothold. This phenomenon is now recognized in the literature on international media assistance in the Western Balkans, according to which economic sustainability is too often simply implied where business models do not correspond to market realities and—even where this was considered—the overall deteriorating economic situation endangered what was earlier viable media business.[19]

---

[19] Cf. Rhodes, "Ten Years of Media Support," 19; Sorge, "Media in Kosovo," 42; Johnson, "Model Interventions," 29f.

While building capacity in media management and diversification of business models was added at a later stage to the menus of professional training this could not reverse the overall trend that for the time being there is extremely little business with media in the region.

Second, liberalization of local media markets featured high on the agendas for international media assistance and was reinforced by a very liberal interpretation of open media market access as a tenet of exercising freedom of expression. This has arguably augmented oversaturation of local media markets because structural measures did not find favor with the international community.[20] Instead there has been a false reliance on the cleansing effect of market forces, which was thought to lead to consolidation and competition on the merits of journalistic quality and innovation.[21] The overall confused funding practice during international media assistance has further contributed to the congestion of local media markets, as is very well portrayed in the chapter on Kosovo.

This leads to the third and last issue—that the international financing of media operations is an additional source of revenue that can become the objective for local media. Development literature recognizes that aid functions similar to a market and can provoke artificial demands from beneficiaries locally. Without attempting to devalue the objectives of international media assistance what emerges from the chapters on Bosnia-Herzegovina, Kosovo, Macedonia and Serbia is that during its peak too many local media outlets could access funding for their operational activities from a large diversity of international donors, only to collapse again when the funding dried out.[22]

Instead of instigating commercial media, what was often fostered was a symbiosis between international media assistance and their local project partners that did not bring economic sustainability. This finding extends to the numerous supporting institutions that were intended to institute media self-regulatory bodies and professional associations, and even to some extent to the media watchdogs. Without donor coordination and media assistance based on realistic assumptions about the economic viability of media organizations and corresponding funds over a time horizon adequate for institution building, the international media assistance in

---

[20] Cf. Sorge, "Media in Kosovo," 36.
[21] Franqué, "The Other Frontier," 94.
[22] Illustrative is the OBN case study in Jusić and Ahmetašević, in this volume. However, there are some notable exception, cf. the case study on radio and TV B92 in Serbia in Marko, in this volume.

the Western Balkans was characterized by numerous premature exits of donors which negatively influenced the outlook of such assistance projects.

Local Contextualization and Deliberation

In the presence of international development and assistance, efforts invested in building democratic institutions in transitional settings are contingent upon local acceptance and the fit of the imported models. This is the reason why building effective media institutions can be seen as a function between domestic demand and external influence that is discernible from the level of confrontation or partnership during their introduction and the ongoing levels of local support and acceptance. It is therefore valid to emphasize the process of introducing institutions over their content and formal provisions.[23]

Many examples from the country-level chapters provide evidence that international media assistance in the Western Balkans was conscious of the principal need to work closely with local stakeholders and to align media reforms with the local context. Such was the case in Albania where the 1998 Law on Public and Private Radio and Television was drafted by a parliamentary commission in collaboration with a local expert group and the help of international expertise.[24] The Macedonian Broadcasting Law from 1997 is also cited "as an exemplary form of cooperation between international bodies [and donors] and the Macedonian authorities."[25]

Yet, in many situations the very purpose of the deliberation, that is, customizing legislation to the sociopolitical and cultural context as well as raising local acceptance, was not fully achieved, though for very different reasons. Whereas European media values and institutions pervaded local stakeholders' deliberations, little consideration was given to their meaningful interpretation or to measures that would compensate for a lack of tradition that would, for example, sustain formally independent media institutions, that is, the media supervisory authority and the public service broadcasting organization. Occasionally, international consultants dominated deliberations providing expertise which did not correspond to local

---

[23] For effective legal institutions, see Berkowitz, Pistor, and Richard, "The Transplant Effect," 178f.

[24] Londo, in this volume.

[25] Price, Davis Noll, and De Luce, "Mapping Media Assistance," 57.

circumstances, interests or organizational cultures, as evidenced by the unaccomplished organizational reform of the public service broadcasting organization in Bosnia and Herzegovina[26] or the much criticized study of the EU on the Serbian media.[27]

Contrary to good government practices, while international expertise is invited in some situations, local governments did not properly consult draft laws or, when they did so, neglected consultation outcomes leaving local stakeholders no venue to influence the policy-making process. This is exposed in the chapter on Serbian with regard to the Public Information Law, as well as in Bosnia and Herzegovina where local expertise was, in quite a few cases, not invited.

Every so often, well-intentioned initiatives to construct media-supporting institutions, such as professional organizations and self-regulatory bodies, were welcomed by local stakeholders who failed to support them in practice, as was the case, for example, with the Council of Ethics in Albania. Probably a reflection of the rather weak role of civil society, media as a public interest goal did not permeate well the concerns of the society at large, which is well illustrated by the rather dispassionate relationship between the societies of the Western Balkans and their public service media.

Entirely different was the situation in postconflict Bosnia and Herzegovina and Kosovo where the OHR and UNMIK used their powers to institute media legislation and institutions at a time when these modern states were still under construction, and later due to legislative stalemate by local governments. While some of the so created media institutions functioned reasonably well under the international protectorate, such as the independent supervisory authority CRA in Bosnia and Herzegovina, local politics remains a real and lingering threat. Moreover, the case study delineating the establishment of a system of public service broadcasting in Bosnia and Herzegovina is an account of local resistance that was overruled by a series of OHR decisions, important elements of which are to date not effective.[28]

---

[26] It was modeled after the UK equivalent, the BBC. See Jusić and Ahmetašević, in this volume.

[27] Marko, in this volume.

[28] Jusić and Ahmetašević, in this volume.

Minority Media and the Interethnic Mediated Public Sphere

One priority of international media assistance which still continues during the phasing-out of international media assistance is support to minority media. In multiethnic countries like Bosnia and Herzegovina, Kosovo and Macedonia international donors have been supporting underrepresented people and minorities in the media to launch media outlets, such as print publications, local radio and sometimes TV programs, in their language and for their constituency. Determining the appropriate strategy to promote minority media while preserving an integrated local media sphere appears to be particularly challenging. As it is well captured in the Macedonian chapter this may cement into an ethnically divided media sphere and the danger that this spirals into ethnically biased reporting and polarization.[29] In addition, Serbia's media content reflects political, ethnic, and territorial divisions within society.[30]

Moreover, in public service media international assistance did not discourage ethnically motivated divisions and spheres of influence, frustrating later efforts to foster an interethnic national identity and dialogue mediated by an integrated media sphere. Subsequent attempts to promote adjustment to the public service media in particular faced enormous difficulties because it would endanger the already acquired positions of control and influence (see, for example, the case studies on the local public service broadcaster in the chapters on Bosnia and Herzegovina and Macedonia). Thus, the focus of international media assistance should always be to support public institutions and structures that could effectively facilitate interethnic dialogue in a country in addition to serving specific constituencies.

International Monitoring

In addition to local efforts, international media assistance has an important role to play in monitoring the state of democratic media transformation and media institution building in the countries of the Western Balkans. From the outset there was no shortage of international moni-

---

[29] Dimitrijevska-Markoski and Daskalovski, in this volume.
[30] Marko, in this volume.

toring tackling the media sector or specific media institutions, such as the legal frameworks, the media supervisory authority and the public service media organizations. Albeit with different foci, regular reports are produced—the European Commission's annual progress reports for the Western Balkan countries, the IREX Media Sustainability Index and reports by Reporters without Borders and Freedom House. Other international actors engage in ad hoc monitoring, especially the Council of Europe and the OSCE, among others.

Probably the most influential, the European Commission's annual progress reports cover the media as an aspect of guaranteeing freedom of expression and media institutions within the policy on information society and the media. Relative to its scope, the report has to be very concise on these issues and it does not amount to detailed monitoring. The Serbian country reports offer an illustrative example of the general nature of this exercise.[31] For Macedonia it is noted that criticism from the EU attracts the widest public attention, but repeated concerns in the progress reports have not been sufficient to bring about change.[32]

In substance, international monitoring too often questions formal arrangements but pays too little attention to the implementation of media reforms and the informal practices that are equally decisive for the functioning of media institutions. In spite of the prevailing diplomacy there must be clues as to who is accountable, what concrete action is required to improve a situation, and who is responsible to take action. It is also important that international media assistance defends the principles of media freedom and critically engages with its own theoretical concepts. Contrary to the widespread practice of assessing progress against benchmarks that presuppose a consolidated democracy, it would be more useful to assess the risks to local media freedoms and independent media institutions.

International monitoring is not an end in itself and requires diplomatic follow-up and, when necessary, political pressure. A good example is the international scrutiny over attempts to interfere with the independence of the media supervisory authority, CRA, in Bosnia and Herzegovina.[33] In addition to the actions taken by the OHR, other key international actors regularly issued warnings and protest letters to the local government in order to voice concrete concerns over the independence of the regulator.

---

[31] Ibid.
[32] Dimitrijevska-Markoski and Daskalovski, in this volume.
[33] Jusić and Ahmetašević, in this volume.

Now that international pressure has weakened, the CRA is facing many attempts at political capture.[34] In other Western Balkan countries international media assistance has not used its political leverage systematically in an effort to protect key media institutions from political interference.

Achievements and Pitfalls of Media Democratization

The following cross-national comparison of the achievements and pitfalls of democratic media transition in the five Western Balkan countries is used to examine the role and influence of international media assistance and conditionality.

Media freedoms and European Best Practices

In all five countries, there is a common high level of formal compliance of local media laws and institutions with European best practices issued by the Council of Europe, the OSCE and the EU that can be attributed to their involvement during the legislative process. For the two countries that underwent media intervention, that is, Bosnia and Herzegovina and Kosovo, the international protectorate charged the OSCE directly with drafting or even instituting local media laws. But the international community also provided expertise, consultation and evaluations of draft media laws in Albania, Macedonia, and Serbia, to the effect that these laws adhere to European best practices. For example, in many aspects the governing legislation for the independent media supervisory authorities would excel those of old EU member states. But to what effect?

Such media policy transfer would be a very impressive result of international media assistance in the Western Balkan region were these laws effectively implemented and complied with. However, with only a handful of exceptions, the country studies reveal that there is a general mismatch between the quality of the legislation and its practical consequences, which is explained by a general implementation deficit that in some cases results from deliberate obstruction by local elites.[35] Nonetheless, there are achievements that ought to be recognized, in particular that countries of

---

[34] Ibid.
[35] Cf. Rhodes, "Ten Years of Media Support," 12, 27.

the Western Balkans now have a pluralistic media landscape, broadcast licensing has confined the previous chaos in the ether, regulation effectively condemns hate speech, and the media and journalists are no longer criminalized for alleged defamation, among others.[36] All of this, to different degrees, has been influenced by international media assistance in the pursuit of bringing to life the universal value of freedom of expression and infusing European best practices in media regulation and institutions.

Beyond the progress noted, there are a number of arguments why formal arrangements that outperform their local context should not be defied. Are not such discrepancies characteristic for countries in the process of democratic transition? As representative of the other countries, in the chapter on Serbia, Davor Marko notes that the transposition of European standards for the media set the path for the Serbian media transition, and enabled international actors to monitor the degree of transition.[37] While it is not wrong to emphasize the development path, however, it does not suffice to rely on media institutions that have democratic potential encoded in their institutional design.[38] A normative framework alone cannot entrench against capture and informality, in particular the worrying tendency in Western Balkan countries for media, politics and business to form an iron triangle, that is, a self-enforcing power structure serving local, albeit sometimes competing, elites. Nonetheless, formal guarantees are crucial to prevent even more blatant attempts to deputize media; they should be invoked by individuals and media advocates to defend local media institutions and, in principle, they keep the marketplace of ideas open.

Top-Down versus Bottom-Up

Western Balkan countries have different track histories when it comes to media institution building, but also within a country some subsystems appear to flow easier through transition than others. When comparing the experiences across all five countries, it emerges that top-down legal reforms are at face value comparatively easier to accomplish than bottom-up initiatives.

---

[36] Ibid., 28; Cf. Londo, in this volume.
[37] Marko, in this volume.
[38] Jakubowicz and Sükösd, "Twelve Concepts," 12.

Typical examples for top-down media institutions are the establishment of a media supervisory authority or issuing media legislation, but with mixed results in practice (see below). These findings are amplified whenever media reforms take place in the presence of international custody such as earlier in Bosnia and Herzegovina or in Kosovo. In both countries, initial media reforms were fast-tracked or were issued entirely under international authority, for example, the media decrees issued by the Office of the High Representative in Bosnia and Herzegovina.[39] With domestication and local ownership the initial headway of top-down media institution building in countries undergoing media intervention (such as Bosnia and Herzegovina and Kosovo) levels out compared to those countries which experienced more domestically driven changes in the media system, such as Macedonia, Albania and Serbia.

The building of media institutions from the bottom up, which requires local acceptance, as is the case with membership-based organizations such as media self-regulation bodies, is much more time-consuming and the prospects are uncertain. Attempts to root press and journalistic self-regulation in the countries of the Western Balkans have led to the creation of institutional empty shells: For Albania, the introduction of member-based organizations in the media has been by and large unsuccessful. In Macedonia, press outlets and groups of journalists do not subscribe to the authority of the Council of Honor that was charged with defending media ethics. In Kosovo, the OSCE attempt to set up a journalists' association in 2000 failed, while subsequent self-regulatory bodies never became self-sustainable. Despite the 2006 Code of Ethics and the Press Council, institutionalized self-regulation remains weak in Serbia. Hence, the experience of supporting media institutions is fairly similar in all the countries studied in the framework of this research project; that is, with very few exceptions they do not (yet) root in the local media systems. Notable exemptions are a few commercial broadcasters which, after initial operational support from international donors, matured into locally accepted ventures, such as the Serbian B92.

The transformation of state broadcasters into public service broadcasting bears characteristics of both because their inception is based on a top-down legal reform but their success nevertheless rests on acceptance by the local population as well as stakeholders. The experiences with public service broadcasting institutions in the five Western Balkan coun-

---

[39] For a complete list, see Jusić and Ahmetašević, in this volume.

tries show that achievements at the formal level do not automatically guarantee their independence and the fulfillment of the public service mission. Without exception public service media organizations are perceived as government-friendly media and newly elected governments rush to institute their influence over the management and the content of these institutions. Moreover, as examples in Macedonia show, local constituencies do not easily accept funding their public service broadcasting with a license fee, which is unlikely to change in the short-term even if the programs were of better journalistic quality and the reporting more objective and diverse.

Implementation and Domestication: (Re)politicization of Media Institutions

Across the region, it emerges that in addition to the sizeable implementation deficit and the culture of informality eroding democratic institutions there is a new and rather open tendency to (re)politicize public media institutions. These issues are mutually reinforcing and pose a very serious threat to democratic media transition and media institution building in the Western Balkan countries. At the time when international media assistance was phasing out, local and international observers recognized a growing political saliency of media, policy and regulation. "As soon as foreign donors withdrew their (financial and practical) support the newly implemented institutions dwindle or are being hijacked by particularistic interests."[40] After 2010, international reports documented the dramatic deterioration in the Macedonian media sphere, which has even led to the reintensifying of international media assistance.[41]

The trade-offs between local ownership and democratic media transition are most visible in public service media reforms and with independent media supervisory authorities, both raising critical issues in relation to the *actual independence of* the organizations. The deadlock when appointments of decision-makers to media supervisory authorities or the public service media are due serves as an illustration. In Bosnia and Herzegovina, Albania and Kosovo years can pass by without the elected politicians making effective appointments because such decisions are highly

---

[40] Voltmer, in this volume.
[41] Dimitrijevska-Markoski and Daskalovski, in this volume.

politicized. Likewise, these media institutions are exposed to postelectoral vulnerabilities when every new government in power attempts to change legislation in order to influence the composition of the boards and senior management. In Bosnia and Herzegovina and Kosovo initial progress during international media intervention has been partially offset during the subsequent process of domestication, that is, when ownership, control and oversight over local media institutions was handed back to local stakeholders. In Kosovo, "the issue of political interference in media institutions has intensified following 'Kosovarization'."[42] In Bosnia and Herzegovina, government increasingly ignores international criticisms over the independence of the regulatory authority CRA.[43] Public service media's dependency on the state budget, as highlighted in Serbia and Kosovo, can equally be used to leverage political influence.

It would be too early to assume that in the Western Balkan countries these alarming trends have already consolidated into hybrid or "atavistic" media systems in which the imported European media models are irreversibly tweaked by political parallelism. International media assistance should accept the political nature of media policy when formulating responses that are sensitive to local interests and positive incentives that would ensure political support locally. International media assistance is crucially needed to accompany the process of localization and domestication of local key media institutions with expertise and international scrutiny. International monitoring should place renewed focus on the implementation of media reforms and focus more closely on local practices. EU conditionality and diplomatic efforts must work together when promoting media freedoms, policy stability and credible media reform in these countries.

By contrast, business parallelism is nurtured by local media economics and the lack of transparency, and above all is perfectly legal. In private media where owners and editors—albeit constrained economically—are free to define their editorial line political allegiances and partisan reporting have increased. Media policy can however provide incentives for the production of quality content and the dissemination of news and current affairs. Instead of contributing to the operational costs of mainstream media, and in addition to stimulating minority media, international media assistance could place new emphasis on investigatory journalism, quality content production and sharing, as well as facilitate access to European audiovisual content.

---

[42] Miftari, in this volume.
[43] Jusić and Ahmetašević, in this volume.

Nontransparent Media

Similar to other countries in Central and Eastern Europe, the media sectors of Western Balkan countries are characterized by fuzzy ownership, which describes a situation in which transparency about media owners and their interests is lacking. Fuzzy ownership is more complex than understanding who owns which media. Londo summarizes for Albania that media owners and moguls are "persons with economic interests in other businesses, lacking media experience and with little transparency of their media funding practices."[44] More direct transparency concerning media ownership and funding would be crucial therefore in order to expose the rampant cross-subsidization to media outlets as well as partisan public sector funding and procurement of media services.[45]

Throughout the democratic media transition in the Western Balkans there has been no systematic effort to gather and release economic indicators about local media markets, such as operating budgets of media outlets, advertising, subscription and sales revenues, subsidies and public funds. The country chapter on Albania notes the lack of reliable data on the media and the very sketchy evidence available. If local policy makers, but also international media assistance, are not informed, how can it be possible to devise optimal and evidence-based policies? By the same token, transparency of international media assistance should also be strengthened.

Hence, the failure to promote transparency across all aspects of media governance, especially with regard to ownership and the financing of media operations in addition to procedural requirements, should be considered a crucial omission of international media assistance. The same applies to transfers of the state and of state-owned companies to any media outlet, no matter whether this is in exchange for media services or by way of public subsidies. The reason for this blind spot is easy to pinpoint: neither the *acquis* of the Council of Europe nor the European Union provides for the introduction of such far-reaching transparency and procedural requirements. So far, at the European and EU level there are only nonbinding instruments[46] and attempts to introduce transparency of

---

[44] Londo, in this volume.
[45] Irion, "Follow the Money!"
[46] Specifically, Council of Europe, "Resolution 1636 (2008)," para. 8.18–19; Council of Europe, "Recommendation 94(13)."; European Parliament, "Resolution of 25 September 2008."

media ownership in Serbia, for example, were met with fierce resistance by private media.

Internal Culture of Independence through Good Governance Practices

Through an internal culture of independence the resilience of media organizations in the public and the private sector can to a certain extent be strengthened, even in an environment that is not fully enabling, as is the case in the countries of the Western Balkans.[47] Especially in the public sector, a public service culture that embraces the tenets of good governance is believed to improve the overall performance and public standing of key media institutions. Transparency of decision-making, participatory deliberations and accountability are important non-media-specific ingredients for a public service culture that would ultimately foster an internal culture of independence at the local media supervisory authority and the public service media organization. Unfortunately, European best practices that are binding in the media sector do not tie in with good governance practices, although as a value they are promoted throughout international media assistance.

Selectively, international media assistance flagged the role of transparency and accountability, which has promoted some change, for example, by infusing more transparency in the work of the Macedonian media supervisory authority. Another successful element is the integration of local media supervisory authorities into European networks of peer institutions, for example, the European Platform of Regulatory Authorities (EPRA). In another situation, however, the offer to improve the Albanian media supervisory authority's accounting system was not met with interest. International media assistance can help build the internal culture of independence through training, and international monitoring could be better attuned to assess good governance practices.

---

[47] Council of Europe, "Declaration of the Committee of Ministers."

Conclusions

The effects of international media assistance accompanying the democratic transformation of the media in Western Balkan countries is highly constrained by the local context. The experiences of international media assistance in the region suggest that imported solutions have not been very cognitive in all aspects of local conditions; for example, neglecting media economics in these very small markets, and also in regard to the ability of media-supporting institutions to govern themselves. International responses to the political saliency of media policy and media institutions have been rather schematic when prescribing independent institutions as regulators and in public service media. The promoted media reforms did not harness much needed transparency of media ownership and funding, and lacked strategic approaches to promote media policy stability and to keep close tabs on credible media reform and implementation.

In the Western Balkan countries surveyed, the transformation of the media systems and their subsystems has not been linear; all transformation cases studied have experienced retrograde processes and a sliding back after the external push for change weakened. Today, democratic media transition in the surveyed countries is stagnating at a comparative level and in some of them the situation may deteriorate further, for example, Macedonia. Sustainable and functioning media institutions are hard to come by because most of them are repoliticized or at least vulnerable in their dependence on external resources or political cues. We conclude that a decade of international media assistance of varying intensity is not sufficient to construct media institutions when for their proper functioning they have to outperform their local context. In the mid-term, the introduced media institutions and policies will largely depend on the development of the political culture in the five studied countries—an uncertain and slow process of systemic change.[48] The present state of affairs is that locally driven international media assistance will be needed for the foreseeable future to counterbalance politicization and partisanship in the media.

In addition, our cross-national comparison of key media institutions in the Western Balkan countries suggests that—aside from short-term affects—scaling international media assistance does not necessarily improve outcomes. However, it seems that those societies and institutions that received

---

[48] Jakubowicz and Sükösd, "Twelve Concepts," 22–23.

a stronger push through external assistance or even direct intervention were able to "travel" faster and further than those that were primarily driven by domestic, endogenous drives for change. However, the institutions that were reformed more radically and rapidly due to external assistance witnessed a fiercer backlash once they were integrated into the local legal and institutional context, after the external assistance was reduced.

To a certain extent, the loss of international media assistance effectiveness is also self-afflicted due to a number of shortcomings, most importantly the lack of coordination among donors and the absence of a long-term strategy adequate for institution building. From a normative point of view, the exported media model is a patchwork: European best practices are a compilation of binding and nonbinding instruments of the Council of Europe and the OSCE as well as the EU *acquis*. As it stands, scattered international competences and the self-referentiality of the international system do their part to undermine a consistent and coherent approach that would be reinforcing at the normative and implementation levels. The EU conditionality mechanisms are still a very strong incentive for Western Balkan regimes to continue media reforms and institution building, however they do not practically implement formally accepted arrangements. Thus, while at the formal level the introduction of European best practices and key media institutions has apparently succeeded, there is a growing sense of urgency to improve implementation and effectiveness before the locally specific mismatch between form and substance consolidates into hybrid and atavistic media systems.

POLICY RECOMMENDATIONS

This research into democratic media transition in five Western Balkan countries in the presence of international media assistance and conditionality backs a number of policy recommendations which address policies in support of democratic media transition and international media assistance, respectively.

TRANSPARENCY

Promoting transparency should enable local stakeholders and the international community to better assess and evaluate local media markets and assistance needs and provide a basis for enhanced coordination among themselves. For countries which undergo democratic transition, transparency becomes a central requirement for media development at public and private levels, including all state funding in support of public service and private media, public procurement of media services by the state and state-owned companies, as well as media ownership and financing of media operations. Policy-making processes should be transparent and inclusive for local stakeholders and the public. When entering the phase of media reforms and institution building, the international community should make transparency conditional upon receiving external funds and promote it vigorously in media policy making while contributing with their own practices to this end. In particular, international media assistance should make all significant funding and actions transparent and help establish a single public registry to which this information is submitted.

POLICY CONSISTENCY AND STABILITY

In the phase of media reforms and institution building, local stakeholders and the international community should contribute to consistent media policy objectives and jointly foster a healthy degree of policy stability.

- International media assistance that influences local media policy and institution building should reinforce local media policy objectives corresponding to international best practices, while remaining flexible to accommodate different strategies and funding priorities at the operational level.
- International media assistance should aim to enhance the political commitment to local media legislation and key media institutions corresponding to international best practices, as well as identify strategies to limit postelectoral political vulnerabilities and deadlocks concerning key media institutions.
- International media assistance and EU conditionality should reduce external demands for legislative reforms that unnecessarily unsettle media policy stability.
- International media assistance should address local needs as they arise but maintain an outlook and strategy adequate for media institution building and subsequent consolidation.

Contextual Integrity and Local Ownership

In the phase of media reforms and institution building, international media assistance should aim for optimal contextual integrity that recognizes local political and economic circumstances and facilitates local ownership of media reforms and institutions. International media assistance should be attuned to country-specific media economics, refrain from distorting local media markets and be considerate of the economic repercussions of aid. Moreover, international media assistance should not phase out during the process of localization and domestication of local key media institutions but accompany this process strategically, such as by continuously providing expertise and international scrutiny.

Implementation and Compliance

International media assistance should pay more attention to the implementation of local media reforms and compliance with formal arrangements.

- At the stage of policy formulation positive incentives should be considered that would ensure political and professional support locally for the implementation of legal frameworks and the operation of key media institutions.
- Local policy makers should be assisted in devising implementation strategies and accountability mechanisms with clearly defined roles and deliverables.
- International media assistance can play an important role in strengthening an internal culture of independence and promoting professional ethics as well as connecting key media institutions with European and/or international peer networks.

Progress Evaluation and International Scrutiny

Systematic and continuous progress evaluations and international scrutiny should accompany democratic media transition and should inform EU conditionality mechanisms, international relations and international media assistance alike.

- In additional to formal scrutiny, discrepancies between formal guarantees and actual practices should also be followed up diplomatically and trigger political consequences that do not weaken the local media system.

- International monitoring and progress evaluation should be detailed and allow for contextual interpretation of local developments; it should assess risks to media freedoms and independence corresponding to international best practices instead of measuring progress against benchmarks from media theory and Western democracies.

Bibliography

Aday, Sean. "Chasing the Bad News: An Analysis of 2005 Iraq and Afghanistan War Coverage on NBC and Fox News." *Journal of Communication* 61.1 (2010): 144–164.

Ahmetašević, Nidžara. "A House of Cards: Bosnian Media under (Re)Construction: Media Assistance as a Tool of Post-Conflict Democratization and State Building." PhD diss., University of Graz.

Albanian Parliament. *Minutes of Parliamentary Media Commission Discussions of Annual Reports of KKRT 2011.* Tirana: Albanian Parliament, 2012.

Albanian Radio and Television Steering Council. *Annual Report, 2009.* Tirana: RTSH Steering Council, 2010.

Alfa. "MRTV naplaka radiodifuzna taksa za sekoj clen vo semejstvoto" [MRTV enforces payment of the fee for each member of the family]. *Time.mk*, October 20, 2012.

Allen, Tim, and Nicole Stremlau. "Media Policy, Peace and State Reconstruction." Discussion Paper no. 8. Crisis States Development Research Centre, London School of Economics, March 2005. Accessed 2011. http://eprints.lse.ac.uk/28347/.

Almond, Gabriel A., and Sidney Verba. *The Civic Culture.* Boston: Little, Brown, 1965.

Alon. "Novinarite revoltirano ja napustija debatata za Zakonot za medium" [Journalists, revolted, left the debate on the media law]. Accessed October 3, 2013. http://a1on.mk/wordpress/archives/132850.

AMA. "Raporti Vjetor" [Annual report]. Autoriteti i Mediave Audiovizive 2013.

AMI. "Albania Adopts Important Defamation Reform." *AMI Newsletter* (Albanian Media Institute), February 2012.

AMI. "Annual Report 2005." Albanian Media Institute, 2005.

AMI. "Minority Media in Albania in 2009." Albanian Media Institute, 2010.

AMI. "Parliament Approves the Law on Audiovisual Media." *AMI Newsletter* (Albanian Media Institute), March 2013.

Anastasakis, Othon. "The EU's Political Conditionality in the Western Balkans: Towards a More Pragmatic Approach." *Southeast European and Black Sea Studies* 8 (2008): 365–367.

Andersen, Ben. "Serbia after Milošević: A Progress Report." US Helsinki Commission Briefing, 2001.

Anderson, Benedict. *Imagined Communities: Reflections on the Origins and Spread of Nationalism.* London: Verso, 1983.

Anderson, Christopher J., André Blais, Shaun Bowler, Todd Donovan, and Ola Listhaug. *Losers' Consent: Elections and Democratic Legitimacy.* Oxford: Oxford University Press, 2005.

ANEM. *Legal Monitoring of Serbian Media Scene—Reports for December 2012.* Serbia: ANEM, 2012.

Anti-Corruption Council. "Izveštaj o vlasničkoj strukturi i kontroli medija u Srbiji" [Report on ownership structure and control of media in Serbia]. Government of the Republic of Serbia, February 26, 2015. Accessed October 28, 2015. http://www.antikorupcija-savet.gov.rs/Storage/Global/Documents/izvestaji/izvestaj%20mediji%2026%2002.pdf.

Anti-Corruption Council. "Report on Pressures on & Control of Media in Serbia." Government of the Republic of Serbia, September 19, 2011. Accessed October 28, 2015. http://www.antikorupcija-savet.gov.rs/Storage/Global/Documents/mediji/IZVESTAJ%20O%20MEDIJIMA%20PRECISCEN%20ENG..pdf.

Associated Press. "US Sends Electronic Warfare Planes to Bosnia." *New York Times,* September 12, 1997. Accessed October 7, 2017. http://www.nytimes.com/1997/09/12/world/us-sends-electronic-warfare-planes-to-bosnia.html.

Association of Journalists of Macedonia. *Code of the Journalists of Macedonia.* Skopje: Association of Journalists of Macedonia, 2001.

Bacevich, Andrew, and Cohen, Eliot. *War over Kosovo: Politics and Strategy in a Global Age.* New York: Columbia University Press, 2001.

Bagaviki Berisha, Elda. "Ndikimi i programeve të agjensive të ndihmës së huaj në mbështetje të gazetarisë" [Influence of foreign aid agency support in journalism]. In *Mediat shqiptare në tranzicion* [Albanian media in transition], 153–159. Tirana: Faculty of History and Philology, 2010.

Bajraktari, Yll, and Emily Hsu. "Developing Media in Stabilization and Reconstruction Operations." Stabilization and Reconstruction Series No. 7. United States Institute of Peace, October 2007.

Baka, Besnik. "Media vs. Politics: Transition to (in)dependence." Albanian Media Institute, 2011.

Balkan Insight. "Belgrade's Radio B92 Axes Most Remaining Staff." Accessed on October 3, 2015. http://www.balkaninsight.com/en/article/most-employees-fired-from-belgrade-s-radio-b92.

Balkan Peace Team. "Protests in Belgrade and throughout Yugoslavia—1996/1997." December 10, 1996, and January 23, 1997. Accessed February 11, 2013. http://www.hartford-hwp.com/archives/62/063.html.

Ballentine, Karen. "International Assistance and the Development of Independent Mass Media in the Czech and Slovak Republics." In *The Power and Limits of NGOs: A Critical Look at Building Democracy in Eastern Europe and Eurasia,* edited by Sarah E. Mendelson, and John K. Glenn, 91–125. New York: Columbia University Press, 2002.

Bašić-Hrvatin, Sandra, and Mark Thompson. "Public Service Broadcasting in Plural and Divided Societies." In *Divided They Fall: Public Service Broadcasting in*

Multi-Ethnic States, edited by Sandra Bašić-Hrvatin, Mark Thompson, and Tarik Jusić, 7–40. Sarajevo: Mediacentar, 2008.

Basile, Olivier. Kosovo: Still Not Too Late for Press Freedom: An Investigation." Reporters without Borders, 2010. Accessed October 7, 2017. http://files.rsf-es.org/200002833-845a185549/2010_INFORME_KOSOVO_ingles.pdf.

Becker, Lee B., and C. Ann Hollifield. "Market Forces, Media Assistance and Democratization." Paper presented at the International Conference "State and Democracy," University of Belgrade, November 28–29, 2008.

Belicanec, Roberto, and Zoran Ricliev. "Mapping Digital Media: Macedonia." Open Society Foundations, June 5, 2012. Accessed October 31, 2013. http://www.opensocietyfoundations.org/sites/default/files/mapping-digital-media-macedonia-20120625.pdf.

Bennett, Christopher. "How Yugoslavia's Destroyers Harnessed the Media." *Frontline*, 1995. Accessed October 3, 2013. http://www.pbs.org/wgbh/pages/frontline/shows/karadzic/bosnia/media.html.

BeoMedia. "Radio Listening Report, January 5–9, 1997." 1997.

Berger, Peter, and Thomas Luckmann. *The Social Construction of Reality: A Treatise in the Sociology of Knowledge*. Garden City: Doubleday, 1966.

Berisha, Isuf. "Kosovo/a." In *Media Ownership and Its Impact on Media Pluralism and Independence*, edited by Brankica Petković, 219–248. Ljubljana: Peace Institute, Institute for Contemporary Social and Political Studies, 2004.

Berkowitz, Daniel, Pistor, Katharina, and Richard, Jean-Francois. "The Transplant Effect." *American Journal of Comparative Law* 51.1 (2003): 163–203.

Bernhagen, Patrick. "Measuring Democracy and Democratization." In *Democratization*, edited by Christian W. Haerpfer, Patrick Bernhagen, Ronald F. Inglehart, and Christian Welzel, 24–40. Oxford: Oxford University Press, 2009.

Bertelsmann Stiftung. "BTI 2012: Albania Country Report." 2012. Accessed May 14, 2013. https://www.bti-project.org/fileadmin/files/BTI/Downloads/Reports/2012/pdf/BTI_2012_Albania.pdf.

Bildt, Carl. *Peace Journey: The Struggle for Peace in Bosnia*. London: Weidenfeld and Nicolson, 1998.

BIRN. "BIRN." Accessed September 29, 2013. http://birn.eu.com/en/network/birn-kosovo-donors-and-partners.

Börzel, Tanja A. "Towards Convergence in Europe? Institutional Adaptation to Europeanization in Germany and Spain." *Journal of Common Market Studies* 39 (1999): 574–596.

Boyd-Barrett, Oliver, and Terhi Rantanen, eds. *The Globalization of News*. London: Sage, 1998.

Bratić, Vladimir, Susan Dente Ross, and Hyeonjin Kang-Graham. "Bosnia's Open Broadcast Network: A Brief but Illustrative Foray into Peace Journalism Practice." *Global Media Journal* 7.6 (2008). Accessed October 1, 2017. http://www.globalmediajournal.com/open-access/bosnias-open-broadcast-network-a-brief-but-illustrative-foray-into-peace-journalism-practice.php?aid=35218.

Broadcasting Council. "Analiza na pazarot na radiodifuznata dejnost za 2011 godina" [Analysis of the broadcasting activity market for 2011]. Skopje: Broadcasting Council, 2012.

Broadcasting Council. "Izvestaj od Mediumsko Pokrivanje na Izbornata Kampanja za Lokalnite Izbori 2013" [Report on the media coverage of the electoral campaign for the local elections 2013]. Skopje: Broadcasting Council, 2013.

Broadcasting Council. "List of Registered Radio Stations." Skopje: Broadcasting Council, 2013.

Broadcasting Council. "List of Registered TV Outlets." April 2013. Skopje: Broadcasting Council, 2013. Accessed May 1, 2013.

Broadcasting Council. "Report on the Work of the Broadcasting Council of the Republic of Macedonia, for the Period 1.1 2007 to 31.12.2007." Skopje: Broadcasting Council, 2008.

Broadcasting Council. "Report on the Work of the Broadcasting Council of the Republic of Macedonia, for the Period 1.1.2008 to 31.12.2008." Skopje: Broadcasting Council, 2009.

Broadcasting Council. "Report on the Work of the Broadcasting Council of the Republic of Macedonia, for the Period 1.1.2009 to 31.12.2009." Skopje: Broadcasting Council, 2010.

Broadcasting Council. "Report on the Work of the Broadcasting Council of the Republic of Macedonia, for the Period 1.1.2010 to 31.12 2010." Skopje: Broadcasting Council, 2011.

Broughton Micova, Sally. "Finding a Niche: Small States Public Service Broadcasting in Slovenia and Macedonia." Revisionary Interpretations of the Public Enterprise in Media (RIPE), 2010.

Brunner, Roland. "Urgent Media Assistance for Macedonia." *Medienhilfe Ex-Jugoslawien*, May, 2002. Accessed September 29, 2013. http://archiv.medienhilfe.ch/Projekte/MAC/urgent.htm.

Brunwasser, Matthew. "Concerns Grow about Authoritarianism in Macedonia." *New York Times*, October 13, 2011.

Bukovska, Barbora. "Bosnia and Herzegovina: Legislative Framework on the Communications Regulatory Agency." Article 19 and OSCE Representative on Freedom of the Media, September 2012. Accessed January 21, 2013. http://www.osce.org/fom/94101.

B92. "Serbia's Public Broadcaster to Be Financed from Budget." Accessed April 3, 2013. http://www.b92.net/eng/news/comments.php?nav_id=85503.

B92. "Vlasnička struktura" [Ownership structure]. Accessed March 12, 2013. http://www.b92.net/o_nama/vlasnistvo.php.

Carothers, Thomas. *Aiding Democracy Abroad: The Learning Curve.* Washington, DC: Carnegie Endowment for International Peace, 1999.

Cary, Peter, and Rosemary D'Amour. "U.S. Government Funding for Media: Trends and Strategies: A Report to the Center for International Media Assistance." Center for International Media Assistance/National Endowment for Democracy, March 19, 2013. Accessed March 14, 2013. http://www.cima.ned.org/wp-content/uploads/2015/01/U.S.-Government-Funding-for-Media_Trends-and-Strategies.pdf.

Cela, Sefedin. "Mediat elektronike—realitet dhe sfide" [Electronic media—Reality and challenge]. *Media Shqiptare* 8 (2000): 5–26.

Čengić, Nermin. "Zemljotres u Sivom domu" [Earthquake in the grey house]. *Dani*, September 8, 2000.

Center for Public Integrity. "Frequently Asked Questions." Accessed October 31, 2015. http://www.publicintegrity.org/about/our-organization/frequently-asked-questions.

Center for Public Integrity. "Return of Organization Exempt from Income Tax." Accessed October 31, 2015. http://s3.amazonaws.com/propublica/assets/about/propublica_990_2012.pdf.

Center for Public Integrity. "Worldwide Watchdog: Annual Report 2012". Center for Public Integrity, 2012. Accessed October 28, 2015. https://iw-files.s3.amazonaws.com/documents/pdfs/CPI_AnnualReport2012_sm.pdf.

Chadwick, Andrew. *The Hybrid Media System: Politics and Power.* Oxford: Oxford University Press, 2013.

Chandler, David. *Bosnia: Faking Democracy after Dayton.* 2nd ed. London: Pluto Press, 2000.

Chemonics International. *Giving Citizens a Voice—Strengthening Independent Media in Bosnia and Herzegovina: Final Report.* Chemonics International Inc., 2006.

Chetwynd, Eric, Jr., and Frances J. Chetwynd. "Mid-Term Evaluation: Kosovo Media Assistance Program (KMAP)." USAID, February 15, 2007. Accessed September 30, 2013. http://pdf.usaid.gov/pdf_docs/PDACL816.pdf.

Chetwynd, Frances, Jehona Gjurgjeala, and David Smith. "Kosovo Media Assistance Program: Final Evaluation Report." USAID, March 2008. Accessed October 7, 2017. http://democracyinternational.com/media/DI%20Final%20Report-Kosovo%20Media%20Evaluation.pdf.

CIMA. "Empowering Independent Media: Inaugural Report 2008." Center for International Media Assistance/National Endowment for Democracy, 2008. Accessed November 23, 2013. http://www.ned.org/cima/CIMA-Empowering_Independent_Media.pdf https://www.cima.ned.org/publication/empowering-independent-media-u-s-efforts-to-foster-free-and-independent-news-around-the-world/.

Cipa, Aleksander. "Pushteti qe zhvishet nga dinjiteti" [Power devoid of dignity]. *Shqip*, August 26, 2008, 9.

Cipa, Aleksander. "Unioni i Gazetareve Shqiptarë, organizimi sindikalist ne jeten mediatike te vendit" [Union of Albanian Journalists, a trade union organization in the media life of the country]. *Shqip*, May 3, 2008, 7.

Collier, David, and Steven Levitsky. "Democracy with Adjectives: Conceptual Innovations in Comparative Research." *World Politics* 49.3 (1997): 430–451.

"Constitution of the Republic of Kosovo." June 15, 2008.

Cook, Thomas J., and Ivo Spalatin. "Final Evaluation of OTI's Program in Serbia-Montenegro." Development Associates, December 31, 2002. Accessed October 28, 2015. http://pdf.usaid.gov/pdf_docs/pdabx440.pdf.

Council of Europe. "Declaration of the Committee of Ministers on the Independence and Functions of Regulatory Authorities for the Broadcasting Sector." Accessed December 10, 2013. https://wcd.coe.int/ViewDoc.jsp?id=1266737&Site=CM.

Council of Europe. "Recommendation CM/Rec (2012) 1 of the Committee of Ministers to member States on public service media governance." Accessed April 4, 2013. https://wcd.coe.int/ViewDoc.jsp?id=1908265.

Council of Europe. "Recommendation Rec (2000) 23 of the Committee of Ministers to Member States on the Independence and Functions of Regulatory Authorities for the Broadcasting Sector." December 20, 2000.

Council of Europe. "Recommendation 1848." Accessed February 26, 2013. http://
assembly.coe.int/main.asp?Link=/documents/adoptedtext/ta08/erec1848.htm.
Council of Europe. "Recommendation 94(13) on Measures to Promote Media
Transparency." Accessed December 10, 2013. http://www.coe.int/t/dghl/stan-
dardsetting/media/doc/cm/rec(1994)013&expmem_EN.asp.
Council of Europe. "Resolution 1636 (2008) of the Parliamentary Assembly on
Indicators for Media in a Democracy." Strasbourg: Council of Europe, 2008.
Accessed December 10, 2013. http://assembly.coe.int/main.asp?Link=/docu-
ments/adoptedtext/ta08/eres1636.htm.
CRA. "Annual Report of the Communications Regulatory Agency for the Year
2010." Communications Regulatory Agency of Bosnia and Herzegovina, March 2011. Accessed February 15, 2012. http://rak.ba/eng/index.
php?uid=1273696422.
CRA. "Annual Report of the Communications Regulatory Agency for the Year
2014." Communications Regulatory Agency of Bosnia and Herzegovina,
2015.
Croissant, Aurel S., and Wolfgang Merkel, eds. *Consolidation and Defective Democracy? Problems of Regime Change.* Special issue of *Democratization* 11.5 (2004).
Curran, James. "Mass Media and Democracy: A Reappraisal." In *Mass Media and
Society*, edited by James Curran and Michael Gurevitch, 82–117. London: E.
Arnold, 1991.
Darbishire, Helen. *Analiza e ligjit shqiptar mbi mediat elektronike* [Analysis of Alba-
nian law on electronic media]. Tirana: A19 & IFJ, 1997.
Daskalovski, Zhidas. "Language and Identity: The Ohrid Framework Agreement
and Liberal Notions of Citizenship and Nationality in Macedonia." *Journal of
Ethnopolitics and Minority Issues in Europe* 1 (2002): 1–32.
Daskalovski, Zhidas. "Macedonia: A Country Report." In *Nations in Transit 2010:
Democratization from Central Europe to Eurasia*, edited by Jeannette Goehring,
78–96. New York: Freedom House, 2011.
Daskalovski, Zhidas. "Mostovi koji dijele: mediji i manjine u Makedoniji" [The
bridges that divide: Media and minorities in Macedonia]. In *Na marginama:
manjine i mediji u jugoistočnoj Evropi* [On the margins: Minorities and media in
Southeast Europe], edited by Edin Hodžić and Tarik Jusić, 77–203. Sarajevo:
Mediacentar, 2010.
Daskalovski, Zhidas. "A Study of the Legal Framework of the Macedonian Broad-
casting Media (1991–1998): From Deregulation to a European Paradigm."
Balkanistica 14 (2001): 19–42.
Daskalovski, Židas. *Walking on the Edge: Consolidating Multiethnic Macedonia 1989–
2004.* Chapel Hill: Globic, 2006.
Dean, Walter. "Working in Concert: Coordination and Collaboration in International
Media Development." The Center for International Media Assistance at the
National Endowment for Democracy (CIMA)/National Endowment for Democ-
racy, December 18, 2012. Accessed November 23, 2013. http://issuu.com/cima-
publications/docs/cima-working-in-concert-coordination-and-collabora.
Deane, James. "Fragile States: The Role of Media and Communication." Policy
Briefing #10. BBC Media Action, October 2013. Accessed October 31, 2013.
http://downloads.bbc.co.uk/mediaaction/policybriefing/fragile_states_policy_
briefing.pdf.

De Luce, Dan. "Assessment of USAID Media Assistance in Bosnia and Herze-govina, 1996–2002." PPC Evaluation Working Paper No. 6. Bureau for Policy and Program Coordination, USAID, 2003. Accessed November 24, 2013. http://pdf.usaid.gov/pdf_docs/PNACR756.pdf.

Diamond, Larry, and Marc F. Plattner, eds. *The Global Divergence of Democracy.* Baltimore: Johns Hopkins University Press, 2001.

Dietz, Christoph. "International Media Assistance: A Guide to the Liter-ature, 1990–2010." Forum Medien und Entwicklung, September 13, 2010. Accessed October 20, 2016. http://nieman.harvard.edu/wp-content/uploads/pod-assets/pdf/Nieman%20Reports/Spring%202011/Media-Assis-tance-1990-2010.pdf.

Di Lellio, Anna. "Empire Lite as a Swamp." *Transitions* 1 (2005): 63–79. Accessed March 28, 2013. http://dev.ulb.ac.be/cevipol/dossiers_fichiers/7-di-lellio.pdf.

Dimitrijevska-Markoski, Tamara, and Zhidas Daskalovski. "Assisting Media Democratization after Low-Intensity Conflict: The Case of Macedonia." Working Paper 5/2013. Center for Social Research Analitika/Center for Research and Policy Making, 2013. Accessed October 7, 2017. http://www.analitika.ba/sites/default/files/publikacije/tamara_and_zhidas_-_rrpp_macedo-nia_wp05_3dec2013_final_for_publishing.pdf.

Di Palma, Giuseppe. *To Craft Democracies: An Essay on Democratic Transition.* Berkeley: University of California Press, 1990.

Dobek-Ostrowska, Boguslawa, Michał Glowacki, Karol Jakubowicz, and Miklós Sükösd, eds. *Comparative Media Systems: European and Global Perspectives.* Budapest: Central European University Press, 2010.

Downs, Anthony. *An Economic Theory of Democracy.* New York: Harper & Row, 1957.

DSDC. "Analysis of Foreign Assistance Performance 2011–2012." Tirana: Department of Strategy and Donor Coordination, 2012. Accessed May 4, 2013. http://www.dsdc.gov.al/dsdc/pub/analiza_e_donatoreve_2011_2012_final_1363_1.pdf.

DSDC. "External Assistance in Albania 2009–2010: Progress Report." Tirana: Department of Strategy and Donor Coordination, 2011. Accessed May 5, 2013. http://www.dsdc.gov.al./dsdc/pub/2009_2010_progress_report_eng_final_copy_1_1011_1.pdf.

Dzamazovski, Panta. "Novi prepukuvanja pri izborot na novi clenovi na SRD" [New fights about the election of new members of SRD]. *Telma,* August 25, 2011.

Džihana, Amer, Kristina Ćendić, and Meliha Tahmaz. "Mapping Digital Media: Bosnia and Hercegovina." Open Society Foundations, June 11, 2012. Accessed October 31, 2013. http://www.opensocietyfoundations.org/sites/default/files/mapping-digital-media-bosnia-20120706.pdf.

EAR. "Contract List—Signed by EAR from 08/01/2001 to 26/09/2008, Republic of Serbia." European Agency for Reconstruction, 2008.

EAR. "Serbia." European Agency for Reconstruction, 2008. Accessed January 15, 2013.

EAR. "Serbia: Civil Society and Media, EUR 32 Million." European Agency for Reconstruction, 2008. Accessed March 2, 2013.

EBU. "EBU Accuses PM of Interference in Kosovo Broadcaster." European Broad-casting Union, 2009.

EBU. "PSM Correlations: Links between Public Service Media and Societal Well-being." European Broadcasting Union, August 2016.

Ellis, Justin. "ProPublica at Five: How the Nonprofit Collaborates, Builds Apps, and Measures Impact." *Nieman Journalism Lab*, June 10, 2013. Accessed October 28, 2015. http://www.niemanlab.org/2013/06/propublica-at-five-how-the-nonprofit-collaborates-builds-apps-and-measures-impact/.

Elstein, David. "The Licence Fee Is a Fetter on the BBC." *Open Democracy*, January 11, 2013. Accessed August 23, 2013. http://www.opendemocracy.net/our-beeb/david-elstein/licence-fee-is-fetter-on-bbc.

Enda, Jodi. "Staying Alive." *American Journalism Review*, September 5, 2012. Accessed October 28, 2015. http://www.ajr.org/Article.asp?id=5389.

Esser, Frank, and Andrea Umbricht. "Competing Models of Journalism? Political Affairs Coverage in US, British, German, Swiss, French and Italian Newspapers." *Journalism* 14.8 (2013): 989–1007.

European Commission. "Albania 2012 Progress Report." SWD(2012) 334. Brussels: European Commission, 2012.

European Commission. "Bosnia and Herzegovina 2009 Progress Report." SEC(2009) 1338. Brussels: European Commission, 2009. Accessed May 31, 2012. https://ec.europa.eu/neighbourhood-enlargement/sites/near/files/pdf/key_documents/2009/ba_rapport_2009_en.pdf.

European Commission. "Bosnia and Herzegovina 2010 Progress Report." SEC(2010) 1331. Brussels: European Commission, 2010. Accessed October 28, 2015. http://ec.europa.eu/enlargement/pdf/key_documents/2010/package/ba_rapport_2010_en.pdf.

European Commission. "Bosnia and Herzegovina 2011 Progress Report." SEC(2011) 1206. Brussels: European Commission, 2011. Accessed May 31, 2012. http://ec.europa.eu/enlargement/pdf/key_documents/2011/package/ba_rapport_2011_en.pdf.

European Commission. "Bosnia and Herzegovina 2012 Progress Report." SWD(2012) 335. Brussels: European Commission, 2012. Accessed November 24, 2013. http://ec.europa.eu/enlargement/pdf/key_documents/2012/package/ba_rapport_2012_en.pdf.

European Commission. "Bosnia and Herzegovina 2014 Progress Report." SWD(2014) 305. Brussels: European Commission, 2014. Accessed October 28, 2015. https://ec.europa.eu/neighbourhood-enlargement/sites/near/files/pdf/key_documents/2014/20141008-bosnia-and-herzegovina-progress-report_en.pdf.

European Commission. "Commission Staff Working Paper: Analytical Report Accompanying the Document Communication from the Commission to the European Parliament and the Council: Commission Opinion on Serbia's Application for Membership of the European Union." SEC (2011) 1208. Brussels: European Commission, 2011. Accessed October 28, 2015. http://www.ipex.eu/IPEXL-WEB/dossier/document/SEC20111208.do.

European Commission. "The Former Yugoslav Republic of Macedonia 2006 Progress Report." SEC (2006)1387. Brussels: European Commission, 2006. Accessed November 26, 2017. https://ec.europa.eu/neighbourhood-enlargement/sites/near/files/pdf/key_documents/2006/nov/fyrom_sec_1387_en.pdf.

European Commission. "The Former Yugoslav Republic of Macedonia 2007 Progress Report." SEC(2007) 1432. Brussels: European Commission, 2007. Accessed November 26, 2017. https://ec.europa.eu/neighbourhood-enlargement/sites/near/files/pdf/key_documents/2007/nov/fyrom_progress_reports_en.pdf.

European Commission. "The Former Yugoslav Republic of Macedonia 2009 Progress Report." SEC(2009) 1335. Brussels: European Commission, 2009. Accessed November 26, 2017. https://ec.europa.eu/neighbourhood-enlargement/sites/near/files/pdf/key_documents/2009/mk_rapport_2009_en.pdf.

European Commission. "The Former Yugoslav Republic of Macedonia 2010 Progress Report." SEC(2009) 1332. Brussels: European Commission, 2010. Accessed November 26, 2017. https://ec.europa.eu/neighbourhood-enlargement/sites/near/files/pdf/key_documents/2010/package/mk_rapport_2010_en.pdf.

European Commission. "The Former Yugoslav Republic of Macedonia 2012 Progress Report." SWD(2012) 332. Brussels: European Commission, 2012. Accessed May 1, 2013. https://ec.europa.eu/neighbourhood-enlargement/sites/near/files/pdf/key_documents/2012/package/mk_rapport_2012_en.pdf.

European Commission. "Kosovo (under UNSCR 1244) 2005 Progress Report." SEC (2005) 1423. Brussels: European Commission, 2005. Accessed November 26, 2017. https://ec.europa.eu/neighbourhood-enlargement/sites/near/files/archives/pdf/key_documents/2005/package/sec_1423_final_progress_report_ks_en.pdf.

European Commission. "Kosovo (under UNSCR 1244) 2006 Progress Report." SEC (2006) 1386. Brussels: European Commission, 2006. Accessed November 26, 2017. https://ec.europa.eu/neighbourhood-enlargement/sites/near/files/pdf/key_documents/2006/nov/ks_sec_1386_en.pdf.

European Commission. "Kosovo (under UNSCR 1244) 2007 Progress Report." SEC (2007) 1433. Brussels: European Commission, 2007. Accessed November 26, 2017. https://www.mei-ks.net/repository/docs/2007_Commission_Progress_Report_KOSOVO.pdf.

European Commission. "Kosovo (under UNSCR 1244/99) 2008 Progress Report." SEC(2008) 2697. Brussels: European Commission, 2008. Accessed November 10, 2016. http://ec.europa.eu/enlargement/pdf/press_corner/key-documents/reports_nov_2008/kosovo_progress_report_en.pdf .

European Commission. "Kosovo under UNSCR 1244/99 2009 Progress Report." SEC(2009) 1340. Brussels: European Commission, 2009. Accessed November 10, 2016. http://ec.europa.eu/enlargement/pdf/key_documents/2009/ks_rapport_2009_en.pdf.

European Commission. "Kosovo 2010 Progress Report." SEC(2010)1329. Brussels: European Commission, 2010. Accessed November 10, 2016. http://ec.europa.eu/enlargement/pdf/key_documents/2010/package/ks_rapport_2010_en.pdf.

European Commission. "Kosovo 2011 Progress Report." SEC(2011) 1207. Brussels: European Commission, 2011. Accessed November 10, 2016. http://ec.europa.eu/enlargement/pdf/key_documents/2011/package/ks_rapport_2011_en.pdf.

European Commission. "Commission Staff Working Document accompanying the document. Commission Communication on a Feasibility Study for a Stabilisation and Association Agreement between the European Union and Kosovo." SWD(2012) 339 final/2. Brussels: European Commission, 2012. Accessed November 10, 2016. http://ec.europa.eu/enlargement/pdf/key_documents/2012/package/ks_analytical_2012_en.pdf.

European Commission. "Kosovo 2013 Progress Report." SWD(2013) 416. Brussels: European Commission, 2013. Accessed November 10, 2016. http://www.europarl.europa.eu/document/activities/cont/201311/20131105ATT73963/20131105ATT73963EN.pdf.

European Commission. "Kosovo 2014 Progress Report." SWD(2014) 306. Brussels: European Commission, 2014. Accessed November 10, 2016. http://ec.europa.eu/enlargement/pdf/key_documents/2014/20141008-kosovo-progress-report_en.pdf.

European Commission. "Mapping EU Media Support 2000–2010." Brussels: European Commission, 2012. Accessed October 7, 2017. https://ec.europa.eu/europeaid/sites/devco/files/study-mapping-eu-media-support-2000-2010_en_3.pdf.

European Commission. "Recommendation for a Council Decision authorising the opening of negotiations on a Stabilisation and Association Agreement between the European Union and Kosovo." COM(2013) 200. Brussels: European Commission, 2013. Accessed September 30, 2013. http://ec.europa.eu/enlargement/pdf/key_documents/2013/ks_recommendation_2013_en.pdf.

European Commission. "Serbia 2012 Progress Report." SWD(2012) 333. Brussels: European Commission, 2012. Accessed on October 28, 2015. http://ec.europa.eu/enlargement/pdf/key_documents/2012/package/sr_rapport_2012_en.pdf.

European Commission. "Serbia 2014 Progress Report." SWD(2014) 302. Brussels: European Commission, 2014. Accessed November 10, 2016. https://ec.europa.eu/neighbourhood-enlargement/sites/near/files/pdf/key_documents/2014/20140108-serbia-progress-report_en.pdf.

European Commission. "Stabilization and Association Agreement between European Communities and Serbia." Brussels: European Commission, 2008. Accessed March 2, 2013. http://www.europa.rs/upload/documents/key_documents/2008/SAA.pdf.

European Parliament. "Resolution of 25 September 2008 on Concentration and Pluralism in the Media in the European Union." Brussels: European Parliament, 2008. Accessed December 12, 2013. http://www.europarl.europa.eu/sides/getDoc.do?type=TA&reference=P6-TA-20080459&language=EN.

European Parliament and the European Council. "Directive 2010/13/EU of the European Parliament and of the Council of 10 March 2010 on the Coordination of Certain Provisions Laid Down by Law, Regulation or Administrative Action in Member States Concerning the Provision of Audiovisual Media Services (Audiovisual Media Services Directive)." *Official Journal of the European Union* L95/1.

European Union. "The Future of European Regulatory Audiovisual Policy." Accessed February 11, 2013. http://europa.eu/legislation_summaries/audiovisual_and_media_l24107_en.htm.

European Union and A.R.S. Progetti S.P.A. "Technical Assistance for Evaluation of Sector of Civil Society Organizations (CSO), Media and Culture Implemented and Financed by IPA Programme, EU Programmes and other Donors in the Republic of Serbia: Draft Evaluation Report." EU: European Union and A.R.S. Progetti S.P.A, 2013.

Evans, Peter. "Development as Institutional Change: The Pitfalls of Monocropping and the Potentials for Deliberation." *Studies in Comparative International Development* 4 (2004): 30–52.

"Federalna a ne državna" [The federal and not the state broadcaster]. *Oslobođenje*, February 1, 1998.

Fondacioni Shoqëria e Hapur për Shqipërinë. "Përdorimi i Facebook, Twitter, YouTube dhe Blogjeve për ligjërim politik mes të rinjve dhe kandidatëve për bashki e komuna" [Use of Facebook, Twitter, YouTube, and blogging for political deliberation between the youth and candidates for local office]. Accessed October 7, 2017. http://www.osfa.al/njoftime/perdorimi-i-facebook-twitter-youtube-dhe-blogjeve-per-ligjerim-politik-mes-te-rinjve-dhe-kandidat-eve-per-bashki-e-komuna.

Foundation Open Society Macedonia. "Godišen izveštaj 2011" [Annual report for 2011]. Skopje: Foundation Open Society Macedonia, 2011. Accessed October 3, 2013. http://www.soros.org.mk/izvestai/AR2011MK.pdf.

Franqué, Friederike von. "The Other Frontier: Media Assistance by International Organizations." In *Media in the Enlarged Europe: Politics, Policy and Industry*, edited by Alec Charles, 91–97. Bristol: Intellect Books, 2009.

Freedom House. "Freedom of the Press: Macedonia." Accessed October 3, 2013. http://www.freedomhouse.org/report/freedom-press/2012/macedonia.

FRIDE. "Democracy Monitoring Report: Albania 2010." Madrid: Fundación para las Relaciones Internacionales y el Diálogo Exterior, 2010. Accessed May 19, 2013. http://www.fride.org/publication/758/democracy-in-albania.

Gadzovska Spasovska, Zorana. "Partizacija na SRD?" [Partitioning the SRD?]. *Radio Free Europe*, July 13, 2011. Accessed January 24, 2013. http://www.makdenes.org/content/article/24264783.html.

Gadzovska Spasovska, Zorana. "Sovet za radiodifuzija ili lustracija na radiodifuzeri" [Broadcasting Council or lustration for broadcasters]. *Radio Free Europe*, June 14, 2012. Accessed October 7, 2013. http://www.makdenes.org/content/article/24614129.html.

Gap Institute. "RTK's Financial Sustainability: Finding Alternatives to Public Broadcaster Financing." GAP Policy Brief, n.d. Accessed September 30, 2013. http://www.institutigap.org/documents/78229_RTK-English.pdf.

"The General Framework Agreement for Peace in Bosnia and Herzegovina" [Dayton Peace Agreement]. December 14, 1995.

Goetz, Anne Marie. "Manoeuvring Past Clientelism: Institutions and Incentives to Generate Constituencies in Support of Governance Reforms." *Commonwealth & Comparative Politics* 4 (2007): 403–424.

Goga, Thanas. "The Era of 'Cross-Platform' Media and Its Impact on the Market: Case Study: A Profile of Albanian Dailies in the Facebook Social Network." Albanian Media Institute, 2013. Accessed July 14, 2016. http://www.institute-media.org/Documents/PDF/th-goga-english-follow-up.pdf.

Golubović, Zagorka, Bora Kuzmanović, and Mirjana Vasović. *Društveni karakter i društvene promene u svetlu nacionalnih sukoba* [Social character and social change in the light of national conflicts]. Belgrade: Institut za filozofiju i društvenu teoriju "FilipVišnjić," 1995.

Goodman, Emma. "ProPublica: Could the Non-Profit Model be the Saviour of the Newspaper Industry?" *World Association of Newspapers and News Publishers–Editors Weblog*, February 6, 2009. Accessed October 28, 2015. http://www.editorsweblog.org/2009/02/06/propublica-could-the-non-profit-model-be-the-saviour-of-the-newspaper-industry.

Gorinjac, E. "RAK mora dva puta raditi isti posao: Novi Parlament BiH također želi podobne u UO BHRT-a" [CRA has to do it all over again: New BiH parliament wants to appoint politically suitable candidates to the governing board of BHRT]. Sarajevo-x.com, August, 29, 2011. Accessed January 28, 2012. http://www.sarajevo-x.com/bih/novi-parlament-bih-takodjer-zeli-podobne-u-uo-bhrt-a/110829097.

Grade, Michael. "Building Public Value." BBC, 2004. Accessed January 28, 2016. http://www.bbc.co.uk/pressoffice/speeches/stories/bpv_grade.shtml.

Grzymała-Busse, Anna. "Political Competition and the Politicization of the State in East and Central Europe." *Comparative Political Studies* 36.10 (2003): 1123–1147.

Halilović, Mehmed. "Disciplining Independent Regulators: Political Pressures on the Communications Regulatory Agency of Bosnia and Herzegovina." *Puls demokratije*, July 10, 2008. Accessed, May 29, 2012. http://arhiva.pulsdemokratije.net/index.php?id=1060&l=en.

Hallin, Daniel C., and Paolo Mancini. "Americanization, Globalization, and Secularization: Understanding the Convergence of Media Systems and Political Communication." In *Comparing Political Communication: Theories, Cases, and Challenges*, edited by Frank Esser and Barbara Pfetsch, 25–44. Cambridge: Cambridge University Press, 2004.

Hallin, Daniel C., and Paolo Mancini. *Comparing Media Systems: Three Models of Media and Politics*. Cambridge: Cambridge University Press, 2004.

Hallin, Daniel C., and Paolo Mancini, eds. *Comparing Media Systems beyond the Western World*. Cambridge: Cambridge University Press, 2012.

Handwerk, Agnes, and Harrie Willems. "WAZ and the Buy-out of the Macedonian Independent Press." *Media Online: Southeast European Media Journal*, February 23, 2004, 1–39. Accessed October 3, 2013. http://www.mediaonline.ba/en/?ID=298.

Hanretty, Chris. "Public Service Broadcasting's Continued Rude Health." London: British Academy, 2012. Accessed October 31, 2013. http://www.britac.ac.uk/policy/Public-service-broadcasting.cfm.

Hans Bredow Institute for Media Research et al. *INDIREG: Indicators for Independence and Efficient Functioning of Audiovisual Media Services Regulatory Bodies for the Purpose of Enforcing the Rules in the AVMS Directive*. Study conducted on behalf of the European Commission. Final Report. *February 2011*. Accessed October 7, 2017. http://ec.europa.eu/archives/information_society/avpolicy/docs/library/studies/regulators/final_report.pdf.

Haraszti, Miklós. "The Role of the Media in March 2004 Events in Kosovo." Organization for Security and Co-operation in Europe, 2004. Accessed October 7, 2017. http://www.ian.org.rs/kosovo-info/zajednicke/vesti/OSCEviolance.pdf.

Haraszti, Miklós. "The State of Media Freedom in the Yugoslav Republic of Macedonia, Observations and Recommendations." Organization for Security and Co-operation in Europe, 2005.

Hedges, Chris. "TV Station in Bosnia Feeds Serbs Propaganda." *New York Times*, June 9, 1996.

Henderson, Gwyneth, Jasna Kilalic, and Boro Kontic. "The Media Environment in Bosnia and Herzegovina—An Assessment for USAID/Bosnia." USAID, January 2003. Accessed October 7, 2017. http://pdf.usaid.gov/pdf_docs/Pnacy558.pdf.

Hill, Mathew Allan. "Exploring USAID's Democracy Promotion in Bosnia and Afghanistan: A 'Cookie-Cutter Approach'?" *Democratization* 17.1 (2010): 98–124.

Hopin, Jonathan. "Comparative Methods." In *Theory and Methods in Political Science*, edited by David Marsh and Gerry Stoker, 249–267. Houndmills: Palgrave Macmillan, 2002.

Hozić, Aida A. "Democratizing Media, Welcoming Big Brother: Media in Bosnia and Herzegovina." In *Finding the Right Place on the Map: Central and Eastern European Media: Change in a Global Perspective*, edited by Karol Jakubowicz and Miklós Sükösd, 145–163. Bristol: Intellect, 2008.

Human Rights Watch. *Human Rights Watch World Report 1998: Events of 1997*. New York: Human Rights Watch, 1997.

Hume, Ellen. *The Media Missionaries: American Support for Journalism Excellence and Press Freedom around the Globe*. Miami: John S. and James L. Knight Foundation, 2004.

Humphreys, Peter. *Mass Media and Media Policy in Western Europe*. Manchester: Manchester University Press, 1996.

Huntington, Samuel P. "Democracy's Third Wave." *Journal of Democracy* 2 (1991): 12–34.

Huntington, Samuel P. *The Third Wave: Democratization in the Late Twentieth Century*. London: University of Oklahoma Press, 1991.

Huth, Paul K., and Todd L. Allee. *The Democratic Peace and Territorial Conflict in the Twentieth Century*. Cambridge: Cambridge University Press, 2002.

ICG. "Collapse in Kosovo." ICG Europe Report No. 155. International Crisis Group, April 22, 2004. Accessed January 29, 2016. https://www.crisisgroup.org/europe-central-asia/balkans/kosovo/collapse-kosovo.

ICG. "Media in Bosnia and Herzegovina: How International Support Can Be More Effective." ICG Bosnia Report No. 21. International Crisis Group, March 14, 1997. Accessed August, 2010. http://repository.forcedmigration.org/show_metadata.jsp?pid=fmo:1727.

IJNET. "Draft Defamation Legislation Announced for Bosnia-Herzegovina." *IJNET–International Journalists Network*, February 14, 2001. Accessed June 9, 2013. http://ijnet.org/opportunities/draft-defamation-legislation-announced-bosnia-herzegovina.

Ilić, Biljana. "Recenzija: VMRO-DPMNE za kampanja dosega potrosile 730,000 evra" [Review: VMRO-DPMNE spent €730,000 for the campaign]. *Proverka na fakti od mediumite*, March 19, 2013.

IMC. "About the IMC." Independent Media Commission, n.d. Accessed March 11, 2012. http://kpm-ks.org/?faqe=141&gjuha=3.

IMC. "Advertising Market Research and Analysis in Kosovo." Independent Media Commission, September 2013. Accessed November 10, 2016. http://kpm-ks.org/materiale/dokument/1389360328.1626.pdf.

IMC. "Annual Report Presented to the Kosovo Assembly." Independent Media Commission, 2012. accessed October 7, 2013. http://www.kpm-ks.org/materiale/dokument/1337178172.1865.pdf.

IMC. "Draft Strategy: Transition from Analogue to Digital Broadcasting in the Republic of Kosova." Independent Media Commission, 2013. Accessed September 29, 2013. http://www.kpm-ks.org/?pamja=dokumentet&gjuha=3&kerk o=Draft%20Strategy.

IMC. "Komisioni i Pavarur per Media, Raporti vjetor i punes per vitin 2011 drejtuar Kuvendit te Kosoves ne shkurt 2012, IMC." [Independent Media Commission, annual report 2011, submitted to Kosovo Assembly on February 2012]. Independent Media Commission, 2012. Accessed October 7, 2013. http://www.kpm-ks.org/materiale/dokument/1337178172.1865.pdf.

Infocentar. "Gragjanskite organizacii baraat vrakanje na procesot javna debata za noviot zakon za kleveta" [Civic associations demand the return of the public debate on the new law on libel]. NVO Infocentar. 2012.

Infocentar. *Media Mirror Further Deterioration of Media Freedoms and Freedom of Expression: Monitoring of Media in Republic of Macedonia: Report 1–2013.* Skopje: Infocentar, 2013.

Instituti i Medias. "Roli i reklamave në zhvillimin e medias" [Role of advertisement in media development]. Tirana: Instituti i Medias, 2012. Accessed June 4, 2013. http://www.fes-tirana.org/media/publications/pdffiles/2012/pub_ Roli%20i%20reklamave%20ne%20zhvillimin%20e%20medias.pdf.

International Media Freedom Mission. "Macedonia Report." Accessed October 3, 2013. http://www.znm.org.mk/drupal7.7/sites/default/files/International%20 Media%20Freedom%20Mission%20to%20Macedonia%20Report%20 ENG%20May%202012.pdf.

International Press Institute. "Proposed Changes to Broadcasting Council in Republic of Macedonia." July 14, 2011.

IREX. "Albania." In *Media Sustainability Index 2001: Development of Sustainable Independent Media in Europe and Eurasia*, 21–27. Washington, DC: International Research & Exchanges Board, 2001. Accessed February 12, 2013. https://www.irex.org/sites/default/files/pdf/media-sustainability-index-europe-eurasia-2001-full.pdf.pdf.

IREX. "Albania." In *Media Sustainability Index 2003: Development of Sustainable Independent Media in Europe and Eurasia*, 3–12. Washington, DC: International Research & Exchanges Board, 2003. Accessed November 26, 2017. https://www.irex.org/sites/default/files/pdf/media-sustainability-index-europe-eurasia-2003-full.pdf.pdf.

IREX. "Albania." In *Media Sustainability Index 2005: Development of Sustainable Independent Media in Europe and Eurasia*, 3–16. Washington, DC: International Research & Exchanges Board, 2005. Accessed November 26, 2017. https://www.irex.org/sites/default/files/pdf/media-sustainability-index-europe-eurasia-2005-full.pdf.pdf.

IREX. "Albania" In *Media Sustainability Index 2009: Development of Sustainable Independent Media in Europe and Eurasia*, 3–16. Washington, DC: International Research & Exchanges Board, 2009. Accessed November 26, 2017. https://www.irex.org/sites/default/files/pdf/media-sustainability-index-europe-eurasia-2009-full.pdf.pdf.

IREX. "Albania" In *Media Sustainability Index 2010: Development of Sustainable Independent Media in Europe and Eurasia*, 3–16. Washington, DC: International Research & Exchanges Board, 2010. Accessed November 26, 2017. https://www.irex.org/sites/default/files/pdf/media-sustainability-index-europe-eurasia-2010-full.pdf.pdf.

IREX. "Albania." In *Media Sustainability Index 2012: Development of Sustainable Independent Media in Europe and Eurasia*, 3–17. Washington, DC: International Research & Exchanges Board, 2012. Accessed June 5, 2013. https://www.irex.org/sites/default/files/pdf/media-sustainability-index-europe-eurasia-2012-full.pdf.pdf.

IREX. "Albania." In *Media Sustainability Index 2013: Development of Sustainable Independent Media in Europe and Eurasia*, 3–15. Washington, DC: International Research & Exchanges Board, 2013. Accessed June 5, 2013. https://www.irex.org/sites/default/files/pdf/media-sustainability-index-europe-eurasia-2013-full.pdf.pdf.

IREX. "Bosnia and Herzegovina." In *Media Sustainability Index 2013: The Development of Sustainable Independent Media in Europe and Eurasia*, 16–35. Washington, DC: International Research & Exchanges Board, 2013. Accessed October 28, 2015. https://www.irex.org/sites/default/files/pdf/media-sustainability-index-europe-eurasia-2013-full.pdf.pdf.

IREX. "Bosnia and Herzegovina." In *Media Sustainability Index 2014: The Development of Sustainable Independent Media in Europe and Eurasia*, 17–34. Washington, DC: International Research & Exchanges Board, 2014. Accessed March 6, 2016. https://www.irex.org/sites/default/files/pdf/media-sustainability-index-europe-eurasia-2014-full.pdf.

IREX. "Bosnia and Herzegovina." In *Media Sustainability Index 2016: The Development of Sustainable Independent Media in Europe and Eurasia*, 17–32 Washington, DC: International Research & Exchanges Board, 2016. Accessed August 11, 2016. https://www.irex.org/sites/default/files/pdf/media-sustainability-index-europe-eurasia-2016-full.pdf.pdf.

IREX. "Kosovo." In *Media Sustainability Index 2001: The Development of Sustainable Independent Media in Europe and Eurasia*, 123–130. Washington, DC: International Research & Exchanges Board, 2001. Accessed November 13, 2016. https://www.irex.org/sites/default/files/pdf/media-sustainability-index-europe-eurasia-2001-kosovo.pdf.

IREX. "Kosovo." In *Media Sustainability Index 2002: The Development of Sustainable Independent Media in Europe and Eurasia*, 43–52 Washington, DC: International Research & Exchanges Board, 2002. Accessed November 13, 2016. https://www.irex.org/sites/default/files/pdf/media-sustainability-index-europe-eurasia-2002-full.pdf.pdf.

IREX. "Kosovo." In *Media Sustainability Index 2005: The Development of Sustainable Independent Media in Europe and Eurasia*, 55–66. Washington, DC: International Research & Exchanges Board, 2005. Accessed November 13, 2016. https://www.irex.org/sites/default/files/pdf/media-sustainability-index-europe-eurasia-2005-full.pdf.pdf.

IREX. "Kosovo." In *Media Sustainability Index 2009: The Development of Sustainable Independent Media in Europe and Eurasia*, 57–66. Washington, DC: International Research & Exchanges Board, 2009. Accessed November 13, 2016. https://www.irex.org/sites/default/files/pdf/media-sustainability-index-europe-eurasia-2009-full.pdf.pdf.

IREX. "Kosovo." In *Media Sustainability Index 2012: The Development of Sustainable Independent Media in Europe and Eurasia*, 75–86. Washington, DC: International Research & Exchanges Board, 2012. Accessed November 13, 2016. https://www.irex.org/sites/default/files/pdf/media-sustainability-index-europe-eurasia-2012-full.pdf.pdf.

IREX. "Kosovo." In *Media Sustainability Index 2015: The Development of Sustainable Independent Media in Europe and Eurasia*, 59–70. Washington, DC: International Research & Exchanges Board, 2015. Accessed November 13, 2016. https://www.irex.org/sites/default/files/pdf/media-sustainability-index-europe-eurasia-2015-full.pdf.pdf.

IREX. "Macedonia." In *Media Sustainability Index 2012: The Development of Sustainable Independent Media in Europe and Eurasia*, 87–96. Washington, DC: International Research & Exchanges Board, 2012. Accessed January 10, 2013. https://www.irex.org/sites/default/files/pdf/media-sustainability-index-europe-eurasia-2012-full.pdf.pdf.

IREX. "Macedonia." In *Media Sustainability Index 2013: The Development of Sustainable Independent Media in Europe and Eurasia*, 78–89. Washington, DC: International Research & Exchanges Board, 2013. Accessed October 28, 2015. https://www.irex.org/sites/default/files/pdf/media-sustainability-index-europe-eurasia-2013-full.pdf.pdf.

IREX. "Macedonia." In *Media Sustainability Index 2015: The Development of Sustainable Independent Media in Europe and Eurasia*, 71–86. Washington, DC: International Research & Exchanges Board, 2015. Accessed October 3, 2015. https://www.irex.org/sites/default/files/pdf/media-sustainability-index-europe-eurasia-2015-full.pdf.pdf.

IREX. "Methodology." In *Media Sustainability Index 2012: The Development of Sustainable Independent Media in Europe and Eurasia*, xvii–xxi. Washington, DC: International Research & Exchanges Board, 2012. Accessed December 10, 2013. https://www.irex.org/sites/default/files/pdf/media-sustainability-index-europe-eurasia-2012-full.pdf.pdf.

IREX. "Serbia: Building Independent Media—Documentary." International Research & Exchanges Board, 2012. Accessed October 2, 2013. https://www.youtube.com/watch?v=HHBvyM0k8ek.

IREX. " Serbia (Federal Republic of Yugoslavia)." In *Media Sustainability Index 2001: The Development of Sustainable Independent Media in Europe and Eurasia*, 205–214. Washington DC: International Research & Exchanges Board, 2001. Accessed November 26, 2017. https://www.irex.org/sites/default/files/pdf/media-sustainability-index-europe-eurasia-2001-full.pdf.pdf.

IREX. "Serbia." In *Media Sustainability Index 2003: The Development of Sustainable Independent Media in Europe and Eurasia*, 89-96. Washington, DC: International Research & Exchanges Board, 2003. Accessed November 26, 2017. https://www.irex.org/sites/default/files/pdf/media-sustainability-index-europe-eurasia-2003-full.pdf.pdf.

IREX. "Serbia." In *Media Sustainability Index 2005: The Development of Sustainable Independent Media in Europe and Eurasia*, 99-109. Washington, DC: International Research & Exchanges Board, 2005. Accessed November 26, 2017. https://www.irex.org/sites/default/files/pdf/media-sustainability-index-europe-eurasia-2005-full.pdf.pdf.

IREX. "Serbia." In *Media Sustainability Index 2009: The Development of Sustainable Independent Media in Europe and Eurasia*, 103-111. Washington, DC: International Research & Exchanges Board, 2009. https://www.irex.org/sites/default/files/pdf/media-sustainability-index-europe-eurasia-2009-full.pdf.pdf.

IREX. "Serbia." In *Media Sustainability Index 2013: The Development of Sustainable Independent Media in Europe and Eurasia*, 114–129. Washington, DC: International Research & Exchanges Board, 2013. Accessed October 28, 2015. https://www.irex.org/sites/default/files/pdf/media-sustainability-index-europe-eurasia-2013-full.pdf.pdf.

IREX. "Serbia." In *Media Sustainability Index 2015: The Development of Sustainable Independent Media in Europe and Eurasia*, 115-127. Washington, DC: International Research & Exchanges Board, 2015. Accessed 10 May, 2015. https://www.irex.org/sites/default/files/pdf/media-sustainability-index-europe-eurasia-2015-full.pdf.pdf.

IREX. "Strengthening Independent Minority Media (SIMM) in Kosovo, Factsheet." Washington, DC: International Research & Exchanges Board, 2012. Accessed April 15, 2013.

IREX ProMedia/Serbia. *Quarterly Report*, April 1, 2003–June 30, 2003, CA #169-A-00-99-00101-00. Washington DC: International Research & Exchanges Board, 2003. http://pdf.usaid.gov/pdf_docs/Pdabz683.pdf.

Irion, Kristina, Michele Ledger, Sara Svensson, and Nevena Rsumovic. 2014. *The Independence and Functioning of the Audiovisual Media Authority in Albania*. Study commissioned by the Council of Europe, Amsterdam/Brussels/Budapest/Tirana, October, 2014.

Irion, Kristina, Michele Ledger, Sara Svensson, and Nevena Rsumovic. 2017. *The Independence and Functioning of the Regulatory Authority for Electronic Media in Serbia*. Study commissioned by the Council of Europe, Amsterdam/Brussels/Budapest/Belgrade, August, 2017.

Irion, Kristina. "Follow the Money! Ownership & Financial Transparency should be a Media Policy Standard," LSE Media Policy Blog, 30 April 2014 http://blogs.lse.ac.uk/mediapolicyproject/2014/04/30/follow-the-money-ownership-financial-transparency-should-be-a-media-policy-standard/.

Irion, Kristina, and Tarik Jusić. "International Assistance and Media Democratization in the Western Balkans: A Cross-National Comparison." *Global Media Journal* (German edition) 4 (2014). Accessed October 27, 2016. URN:nbn:de:gbv:547-201400711.

Jakimovski, Ljubomir, Vesna Nikodinovska, Petrit Sarachini, and Mirche Adamchevski. *My Choice 2011*. Skopje: Macedonian Institute for Media, 2011.

Jakubowicz, Karol. "Lovebirds? The Media, the State and Politics in Central and Eastern Europe." *Javnost—The Public* 2.1 (1995): 75–91.

Jakubowicz, Karol. "Preface." In *The Independence of the Media and Its Regulatory Agencies: Shedding New Light on Formal and Actual Independence against the*

National Context, edited by Wolfgang Schulz, Peggy Valcke, and Kristina Irion, xi–xxiv. Bristol: Intellect, 2013.

Jakubowicz, Karol. "Public Service Broadcasting: Product (and Victim?) of Public Policy." In *The Handbook of Global Media and Communication Policy,* edited by Robin Mansell and Marc Raboy, 210–229. Malden: Wiley-Blackwell, 2011.

Jakubowicz, Karol. "Social and Media Change in Central and Eastern Europe: Frameworks of Analysis." In *Business as Usual: Continuity and Change in Central and Eastern Europe,* edited by David Paletz and Karol Jakubowicz, 3–43. Cresskill: Hampton Press, 2003.

Jakubowicz, Karol, and Directorate General for Information Society and Media (Audiovisual and Media Policies Unit) of the European Commission. "Analysis and Review of a Draft Law on Broadcasting Activity of 'The Former Yugoslav Republic of Macedonia.'" ATCM(2005)005 (English only). Prepared by the Ministry of Transport and Communications, Council of Europe, May 20, 2005. Accessed October 3, 2013. http://ec.europa.eu/avpolicy/docs/ext/fyrom_en.pdf.

Jakubowicz, Karol, and Miklós Sükösd. "Twelve Concepts Regarding Media System Evolution and Democratization in Post-Communist Societies." In *Finding the Right Place on the Map: Central and Eastern European Media Changes in a Global Perspective,* edited by Karol Jakubowicz and Miklós Sükösd, 9–40. Bristol: Intellect, 2008.

Jakubowicz, Karol, and Miklós Sükösd, eds. *Finding the Right Place on the Map: Central and Eastern European Media Change in a Global Perspective.* Bristol: Intellect, 2008.

Johnson, Hawley M. "Model Interventions: The Evolution of Media Development Strategies in Bosnia Herzegovina, Kosovo, and Macedonia from 2000 to 2007." PhD diss., Columbia University, 2012. Accessed December 15, 2013. http://hdl.handle.net/10022/AC:P:14315.

Jusić, Tarik, and Nidžara Ahmetašević. "Media Reforms through Intervention: International Media Assistance in Bosnia and Herzegovina." Working Paper 3/2013. Sarajevo: Center for Social Research Analitika, 2013. Accessed October 7, 2017. http://www.sze.hu/~smuk/Nyilvanossag_torvenyek_east_south_eur/Szakirodalom,%20egy%C3%A9b%20forr%C3%A1sok/Int%20Media%20Assistance%20BiH.pdf.

Kalathil, Shanthi. *Developing Independent Media as an Institution of Accountable Governance: A How-To Guide.* Washington, DC: World Bank, 2011.

Kaplan, David E. *Empowering Independent Media: US Efforts to Foster a Free Press and an Open Internet around the World,* 2nd ed. Washington, DC: Center for International Media Assistance/National Endowment for Democracy, 2012. Accessed October 28, 2015. http://www.cima.ned.org/resource/empowering-independet-media-u-s-efforts-to-foster-a-free-press-and-an-open-internet-around-the-world-second-edition-2012/.

Kaplan, David E. "Global Investigative Journalism: Strategies for Support: A Report to the Center for International Media Assistance." 2nd ed. Center for International Media Assistance and National Endowment for Democracy, January 14, 2013. Accessed October 28, 2015. http://www.cima.ned.org/resource/global-investigative-journalism-strategies-for-support/.

Karajkov, Risto. "Macedonia: Media Freedom under Threat." *Osservatorio Balcani e Caucaso,* July 5, 2012. Accessed October 3, 2013. http://www.balcanicaucaso.org/eng/Regions-and-countries/Macedonia/Macedonia-Media-Freedom-Under-Threat.

Kaufman, Joshua. "Kosovo Media Assessment: Final Report." USAID Kosovo/ ARD Inc., March 2004. Accessed September 29, 2013. http://pdf.usaid.gov/ pdf_docs/Pnacx726.pdf.

Kelly, Mary, Gianpietro Mazzoleni, and Denis McQuail, eds. *The Media in Europe: The Euromedia Handbook*. London: Sage, 2004.

KIPRED. "Circulation and Politicization of the Print Media in Kosovo." OSCE Mission in Kosovo / Kosovar Institute for Policy Research and Development, 2010. Accessed September 28, 2013. http://www.osce.org/ kosovo/67790?download=true.

KIPRED. "Media Monitoring during the Elections Campaign 2009." Kosovar Institute for Policy Research and Development, 2009.

KIPRED. "Monitorimi i programit informativ të Radiotelevizionit të Kosovës" [Monitoring of the informative program of RTK]. Kosovar Institute for Policy Research and Development, 2011. Accessed September 30, 2013. http://www. kipred.org/repository/docs/Monitorimi%C2%A0i%C2%A0programit%C2%A 0informativ%C2%A0të%C2%A0_Radiotelevizionit%C2%A0të%C2%A0Kos ovës_237448.pdf.

KIPRED. "Monitoring of Media during the Election Campaign in Kosovo (October 26–November 16, 2007)." Kosovar Institute for Policy Research and Development, 2008. Accessed September 28, 2013. http://www.kipred.org/ repository/docs/Monitoring_of_Media_During_the_Election_Campaign_in_ Kosovo__(26_October-_16_November_2007)_262357.pdf.

KIPRED. "RTK Challenge." Kosovar Institute for Policy Research and Development, 2011. Accessed September 29, 2013. http://www.kipred.org/repository/ docs/RTK_Challenge_413092.pdf.

Kiprijanovska, Dragana. "Monitoring the Court Cases against Journalists Accused of Defamation and Insult." Skopje: Coalition of Civil Associations "All for Fair Trials," September 2011.

Kirchheimer, Otto. "The Transformation of West European Party Systems." In *Political Parties and Political Development*, edited by Joseph La Palombara and Myron Weiner, 177–200. Princeton: Princeton University Press, 1966.

KKRT. "Koha e Plote per Subjektet Politike dhe Institucionet Qendrore" [Time on political subjects and main institutions]. Tirana: Këshilli Kombëtar i Radios dhe Televizionit, 2012.

KKRT. "Raporti Vjetor" [Annual report]. Tirana: Këshilli Kombëtar i Radios dhe Televizionit, 2006.

KKRT. "Raporti Vjetor" [Annual report]. Tirana: Këshilli Kombëtar i Radios dhe Televizionit, 2007.

KKRT. "Raporti Vjetor" [Annual report]. Tirana: Këshilli Kombëtar i Radios dhe Televizionit, 2008.

KKRT. "Raporti Vjetor" [Annual report]. Tirana: Këshilli Kombëtar i Radios dhe Televizionit, 2009.

KKRT. "Raporti Vjetor" [Annual report]. Tirana: Këshilli Kombëtar i Radios dhe Televizionit, 2010.

KKRT. "Raporti Vjetor" [Annual report]. Tirana: Këshilli Kombëtar i Radios dhe Televizionit, 2011.

KKRT. "Raporti Vjetor" [Annual report]. Tirana: Këshilli Kombëtar i Radios dhe Televizionit, 2012.

Klekovski, Sašo, Daniela Stojanova, Gonce Jakovleska, and Emina Nuredinoska. "Civil Society Index Report for the Republic of Macedonia." Skopje: Macedonian Center for International Cooperation, 2011.

Knežević, Sofija. "Uloga programa obuke BBC-ja u transformaciji RTS-a u javni servis" [The role of BBC training programs in transformation of RTS into a public service]. *Communication Management Quarterly* 7.22 (2012).

Kolar-Panov, Dona. "Broadcasting in Macedonia: Between the State and the Market." Paper presented at the colloquium on "Media Ownership and Control in East and Central Europe," sponsored by WACC, the Slovenian Broadcasting Council, and the Ministry of Science and Technology of the Republic of Slovenia, Piran, Slovenia, April 8–10, 1999. Accessed on January 20, 2013. http://www.waccglobal.org/en/19993-changing-perspectives-in-europe-today/813-Broadcasting-in-Macedonia-Between-the-State-and-the-Market--.html.

Kornegay, Van. "On the Road to Free Press in Albania: Evaluating outside Aid Efforts." The James M. Cox, Jr., Center for International Mass Communication Training and Research, Henry W. Grady College of Journalism and Mass Communication, the University of Georgia, 1995. Accessed October 7, 2017. http://www.grady.uga.edu/coxcenter/conference_papers/public_tcs/free_press_albania.pdf.

Kosovo Agency of Statistics. "Kosovo Population and Housing Census 2011." Accessed April 1, 2013.

Kremenjak, Slobodan. "Obstacles on the Road towards a New Regulatory Framework for the Media in Serbia." In *Legal Monitoring of Serbian Media Scene: ANEM Publication IV*, 27–29. Serbia: ANEM, 2010. Accessed October 7, 2017. http://www.anem.org.rs/en/aktivnostiAnema/monitoring/story/11548/THE+FOURTH+ANEM+MONITORING+PUBLICATION+.html.

Kremenjak, Slobodan, and Miloš Živković. "Serbia." In *The Media in South-East Europe: A Comparative Media Law and Policy Study*, edited by Beate Martin, Alexander Scheuer, and Christian Bron, 123–130. Berlin: Friedrich Ebert Foundation, 2011. Accessed October 28, 2015. http://library.fes.de/pdf-files/bueros/sofia/08097.pdf.

KRIK. "About Us." Crime and Corruption Reporting Network website. Accessed October 31, 2015. https://www.krik.rs/en/about-us/.

Kumar, Krishna. "International Assistance to Promote Independent Media in Transition and Post-conflict Societies." *Democratization* 13.4 (2006): 652–667.

Kumar, Krishna. "One Size Does Not Fit All: Objectives and Priority Areas for Media Assistance in Different Societies." Washington, DC: Center for International Media Assistance/National Endowment for Democracy, 2009. Accessed October 3, 2013. http://www.cima.ned.org/wp-content/uploads/2015/02/Kumar-One-Size-Does-Not-Fit-All.pdf.

Kurspahić, Kemal. *Zločin u 19:30: Balkanski mediji u ratu i miru* [Prime-time crime: Balkan media in war and peace]. Sarajevo: Mediacentar, 2003. Accessed October 7, 2017. http://www.media.ba/mcsonline/files/shared/Zlocinu1930.pdf.

LaMay, Craig L. *Exporting Press Freedom: Economic and Editorial Dilemmas in International Media Assistance*. New Brunswick: Transaction Publishers, 2009.

Laue, Eberhard. "Local Electronic Media in Kosovo." OSCE Mission in Kosovo, August 2005. Accessed October 7, 2017. http://www.osce.org/kosovo/16355? download=true.

"Law no. 02/L-15 for the Independent Media Commission and Broadcasting." Assembly of Kosovo, April 21, 2005.

"Law no. 04/L-044 on the Independent Media Commission." *Official Gazette of the Republic of Kosovo*, 5/05, April 2012.

"Law no. 02/L-047 on Radio Television of Kosovo." *Official Gazette of the Republic of Kosovo*, April 2006.

"Law no. 04/L-046 on Radio Television of Kosovo." *Official Gazette of the Republic of Kosova*, 012-2012, April 2012.

LeBor, Adam. "Comment: Milošević the Peacemaker." London: Institute for War and Peace Reporting (IWPR), 2005. Accessed October 11, 2013. http://iwpr. net/report-news/comment-milosevic-peacemaker.

"Ligji nr. 8410 Per Radion dhe Televizionin Publik dhe Privat" [Law no. 8410 on public and private radio and television]. *Official Gazette* 20/98, Art. 7 (4).

Lijphart, Arend. "Comparative Politics and the Comparative Method." *American Political Science Review* 65.3 (1971): 682–693.

Lijphart, Arendt. *Democracy in Plural Societies: A Comparative Exploration.* New Haven: Yale University Press, 1977.

Lijphart, Arendt, and Carl H. Waisman, eds. *Institutional Design in New Democracies: Eastern Europe and Latin America.* Boulder: Westview, 1996.

Lindvall, Daniel. "The Public Broadcasting Reform—A Reflection of the Bosnian Dilemma." Unpublished draft paper, November 24, 2005.

Liperi, Ornela. "Special: Advertisement 2010." *Revista Monitor*, March 2011.

Loewenberg, Shira. "United Nations Media Strategy: Recommendations for Improvement in Peacekeeping Operations: Case Study: UN Interim Administration Mission in Kosovo." United Nations, 2006. Accessed October 7, 2017. http://citeseerx.ist.psu.edu/viewdoc/download?doi=10.1.1.554.592&rep=rep1 &type=pdf.

Londo, Ilda. "Albania." In *Freedom of Speech in South East Europe: Media Independence and Self-Regulation*, 20-63 Sofia: Media Development Center; Budapest: South East European Network for Professionalization of Media, 2007.

Londo, Ilda. "Albania." In *Media Ownership and Its Impact on Media Pluralism and Independence*, edited by Brankica Petković, 39–60. Ljubljana: Peace Institute, Institute for Contemporary Social and Political Studies, 2004.

Londo, Ilda. "Albania." In *Television across Europe: More Channels, Less Independence: Follow-up Reports 2008*, edited by Mark Thompson, 67–107. Budapest: Open Society Institute/EU Monitoring and Advocacy Program, 2008.

Londo, Ilda. "Digital Television in Albania: Policies, Development, and Public Debate." Tirana: Albanian Media Institute, May 26, 2006. Accessed October 7, 2017. http://www.institutemedia.org/Documents/PDF/Albania%20 paper%20DTV.pdf.

Londo, Ilda. "Limited Assistance for Limited Impact: International Media Assistance in Albania." Sarajevo: Center for Social Research Analitika, 2013. Accessed October 7, 2017. http://mediaobservatory.net/sites/default/files/Albania_Ilda_Londo.pdf.

Londo, Ilda. "Mapping Digital Media: Albania." Open Society Foundations, January 20, 2012. Accessed October 31, 2013. http://www.institutemedia.org/Documents/PDF/OSF-Media-Report-Albania-02-17-2012-final-WEB.pdf.

Londo, Ilda, and Mirela Shuteriqi. "Albania." In *Television across Europe: More Channels, Less Independence: Monitoring Reports 2005*, Vol. 1, 185–252. Budapest: Open Society Institute/EU Monitoring and Advocacy Program, 2005.

Luković, Petar. "Nemam problema sa svojom prošlosti" [I have no problems with my past]. *BH Dani*, September 6, 2002.

Macedonian Institute for Media. "About Us." Accessed February 14, 2013. http://www.mim.org.mk/index.php/en/about-mim1.

Macedonian Institute for Media. "Development of the Media in Macedonia According to UNESCO Indicators." Skopje: Macedonian Institute for Media, January 2012. Accessed October 7, 2017. http://mediaobservatory.net/sites/default/files/unesko_indikatori_en.pdf.

Macedonian Radio Television. "Godišen izveštaj za finansiskoto rabotenje na JP Makedonska Radio Televizija vo 2011 godina" [Financial report of Macedonian Radio Television for 2011]. Skopje: Macedonian Radio Television, 2012. Accessed February 14, 2013. http://www.mtv.com.mk/upload/Dokumenti/Izvestaj%20MRT%202011%20vtora%20varijanta.pdf.

Malcolm, Noel. *Kosovo: A Short History*. London: Pan, 2002.

Manevski, Borce, and Adriana Skerlev-Cakar. "Macedonia." In *The Media in South-East Europe: A Comparative Media Law and Policy Study*, edited by Beate Martin, Alexander Scheuer, and Christian Bron, 83–89. Berlin: Friedrich Ebert Foundation, 2011. Accessed October 28, 2015. http://library.fes.de/pdf-files/bueros/sofia/08097.pdf.

Marko, Davor. "Bosnia and Herzegovina in Search of Accountability: The Role of Professional Journalist Associations in Generating Professionalism and Accountability of the Media in BiH." Sarajevo: Open Society Foundation, 2012.

Marko, Davor. "Media Reforms in Turbulent Times: The Role of Media Assistance in the Establishment of Independent Media Institutions in Serbia." Working Paper 6/2013. Sarajevo: Centre for Social Research Analitika, 2013. Accessed October 7, 2017. http://mediaobservatory.net/sites/default/files/Marko_Serbia.pdf.

Marko, Davor. "Medijska pomoć i izgradnja medijskih institucija u Srbiji" [Media assistance and the development of functional media institutions in Serbia]. In *Godišnjak 2014*, by the Faculty of Political Sciences, University of Belgrade, 133–147. Belgrade: University of Belgrade, 2014. Accessed October 7, 2017. http://www.fpn.bg.ac.rs/wp-content/uploads/2017/01/Godisnjak-dec-2014.pdf.

Marko, Davor. "The Role of Media Assistance in the Establishment of Public Service Broadcasting in Serbia." *International Journal for Digital Television* 6.6 (2015): 293–310.

Martin, Eric. "Media Reform and Development in Bosnia: An Interorganizational Account of the Media Issues Group." *South East European Journal of Economics and Business* 6.1 (2011): 85–98.

Marusic, Sinisa Jakov. "Libel Law Changes Criticized in Macedonia." *Balkan Insight*, November 13, 2012. Accessed April 1, 2013. http://www.balkaninsight.com/en/article/macedonia-decriminalizes-libel-tightens-rules-on-foreign-media.

Marusic, Sinisa Jakov. "Macedonian Journalists Cry Foul Over Libel Reform." *Balkan Insight*, June 15, 2012. Accessed April 1, 2013. http://www.balkaninsight.com/en/article/macedonian-journalists-cry-foul-over-libel-reform

Mastilović Jasnić, Ivana. "Matić: Model devedestih je ponovo zaživeo" [Matić: Model of 1990s lives again]. *Blic*, December 30, 2012. Accessed March 10, 2013. http://www.blic.rs/Vesti/Drustvo/360281/Veran-Matic-Model-devedesetih-je-ponovo-zaziveo.

Matić, Jovanka. "Post-komunističke medijske reforme iz ptičje perspective" [Postcommunist media reforms from a broader perspective]. In *Legal Monitoring of Serbian Media Scene ANEM Publication VI*, 17–20. Serbia: ANEM, 2012. Accessed October 7, 2017. http://www.anem.rs/en/aktivnostiAnema/monitoring/story/13551/THE+SIXTH+ANEM+MONITORING+PUBLICATION.html.

Matić, Jovanka. "Raznovrsnost TV programa u Srbiji" [Diversity of TV programs in Serbia]. In *Medijski skener*, edited by Dubravka Valić-Nedeljković, 24–69. Novi Sad: Novosadska novinarska škola, 2009.

Matić, Jovanka. "Serbian Media Scene vs. European Standards: Report Based on Council of Europe's Indicators for Media in a Democracy." Belgrade: Association of Independent Electronic Media (ANEM), 2012. Accessed October 28, 2015. http://www.anem.rs/en/aktivnostiAnema/AktivnostiAnema/story/13442/Publication+%22Serbian+Media+Scene+VS+European+Standards%22.html.

Matić, Jovanka. "Servis građana ili servis vlasti: Pluralizam mišljenja u informativnom programu javnog TV servisa u Srbiji" [Serving the public or the government: Pluralism of opinion in the news programs of the public TV service in Serbia]. Belgrade: Dobar naslov, 2014.

Matić, Jovanka. "(Too) High Expectations of Democracy in Serbia? Interpretation of Empirical Research." *Southeastern Europe* 36.3 (2012): 304–327.

Matić, Jovanka, and Larisa Ranković. "Serbia." In *Media Landscapes*, European Journalism Centre. Accessed October 28, 2015. http://ejc.net/media_landscapes/serbia.

Matic, Veran. "Media Cannot Survive on Donations Alone" (interview), *Balkan Insight*, September 2007. Accessed on February 5, 2013. Available at: http://www.balkaninsight.com/en/article/interview-media-cannot-survive-on-donations-alone.

Mazowiecki, Tadeusz. "Specijalni izveštaj o medijima izvještača UN-a imenovanog Rezolucijom 1994/72 Komisije za ljudska prava UN-a, E/CN 4/1995/54" [Special report on the media: Report of the special rapporteur submitted pursuant to Commission resolution, 1994/72, E/CN.4/1995/54. UN Commission on Human Rights]. Geneva: UN Commission on Human Rights, 1994.

McClear, Rich, Suzi McClear, and Peter Graves. "US Media Assistance in Serbia July 1997–June 2002." Washington, DC: United States Agency for International Development, Bureau for Policy and Program Coordination, 2003. Accessed October 28, 2015. http://pdf.usaid.gov/pdf_docs/PNACT553.pdf.

Mcloughlin, Claire, and Zoë Scott. "Topic Guide on Communications and Governance." International Development Department, University of Birmingham, Communication for Governance and Accountability Program, 2010. Accessed October 7, 2017. http://www.gsdrc.org/docs/open/commgap1.pdf.

McQuail, Denis. *Media Performance: Mass Communication and the Public Interest.* London: Sage, 1992.

Media Experts Commission. "Završni izvještaj: Mediji u izborima" [Final report: Media in elections]. OSCE Mission in Bosnia and Herzegovina, 1998.

Mediaonline. "Novosti u medijima" [News in the media]. Accessed December 13, 2012. http://www.mediaonline.ba/ba/arhiva/arhiva/pdf/1998/mnbr07bh.pdf.

Media Task Force. "Overview of Media Support to SEE." 2003.

Media Task Force. "Stability Pact for SEE Overall Strategy for Media Assistance." Media Task Force, Stability Pact for SEE, October 2001.

Medienhilfe. "Crisis Assistance for Local Independent Broadcasters in Macedonia." Accessed September 29, 2013. http://archiv2.medienhilfe.ch/Partner/MAC/IMF/IMF-CAP2.htm.

Medienhilfe. "International Media Fund for Macedonia—Fact Sheet." October 2001. Accessed September 29, 2013. http://archiv2.medienhilfe.ch/Partner/MAC/IMF/index.htm.

Medija centar. "EAR Media Fund." Accessed October 28, 2015. http://212.62.51.2/ear-media-fund.6.html?eventId=26517

"Memorandum of Understanding between Telecommunications Regulatory Agency and Independent Media Commission, no. 376\2\10." October 7, 2010.

Miftari, Naser. "Starting from Scratch: The Role of Media Assistance in the Establishment of Independent Media Institutions in Kosovo." Working Paper 4/2013. Sarajevo: Center for Social Research Analitika/Pristina: Democracy for Development, 2013. Accessed October 7, 2017. http://www.analitika.ba/sites/default/files/publikacije/miftari_n_-_rrpp_kosovo_wp04_3dec2013_final_for_publishing.pdf.

Miftari, Naser, and Surroi Flaka, eds. *Koha Ditore—10 vjetët e parë Monografi* [*Koha Ditore*—The first ten years]. Pristina: Koha Ditore, 2007.

Mihajloski, Goce. "VMRO-DPMNE za kampanja dosega potrosile 730,000 evra" [VMRO-DPMNE for the campaign spent so far 730,000 Euros]. *24 Vesti*, April 9, 2013. Accessed May 1, 2013. http://24vesti.mk/vmro-dpmne-za-kampanja-dosega-potroshile-730000-evra.

Mill, John Stuart. *On Liberty.* London: Penguin, 1972.

Milivojević, Snježana. "Strategy, Study, Summary." In *Legal Monitoring of Serbian Media Scene ANEM Publication IV*, 33–37. Serbia: ANEM, 2010. Accessed October 7, 2017. http://www.anem.org.rs/en/aktivnostiAnema/monitoring/story/11548/THE+FOURTH+ANEM+MONITORING+PUBLICATION+.html.

Milton, Andrew K. *The Rational Politician: Exploiting the Media in New Democracies.* Aldershot: Ashgate, 2000.

Mutz, Diana C. *Hearing the Other Side: Deliberative Versus Participatory Democracy.* Cambridge: Cambridge University Press, 2006.

Mutz, Diana C., and Paul S. Martin. "Facilitating Communication across Lines of Political Difference: The Role of Mass Media." *American Political Science Review* 95.1 (2001): 97–114

Myers, Mary, Christoph Dietz, and Marie-Soleil Frère. "International Media Assistance: Experiences and Prospects." *Global Media Journal* (German edition) 4 (2014): 1–7. Accessed October 27, 2016. URN:nbn:de:gbv:547-201400686.

Napoli, Philip M. "The Marketplace of Ideas Metaphor in Communications regulation." *Journal of Communication* 49.4 (1999): 151–169.

National Endowment for Democracy. "Annual Reports 1984–2004." Accessed on March 18, 2013. http://www.ned.org/publications/annual-reports/.

Netpress. "ZNM: Novinarite vo Brisel ja posramotija i diskreditiraa profesijata" [ZNM: Journalists in Brussels shamed and discredited the profession]. *Time. mk*, September 22, 2011.

Nigel, Thomas. *The Yugoslav Wars (2): Bosnia, Kosovo and Macedonia 1992-2001.* Oxford: Osprey Publishing, 2006.

Nikodinovska, Vesna, Snezana Trpevska, Petrit Sarachini, Biljana Petkovska, Zaneta Trajkoska, Slagjana Dimiskova, Tamara Causidis, and Naser Selmani. "Analysis Development of the Media in Macedonia According to UNESCO Indicators." Skopje: Macedonian Institute for Media, 2012.

Norris, Pippa, ed. *Public Sentinel: News Media & Governance Reform.* Washington, DC: The International Bank for Reconstruction and Development/The World Bank, 2010.

NUNS. "TV Pink i RTS najgledanije u Srbiji" [TV Pink and RTS are the most watched in Serbia]. Accessed March 22, 2013. http://nuns.rs/info/news/3941/tv-pink-i-rts-1-najgledanije-u-srbiji.html.

N1. "Bujošević: Pretplata za RTS treba da bude obavezna." Accessed October 9, 2015. http://rs.n1info.com/a98726/Vesti/Bujosevic-Pretplata-za-RTS-treba-da-bude-obavezna.html.

OCCRP. "About Us." Organized Crime and Corruption Reporting Project, n.d. Accessed October 31, 2015. https://reportingproject.net/occrp/index.php/en/about-us.

OHR. "Decision Imposing the Law on the Basis of the Public Broadcasting System and on the Public Broadcasting Service of Bosnia and Herzegovina." Office of the High Representative, May 23, 2002. Accessed November 5, 2012. http://www.ohr.int/decisions/mediadec/default.asp?content_id=8359

OHR. "Decision Imposing the Law on Radio-Television of Republika Srpska." Office of the High Representative, May 24, 2002. Accessed November 5, 2012. http://www.ohr.int/decisions/mediadec/default.asp?content_id=8361.

OHR. "Decision on the Liquidation Procedure to be Applied in Winding-up the Public Enterprise Radio and Television of Bosnia and Herzegovina." Office of the High Representative, May 24, 2002. Accessed November 5, 2012. http://www.ohr.int/decisions/mediadec/default.asp?content_id=8362.

OHR. "Decision Amending the Structures of Expenditures of the Communications Regulatory Agency for 2002." Office of the High Representative, December 2, 2002.

OHR. "Decision Combining the Competencies of the Independent Media Commission and the Telecommunications Regulatory Agency." Office of the High Representative, February 3, 2001. Accessed September, 2011. http://www.ohr.int/?p=67881.

OHR. "Decision on the Appointment of the Transfer Agent and the Expert Team for the Establishment of Public Service Broadcasting." Office of the High Representative, April 15, 2000. Accessed November 24, 2012. http://www.ohr.int/?p=67865&print=pdf.

OHR. "Decision on the Establishment of the Independent Media Commission." Office of the High Representative, June 11, 1998. Accessed January, 2012. http://www.ohr.int/?p=67833.

OHR. "Decisions on the Restructuring of the Public Broadcasting System in BiH and on Freedom of Information and Decriminalisation of Libel and Defamation." Office of the High Representative, July 30, 1999. Accessed June 9, 2013. http://www.ohr.int/?p=67821.

OHR. "Decision Enacting the Law on Communications of Bosnia and Herzegovina." No. 52/02. Office of the High Representative, October 21, 2002.

OHR. "Peace Implementation Council Decisions and Communiqués." Office of the High Representative. Accessed on June 9, 2013. http://www.ohr.int/?cat=244

OHR. "Second Decision on Restructuring the Public Broadcasting System in BiH." Office of the High Representative, October 23, 2000. Accessed November 28, 2012. http://www.ohr.int/?p=67845.

OHR. "Decision Amending the Law on Radio-Television of the RS." Office of the High Representative, January 9, 1999. Accessed December 25, 2013. http://www.ohr.int/?p=67817

Ohrid News. "Novinarite baraat otvorena debata za zakonot za mediumi" [Journalists demand open debate the media law]. Association of Journalists of Macedonia, April 8, 2013. Accessed October 3, 2013. http://www.znm.org.mk/drupal-7.7/mk/node/583.

O'Neill, Onora. "Practices of Toleration." In *Democracy and the Mass Media*, edited by Judith Lichtenberg, 155–185. Cambridge: Cambridge University Press, 1990.

O'Neill, Onora. "What Is Public about Public Service Broadcasting?" In *Concepts of Public Service Broadcasting in a Changing Policy Context*, 2–5. London: British Academy, 2016. Accessed August 28, 2016. https://www.britac.ac.uk/sites/default/files/BRIJ4610%20Public%20service%20Broadcasting%2006_16_WEB_0.pdf.

Open Society Institute. *Television across Europe: Regulation, Policy, and Independence—Monitoring Reports 2005, Vol. 1*. Budapest: Open Society Institute/EU Monitoring and Advocacy Program, 2005. Accessed October 7, 2017. https://www.opensocietyfoundations.org/sites/default/files/volone_20051011_0.pdf.

OSCE. "OSCE Media Freedom Representative Welcomes New Macedonian Broadcast Law." Organization for Security and Co-operation in Europe, November 11, 2005. Accessed October 3, 2013. http://www.osce.org/fom/46888.

OSCE. "OSCE Media Freedom Representative Welcomes Skopje Authorities' Decriminalization of Libel." Organization for Security and Co-operation in Europe, November 14, 2012. Accessed May 1, 2013. http://www.osce.org/fom/97244.

OSCE. "OSCE Mission to Skopje Donation Helps Broadcasting Council Monitor Media's Election Coverage." Organization for Security and Co-operation in Europe, November 25, 2008. Accessed January 20, 2013. http://www.osce.org/skopje/50413.

OSCE and ODIHR. "Republic of Albania: Parliamentary Elections 28 June 2009: OSCE/ODIHR Election Observation Mission Final Report 2009." Organization for Security and Co-operation in Europe/Office of Democratic Institutions and Human Rights, September 14, 2009. Viewed October 7, 2017. http://www.osce.org/odihr/elections/albania/38598?download=true.

OSCE Mission in Bosnia and Herzegovina. "Rules and Regulations: Decisions until July 16, 1996." OSCE Mission in Bosnia and Herzegovina - Provisional Election Commission, July 16, 1996.

OSCE Mission in Kosovo. "Broadcast and Print Regulations for Kosovo Media Approved." Organization for Security and Co-operation in Europe, June 21, 2000. Accessed April 30, 2013. http://www.osce.org/kosovo/52681.

OSCE Mission in Kosovo. "Freedom of Media and Safety of Journalists in Kosovo." Organization for Security and Co-operation in Europe, June 2014. Accessed November 10, 2016. https://www.osce.org/kosovo/122390?download=true.

OSCE Mission in Kosovo. "Kosovo Broadcasters to Apply for Frequencies." Organization for Security and Co-operation in Europe, June 21, 2000. Accessed September 30, 2013. http://www.osce.org/kosovo/52680.

OSCE Mission in Kosovo. "Kosovo's Temporary Media Commissioner Not to Issue Any Further Broadcast Licenses." Organization for Security and Co-operation in Europe, March 28, 2003. Accessed April 2, 2013. http://www.osce.org/kosovo/55163.

OSCE Mission to Serbia. "Draft Strategy for the Development of the Public Information System in the Republic of Serbia until 2016." Organization for Security and Co-operation in Europe, June 3, 2011. Accessed January 15, 2013. http://www.osce.org/serbia/78448.

OSCE Mission to Serbia. "OSCE Opens Office within Radio-Television Serbia." Organization for Security and Co-operation in Europe, February 21, 2002. Accessed March 2, 2013. http://www.osce.org/serbia/54174.

Ozimec, Kristina. "Vladata se reklamira po nepoznata pravila na igra" [The government advertises using unknown market rules]. *Kapital,* February 15, 2012. Accessed January 23, 2013. http://www.kapital.mk/MK/dneven_vesnik/80114/mim__vladata_se_reklamira_po_nepoznati_pravila_na_igra!.aspx?iId=2597.

Palmer, L. Kendall. "Power-Sharing in Media—Integration of the Public?" In *Arranged Marriage: International Community and Media Reforms in BiH, Media Online Selections,* edited by Svjetlana Nedimović, 32–38. Sarajevo: Media Plan Institute, 2001.

Pavli, Darian. "Running the Marathon: The Effort to Reform Albania's Defamation Laws." Albanian Media Institute, 2013. Accessed October 7, 2017. http://www.institutemedia.org/Documents/PDF/D.%20Pavli%20English%20follow-up-1.pdf.

Peacock, Alan T., ed. *Public Service Broadcasting without the BBC?* London: Institute of Economic Affairs, 2004.

Peace Implementation Council. "PIC Bonn Conclusions - Bosnia and Herzegovina 1998: Self-sustaining Structures ." PIC Main Meeting Bonn, October 12, 1997. Accessed November 25, 2017. http://www.ohr.int/?p=54137

Peace Implementation Council Steering Board, PIC Steering Board Press Communique: Broadcast Media Statement. Office of the High Representative, April 24, 1996. Accessed November 25, 2017. http://www.ohr.int/?p=52817.

"Për disa shtesa dhe ndryshime në ligjin nr. 8410, datë 30.9.1998 "Për radion dhe televizionin publik e privat në Republikën e Shqipërisë", të ndryshuar"

[Law no. 9531 on some additions and amendments to Law no. 8410, dated 30.9.1998, on public and private radio and television in the Republic of Albania]. *Official Gazette* 65/06.

"Për mediat audiovizive në Republikën e Shqipërisë" [Law no. 97/2013 on audiovisual media in the Republic of Albania]. *Official Gazette* 37/13.

Popovic, Mirjana. "Covering Bosnia and Herzegovina: Media Reform." In *10 Years of OSCE Mission in Bosnia and Herzegovina 1995–2005*, 125–133. Sarajevo: Organization for Security and Co-operation in Europe, 2005.

Popovic, Tanja. "The Former Yugoslav Republic of Macedonia." In *Media in Multilingual Societies: Freedom and Responsibility*, edited by Ana Karlsreiter, 21–49. Vienna: Organization for Security and Co-operation in Europe, 2003.

Presnall, Aaron. "Which Way the Wind Blows: Democracy Promotion and International Actors in Serbia." *Democratization* 16.4 (2009): 661–681.

Press Council of Kosovo. "OSCE Mission in Kosovo Supports PCK Awareness Campaign." July 26, 2012. Accessed September 29, 2013. http://www.presscouncil-ks.org/osce-mission-in-kosovo-supports-pck-awareness-campaign/?lang=en.

Price, Monroe E., and Peter Krug. "The Enabling Environment for Free and Independent Media: Contribution to Transparent and Accountable Governance." Occasional Papers Series, PN-ACM-006. Washington, DC: Office of Democracy and Governance, Bureau for Democracy, Conflict, and Humanitarian Assistance, US Agency for International Development, January 2002. Accessed November 23, 2013. http://www.global.asc.upenn.edu/app/uploads/2014/06/ENABLING_ENV.pdf.

Price, Monroe, and Peter Krug. "The Enabling Environment for Free and Independent Media." In *Media Matters: Perspectives on Advancing Governance and Development from the Global Forum for Media Development*, edited by Mark Harvey, 95–102. Paris: Internews Europe, 2006.

Price, Monroe E., Bethany Davis Noll, and Daniel De Luce. "Mapping Media Assistance." Centre for Socio-Legal Studies, University of Oxford, February 1, 2002. http://repository.upenn.edu/asc_papers/62.

ProPublica. "Annual Report 2012." ProPublica, January 2013. Accessed October 31, 2015. http://propublica.s3.amazonaws.com/assets/about/propublica_2012 report_final_170210_164448.pdf?_ga=2.208172561.2054798429.151161219 2- 1564442349.1511612191.

ProPublica. "Steal Our Stories." N.d. Accessed October 31, 2015. http://www.propublica.org/about/steal-our-stories/.

Putzel, James, and Joost van der Zwan. "Why Templates for Media Development Do Not Work in Crisis States: Defining and Understanding Media Development Strategies in Post-War and Crisis States." Crisis States Research Centre, London School of Economics and Political Science, 2006. Accessed July 2011. http://eprints.lse.ac.uk/archive/00000837.

Qavdarbasha, Shkamb. "The State of the Media in Kosovo." Edited by Krenar Gashi. Institute for Development Policy, 2012.

Rakner, Lise, Alina Rocha Menocal, and Verena Fritz. *Democratisation's Third Wave and the Challenges of Democratic Deepening: Assessing International Democracy Assistance and Lessons Learned*. London: Overseas Development Institute, 2007.

Ranson, Jenny. "International Intervention in Media: The Open Broadcast Network: A Case Study in Bosnia and Herzegovina." Institute for Peace, Media and Security, University of Peace, 2005.

"Regulation on the Conduct of Print Media in Kosovo." UNMIK 2000/37, June 17, 2000.

"Regulation on the Licensing and Regulation of Broadcast Media and on the Code of Conduct for Print Media in Kosovo." UNMIK 2000/36, June 17, 2000.

"Regulation on the Prohibition against Inciting to National, Racial, Religious or Ethnic Hatred, Discord or Intolerance." UNMIK 2000/4, February 1, 2000.

Reljić, Dušan. "Killing Screens: Media in Times of Conflict." Dusseldorf and Paris: European Institute for the Media, 2001.

Republic Broadcasting Agency. "Komercijalni emiteri sa nacionalnim pokrivanjem: Načini ispunjavanja zakonskih i programskih obaveza" [Commercial broadcasters with national scope: How they meet legislative and program demands]. Belgrade: The Republic Broadcasting Agency, 2012.

"Rezultati konkursa 'Jačanje dijaloga između organizacija civilnog društva Srbije i EU' i 'Medijski fond u oblasti evropskih integracija'" [Results of the competition "Strengthening dialogue between the organizations of the civil society of Serbia and the EU" and "Media fund in the field of European integration"]. Accessed January 30, 2013. http://www.europa.rs/upload/documents/documents/news/20100618%20-%20Objedinjena%20Lista%20pobednika%20konkursa%20MF%20i%20CSF.pdf.

Rhodes, Aaron. "Ten Years of Media Support to the Balkans: An Assessment." Amsterdam: Media Task Force of the Stability Pact for South Eastern Europe, June 2007. Accessed December 10, 2013. http://www.medienhilfe.ch/fileadmin/media/images/dossier/mediasupport_Balkan.pdf.

Riley, Chris. "Painstaking Efforts—OHR Media Development Strategy In Post-Dayton BiH." In *Arranged Marriage: International Community and Media Reforms in BiH, Media Online Selections*, edited by Svjetlana Nedimović, 39–45. Sarajevo: Media Plan Institute, 2001.

Ross, Howard. "International Media Assistance: A Review of Donor Activities and Lessons Learned." Working Paper 19. Hague: Netherlands Institute of International Relations "Clingedael," 2003.

Rrokum Television. "Rrokum Television: Investigative Journalism Section." Rrokum, November 2011. Accessed November 25, 2017. https://www.yumpu.com/en/document/view/7314616/dossier-kijac-eng-rrokum-tv.

RTK. "Raport Vjetor per vitin 2005—Radio Televizioni i Kosoves" [RTK annual report 2005]. Accessed September 30, 2013. http://www.rtklive.com/rtk/rp_ad_sq/2005_sq.pdf.

RTK. "Raport Vjetor per vitin 2007—Radio Televizioni i Kosoves" [RTK annual report 2007]. Accessed September 30, 2013. http://www.rtklive.com/rtk/rp_ad_sq/2007_sq.pdf.

Sakwa, Richard. *Postcommunism*. Buckingham: Open University Press, 1999.

Sartori, Giovanni. "Comparing and Miscomparing." *Journal of Theoretical Politics* 3 (1991): 243–257.

Schimmelfennig, Frank, and Ulrik Sedelmeier. "Governance by Conditionality: EU Rule Transfer to the Candidate Countries of Central and Eastern Europe." *Journal of European Public Policy* 11 (2004): 669–687.

Schudson, Michael. *Discovering the News: A Social History of American Newspapers.* New York: Basic Books, 1978.

Searle, John R. *The Construction of Social Reality.* Harmondsworth: Penguin, 1995.

Seymour-Ure, Colin. *The Political Impact of Mass Media.* London: Constable, 1974.

Shirley, Mary M. *Institutions and Development.* Cheltenham: Edward Elgar, 2008.

Shirley, Mary M. "Institutions and Development." Working Paper. The International Institute of Management and Economic Education, University of Flensburg, 2003. Accessed February 4, 2012. http://www.iim.uni-flensburg.de/vwl/upload/lehre/sose08/MaEuS/w-shirley2003institutionsanddevelopment.pdf.

Smit, Margo, Brigitte Alfter, Mar Cabra, Annamarie Cumiskey, Ides Debruyne, Marcos García Rey, Rafael Njotea, and Albrecht Ude. *Deterrence of Fraud with EU Funds through Investigative Journalism in EU-27.* Brussels: European Parliament, Directorate General for Internal Policies, Policy Department D: Budgetary Affairs, 2012. Accessed October 28, 2015. http://www.europarl.europa.eu/document/activities/cont/201210/20121002ATT52809/20121002ATT52809EN.pdf.

SNP NAŠI. "Tražimo gašenje antisrpskih medija" [We are demanding the termination of anti-Serbian media]. Accessed October 12, 2013. http://nasisrbija.org/index.php/2012/12/02/trazimo-gasenjeantisrpskih-medija/.

Šopar, Vesna. "Macedonia." In *Divided They Fall: Public Service Broadcasting in Multiethnic States,* edited by Sandra Bašić-Hrvatin, Mark Thompson, and Tarik Jusić, 119–157. Sarajevo: Mediacentar, 2008.

Šopar, Vesna. "Republic of Macedonia." In *Television across Europe: More Channels, Less Independence: Follow-up Reports 2008,* 314–363. Budapest: Open Society Institute/EU Monitoring and Advocacy Program, 2008.

Sorge, Petra. "Media in Kosovo—Long Walk to Modernity." *Südosteuropa Mitteilungen* 52.4 (2012): 32–47.

Soros Files. "Media Development Loan Fund." October 19, 2011. Accessed July 11, 2013. http://sorosfiles.com/soros/2011/10/media-development-loan-fund.html.

Soros Foundation. "Albania Annual Report 1994." Tirana: Soros Foundation, 1994.

Soros Foundation. "Albania Annual Report 1995." Tirana: Soros Foundation, 1995.

Soros Foundation. "Albania Annual Report 1996." Tirana: Soros Foundation, 1996.

Soros Foundation. "Albania Annual Report 1997." Tirana: Soros Foundation, 1997.

Soros Foundation. "Albania Annual Report 1998." Tirana: Soros Foundation, 1998.

Soros Foundation. "Albania Annual Report 1999." Tirana: Soros Foundation, 1999.

Sparks, Colin. "Media Theory after the Fall of European Communism: Why the Old Models from East and West Won't Do Anymore." In *De-Westernizing Media Studies,* edited by James Curran and Myung-Jin Park, 35–49. London: Routledge, 2000.

Spasovska, Mirjana. "Novinarite se bunat, SRD se siri" [Journalists complain, SRD expands]. *Radio Free Europe,* August 24, 2011, Accessed February 1, 2013. http://www.makdenes.org/content/article/24306613.html.

Stability Pact for South Eastern Europe. "Media Task Force: Progress and Problems for the Media in South Eastern Europe." September 6, 2004. Accessed January 20, 2013. http://www.stabilitypact.org/media/info.asp.

State Statistical Office. *Census of Population, Households, and Dwellings in the Republic of Macedonia, 2002, Book III.* Skopje: State Statistical Office, 2005.

Stern, Ulrike, and Sarah Wohlfield. "Albania's Long Road into the European Union: Internal Political Power Struggle Blocks Central Reforms." DGAP-analyse 11, Deutsche Gesellschaft für Auswärtige Politik, September 2012. Accessed June 5, 2013. https://dgap.org/en/think-tank/publications/dgapanaly-sis/albania%E2%80%99s-long-road-european-union.

Stiglmayer, Filip. "OSCE-Supported Press Council Helps Improve Kosovo's Media Landscape." Organization for Security and Co-operation in Europe, March 8, 2007. Accessed April 30, 2013. http://www.osce.org/kosovo/57584.

Sullivan, Drew. "Investigative Reporting in Emerging Democracies: Models, Challenges, and Lessons Learned." Center for International Media Assistance and National Endowment for Democracy, January 14, 2013. Accessed October 28, 2015. http://www.cima.ned.org/resource/investigative-reporting-in-emerging-democracies-models-challenges-and-lessons-learned/.

Sullivan, Stacy. "Restructuring the Media in Post-Conflict Societies: Four Perspectives—The Experience of Intergovernmental and Non-Governmental Organizations." Paper presented at the UNESCO "World Press Day" conference, Geneva, May 2000.

Surčulija, Jelena, Biljana Pavlović and Đurđa Jovanović Padejski. "Mapping Digital Media: Serbia." Open Society Foundations, October 15, 2011. Accessed October 31, 2013. http://www.opensocietyfoundations.org/sites/default/files/mapping-digital-media-serbia-20111215.pdf.

Susman-Peña, Tara. "Making Media Development More Effective." Washington, DC: Center for International Media Assistance, 2012.

Taylor, Bill. "Setting Media Standards: Public Awareness and Effectiveness of the Independent Media Commission and the Press Council of Kosovo." Thomson Foundation, September 2014. Accessed November 10, 2016. http://www.thomsonfoundation.org/media/33424/kosovo_report_setting_media_stand-ards_2015.pdf.

Taylor, Maureen, and Michael L. Kent. "Media Transitions in Bosnia: From Propagandistic Past to Uncertain Future." *Gazette* 62.5 (2000): 355–378. Accessed December 20, 2013. http://citeseerx.ist.psu.edu/viewdoc/download?doi=10.1.1.129.6690&rep=rep1&type=pdf.

Thompson, Mark. *Forging War: The Media in Serbia, Croatia, Bosnia and Herzegovina.* London: University of Luton Press, 1999.

Thompson, Mark. "Slovenia, Croatia, Bosnia and Herzegovina, Macedonia (FYROM) and Kosovo: International Assistance to Media." Office of the Representative on Freedom of the Media, Organization for Security and Co-operation in Europe, 2000. Accessed October 7, 2017. http://www.osce.org/fom/25448?download=true.

Thompson, Mark, and Article 19. *Kovanje rata: Mediji u Srbiji, Hrvatskoj i Bosni i Hercegovini* [Forging war: The media in Serbia, Croatia, Bosnia and Herce-govina]. Trans. Miodrag Pavić. Zagreb: Hrvatski helsinški odbor za ljudska prava; Građanska inicijativa za slobodu javne riječi, 1995.

Thompson, Mark, and Dan De Luce. "Escalating to Success? The Media Intervention in Bosnia and Herzegovina." In *Forging Peace: Intervention, Human Rights and the Management of Media Space,* edited by Monroe E. Price and Mark Thompson, 201–235. Edinburgh: Edinburgh University Press, 2002.

Thussu, Daya. *International Communication: Continuity and Change*. London: Bloomsbury, 2006.

Topić, Tanja. "Electronic Media: Regulation Efforts in Semi-Protectorate." In *Peace Building and Civil Society in Bosnia—Ten Years after Dayton*, edited by Martina Fischer, 157–184. Munich: Lit Verlag, 2006.

Trajanovski, Mirko. "Što znači kandidiranjeto na novinari od A1 na listite na SDSM?" [What does it mean to nominate journalists from A1 to the SDSM electoral lists?]. *Telma*, May 3, 2011.

Trpevska, Snežana, and Igor Micevski. "Macedonia." In *Media Integrity Matters: Reclaiming Public Service Values in Media and Journalism*, edited by Brankica Petković and Jovana Mihajlović Trbovc, 257–326. Ljubljana: Peace Institute, 2014. Accessed October 7, 2017. http://mediaobservatory.net/sites/default/files/media%20integrity%20matters_za%20web_2.pdf.

Tsebelis, George. *Veto Players: How Political Institutions Work*. Princeton: Princeton University Press, 2002.

Tuchman, Gaye. "Objectivity as Strategic Ritual: An Examination of Newsmen's Notions of Objectivity." *American Journal of Sociology* 77.4 (1972): 660–679.

Udovičić, Radenko. "Bosnia and Herzegovina." In *Country Reports on Media Freedom*. South East European Network for Professionalisation of Media (SEENPM), 2012. Accessed October 28, 2015. http://www.seenpm.org/wp-content/uploads/2012/08/SEENPM_Media_ freedom_report_final.pdf.

Udovičić, Radenko. "Bosnia-Herzegovina." In *The Media in South-East Europe: A Comparative Media Law and Policy Study*, edited by Beate Martin, Alexander Scheuer, and Christian Bron, 41–54. Berlin: Friedrich Ebert Foundation, 2011. Accessed October 28, 2015. http://library.fes.de/pdf-files/bueros/sofia/08097.pdf.

Udovičić, Zoran. "Media in B-H: The Scope of International Community Intervention." In *International Support Policies to South-East European Countries: Lessons (Not) Learned in B-H*, edited by Žarko Papić, 195–207. Sarajevo: Müller, 2001.

Umbricht, Andrea, and Frank Esser. "Changing Political News? Long-term Trends in American, British, French, Italian, German and Swiss Press Reporting." In *Political Journalism in Transition: Western Europe in a Comparative Perspective*, edited by Raymond Kuhn and Rasmus Kleis Nielsen, 195-218. London: I. B. Tauris, 2013.

UNDEF. "Evaluation Report." United Nations Democracy Fund, March 25, 2011.

UNDP. "Supporting Public Service Broadcasting: Learning from Bosnia and Herzegovina's Experience." United Nations Development Programme-Bureau for Development Policy-Democratic Governance Group, 2004. Accessed November 24, 2013. http://www.gsdrc.org/document-library/supporting-public-service-broadcasting-learning-from-bosnia-and-herzegovinas-experience/.

UNDP and USAID. "Action Paper on Association of Professional Journalists in Kosovo: Freedom of Expression in the Media and the Role of the Association of Professional Journalists of Kosovo." United Nations Development Programme, March 29, 2012. Accessed September 30, 2013. http://www.ks.undp.org/content/kosovo/en/home/library/democratic_governance/action-paper-on-association-of-professional-journalists-in-kosov.html.

Unioni i Gazetarëve Shqiptarë. "Statuti i unionit të gazetarëve të Shqipërisë" [Statute of the Union of Albanian Journalists], 2005.

United States Department of State, Bureau of Democracy, Human Rights and Labor. "Bosnia and Herzegovina." In *Country Reports on Human Rights Practices 2014*. 2014. Accessed October 28, 2015. http://www.state.gov/j/drl/rls/hrrpt/humanrightsreport/index.htm?year= 2014&dlid=236506.

United States Department of State, Bureau of Democracy, Human Rights and Labor. "Bosnia and Herzegovina 2012 Human Rights Report." 2012. Accessed October 28, 2015. http://www.state.gov/documents/organization/204478.pdf.

UNMIK. "UNMIK Sets out Plans for Revival and Development of RTP and Independent Media in Kosovo." Press release, 21 July 1999.

USAID. "Bosnia-Herzegovina Democracy and Governance Assessment." United States Agency for International Development, May 2007. Accessed October 28, 2015. http://pdf.usaid.gov/pdf_docs/PNADK585.pdf.

USAID. "Giving Citizens a Voice: Strengthening Independent Media in Bosnia and Herzegovina: Final Report." United States Agency for International Development, December 31, 2006. Accessed October 28, 2015. http://pdf.usaid.gov/pdf_docs/Pdack302.pdf.

USAID. "ProMedia II/Bosnia and Herzegovina Program Report: Quarter 3, FY 2003, April 1–June 30, 2003, Cooperative Agreement No. 168-A-00-99-00103-00." United States Agency for International Development, July 31, 2003. Accessed November 24, 2013. http://pdf.usaid.gov/pdf_docs/PDABZ686.pdf.

Valić-Nedeljković, Dubravka, and Višnja Baćanović. "From Emotional Approach to the Fate of Kosovo to Progressive Civil Activism." In *Indicator of Public Interest*, edited by Radenko Udovičić, 197–230. Sarajevo: Media Plan Institute, 2007.

Van Zweeden, Cees. "The State of the Media in Kosovo." *Helsinki Monitor: Security and Human Rights* 18.2 (2007): 138–149. Accessed March 28, 2013. http://www.uio.no/studier/emner/hf/imk/JOUR4330/h07/Zweeden%20The%20state%20of%20media%20in%20Kosovo.pdf.

Večer. "OBSE ke mu pomaga na Sovetot za radiodifuzija" [OSCE will help the Broadcasting Council]. Večer, 2007.

Veljanovski, Rade. "Medijska strategija—bliže ili dalje od medijskog servisa" [Media strategy—Closer or more far away from media service]. *Izazovi evropskih integracija* 11 (2011).

Veljanovski, Rade. *Javni RTV servis u službi građana* [Public RTV service serving citizens]. Belgrade: Clio, 2005.

Veljanovski, Rade. *Medijski sistem Srbije* [Media system of Serbia]. Belgrade: Čigoja, 2009.

Vidimliski, Mihajlo. "Eksperti—noviot zakon za medium se nosi zad zatvoreni vrati" [Experts—The new law should not be passed behind closed doors]. *24 Vesti*, November 12, 2012. Accessed October 3, 2013. http://24vesti.mk/eksperti-%E2%80%93-noviot-zakon-za-mediumi-se-nosi-zad-zatvoreni-vrati.

Voltmer, Katrin. "How Far Can Media Systems Travel? Applying Hallin and Mancini's Comparative Framework outside the Western World." In *Comparing Media Systems beyond the Western World*, edited by Daniel C. Hallin and Paolo Mancini, 224–245. Cambridge: Cambridge University Press, 2012.

Voltmer, Katrin. *The Media in Transitional Democracies*. Cambridge: Polity, 2013.

Voltmer, Katrin, and Mansur Lalljee. "Agree to Disagree: Respect for Political Opponents." In *British Social Attitudes: The 23rd Report*, edited by Alison Park, John Curtice, Katarina Thomson, Miranda Phillips, and Mark Johnson, 95–118. London: Sage, 2007.

Voltmer, Katrin, and Herman Wasserman. "Journalistic Norms between Universality and Domestication: Journalists' Interpretation of Press Freedom in Six New Democracies." *Global Media and Communication* 10.2 (2014): 1–16.

Waisbord, Silvio. "In Journalism We Trust? Credibility and Fragmented Journalism in Latin America." In *Mass Media and Political Communication in New Democracies*, edited by Katrin Voltmer, 76–91. Abingdon: Routledge, 2006.

Wattenberg, Martin P. *The Decline of American Political Parties, 1952–1996*. Cambridge, MA: Harvard University Press, 1998.

Weber, Max. *The Methodology of the Social Sciences*. Glencoe: Free Press, 1949.

Weber, Max. "The Three Types of Legitimate Rule." *Berkeley Publications in Society and Institutions* 4.1 (1958): 1–11.

Wheeler, Mark. *Monitoring the Media: The Bosnian Elections 1996*. Sarajevo: Media Plan Institute and IWPR, 1997.

Whitehead, Laurence. *Democratization: Theory and Experience*. Oxford: Oxford University Press, 2002.

YIHR. "State of Constriction? Governance and Free Expression in Kosovo." Pristina: Youth Initiative for Human Rights, May 24, 2010. Accessed March 15, 2013. http://www.yihr.org/public/fck_files/ksfile/STATE%20of%20CON-STRICTION.pdf.

"Zakon o izmenama i dopunama krivičnog zakonika" [Law amending the Criminal Code]. *Official Gazette of the Republic of Serbia* 121/2012.

"Zakon o izmenama i dopunama zakona o javnim medijskim servisima" [Law on amendments to the law on public media services]. *Official Gazette of the Republic of Serbia* 58/2015.

"Zakon o javnim medijskim servisima" [Law on public media services]. *Official Gazette of the Republic of Serbia* 83/2014.

"Zakon o javnom informisanju" [Law on public information]. *Official Gazette of the Republic of Serbia*, no. 43/2003, 61/2005.

"Zakon o javnom radiotelevizijskom servisu Bosne i Hercegovine" [Law on the public broadcasting system of BiH]. *Official Gazette of BiH* 92/05.

"Zakon o javnom radio-televizijskom sistemu BiH" [Law on the public service broadcasting system of BiH]. *Official Gazette of BiH* 78/05.

"Zakon o javnom servisu radio-televizije Federacije BiH" [Law on the public broadcasting service of the Federation of BiH]. *Official Gazette of FBiH* 01-02-401/08.

"Zakon o komunikacijama BiH" [Law on communications of Bosnia and Herzegovina]. *Official Gazette of Bosnia and Herzegovina* 31/03.

"Zakon o oglašavanju" [Law on advertising]. *Official Gazette of the Republic of Serbia* 79/2005.

"Zakon o osnovama javnog radio-televizijskog sistema i o javnom radio-televizijskom servisu BiH" [Law on the basis of public broadcasting system and public broadcasting service of Bosnia and Herzegovina]. *Official Gazette of BiH* 29/02.

"Zakon o radiodifuziji" [Broadcasting act]. *Official Gazette of the Republic of Serbia.* 42/2002, 97/2004, 76/2005, 79/2005, 62/2006, 85/2006, 86/2006.

"Zakon o Radio-Televiziji Republike Srpske" [Law on the Radio Television of Republika Srpska]. *Official Gazette of RS* 22/03, 49/06.

"Zakon o slobodnom pristupu informacijama od javnog značaja" [Law on free access to information of public Importance]. *Official Gazette of the Republic of Serbia* 120/2004, 54/2007.

"Zakon za osnovanje na javno pretprijatie Makedonska Radiodifuzija" [Law on the establishment of the public enterprise Macedonian Radio Television]. *Official Gazette of the Republic of Macedonia* 6/1998, 98/2000 and 78/2004.

"Zakon za radiodifuznata dejnost" [Law on broadcasting activity]. *Official Gazette of the Republic of Macedonia* 20/1997.

"Zakon za radiodifuznata dejnost" [Law on broadcasting activity]. *Official Gazette of the Republic of Macedonia* 100/2005.

Zielonka, Jan, and Paolo Mancini. "Executive Summary: A Media Map of Central and Eastern Europe." Media and Democracy in Central and Eastern Europe, Department of Politics and International Relations, University of Oxford, 2011. Accessed December 5, 2013. http://mde.politics.ox.ac.uk/images/stories/summary_mdcee_2011.pdf.

Zikov, Ljupčo. "Dragane Pavlovicu-Latas . . . vidi vaka" [Dragane Pavlovicu-Latas . . . look, it is like this]. *Kapital,* May 2, 2012. Accessed October 3, 2013. http://kapital.mk/mk/makedonija/83499/dragane_pavlovichu-latas_____vidi_vaka!.aspx

Zurovac, Ljiljana, and Borka Rudić, eds. "Shadow Report for Bosnia and Herzegovina: Indicators for Measuring Media Freedoms in the Countries Members of the Council of Europe." Press Council in Bosnia and Herzegovina/Association of BH Journalists, 2012. Accessed October 28, 2015. http://www.civilrightsdefenders.org/files/Indicators-for-Media-in-a-Democracy-Bosnia-and-Herzegovina-report.pdf.

About the Authors

Dr. NIDŽARA AHMETAŠEVIĆ holds a PhD degree from the Joint Programme in Diversity Management and Governance at the University in Graz, Austria. Her field of research is on democratization and media development in postconflict countries. Before coming to Graz, she spent a year at the University of Kent, UK, on a Chevening Scholarship. Ahmetašević holds a Masters in Human Rights and Democratization in South East Europe, a joint program of the Centre for Intedisciplinary Studies of the Universities of Sarajevo and Bologna. Her thesis was on political propaganda in broadcast media in Serbia, Croatia and Bosnia and Herzegovina during the wars of the 1990s. Before her master studies, as a Ron Brown Fellow (a US State Department award supporting young professionals from Central and Eastern Europe), she spent a year at the DeWitt Wallace Center for Media & Democracy, Duke University, North Carolina. Ahmetašević has had a long career as a journalist, covering human rights, foreign policy, and transitional justice issues, in particular.

Dr. ZHIDAS DASKALOVSKI holds a PhD from the Political Science Department, Central European University. He has published numerous scholarly articles on politics in the Southeast European region, as well as co-edited books, including *Understanding the War in Kosovo* (Frank Cass, 2003) and *Ten Years after the Ohrid Framework Agreement: Lessons (to Be) Learned from the Macedonian Experience* (CRPM and Friedrich Ebert Stiftung, 2012). He is a full professor at the Faculty of Security Studies, University of Kliment Ohridski, and is Director of the Council of Europe–supported Mother Teresa School of Public Policy. Daskalovski is a public advocate of REKOM initiative. He was the 2008 Young Scientist of the Year of the Macedonian Academy of Science, a recipient of Lord Dahrendorf Fellowship at Oxford University, a SSEES Fellowship, and a Social Science Research Council Fellowship at the University of North Carolina.

Dr. TAMARA DIMITRIJEVSKA-MARKOSKI is an Assistant Professor of Public Administration and Public Policy in the department of Political Science and Public Administration at Mississippi State University. Her primary research interests are performance measurement and management of local governments and social impact bonds. Her doctoral dissertation: Use of Performance Information by Local Government Administrators: Evidence from Florida examined the factors that facilitate and hinder the use of performance data by local governments. Her work appears in the International Journal of Public Policy and she has presented at number of national and international conferences including ASPA, APPAM and PMRC. Dr. Dimitrijevska-Markoski earned her Ph.D. in Public Affairs at the University of Central Florida. She also holds MA in Human Rights from the Central European University in Hungary and a dual BA in Political Science & International Relations, and European Studies from the American University in Bulgaria.

Dr. KRISTINA IRION is Senior Researcher at the Institute for Information Law (IViR) at the University of Amsterdam. She coordinates and teaches in the Research Master's Information Law and is the faculty organiser of the Annual IViR Summer Course on Privacy Law and Policy. She is Associate Professor (on research leave) at the School of Public Policy at Central European University in Budapest (Hungary). Kristina obtained her Dr. iuris degree from Martin Luther University, Halle-Wittenberg (Germany), and holds a Master's degree in Information Technology and Telecommunications Law from the University of Strathclyde, Glasgow (UK). Her research covers EU law, regulation and public policy in the fields of electronic communications, online media, content and services as well as privacy and data protection. Kristina was key personnel of four collaborative European research projects on privacy, independent media supervisory authorities, and building functioning media institutions. She has been the key public policy expert in the INDIREG study which developed a set of indicators for assessing the independence and efficient functioning of media regulatory bodies in European countries. She led the application of this methodology to the Albanian and Serbian authorities charged with media supervision. She was the scientific advisor to the cross-national project on international assistance and media democratization in the Western Balkans of which this edited volume it an output. Kristina provided expertise to the European Commission and the European Parliament, the Council of Europe, the OECD and ENISA as well as advising various civil society organizations.

Dr. TARIK JUSIĆ is Managing Director at the Center for Social Research Analitika in Sarajevo and a non-resident fellow at the Center for Media, Data and Society (CMDS), Central European University, Budapest. He holds a doctoral degree from the Institute for Media and Communication Studies, University of Vienna, Austria, an MA degree in Political Science from Central European University, and an Executive MBA degree, also from Central Europea University. He was an Assistant Professor at the Department of Political Science and International Relations, Sarajevo School of Science and Technology, and a guest lecturer at the European Regional Master's Degree in Human Rights and Democracy in South East Europe (ERMA) of the Center for Interdisciplinary Postgraduate Studies at the University of Sarajevo. From 2014 to 2017 Tarik was supervisor for the Local Coordination Unit for Bosnia and Herzegovina within the Regional Research Promotion Program in the Western Balkans (RRPP), aimed at promoting social science research in the Western Balkans, funded by the Swiss Agency for Development and Cooperation. He also worked as a program director at Mediacentar Sarajevo from 2002 until 2011. Tarik participated in various research projects, including the most recent comparative study on the prospect of public service media in the Western Balkans, implemented by the University of Fribourg and the Center for Social Research Analitika. He has published a number of papers and reports and has edited several books dealing with the media democratization in Southeast European region.

ILDA LONDO works as a research coordinator at the Albanian Media Institute since 2001. She has dealt with various research projects where AMI has been involved, such as a study of trends that affect media freedom and independence, research on media ownership and concentration, monitoring performance of regulatory authorities and independent institutions on media development, coverage of ethnic minorities, media landscape surveys, broadcasting development trends, self-regulation and ethical issues. Titles of her research reports and articles include "Main Trends in Media Development in Post-Communist Albania," "Mapping Digital Media in Albania," "Media and Information Society in Albania," "Monitoring Access to Public Institutions," "The Role of the Regulator in Digital Switchover," "Reform of PBS in the Digital Era," "TV across Europe: Regulation, Policy and Independence: Albania," and "Media Ownership, Independence, and Pluralism."

DAVOR MARKO is non-resident research fellow at the Analitika—Center for Social Research, Sarajevo (BiH) and a non-resident fellow at the Center for Media, Data and Society, of the Central European University, Budapest (Hungary). He is PhD candidate in culture and communication at the Faculty of Political Sciences, University of Belgrade. He holds MA in Democracy and Human Rights, a joint-degree awarded by the University of Sarajevo (Bosnia and Herzegovina) and the University of Bologna (Italy). For more than fourteen years he has worked as a media researcher, analyst, and consultant in media and communications. He has collaborated with Mediaplan, the Mediacenter, the Center for Human Rights, the Novi Sad School of Journalism, the Center for Social Research Analitika, OSCE Mission in Serbia and USAID BiH to conduct numerous research projects on media and communication practices in the region of Western Balkans. As research fellow and research coordinator, he has worked with the University of Edinburgh (School of Law, School of Divinity), the Open Society Fund BiH, ZET Stiftung Hamburg, and the UNESCO–Keizo Obuchi program.

Dr. NASER MIFTARI holds a doctorate in Political Science from University of Nebraska-Lincoln and a Master's in Journalism (MJ) from Temple University in Philadelphia. His research focus are political communication and media governance. In recent years he has written extensively on public broadcasting and sustainability of media institutions in new democracies.

NEVENA RŠUMOVIĆ holds an MA in Political Science (certificate in Political Communication) from the Central European University (CEU) in Budapest. She also holds an MA in Media Innovation Management from the Berlin University of Professional Studies (DUW Berlin/Steinbeis Hochschule). She has more than fifteen years of professional experience in media development having worked as a project coordinator for international and local organizations in Bosnia and Herzegovina and Serbia. Working for UNDP Serbia, she implemented activities toward furthering freedom of information. She was editor-in-chief of Mediacentar Sarajevo's online publication Media.ba, targeting media professionals. She served as a consultant on several media- and journalism-related initiatives, including some by UNDP and IREX Serbia. Ršumović works as project manager for the Center for Investigative Journalism of Serbia (CINS) and as communications officer for the South East European Network for Professionalization of Media (SEENPM).

Dr. MARK THOMPSON (PhD Cantab) worked in the former Yugoslavia as a media analyst for the United Nations and a mission spokesman for the OSCE. He spent seven years with the Media Program of the Open Society Foundations, overseeing policy research and giving grants. He now teaches modern European history at the University of East Anglia. His books include *Forging War: The Media in Serbia, Croatia, Bosnia and Herzegovina* (1994, 1999) and—coedited with Monroe Price—*Forging Peace: Intervention, Human Rights and the Management of Media Space* (2002). His biography of the writer Danilo Kiš (*Birth Certificate*, 2013) was awarded the Jan Michalski Prize and the Laura Shannon Prize in Contemporary European Studies.

Prof. KATRIN VOLTMER holds the Chair in Communication and Democracy at the School of Media and Communication, University of Leeds. Her research interests focus on the role of the media in emerging democracies in a comparative perspective. She has also widely published on the changing relationship between citizens, politics, and the media in established Western democracies. Recent books include *The Media in Transitional Democracies* (Polity, 2013) and *Political Communication in Postmodern Democracy: Challenging the Primacy of Politics* (ed. with Kees Brants; Palgrave, 2011). She has been Principal Investigator of the EU-funded FP7 project "Media, Conflict and Democratisation" (http://www.mecodem.eu/). She is currently Global Fellow of the Peace Reasearch Institute Oslo (PRIO) and serves on the Editorial Board of the Reuters Institute for the Study of Journalism, University of Oxford.

Index

Index